Texts and Contexts of the Book of Sirach

Texte und Kontexte des Sirachbuches

Septuagint and Cognate Studies

Wolfgang Kraus, General Editor

Number 66

Texts and Contexts of the Book of Sirach

Texte und Kontexte des Sirachbuches

Edited by

Gerhard Karner, Frank Ueberschaer, and Burkard M. Zapff

SBL PRESS

Atlanta

Library of Congress Cataloging-in-Publication Data

Names: Karner, Gerhard. | Ueberschaer, Frank, editor. | Zapff, Burkard M., editor.
Title: Texts and contexts of the Book of Sirach = Texte und kontexte des Sirachbuches / edited by Gerhard Karner, Frank Ueberschaer, and Burkard M. Zapff.
Description: Atlanta : SBL Press, [2017] | Series: Septuagint and cognate studies ; number 66 | Includes bibliographical references and index.
Identifiers: LCCN 2017009198 (print) | LCCN 2017011089 (ebook) | ISBN 9781628371826 (pbk. : alk. paper) | ISBN 9780884142300 (hardcover : alk. paper) | ISBN 9780884142294 (ebook)
Subjects: LCSH: Bible. Ecclesiasticus—Criticism, interpretation, etc.—Congresses.
Classification: LCC BS1765.52 .T48 2017 (print) | LCC BS1765.52 (ebook) | DDC 229/.40446—dc23
LC record available at https://lccn.loc.gov/2017009198

Printed on acid-free paper.

Contents

Vorwort

Vom 12.–14. September 2014 fand an der Katholischen Universität Eichstätt-Ingolstadt ein von der Deutschen Forschungsgemeinschaft geförderter internationaler Kongress unter dem Titel „*Texte, Kontexte, Lebenswelten: Textformen des Sirachbuches im geistes- und kulturgeschichtlichen Horizont des Hellenismus*“ statt. Die Idee dazu entstand im Zuge von Vorarbeiten zu einem seit Juli 2015 mittlerweile ebenfalls von der Deutschen Forschungsgemeinschaft geförderten Projekt, welches das Ziel verfolgt, eine polyglotte Synopse der hebräischen, syrischen, griechischen und lateinischen Textüberlieferung des Sirachbuches jeweils mit deutscher Übersetzung zu erstellen. Ziel des Sirachkongresses in Eichstätt war es, den aktuellen Stand der Sirachforschung im internationalen Fachdiskurs zu dokumentieren, und zwar im Blick auf die drei Themenbereiche

1. des soziokulturellen und geistesgeschichtlichen Hintergrundes des Sirachbuches,
2. der philologischen und textgeschichtlichen Probleme der verschiedenen sprachlichen Fassungen, in denen das Sirachbuch überliefert ist (Hebräisch, Griechisch, Syrisch, Lateinisch), sowie
3. der den griechischen, syrischen und lateinischen Texttraditionen zugrundeliegenden Übersetzungsstrategien und damit verbundenen hermeneutischen Fragen.

Bei den im vorliegenden Band versammelten Beiträgen handelt es sich um die im Rahmen des Sirachkongresses in Eichstätt 2014 gehaltenen Vorträge, zum Teil in überarbeiteter und erweiterter Fassung. Die Anordnung der Beiträge folgt der Reihenfolge der Vorträge und bietet damit zugleich einen Durchgang durch die drei oben genannten Themenbereiche, vom kulturhistorischen Kontext des Sirachbuches, über textgeschichtliche und philologische Einzelfragen bis hin zu Fragen der Übersetzung und Hermeneutik.

Unser Dank gilt zunächst natürlich der Autorin und den Autoren, die einer Veröffentlichung ihrer Beiträge zugestimmt haben, nicht zuletzt auch für die Geduld, da sich die Drucklegung aus verschiedenen Gründen immer wieder verzögert hat. Der Katholischen Universität Eichstätt-Ingolstadt und dem Collegium Willibaldinum danken wir für die Gastfreundschaft. Frau Anneliese Knör hatte als Sekretärin des Lehrstuhls für Alttestamentliche Wissenschaft an der Katholischen Universität Eichstätt-Ingolstadt maßgeblichen Anteil am Gelingen der Tagung. Die wissenschaftlichen Hilfskräfte Frau Maria Reith und Frau Angelika Nießlbeck des Lehrstuhls für Alttestamentliche Wissenschaft in Eichstätt haben sich um die Erstellung des Manuskripts verdient gemacht. Für die Aufnahme des Bandes in die Reihe der *Septuaginta and Cognate Studies* danken wir den Herausgebern, Fr. Nicole Tilford für die verlegerische Betreuung seitens des Verlags.

Die Herausgeber

Key Aspects and Themes in Recent Scholarship on the Book of Ben Sira

Markus Witte

1. Five Reasons for the Current Blossoming in the Scholarship of Ben Sira

Ben Sira scholarship finds itself in a time of considerable bloom. There are manifold reasons for this. First, it is participating in the current blossoming of Qumran and Septuagint scholarship that started with the publication of almost all the Qumran texts known at that time in the early 1990s and with the large Septuagint translation projects of Bible d'Alexandrie, New English Translation of the Septuagint, Septuaginta Deutsch, and La Biblia griega.[1] Second, because of the relatively solid date of its putative Hebrew original version and its first Greek translation to around 180 BCE and 120 BCE respectively, it has come to be viewed in literary-historical terms, like Deuteronomy, as something of an Archimedean Point for Israelite-Jewish literature. Third, in terms of methodology, the foundationally new understanding of the relationships between text criticism and compositional criticism, as well as from textual history and literary history in Old Testament studies has led to viewing the divergences in textual traditions as valuable for something other than the reconstruction of a hypothetical "Urtext." Text variants are instead viewed as empirical literary-historical

1. Marguerite Harl, ed., *La Bible d'Alexandrie: Traduction et annotation des livres de la Septante* (Paris: Cerf, 1986); Albert Pietersma and Benjamin G. Wright, eds., *A New English Translation of the Septuagint and the Other Greek Translations Traditionally Included under That Title* (New York: Oxford University Press, 2007); Wolfgang Kraus and Martin Karrer, eds., *Septuaginta Deutsch: Das griechische Alte Testament in deutscher Übersetzung* (Stuttgart: Deutsche Bibelgesellschaft, 2009; 2nd ed. 2010); Natalio Fernández Marcos and María Victoria Spottorno Díaz-Caro, eds., *La Biblia griega: Septuaginta* (Salamanca: Sígueme, 2008).

evidence for the redaction history of a book. The various ancient versions are now understood in terms of composition and reception history as distinct literary works containing their own structures, statements, and histories of effects. Fourth, current biblical studies, ancient history, and Jewish studies have developed a particular interest in the Greco-Roman period as the formative epoch for the history, culture, and religion of ancient Judaism and early Christianity.[2] Fifth, the blossoming of Ben Sira scholarship is also conditioned by the religious confessions of researchers. While the literary-historical, reception-historical, and theological value of the Apocrypha, or rather the deuterocanonical works, was with few exceptions only appreciated by Roman-Catholic scholarship until the early 1970s, since then Protestant biblical scholarship has also dedicated itself extensively to investigating the Apocrypha. Several examples include (1) the establishment of the series Jüdische Schriften aus Hellenistisch-Römischer Zeit by the Marburg New Testament scholar Werner Georg Kümmel (together with Christian Habicht, Otto Kaiser, Otto Plöger, and Josef Schreiner), continued by the Tübingen New Testament scholar Hermann Lichtenberger; (2) the expansion of the commentary series Altes Testament Deutsch to include commentaries on the Apocrypha—Georg Sauer authored the Ben Sira volume (2000),[3] which represents the first comprehensive Protestant commentary on Ben Sira since the primarily text-critically concentrated elucidations by Otto Zöckler (1891), Victor Ryssel (1900), and Rudolf Smend (1906);[4] and (3) the seminal revision of the Apocrypha within the context of the review of the Luther translation for 2017, which is the first time in the context of the Luther-Bibel that the complete, that is, the expanded, later Greek text (G-II) that includes the Prologue will serve as the textual basis for the translation.[5] It is necessary to keep in mind

2. On this, see the contribution by Oda Wischmeyer in this volume.

3. Georg Sauer, *Jesus Sirach/Ben Sira*, ATD Apokryphen 1 (Göttingen: Vandenhoeck & Ruprecht, 2000).

4. Otto Zöckler, *Die Weisheit Jesus Sirachs*, in *Die Apokryphen des Alten Testaments: Nebst einem Anhang über die Pseudepigraphenliteratur*, Kurzgefaßter Kommentar zu den heiligen Schriften Alten und Neuen Testamentes sowie zu den Apokryphen, Altes Testament 9 (Munich: Beck, 1891), 255–354; Victor Ryssel, *Die Sprüche Jesus, des Sohnes Jesus Sirachs*, APAT 1 (Tübingen: Mohr Siebeck, 1900), 230–475; Rudolf Smend, *Die Weisheit des Jesus Sirach erklärt* (Berlin: Reimer, 1906); Smend, *Die Weisheit des Jesus Sirach: Hebräisch und deutsch; Mit einem hebräischen Glossar* (Berlin: Reimer, 1906).

5. Cf. Markus Witte, "'Es hat nämlich nicht die gleiche Kraft, wenn etwas in der

here that a revised translation of the prayer of Sir 51:12a–o (cf. Ps 136) that only appears in Hebrew and in the B manuscript that is important in terms of liturgy and literary history as well as theology (though perhaps secondary),[6] will be added in an appendix. The *Einheitsübersetzung* (1980; rev. ed. 2016/2017), the New Revised Standard Version (1989/1992), and La Bible—Traduction Oecuménique (2010) also include it.

In the following, I will sketch five subfields within recent Ben Sira scholarship. My intention is not to offer the history of scholarship, but rather to name central questions, to provide a short presentation of selected studies from the past fifteen years that I view as seminal, and to formulate several pressing challenges. This will be carried out in connection with the more recent introductions to the book of Ben Sira and the recent histories of scholarship provided by Friedrich V. Reiterer, Johannes Marböck, Pancratius C. Beentjes, Frank Ueberschaer, and Maurice Gilbert.[7]

---

eigenen Sprache auf Hebräisch gesagt wird und wenn es in eine andere Sprache übersetzt wird' (SirProl 21f.): Anmerkungen zur Übersetzung der Apokryphen in der Revision der Lutherbibel 2017," in *"Was Dolmetschen für Kunst und Arbeit sei": Die Lutherbibel und andere deutsche Bibelübersetzungen, Beiträge der Rostocker Konferenz 2013*, ed. M. Lange and M. Rösel (Stuttgart: Deutsche Bibelgesellschaft, 2014), 273–89.

6. See Otto Mulder, "Three Psalms or Two Prayers in Sirach 51? The End of Ben Sira's Book of Wisdom," *DCLY* 2004: 171–201, esp. 182–87 (what counts for Mulder is Sir 51:12e+–zj+); Burkard M. Zapff, *Jesus Sirach 25–51*, NechtB AT 39 (Würzburg: Echter, 2010), 392–94. On the anthology like character of the prayer, which adopts material from numerous older biblical texts, see already Norbert Peters, *Das Buch Jesus Sirach oder Ecclesiasticus*, EHAT 25 (Münster: Aschendorff, 1913), 442–45, as well as more recently Françoise Mies, "Le Psaume de Ben Sira 51,12a–o Hébreu," *RB* 116 (2009): 336–67, 481–504.

7. Friedrich V. Reiterer, "Review of Recent Research on the Book of Ben Sira (1980–1996)," in *The Book of Ben Sira in Modern Research*, ed. Pancratius C. Beentjes, BZAW 255 (Berlin: de Gruyter, 1997), 23–60; Reiterer, "Text und Buch Ben Sira in Tradition und Forschung: Eine Einführung," in *Bibliographie zu Ben Sira*, ed. Friedrich V. Reiterer, BZAW 266 (Berlin: de Gruyter, 1998), 1–42; Reiterer et al., *Zählsynopse zum Buch Ben Sira*, FSBP 1 (Berlin: de Gruyter, 2003), 1–77; Johannes Marböck, "Zur Einführung—Neuere Studien und Hilfsmittel zur Arbeit am Sirachbuch," in *Weisheit und Frömmigkeit: Studien zur alttestamentlichen Literatur der Spätzeit*, ed. Johannes Marböck, ÖBS 29 (Frankfurt: Lang, 2006), 11–13; Marböck, "Sirach/Sirachbuch," in Marböck, *Frömmigkeit*, 15–21; Marböck, *Jesus Sirach 1–23 übersetzt und ausgelegt*, HTKAT (Freiburg: Herder, 2010), 21–34; Pancratius C. Beentjes, "Some Major Topics in Ben Sira Research," in *"Happy the One Who Meditates on Wisdom" (Sir. 14,20): Collected Essays on the Book of Ben Sira*, ed. Pancratius C. Beentjes, CBET 43 (Leuven: Peeters, 2006), 3–16; Frank Ueberschaer, *Weisheit aus der Begegnung: Bildung nach*

2. Five Fields of Study in Recent Ben Sira Scholarship

2.1. Text and Language

2.1.1. Text

The most important challenge facing current scholarship on Ben Sira consists of the preparation of a critical edition of the Hebrew text. While Joseph Ziegler prepared a critical-eclectic edition for the Greek Text (G) in 1980[8] and one was begun for the Latin text (La) that was completed as far as Sir 28:24 by Walter Thiele (1987–2005) and is being continued by Anthony J. Forte (2014–) for the Vetus Latina,[9] critical editions are missing for the Hebrew and the Syriac texts. With regard to the Hebrew text (H), this is compensated on a provision basis by the diplomatic edition of the Hebrew fragments presented by Beentjes (1997, revised 2006).[10] In the case of the Syriac text (Syr), there is the diplomatic edition on the basis of the facsimile edition of Codex Ambrosianus (7a1), the oldest extant codex of the Peshitta (seventh century CE) edited by Núria Calduch-Benages, Joan Ferrer, and Jan Liesen (2003).[11] The critical edition in preparation by W. Th. van Peursen and K. D. Jenner as part of the Leiden Peshitta will also be a diplomatic edition based on Codex Ambrosianus.

The edition by Calduch-Benages, Ferrer, and Liesen provides Syr in an easily accessible form. The text is printed in two columns and contains

---

dem Buch Ben Sira, BZAW 379 (Berlin: de Gruyter, 2007), 3–24; Maurice Gilbert, "Methodological and Hermeneutical Trends in Modern Exegesis on the Book of Ben Sira," in *The Wisdom of Ben Sira: Studies on Tradition, Redaction, and Theology*, ed. A. Passaro and G. Bellia, DCLS 1 (Berlin: de Gruyter, 2008), 1–20; Gilbert, "Où en sont les études sur le Siracide?," *Bib* 92 (2011): 161–81.

8. Joseph Ziegler, *Sapientia Iesu Filii Sirach*, 2nd. ed., SVTG 12.2 (Göttingen: Vandenhoeck & Ruprecht, 1980).

9. Walter Thiele, *Sirach (Ecclesiasticus)*, VLB 11.2 (Freiburg: Herder, 1987–2005); Anthony J. Forte, *Sir 25,1–28,24*, part 1 of *Sirach (Ecclesiasticus): Pars altera*, VLB 11.2 (Freiburg: Herder, 2014).

10. Pancratius C. Beentjes, *The Book of Ben Sira in Hebrew: A Text Edition of All Extant Hebrew Manuscripts and a Synopsis of All Parallel Hebrew Ben Sira Texts*, VTSup 68 (Leiden: Brill, 1997; Atlanta: Society of Biblical Literature, 2006).

11. Núria Calduch-Benages, *La sabiduría del escriba/Wisdom of the Scribe: Edición diplomática de la versión siriaca del libro de Ben Sira según el Códice Ambrosiano, con traducción española e inglesia/Diplomatic Edition of the Syriac Version of the Book of Ben Sira according to Codex Ambrosianus with Translations in Spanish and English*, Biblioteca Midrásica 26 (Estella, Navarra: Verbo Divino, 2003; 2nd ed., 2015).

the readings in continuous text of the respective columns of the codex as well as the verse and chapter numbers oriented toward to the Greek version edited by Ziegler. Line numbers for every five lines appear in the margin. The footnotes mention the obvious textual errors of the Milan Codex and provide suggested emendations as well as explanations of the English and Spanish translations. A likewise bilingual introduction guides the reader into the text, the nature of the translation, and the most important editions of Syr, while also listing idiomatic expressions with their translation equivalents.

The preparation of a critical edition of H would, however, presuppose a new viewing of all the Hebrew documents, which are the fragments from the Cairo Genizah, from Qumran, and from Masada. As is seen by the new fragments of manuscripts C and D of the Cairo Genizah published in 2007/2008 und 2011,[12] it can be expected that further new Ben Sira texts will be found in the collection of fragments from Cairo. This also raises hope that Hebrew equivalents will be found to the central chapters 1, 17, and 24, which have so far only surfaced in G, Syr, and La. Even when there are very high quality photographs of all known Ben Sira fragments from the Cairo Genizah, Qumran, and Masada are available online,[13] the preparation of a critical edition still requires viewing the fragments on site, though in spite of the high quality conservation efforts will become successively more difficult to read.

The fundamental problem of preparing a critical edition of H is, as is well known, that none of the six manuscripts of A–F features a complete

12. On C: Shulamit Elizur, "A New Fragment from the Hebrew Text of the Book of Ben Sira," *Tarbiz* 76 (2007):17–28; Elizur, "Two New Leaves of the Hebrew Version of Ben Sira," *DSD* 17 (2010):13–29; Renate Egger-Wenzel, "Ein neues Sira-Fragment MS^{C}," *BN* 138 (2008):107–14; Jean-Sébastian Rey, "Un nouveau bifeuillet du manuscrit C de la Genizah du Caire," in *Florilegium Lovaniense: Studies in Septuagint and Textual Criticism in Honour of F. García Martínez*, ed. M. Vervenne et al., BETL 224 (Leuven: Peeters, 2008), 387–415. The fragment contains the cola 3:27a.b (cf. H^{A}); 6:5a–10b (cf. H^{A}); 6:12a–15b (cf. H^{A}); 6:18a, ba; 20:30a–31b; 21:22a–23b, 26a, b; 22:11a–12b, 21a–22b; 23:11a, b; 25:7c, d; 36:24b (cf. H$^{A/Bmg}$); 37:1a.2–2b (cf. H$^{B/Bm/D}$).

On D: Shulamit Elizur and Michael Rand, "A New Fragment of the Book of Ben Sira," *DSD* 18 (2011): 200–205; Jean-Sébastien Rey, "Un nouveau feuillet du manuscrit D de Ben Sira," *RevQ* 25 (2012):395–422. The new fragment contains the text of Sir 7:18–8:18 (cf. H^{A}: 7:20–21, 23–25; 8:7, and H^{C}).

13. http://tinyurl.com/SBL060467h; http://tinyurl.com/SBL060467j; http://tinyurl.com/SBL060467i.

text. If one desires, as a result, to do more than simply print the manuscripts separately or synoptically in cases where they overlap like Beentjes's edition,[14] then the only remaining possibility is a mixed text like the editions by Francesco Vattioni (1968) and Ze'ev Ben-Ḥayyim (1973).[15] This means that in succession, at any one time, *each* manuscript is printed where it contains the relevant text. When variants from another manuscript are extant, these are noted in an apparatus. This apparatus would also include the divergences from H in G, Syr, and La. The recovery of the as yet unattested Hebrew texts through the reverse translation from the Greek short text (G-I) as the oldest representative of a full version of the book, as undertaken by, for example, Moshe Z. Segal (1933) and Abraham Kahana (1936/1937),[16] is problematic for two reasons. First, as the pertinent investigations by Benjamin G. Wright and Antonino Minissale prove, G constitutes a relatively free translation.[17] Second, G is also extant only in later recensions.

The fact that Ben Sira texts were also found among the texts from Qumran and Masada indicates that scholarship on Ben Sira should be closely interlocked with Qumran scholarship.[18] This includes a systematic

---

14. Cf. also the older editions by Pietro Boccaccio and Guido Berardi, *Ecclesiasticus: Textus Hebraeus secundum fragmenta reperta* (Rome: Pontifical Biblical Institute, 1986).

15. Francesco Vattioni, *Ecclesiastico: Testo ebraico con apparato critico e versioni greca, latina e siriaca*, Pubblicazioni del Seminario di Semitistica 1 (Neapel: Istituto Orientale di Napoli, 1968); Ze'ev Ben-Ḥayyim, *The Book of Ben Sira: Text, Concordance and an Analysis of the Vocabulary*, The Historical Dictionary of the Hebrew Language (Jerusalem: The Academy of the Hebrew Language and the Shrine of the Book, 1973).

16. Moshe Z. Segal, ספר בן סירא השלם [*The Complete Book of Ben Sira*], 3rd ed. (Jerusalem: Bialik Foundation, 1972); Abraham Kahana, "דברי שמעון בן־סירא," in הספרים החיצונים, 2 vols. (repr., Raanana: Ben Zion Kahana, 2006), 2:435–530.

17. Benjamin G. Wright, *No Small Difference: Sirach's Relationship to Its Hebrew Parent Text*, SCS 26 (Atlanta: Scholars Press, 1989); Wright, "Access to the Source: Cicero, Ben Sira, the Septuagint and their Audiences," in *Praise Israel for Wisdom and Instruction: Essays on Ben Sira and Wisdom, the Letter of Aristeas and the Septuagint*, ed. Benjamin G. Wright, JSJSup 131 (Leiden: Brill, 2008), 247–73; Antonino Minissale, *La versione greca del Siracide: Confronto con il testo ebraico alla luce dell' attività midrascica e del metodo targumico*, AnBib 133 (Rome: Pontificio Istituto Biblico, 1995); cf. also Beentjes, "Topics," in *Happy*, 6.

18. 2Q18 with minimal remains from Sir 1:19–20 or more likely from 6:14a–15 and 6:20a–22b, 26a–31b (first century BCE), 11QPs^{a}/11Q05 XXI with sections not

view of all possible citations or allusions from the book of Ben Sira in the extant Qumran texts corpus in the manner that has already been accomplished (in part) for the rabbinic literature. The first detailed studies for the Qumran texts are available, of exemplary nature are the essay by Émile Puech on 4Q525 2 II, 2 and 4QInstruction as well as the comprehensive study by Jean-Sébastien Rey on 4QInstruction.[19]

A special note for future scholarship on the text lies in the analysis of the additions to the Hebrew (Long-) Text (H-II) and in the Greek (Long-) Text (G-II), as well as on the plusses exhibited by La and Syr. In addition to the direct contribution to the textual history, this work would also clarify the literary, social, and religious-historical backgrounds of the ancient versions. The fact that the dissertation completed in 1951 by Conleth Kearns (1902–1985) on the Greek long text was (first) published in 2011 signals the need for further research.[20] Kearns offers a careful investigation of G-II, namely, on how it is reflected in Codex Vaticanus and in several Greek minuscules, on the one hand, and on how it is mirrored in the Vetus Latina which is integrated in the Vulgata and—with characteristic modifications—in Syr, on the other.[21] In this respect Kearns represents the

written in verse of 51:13–20, 30b (early first century CE) and Mas/H^M/Mas 1^h with seven columns written in verse, representing 39:27–44:17 (between 125/100 and 50/25 BCE); cf. Beentjes, "Book," 19, 113–25; Eugene Ulrich, ed., *The Biblical Qumran Scrolls: Transcriptions and Textual Variants*, VTSup 134 (Leiden: Brill, 2010), 719–20.

19. Émile Puech, "Ben Sira and Qumran," in *The Wisdom of Ben Sira: Studies on Tradition, Redaction, and Theology*, ed. A. Passaro and G. Bellia, DCLS 1 (Berlin: de Gruyter, 2008), 79–118; Jean-Sébastien Rey, *4QInstruction: Sagesse et eschatologie*, STDJ 81 (Leiden: Brill, 2009), 17–21, 333–34.

20. Conleth Kearns, *The Expanded Text of Ecclesiasticus: Its Teaching on the Future Life as a Clue to Its Origin: Enlarged with a Biographical Sketch of Kearns by Gerard Norton, an Introduction to Kearn's Dissertation by Maurice Gilbert, Bibliographical Updates (1951–2010) by Núria Calduch-Benages*, ed. Pancratius C. Beentjes, DCLS 11 (Berlin: de Gruyter, 2011).

21. On the importance of La for the history of the text, especially for the textual history of G, see also Maurice Gilbert, "The Vetus Latina of Ecclesiasticus," in *Studies in the Book of Ben Sira*, ed. G. G. Xeravits and J. Zsengellér, JSJSup 127 (Leiden: Brill, 2008), 1–9, as well as Anthony J. Forte, "The Old Latin Version of Sirach: Editio Critica and Textual Problems," in *The Texts and Versions of the Book of Ben Sira: Transmissions and Interpretation*, ed. Jan Joosten and Jean-Sébastien Rey, JSJSup 15 (Leiden: Brill, 2011), 199–214; Forte, "Veteris Latinae Ecclesiastici: Apologia pro interprete latino," *JSCS* 47 (2014): 69–92; Thierry Legrand, "La version latine de Ben Sira: État de la question, essai de classement thématique des 'additions,'" in Joosten and Rey, *Texts and*

first attempt to classify the expansions that G-II manifests in comparison with the older and more original short text (G-I) and locate them in terms of the religious-historical setting on the backdrop of the Jewish writings from the Greco-Roman period (esp. in comparison to Dan 12, 1 Enoch, Jubilees, Wisdom of Solomon, and Psalms of Solomon). His investigation remains quite relevant for the understanding of Judaism during the period from 200 BCE to 100 CE. Even though Kearns was not able to draw upon the presently available critical editions and diplomatic versions of G, Syr, La, and H, and the fact that his argument for the Essene provenance of the G-II text as a systematic eschatological revision of the G-I text hardly remains convincing in light of the present state of Qumran scholarship—Kearns wrote in the early days of this development[22]—scholarship is still in debt to Beentjes for preparing Kearns's manuscript for publication. Also helpful is the bibliographic supplement provided by Calduch-Benages on the main themes treated in the dissertation such as the long text of G-II, Ben Sira's view of death, his view of the afterlife, and Ben Sira's conceptions of resurrection and messianism. With regard to the additions in La and Syr, one can expect that there will be further insights on the nature of writing and the hermeneutics of early Christianity and its relationships to Jewish understandings of writing as well as the theological peculiarities of these versions.

A final desideratum is a critical edition of the Coptic text of Ben Sira, which according to the analysis by Frank Feder belongs to the text types represented by the Greek uncial manuscripts of B, S, and A.[23]

The work on the text of Ben Sira would ideally end with a critical polyglot that would replace the synopsis by Vattioni (1968). The numbering synopsis prepared in 2003 by Reiterer and his team at the Salzburg Sirach Research Center is an irreplaceable aid for such a synopsis and in handling the chaos of the numbering, which has especially been generated by the transposition of pages in the regular codex of G in range of chapters 30–36 as well as the

---

Versions of the Book of Ben Sira, 215–34; Bonifatia Gesche, "Die Vetus Latina-Version des Buchs Jesus Sirach als Zeuge für die Version Griechisch II," in *Die Septuaginta—Text, Wirkung, Rezeption*, ed. W. Kraus and S. Kreuzer, WUNT 32 (Tübingen: Mohr Siebeck, 2014), 698–712.

22. On the relationship between texts of Essene origins and Sira, see Puech, "Ben Sira and Qumran."

23. Frank Feder, "The Coptic Version(s) of the Book of Jesus Sirach," in Joosten and Rey, *Texts and Versions of the Book of Ben Sira*, 11–20.

different verse numbering in La.[24] Reiterer's work offers a synopsis of the differing verse and chapter numbers in H, G, Syr, and Vg/La as well as in four modern translations. The numbering as a whole is aligned to the polyglot text-critical edition of the book on the basis of the numbering in G-I, which is currently in preparation by Reiterer. It includes all passages contained in G-II, in the Hebrew fragments from Qumran, Masada, and the Cairo Genizah, in Syr, and in La. The textual plusses of the individual versions are marked. For H it will list the editions by Ben-Ḥayyim and Beentjes;[25] for Syr the editions of Calduch-Benages, Ferrer, and Liesen,[26] Paul de Lagarde, and the Mosul edition;[27] for G the editions of Ziegler, Alfred Rahlfs, and Henry Barclay Swete;[28] for Vg/La, the Roman edition and the edition of the Stuttgart Bible Society.[29] The modern translations are represented by the New Revised Standard Version, the *Einheitsübersetzung*, the *revidierte Lutherübersetzung* (2017), and the transmission by Sauer (1981).[30]

24. Reiterer, *Zählsynopse*, 174–96. On the problem of the transposition of pages, see also Christian Wagner, *Die Septuaginta-Hapaxlegomena im Buch Jesus Sirach: Untersuchungen zu Wortwahl und Wortbildung unter besonderer Berücksichtigung des textkritischen und übersetzungstechnischen Aspekts*, BZAW 282 (Berlin: de Gruyter, 1999), 33–35; and Franz Böhmisch, "Die Blattvertauschung (Lage 12 und 13) im griechischen Sirachbuch," *PzB* 14 (2005): 17–22.

25. See nn. 15 and 10.

26. See n. 11.

27. Paul Anton de Lagarde, ed., *Libri Veteris Testamenti Apocryphi Syriace* (Leipzig: Brockhaus, 1861), 2–51; *Biblia Sacra iuxta versionem simplicem quae dicitur Pschitta*, 2nd ed. (Beirut: Imprimerie Catholique, 1951), 2:204–55.

28. See n. 8 as well as Alfred Rahlfs, ed., *Septuaginta: Id est Vetus Testamentum graece iuxta LXX interpretes, Duo volumina in uno*, 9th ed. (Stuttgart: Deutsche Bibelgesellschaft, 1979); Henry Barclay Swete, *The Old Testament in Greek according to the Septuagint*, 3rd ed. (Cambridge: University Press, 1907; repr., 4th. ed, 1922), 2:604–754.

29. *Sapientia Salomonis; Liber Hiesu Filii Sirach cum praefationibus et variis capitulorum seriebus; Biblia Sacra, iuxta latinam Vulgatam versionem ad codicum fidem iussu Pauli PP. VI cura et studio monachorum Abbatiae Pontificiae Sancti Hieronymi in Urbe Ordinis Sancti Benedicti edita XII* (Rome: Typis Polyglottis Vaticanis, 1964); Robert Weber, ed., *Biblia Sacra iuxta Vulgatam versionem*, 2nd ed. (Stuttgart: Württembergische Bibelanstalt, 1975), 1028–95.

30. Georg Sauer, *Jesus Sirach*, JSHRZ 3.5 (Gütersloh: Gütersloher Verlagshaus, 1981).

2.1.2. Language

Belonging also to the field of study of Text is the special exploration of the nature of language, primarily of H, but also of G and Syr, in the latter especially from the perspective of its translation technique.

H is especially consulted as a witness for the evaluation of the Hebrew between the Hebrew of the latest books that became part of the canon of the Hebrew Bible and the Mishnah and in comparison to the diverse Hebrew of the nonbiblical texts from Qumran. For the study of Ben Sira's Hebrew in recent scholarship, reference should be made especially to the comprehensive study by van Peursen on the verbal system (2004) and to two volumes of essays edited by Jan Joosten and Rey (2008/2011), but also to the detailed investigation by Johannes F. Diehl on Ben Sira's use of אשרי (2013).[31] Particularly the volume edited by Joosten and Rey in 2011 provides for the development within the history of scholarship with regard to the appreciation of the language and literature of the various versions as discrete texts,[32] rather than merely as quarries for filling in the lacuna of the Hebrew fragments.[33] To that effect, this volume offers separate linguistically oriented studies of select Hebrew manuscripts, studies of translation techniques of various Greek versions, as well as studies on the tradition-historical and theological nature of Syr and the shape of the text of La.

For G, the important studies by Christian Wagner on the Septuagint hapax legomena (1999) as well as the useful concordance on the 135 (in Ziegler's counting) additional lines of the G-II Text by Jean Marie Auwers

---

31. W. Th. van Peursen, *The Verbal System in the Hebrew Text of Ben Sira*, Studies in Semitic Languages and Linguistics 41 (Leiden: Brill, 2004); Jan Joosten and Jean-Sébastien Rey, eds., *Conservatism and Innovation in the Hebrew Language of the Hellenistic Period: Proceedings of a Fourth International Symposium on the Hebrew of the Dead Sea Scrolls and Ben Sira*, STDJ 73 (Leiden: Brill, 2008); Johannes F. Diehl, "'*ʾšry ʾnwš*, der über Weisheit meditiert und zur Einsicht aufschaut' Sir 14,20: Überlegungen zur 'ašrê-Formel bei Ben Sira, in der Hebräischen Bibel und in Qumran," in *Weisheit als Lebensgrundlage*, ed. R. Egger-Wenzel, DCLS 15 (Berlin: de Gruyter, 2013), 47–64.

32. Jan Joosten and Jean-Sébastien Rey, eds., *The Texts and Versions of the Book of Ben Sira: Transmissions and Interpretation*, JSJSup 150 (Leiden: Brill, 2011).

33. Cf. the exemplary work of Friedrich V. Reiterer, "Die Differenz zwischen Urtext und Ausgangstext: Beispiele zur Entwicklung der sirazidischen Versionen," in *From Qumran to Aleppo: A Discussion with E. Tov about the Textual History of Jewish Scriptures in Honor of His Sixty-Fifth Birthday*, FRLANT 230 (Göttingen: Vandenhoeck & Ruprecht, 2009), 123–40.

(2005) should be named.[34] Nonetheless, further investigations on the Greek of G-I and G-II, both in light of the nature of the translation and their location in the context of the contemporary Greek are necessary. A thorough analysis of the prologue by the grandson would be desirable, which examines its linguistic-historical placement, its approach to translation, its text-pragmatics, and its cultural-historical location within the context of ancient paganism and Jewish translation and early Jewish diaspora literature. One can provisionally refer to the shorter studies by Stefan Schorch (2008), Siegfried Kreuzer (2009), Wright (2011), and Stephan Lauber (2013).[35]

On Syr, mention should be made of the comprehensive investigation by van Peursen (2007).[36] His book represents the fruit of the Leiden project "Computer-Assisted Linguistic Analysis of the Peshitta" (CALAP). Part 1 offers a traditional description of the textual history, the translation technique, and the religious characteristics of Syr. It argues that it is a free translation not influenced by G, but with tendencies like the Targums from a Jewish-Christian milieu of the second/third century CE. Part 2 presents the methodology of CALAP, an attempt to attain an objective synchronic version of the text and description of it that requires rather than presenting the antithesis of classical philological analysis, supplementing classical philology in places where exegetes' intuition fails. The focus of the computer-sup-

---

34. Wagner, *Septuaginta-Hapaxlegomena*; Jean Marie Auwers and Églantine Proksch-Strajtmann, *Concordance du Siracide (Grec II et Sacra Parallela)*, CahRB 58 (Paris: Gabalda, 2005).

35. Stefan Schorch, "The Pre-eminence of the Hebrew Language and the Emerging Concept of the 'Ideal Text' in Late Second Temple Judaism," in Xeravits and Zsengellér, *Studies in the Book of Ben Sira*, 43–54; Siegfried Kreuzer, "Der Prolog des Buchs Ben Sira (Weisheit des Jesus Sirach) im Horizont seiner Gattung: Ein Vergleich mit dem Euagoras des Isokrates," in *Geschehen und Gedächtnis: Die hellenistische Welt und ihre Wirkung*, ed. J.-F. Eckholdt, Antike Kultur und Geschichte 13 (Münster: LIT, 2009), 135–60; Benjamin G. Wright, "Why a Prologue? Ben Sira's Grandson and His Greek Translation," in *Emanuel: Studies in the Hebrew Bible, Septuagint and Dead Sea Scrolls*, ed. S. M. Paul, VTSup 14 (Leiden: Brill, 2003), 633–44; Wright, "Translation Greek in Sirach in Light of the Grandsons's Prologue," in Joosten and Rey, *Texts and Versions of the Book of Ben Sira*, 75–94; Stephan Lauber, "Hi 32 als hellenistisches Proömium," *ZAW* 125 (2013): 607–21; cf. the article of Knut Usener in this volume.

36. W. Th. van Peursen, *Language and Interpretation in the Syriac Text of Ben Sira: A Comparative Lingustic and Literary Study*, MPIL 16 (Leiden: Brill, 2007); van Peursen, "Ben Sira in the Syriac Tradition," in Joosten and Rey, *Texts and Versions of the Book of Ben Sira*, 143–65.

ported analysis carried out by van Peursen lies on the graphic, syntactical, and grammatical form of Syr. In addition, the text is completely transliterated, segmented, and analyzed morphologically according to the smallest grammatical units, in order to then describe it in terms of its phrases, clauses, and sentences. In so doing, the computer-supported investigation also incorporates H and G. Van Peursen assigns Syr to a relatively early stage of classical Syriac in terms of its language. His work constitutes a quite helpful aid, which can foster further insights with regard to the composition and interpretation of larger sections such as, for example, the "praise of the fathers" (Sir 44–49, 50). The study is important for the entire field of the exegesis of the Hebrew Bible because of its achievements with regard to translation theory, to translation technique, and to the literary and religious characteristics of the Peshitta as well as to the comparative Semitics (of note here, among others, is the discussion on nominal clauses). However, in contrast to van Peursen, Giovanni Rizzi (2008) argues, after critical review of the main points in favor of the composition of the Peshitta of Ben Sira in Jewish and/or various Christian settings, for its derivation from Syriac Christianity in the fourth century, which—like Aphrahat and Ephraim—was conversant with Jewish exegesis and haggadah.[37] In principle, then, there is need of further research to clarify the linguistic and religious-historical character and provenance of the *Vorlage(n)*, the textual layers, and the influences on Syr. Most recently Jan Joosten presents the view that Syr goes back to a Jewish Targum on Ben Sira, as seen in several West Aramaic words, which in a second stage was "syriacized in a purely Christian milieu."[38]

On the border between the study of language and the study of form are investigations of poetics and rhetoric. Noteworthy here is the work of Eric D. Reymond (2004).[39] The study, which arises from a dissertation completed under the direction of Dennis Pardee at the University of Chicago, offers a poetic analysis of H^{Mas}. After a short introduction to and history of scholarship and methodology into the poetry of the Old Testament

37. Giovanni Rizzi, "Christian interpretations in the Syriac Version of Sirach," in *The Wisdom of Ben Sira: Studies on Tradition, Redaction, and Theology*, ed. A. Passaro and G. Bellia, DCLS 1 (Berlin: de Gruyter, 2008), 277–308.

38. Jan Joosten, "Archaic Elements in the Syriac Version of Ben Sira," in Joosten and Rey, *Texts and Versions of the Book of Ben Sira*, 175; see also the contribution by Jan Joosten in this volume.

39. Eric D. Reymond, *Innovations in Hebrew Poetry: Parallelism and the Poems of Sirach*, StBibLit 9 (Leiden: Brill, 2004).

wisdom books, Reymond describes the poetic characteristics of Sir 40:11–17; 40:18–27; 40:28–30; 41:1–4; 41:5–13; 41:14b–15; 41:14a [*sic*]–42:8; 42:9–14; 42:15–43:33; 44:1–15. He identifies as marks of Ben Sira's poetics as (1) the bicolon is the basic pattern of a verse; (2) the largely equivalence in verse length; (3) the high frequency of grammatical parallelism; (4) the infrequent appearance of semantic parallelism in comparison to the proto-canonical wisdom books; and (5) the oft encountered grammatical, repetitive, or semantic parallelism between contiguous verses. Reymond recognizes Ben Sira's innovation in comparison to the patterns of Proverbs, Psalms, and the book of Job in its creation of new word pairs and metaphors. Comparison between other sections of Ben Sira (5:12–6:1; 10:1–31; 15:1–20; 45:1–22) and Prov 2; Pss 23; 89; 111; and Job 4–5 continue to illustrate Ben Sira's poetics. In view of the concentration of grammatical parallelism in favor of semantic parallelism and traditional word pairs, Reymond proposes the closeness of Ben Sira's poetry with that of the author of the Wisdom of Solomon.[40]

2.2. Form and Composition

Scholarship and questions concerning the composition of Ben Sira primarily center around three topics: the genres in the book, the genre of the book, and the source-critical and redaction history of the book.

2.2.1. Genres in the Book of Ben Sira

In line with a generally observed focus within biblical studies on the study of genre, discussion here centers on the identification of the *literary* form, function, and transformation of the genres present in Ben Sira. An emphasis of the pertinent works from recent years lies on the self praise of cosmic wisdom in chapter 24, for which a certain amount of consensus has arisen in identifying it as a song of praise akin to the aretalogies for the Egyptian goddess Isis, whose rose to the status of an universal goddess in the Hellenistic period.[41] Attention has also been accorded to the "Praise of

40. On the poetics of Ben Sira, see also Jeremy Corley, "Rhyme in the Hebrew Prophets and Wisdom Poetry," *BN* 132 (2006): 55–69. The Tartu dissertation by Jonas Jakobson, likewise dedicated to the peculiar poetics and the parallelism in Ben Sira and strongly marked by a focus on the metrics of the cola, is close to being finished.

41. Cf. basically Johannes Marböck, *Weisheit im Wandel: Untersuchungen zur Weisheitstheologie bei Ben Sira*, BBB 37 (Bonn: Hanstein, 1971); Marböck, "Gottes

the Fathers" in chapters 44–49 (the publications here are legion).[42] Finally there is the encomium of the High Priest Simeon in chapter 50—here the comprehensive and highly-respected study by Otto Mulder (2003) should especially be noted, which interpreted Sir 50 itself as "remembrance discourse/Zichronot" for a Rosh Hashanah liturgy,[43] along with the prayers scattered throughout the book (see below, section 2.4).

2.2.2. The Genre of the Book of Ben Sira

Following upon these discussions are questions concerning the genre of the book as a whole and the current structure of its composition.[44] Though the questions of composition and outline are controversial,[45] there is a consensus that the book should not be seen as a more or less arbitrary

---

Weisheit unter uns: Sir 24 als Beitrag zur biblischen Theologie," in *Gottes Weisheit unter uns: Zur Theologie des Buchs Sirach*, I. Fischer, HBSStudien 6 (Freiburg: Herder, 1995), 73–87; Marböck, "Einwohnung der Weisheit und das Hauptgebot: Schöpferischer Umgang mit Traditionen im Sirachbuch," *BN* 154 (2012): 69–81; Bernd Janowski, "Gottes Weisheit in Jerusalem: Sirach 24 und die biblische Schekina-Theologie," *DCLY* 2008: 1–29; Pancratius C. Beentjes, "'Come to Me, You Who Desire Me…': Lady Wisdom's Invitation in Ben Sira 24,19–22," in *Weisheit als Lebensgrundlage*, ed. R. Egger-Wenzel, DCLS 15 (Berlin: de Gruyter, 2013), 1–11.

42. Cf. the classic works by Burton L. Mack, *Wisdom and the Hebrew Epic: Ben Sira's Hymn in Praise of the Fathers*, CSJH (Chicago: University of Chicago Press, 1986); and Thomas R. Lee, *Studies in the Form of Sirach 44–50*, SBLDS 75 (Atlanta: Scholar Press, 1986) as well as the more recent relevant essays by Pancratius C. Beentjes in his collected essays *Happy*, 123–65; Beentjes, "Ben Sira 44:19–23—The Patriarchs: Text, Tradition, Theology," in Xeravits and Zsengellér, *Studies in the Book of Ben Sira*, 209–28; Jeremy Corley, "Sirach 44:1–15 as Introduction to the Praise of the Ancestors," in Xeravits and Zsengellér, *Studies in the Book of Ben Sira*, 151–81; Corley, "A Numerical Structure in Sirach 44:1–50:24," *CBQ* 69 (2007): 43–63; Corley, "The Portrait of Samuel in Hebrew Ben Sira 46:13–20," *DCLY* 2008: 31–56; Benjamin G. Wright, "The Use and Interpretation of Biblical Tradition in Ben Sira's Praise of the Ancestors," in Xeravits and Zsengellér, *Studies in the Book of Ben Sira*, 183–207.

43. Otto Mulder, *Simon the High Priest in Sirach 50: An Exegetical Study of the Significance of Simon the High Priest as Climax to the Praise of the Fathers in Ben Sira's Concept of the History of Israel*, JSJSup 78 (Leiden: Brill, 2003); adopted by Corley, "Sirach 44:1–15," 151–81.

44. Cf. Christine Mitchell, "Chronicles and Ben Sira: Questions of Genre," in *Rewriting Biblical History: Essays on Chronicles and Ben Sira*, ed. J. Corley and H. van Grol, DCLS 7 (Berlin: de Gruyter, 2011), 1–25.

45. Cf. Johannes Marböck, "Structure and Redaction History of the Book of Ben Sira—Review and Prospects," in *Frömmigkeit*, 31–45; Gilbert, "Les études."

compilation of sapiential poems and instructions, but a well-planned composition. The location of this composition in the sense of a wisdom book of instruction could be found in the small circle of Ben Sira's students. The question of the social and institutional localization of the circle of disciples is connected to the question of actors, forms, and places for the transmission of education and knowledge—not only—in Hellenistic Judaism.

2.2.3. Composition-Critical and Redaction History of the Book of Ben Sira

It remains open whether the well-planned composition of the book goes back to an author, namely, Ben Sira, or whether this is the product of purposeful scribal expansion that therefore demonstrates literary-historical growth. G-II, Syr, and La show that the book of Ben Sira underwent expansions (and abridgment). Moving on from this point, seldom has scholarship raised the question of the composition and redaction history of the book as a whole. Aside from the assumption of select expansions (especially the prayer and the rescue of Zion in 36:1–22 [G: 33:1–13a; 36:16b–22];[46] 44:16; 46:12; 48:11*; 49:12*; 51:12a–o are repeatedly named in this context), the actual composition-critical and redaction-historical analysis of the book remains to be done. The model sketched by Jeremy Corley (2008) presents a beginning.[47] Corley compares the composition of the book with the structures of Proverbs, Job, the Papyrus Insinger, the collection of maxims by Theognis of Megara, and the pre-Maccabean passages of 1 Enoch. He proposes an outline consisting of eight main sections (Sir 1:1–4:10; 4:11–6:17; 6:18–14:19; 14:20–23:27; 24:1–32:13; 32:14–38:23; 38:24–43:33; 44:1–50:24) with an appendix (50:25–51:30) and uses formal criteria to develop a five-stage model for the growth of the book (A: 1:1–23:17 + 51:13–30; B: + 24:1–32:13; C: + 32:14–38:23; 51:1–12; D: + 38:24–43:33; E: + 44:1–50:24; 50:25–26; 50:27–29).

---

46. In more recent times, again by Zapff, *Jesus Sirach*, 236; for discussion and defense of authorship by Ben Sira, see Maria Carmela Palmisano, "*Salvaci, Dio dell' universo!" Studio dell' eucologia di Sir 36H,1–17*, AnBib 163 (Rome: Pontificial Biblical Istitute, 2006), 15–49.

47. Jeremy Corley, "Searching for Structure and Redaction in Ben Sira: An Investigation of Beginnings and Endings," in *The Wisdom of Ben Sira: Studies on Tradition, Redaction, and Theology*, ed. A. Passaro and G. Bellia, DCLS 1 (Berlin: de Gruyter, 2008), 21–47.

2.3. Situation and Tradition

Ben Sira offers an outstanding source for Jewish cultural and religious history in the Hellenistic period because of its relatively certain date and localization in Jerusalem during the first quarter of the second century BCE and its Greek translation in Alexandria during the last quarter of the second century BCE. As a great synthesis of wisdom, cultic, historiographic and prophetic, and legal traditions in ancient Judaism that stands in direct contact with pagan traditions, the book itself provokes a more exact identification of its treatment of the older Jewish traditions and the contemporary pagan philosophical currents. This is especially reflected in current scholarship in four tradition-historically oriented domains.

2.3.1. Ben Sira/Jesus Sirach and the "Biblical Canon"

Both the work of Ben Sira itself and the Greek translation by his grandson support the esteem, one could also say the authoritative standing, of certain traditions within distinct communities of faith that was accorded to writings that became noncanonical in later Judaism, such as the Enoch writings. Ben Sira and his grandson do not attest to the canonicity, in the strict sense of the word, to any Jewish texts except the Torah. Ben Sira and his grandson are still quite distant from an unchangeable text in the sense of a standardized textual tradition,[48] as is apparent in their free interaction with citations of tradition. At the same time, on a macro level, Ben Sira assumes the Torah and the Prophets as Holy Scripture and explicitly accesses texts from the Torah and the Prophets especially within chapters 16–17, 24, and 44–49.[49] As a result, numerous recent studies are dedicated

---

48. Following Philip R. Davies, "How to Get Into the *Canon* and Stay There Or: The Philosophy of an Acquisitive Society," in *The Canon of Scripture in Jewish and Christian Tradition*, ed. P. S. Alexander and J.-D. Kaestli, Publications de l'Institut Romand des Sciences Bibliques 4 (Lausanne: Zèbre, 2007), 11–25, one could speak here of a "tertiary canonization" or a "canon of the third order." On the question of when this process concluded within Judaism, see Philip S. Alexander, "The Formation of the Biblical Canon in Rabbinic Judaism," in *The Canon of Scripture in Jewish and Christian Tradition*, ed. P. S. Alexander and J.-D. Kaestli, Publications de l'Institut Romand des Sciences Bibliques 4 (Lausanne: Zèbre, 2007), 72–74.

49. Markus Witte, "Der 'Kanon' heiliger Schriften des antiken Judentums im Spiegel des Buchs Ben Sira/Jesus Sirach," in *Kanon in Konstruktion und Dekonstruktion: Kanonisierungsprozesse religiöser Texte von der Antike bis zur Gegenwart—Ein Handbuch*, ed. E.-M. Becker and S. Scholz (Berlin: de Gruyter, 2011), 215–41.

to Ben Sira's relationship with the Jewish writings that became canonical (and those that did not become canonical). In connection with this, note should again be made of the works by Beentjes, who has published numerous case studies on scriptural exegesis in the book of Ben Sira since his dissertation (1981),[50] not to mention the overviews provided by Wright and Reiterer.[51]

Ben Sira cites selections especially from the Torah and the Prophets, though the term "citation" must be understood broadly as an allusion to the Torah and the Prophets, combining afresh the formulas and motifs from the Jewish texts that had become canonical and integrating them into his own wisdom argumentation. It also explicitly demonstrates a critical discussion with the wisdom discourses of the books of Job, Qoheleth, and Proverbs.[52] Ben Sira provides an exemplary intertextual work in his inter-

---

50. Pancratius C. Beentjes, *Jesus Sirach en Tenach: Een onderzoek naar en een classificatie van parallellen, met bijzondere aandacht voor hun functie in Sirach 45:6–26* (Ph.D. diss; University of Nieuwegein, 1981). In addition to the relevant contributions in Beentjes's volume *Happy*, the following essays of his should be noted: Beentjes, "A Rereading of the Primeval Narratives: Ben Sira 40:1–17 and 16:26–17:4," in *Wisdom for Life*, ed. N. Calduch-Benages, BZAW 445 (Berlin: de Gruyter, 2014), 201–17; Beentjes, "The Book of Ben Sira and Deuteronomistic Heritage: A Critical Approach," in *Changes in Scripture: Rewriting and Interpreting Authoritative Traditions in the Second Temple Period*, ed. H. von Weissenberg, BZAW 419 (Berlin: de Gruyter, 2011), 275–96; Beentjes, "Ben Sira and the Book of Deuteronomy," in *Houses Full of All Good Things*, ed. J. Pakkala and M. Nissinen, Publications of the Finnish Exegetical Society 95 (Göttingen: Vandenhoeck & Ruprecht, 2008), 413–33; Beentjes, "In Search of Parallels: Ben Sira and the Book of Kings," in *Intertextual Studies in Ben Sira and Tobit*, ed. J. Corley, CBQMS 38 (Washington: The Catholic Biblical Association of America, 2005), 118–31.

51. Benjamin G. Wright, "Biblical Interpretation in the Book of Ben Sira," in *A Companion to Biblical Interpretation in Early Judaism*, ed. M. Henze (Grand Rapids: Eerdmans, 2012), 363–88; Friedrich V. Reiterer, "Sira und seine Bibel," in *"Die Vollendung der Gottesfurcht ist Weisheit" (Sir 21,11): Studien zum Buch Ben Sira (Jesus Sirach)*, ed. Friedrich V. Reiterer, SBA 50 (Stuttgart: Katholisches Bibelwerk, 2011), 43–99.

52. On Job: Friedrich V. Reiterer, "Das Verhältnis Ijobs und Ben Siras," in *"Alle Weisheit stammt vom Herrn ..." Gesammelte Studien zu Ben Sira*, ed. R. Egger-Wenzel, BZAW 375 (Berlin: de Gruyter, 2007), 345–75; Renate Egger-Wenzel, "Der Gebrauch von תמם bei Ijob und Ben Sira: Ein Vergleich zweier Weisheitsbücher," in *Freundschaft bei Ben Sira*, ed. Friedrich V. Reiterer, BZAW 244 (Berlin: de Gruyter, 1996), 203–38; Egger-Wenzel, "'Faith in God' Rather Than 'Fear of God' in Ben Sira and Job," in *Intertextual Studies in Ben Sira and Tobit*, ed. J. Corley and V. Skemp, CBQMS 38 (Washington, DC: Catholic Biblical Association of America, 2005), 211–26.

action with Israelite-Jewish literature that interprets scripture in the mode of new literature, in contrast to the commentaries (pesharim) and Florilegia (see, e.g., 4Q174) known from Qumran. The degree to which this represents a pre-form of midrashic exegesis is controversial in scholarship.[53] The use of Scripture and the related interpretation of Scripture should be surveyed for each particular version, in as much as G, Syr, and La each had available to them a specific corpus of holy writings that had grown beyond their (Hebrew) *Vorlagen* and their own individual networks of scriptural references. At least with regard to La and Syr, the New Testament should also be taken into account (see below, §2.5). Also to be identified is the manner in which G, Syr, and La interpret their supposed *Vorlage*(*n*) with recourse to other writings and each construct their own theological system of references. Marböck has carried this out in an exemplary fashion for H and G in their use of the term ברית resp. διαθήκη. Burkard M. Zapff has shown this most recently in several examples for Syr.[54]

In addition to the question regarding Ben Sira's treatment (in its various forms) of the texts that were becoming, or, as the case may be, had become canonical, the question of its own canonical status arises. The transmission of two different Greek versions, both as canonical texts, shows that, in addition to its canonicity for Syr and La, there is not *one* canonical book of Ben Sira. Primarily Roman-Catholic exegetes like Gilbert, Calduch-Benages, Franz Böhmisch, and Marböck have shown through diverse studies that the book of Ben Sira, like the books of Jeremiah, Daniel, Tobit, and Esther, does not have a *single* canonical text.[55] It instead—like all biblical books—assumes a canonical pluralism.

On Qoheleth: Maurice Gilbert, "Qohelet et Ben Sira," in *Qohelet in the Context of Wisdom*, ed. A. Schoors, BETL 136 (Leuven: Peeters, 1998), 161–79; Jeremy Corley, "Qohelet and Sirach: A Comparison," in *Wisdom for Life*, ed. N. Calduch-Benages, BZAW 445 (Berlin: de Gruyter, 2014), 145–55.

On Proverbs: Jeremy Corley, "An Intertextual Study of Proverbs and Ben Sira," in Corley and Skemp, *Intertextual Studies in Ben Sira and Tobit*, 155–82.

53. Minissale, *La versione greca*.

54. See the contribution by Burkard M. Zapff in this volume.

55. Maurice Gilbert, "L'Ecclésiastique: Quel texte? Quelle autorité?," *RB* 94 (1987): 233–50; Gilbert, *Les études*, 179–80; Núria Calduch-Benages, "Ben Sira y el Canon de las Escrituras," *Greg* 78 (1997): 359–70; Franz Böhmisch, "Die Textformen des Sirachbuchs und ihre Zielgruppen," *PzB* 6 (1997): 87–122; Johannes Marböck, "Fragen und Impulse eines Buchs an einer Wende," *PzB* 19 (2010): 77–88. However, see the earlier discussion of Peter Rüger, "Le Siracide: Un livre à la frontiere du canon," in *Le canon*

While this notion of a flexible understanding of canon (at least for Ben Sira) seems generally to have prevailed within biblical studies, the question remains open as to why the book of Ben Sira itself did not make it into the Tanak. The late date of its composition could not be the reason, given the even later date of the final form of the book of Daniel and the continual expansion of individual Psalms into the Hasmonean period. Neither is the omission of Ben Sira from the Tanak to be explained by its possible critical view of Ezra that could be concluded from Ezra's omission from the "Praise of the Fathers," given the acceptance of the Ezra-critical book of Ruth into the Ketuvim. One reason could be that Ben Sira does not place his wisdom under the authority of Solomon like the books of Proverbs and Qoheleth and wrote in his own name. However, on the other hand, there are also anonymous wisdom writings, like, for example, 4Q524 and 4QInstruction, which were left out of the Tanak.[56] Therefore, the nonadoption of Ben Sira by the Hebrew Holy Scriptures is perhaps connected to the conflict over the Jerusalem high priesthood in the beginning of the second century BCE that culminated in the Zadokite-Aaronide priesthood that was so highly valued by Ben Sira being taken over by non-Zadokites in 175/172 BCE. Further investigation is necessary, which should also incorporate the competition between different priestly circles in Jerusalem mirrored in the latest layers of the Pentateuch in its consideration.[57]

---

de l'Ancien Testament, ed. J. D. Kaestli and O. Wermelingen (Geneva: Labor et Fides, 1984), 47–69.

56. Charlotte Hempel et al., eds., *The Wisdom Texts From Qumran and the Development of Sapiential Thought*, BETL 159 (Leuven: Peeters, 2002); Matthew J. Goff, *Discerning Wisdom: The Sapiential Literature of the Dead Sea Scrolls*, VTSup 116 (Leiden: Brill, 2007); Rey, *4QInstruction*.

57. See Reinhard Achenbach, *Die Vollendung der Tora: Studien zur Redaktionsgeschichte des Numeribuches im Kontext von Hexateuch und Pentateuch*, BZAR 3 (Wiesbaden: Harrassowitz, 2003); and Christoph Berner, "Vom Aufstand Datans und Abirams zum Aufbegehren der 250 Männer: Eine redaktionsgeschichtliche Studie zu den Anfängen der literarischen Genese von Num 16–17," *BN* 150 (2011): 9–33; Berner, "Wie Laien zu Leviten wurden: Zum Ort der Korachbearbeitung innerhalb der Redaktionsgeschichte von Num 16–17," *BN* 152 (2012): 3–28.

2.3.2. Ben Sira/Jesus Sirach and Pagan Wisdom

Three generations after Alexander the Great's campaign, the Palestinian interior was also completely in the grip of Hellenism.[58] Ben Sira therefore lived in a world thoroughly saturated with pagan Greek urban, cultural, and intellectual conceptions. This is clearly reflected and uncontested in his work—even heightened in the translation arising in the unrivaled Hellenistic metropolis of Alexandria.[59] At the same time, the autochthonous traditions of Egypt and Syria remain formative within the culture of Palestine. Therefore, the question as to what degree Ben Sira adopts gentile wisdom extends over three regions that, although merging in the Hellenistic period, stem from distinct tradition-historical and linguistic backgrounds.

(1) From its very inception, *Egyptian along with Mesopotamian wisdom* formed the most important extrabiblical frame of reference for Israelite-Jewish wisdom literature. This was especially the case for Ben Sira, who not only transmitted the well-known "instructions" that reached back to the Old Kingdom and in part forward into the Hellenistic period, but also Demotic wisdom. Through the translations by Miriam Lichtheim, Joachim Quack, and Heinz Thissen, these texts are now easily accessible.[60] A special note here should be made of the Instruction of Ankhsheshonq[61]

58. Cf. John J. Collins and Gregory E. Sterling, eds., *Hellenism in the Land of Israel*, CJA 13 (Notre Dame, IN: University of Notre Dame Press, 2001); Hans-Peter Kuhnen, "Israel unmittelbar vor und nach Alexander dem Großen: Geschichtlicher Wandel und archäologischer Befund," in *Die Griechen und das antike Israel: Interdisziplinäre Studien zur Religions- und Kulturgeschichte des Heiligen Landes*, ed. S. Alkier and M. Witte, OBO 201 (Fribourg: Academic Press, 2004).

59. On Alexandria, see Tobias Georges et al., eds., *Alexandria*, Civitatum Orbis Mediterranei Studia 1 (Tübingen: Mohr Siebeck, 2013).

60. Miriam Lichtheim, *The Late Period*, vol. 3 of *Ancient Egyptian Literature: A Book of Readings* (Berkeley: University of California Press, 1980), 159–217; Lichtheim, *Late Egyptian Wisdom Literature in the International Context: A Study of Demotic Instructions*, OBO 52 (Fribourg: Universitätsverlag, 1983), 13–92, 107–304; Joachim Friedrich Quack, *Einführung in die altägyptische Literaturgeschichte III: Die demotische und gräko-ägyptische Literatur*, 2nd ed., Einführungen und Quellentexte zur Ägyptologie 3 (Berlin: LIT, 2009), 113–38; Friedhelm Hoffmann and Joachim Friedrich Quack, *Anthologie der Demotischen Literatur*, Einführungen und Quellentexte zur Ägyptologie 4 (Berlin: LIT, 2007), 239–304; Heinz Thissen, "Die Lehre des Anchscheschonki," in *TUAT* 3:251–277, 280–319.

61. The manuscripts are from the Ptolemaic period. Quack (*Anthologie der Demotischen Literatur*, 273) places their formation possibly in the sixth/fifth century BCE.

and the instructions transmitted in the Papyrus Insinger ("Phibis"/"The Great Demotic Book of Wisdom"), which was widely disseminated.[62] The focus for "Phibis" lies on the ethical ideal of maintaining the golden mean and the righteousness of God as the one who determines all things and therefore appears as an inscrutable being and the dispenser of all human fortune.

(2) No later than the work of Theophil Middendorp (1973) and the studies by Martin Hengel, Kaiser, John J. Collins, and Erich S. Gruen on the relationship between Judaism and Hellenism, the question about the influence *of pagan Greek literature and classical Greek education* on Ben Sira has been discussed.[63] Homer, the tragic poets, Theognis of Megara, Menander, Plato, Aristotle, the Stoics, as well as the Alexandrian schools of poets and didactic poetry (Aratus of Soli) now belong to the fixed quantities that must be taken into account for understanding Ben Sira's anthropology, cosmology, theology, and also his culture. The recent standard works on these topics are the studies by Oda Wischmeyer (1997), Ursel Wicke-Reuter (2000), and Ueberschaer (2007).[64] Worth consid-

---

According to Lichtheim (*The Late Period*, 159) and Thissen ("Die Lehre des Anchscheschonki," 251), they cannot be dated.

62. The main manuscript is late Ptolemaic. Parallel manuscripts come from the first/second century CE. While Quack (*Anthologie der Demotischen Literatur*, 239) considers composition in the seventh century BCE possible, Lichtheim (*The Late Period*, 184) argues for composition in the Ptolemaic period.

63. Theophil Middendorp, *Die Stellung Jesu Ben Siras zwischen Judentum und Hellenismus* (Leiden: Brill, 1973); Martin Hengel, *Judentum und Hellenismus: Studien zu ihrer Begegnung unter besonderer Berücksichtigung Palästinas bis zur Mitte des 2. Jh.s v. Chr.*, 3rd ed., WUNT 10 (Tübingen: Mohr Siebeck, 1988); Otto Kaiser, *Der Mensch unter dem Schicksal: Studien zur Geschichte, Theologie und Gegenwartsbedeutung der Weisheit*, BZAW 161 (Berlin: de Gruyter, 1985); Kaiser, *Vom offenbaren und verborgenen Gott: Studien zur spätbiblischen Weisheit und Hermeneutik*, BZAW 392 (Berlin: de Gruyter, 2008); John J. Collins, *Jewish Wisdom in the Hellenistic Age*, OTL (Louisville: Westminster John Knox, 1997); Collins, *Jewish Cult and Hellenistic Culture: Essays on the Jewish Encounter with Hellenism and Roman Rule*, JSJSup 100 (Leiden: Brill, 2005); Erich S. Gruen, *Heritage and Hellenism: The Reinvention of Jewish Tradition*, HCS 30 (Berkeley: University of California Press, 1998). On the predecessors of this line of scholarship (Jakob Freudenthal, Moses Hadas, and Victor Tcherikover) see the contribution by Oda Wischmeyer in this volume.

64. Oda Wischmeyer, *Die Kultur des Buchs Jesus Sirach*, BZNW 77 (Berlin: de Gruyter, 1997); Ursel Wicke-Reuter, *Göttliche Providenz und menschliche Verant-*

eration is whether the paradigm of Judaism and Hellenism should not instead be termed Judaism *in* Hellenism.

In his dissertation under Kreuzer at the Kirchliche Hochschule Wuppertal, Ueberschaer furnishes an overview of the nature of schools and education in the ancient Near East, including ancient Israel, and in classical antiquity, and he provides an interpretation of the texts in Ben Sira that present his "educational theory." Ueberschaer investigates the anthropological statements, identifies the target audience for Ben Sira as young men from the Jewish upper class at the beginning of the second century BCE, develops Ben Sira's instructional method and content on the basis of his generic choices, describes the roles of God and wisdom as teachers, shows Ben Sira's self-image to be of pious (not priestly) nature, and specifies the boundaries of knowledge. The aim of the education that Ben Sira communicates, which is only achievable through encountering the wise and their unlocking of wisdom, is passing on wisdom in and for the Jewish community. It is possible that the theme of leisure results from Hellenistic influence, while in contrast to Hellenism's educational ideal, athletics receive no attention.

While Ben Sira's references to pagan Greek literature and philosophy have already been extensively if not exhaustively investigated, the mundane texts and images that appear in Greek papyri, ostraca, building, dedication, and funerary inscriptions, seals, bullae, and coins have to this point received little analysis as educational objects and as literary and visual references.

Naturally it is also important here to consider the relationships to pagan Greek literature and education in a differentiated manner with regard to the various versions of the book, especially given the different locations of their composition (Jerusalem, Alexandria).

(3) In addition to the Egyptian and Greek wisdom, recent scholarly insights in the history of Israel and the role of the Arameans in the cultural transfer between Mesopotamia and Syria-Palestine, as well as new editions of the text have brought forth the importance of *Aramaic wisdom* as reference works for Israelite-Jewish wisdom. This is especially the case for the Story of Ahiqar, which is also the largest Aramaic text from the first millennium BCE[65] and along with the Gilgamesh Epic belongs to the

---

wortung bei Ben Sira und in der Frühen Stoa, BZAW 298 (Berlin: de Gruyter, 2000); Ueberschaer, *Weisheit*.

65. Max Küchler, *Frühjüdische Weisheitstraditionen: Zum Fortgang weisheitlichen*

most beloved material of the ancient Near East. Most noteworthy here is the *opus magnum* by Michael Weigl (2010), which offers a detailed evaluation of the points of contact between the Ahiqar proverbs and Proverbs (esp. Prov 22:17–24:22), Qoheleth, Ben Sira, Job, and the Joseph story (and several passages in the book of Jeremiah).[66]

For a quick overview of Sirach's multifaceted literary interconnectedness with Greek wisdom as well as the wisdom of the Levant and the ancient Near East, the index of parallels accompanying Kaiser's translation of the book of Ben Sira (2005) proves helpful.[67]

2.4. Themes of the Book of Ben Sira

In light of the abundance of themes that Sirach treats and that Martin Luther (1545) describes with the beautiful image of bees that "aus mancherley Blumen / jr sefftlin seuget / vnd inenander menget" ("from various flowers / suck their nectar / and mingle together")[68] there are numerous studies of individual themes in recent scholarship. These especially focus on several key topics.

Denkens im Bereich des frühjüdischen Jahweglaubens, OBO 26 (Fribourg: Universitätsverlag, 1979), 319–413; Ingo Kottsieper, *Die Sprache der Aḥiqarsprüche*, BZAW 194 (Berlin: de Gruyter, 1990); Kottsieper, "Die alttestamentliche Weisheit im Licht aramäischer Weisheitstraditionen," in *Weisheit außerhalb der kanonischen Weisheitsschriften*, ed. B. Janowski, Veröffentlichung der Wissenschaftlichen Gesellschaft für Theologie 10 (Gütersloh: Gütersloher Verlagshaus, 1996), 128–62; Jonas C. Greenfield, "The Wisdom of Ahiqar," in *Wisdom in Ancient Israel: Essays in Honour of J. A. Emerton*, ed. J. Day et al. (Cambridge: Cambridge University Press, 1995), 43–52; Michael Weigl, *Die aramäischen Achikar-Sprüche aus Elephantine und die alttestamentliche Weisheitsliteratur*, BZAW 399 (Berlin: de Gruyter, 2010).

66. E.g., the Ahiqar proverbs (1, 97; numbering according to Weigl, *Achikar-Sprüche*, 73–79; 507–9) are also familiar with praise of heavenly wisdom, which can be compared in terms of tradition history with Job 28; Prov 8:22–31; Sir 1:9–10; 24; Wis 7, and 1 En. 42; cf. Küchler, *Weisheitstraditionen*, 46, 380–412; Markus Witte, *Vom Leiden zur Lehre: Der dritte Redegang (Hiob 21–27) und die Redaktionsgeschichte des Hiobbuchs*, BZAW 230 (Berlin: de Gruyter, 1994), 210–11.

67. Otto Kaiser, *Weisheit für das Leben: Das Buch Jesus Sirach übersetzt und eingeleitet* (Stuttgart: Radius, 2005).

68. Martin Luther, *Die gantze Heilige Schrifft Deudsch Wittenberg 1545*, ed. H. Volz (Munich: Rogner & Bernhard, 1972), 2:1751.

(1) *Conception of God and theology*, including the question of divine justice.[69]

(2) *Conception of humanity and ethics*, with an emphasis on questions of creatureliness, the relationships between genders, and dealing with poverty and wealth. Special mention should be made here of the study by Bradley C. Gregory (2010).[70] In his University of Notre Dame dissertation under the guidance of Gary A. Anderson, Gregory offers a foundational philological, tradition-historical, and social-historical analysis of Ben Sira's most important statements about possessions. The center of the study is the interpretive description of Ben Sira's basic approach to poor and rich as well as his specific explanations of the granting of loans, pledges, and alms. Through the essential theological and anthropological coordination of the remarks in Sir 4:1–10; 7:11; 7:29–36; 8:12–13; 10:19–24, 30–11:1; 11:4–6; 11:11–13, 20–22; 12:1–6; 13:2–23; 14:3–19; 21:5; 29:1–20; 35:1–5, and 35:20–22, Gregory identifies the beliefs of God's just retribution and the conviction of the finality of death. Human generosity appears as the fulfillment of the carpe diem motif in Ben Sira, where it is a means to acquiring heavenly riches, which God distributes in just retribution from his reservoir. Generosity is also a means of atonement for sin. On one hand, Ben Sira relativizes the importance of wealth in light of other values, on the other, however, he ascribes it a special cultic function. Human generosity with material goods mirrors Ben Sira's understanding of *imitatio dei* as ethical norm.[71] As is proper for the comprehensive study, appropri-

---

69. Renate Egger-Wenzel, ed., *Ben Sira's God: Proceedings of the International Ben Sira Conference, Durham, Ushaw College 2001*, BZAW 321 (Berlin: de Gruyter, 2002); Pancratius C. Beentjes, "Theodicy in Wisdom of Ben Sira," in *Happy*, 265–79; Markus Witte, "Theologien im Buch Jesus Sirach," in *Die theologische Bedeutung der alttestamentlichen Weisheitsliteratur*, ed. M. Saur, Biblisch-theologische Studien 125 (Neukirchen-Vluyn: Neukirchener Verlag, 2012), 91–128.

70. Bradley C. Gregory, *Like an Everlasting Signet Ring: Generosity in the Book of Sirach*, DCLS 2 (Berlin: de Gruyter, 2010); cf. also Benjamin G. Wright and Claudia V. Camp, "'Who Has Been Tested by Gold and Found Perfect?': Ben Sira's Discourse of Riches and Poverty," in *Praise*, 71–96; Otto Kaiser, "Arm und Reich bei Jesus Sirach," in *Vom offenbaren und verborgenen Gott: Studien zur spätbiblischen Weisheit und Hermeneutik*, ed. Otto Kaiser, BZAW 392 (Berlin: de Gruyter, 2008), 144–60.

71. Cf. Markus Witte, "Begründungen der Barmherzigkeit gegenüber den Bedürftigen in jüdischen Weisheitsschriften aus hellenistisch-römischer Zeit," in *Anthropologie und Ethik im Frühjudentum und im Neuen Testament*, ed. M. Konradt and E. Schläpfer, WUNT 322 (Tübingen: Mohr Siebeck, 2014), 387–412.

ate statements on riches and poverty in the Jewish literature of the Hellenistic period, especially in Proverbs and in Tobit, as well as the history of the period and the social-historical context of the early second century BCE all appear.

(3) *Understanding of history*, including the question of eschatology and then connected of messianic conceptions in Ben Sira.[72]

(4) *Cult and piety*, with an emphasis on the relationship to the Jerusalem priesthood and the temple,[73] to fear of God, and the meaning of prayer.

On the final topic, reference should be made to the dissertation by Werner Urbanz (2009) at the University of Graz, directed by Marböck.[74] After a chronologically organized history of scholarship on the topic of "prayer in the book of Jesus Sirach," Urbanz offers an overview of all lexemes belonging to the semantic field of "prayer" in G and—as far as it is possible—also of their Hebrew equivalents. He lists their statistical distribution in the book and in each case provides a short localization of the various lexemes in the composition as a whole. In keeping with Claus

72. Jeremy Corley, "Seeds of Messianism in Hebrew Ben Sira and Greek Sirach," in *The Septuagint and Messianism*, ed. M. A. Knibb, BETL 195 (Leuven: Leuven University Press, 2006), 301–12; Benjamin G. Wright, "Eschatology without a Messiah in the Wisdom of Ben Sira," in *The Septuagint and Messianism*, ed. M. A. Knibb, BETL 195 (Leuven: Leuven University Press, 2006), 313–23; Rey, *4QInstruction*; Rey, "L'espérance post-mortem dans le différentes versions du Siracide," in Joosten and Rey, *Texts and Versions of the Book of Ben Sira: Transmissions and Interpretation*, 257–79; Friedrich V. Reiterer, "Aspekte der Messianologie der Septuaginta," in *"Die Vollendung der Gottesfurcht ist Weisheit" (Sir 21,11): Studien zum Buch Ben Sira (Jesus Sirach)*, SBA 50 (Stuttgart: Katholisches Bibelwerk, 2011), 265–83.

73. Mulder, *Simon*; Heinz-Josef Fabry, "Jesus Sirach und das Priestertum," in *Auf den Spuren der schriftgelehrten Weisen*, ed I. Fischer et al., BZAW 331 (Berlin: de Gruyter, 2003), 265–82; Benjamin G. Wright, "'Fear the Lord and Honor the Priest?': Ben Sira as Defender of the Jerusalem Priesthood," in *Praise*, 97–126.

74. Werner Urbanz, *Gebet im Sirachbuch: Zur Terminologie von Klage und Lob in der griechischen Texttradition*, HBS 60 (Freiburg: Herder, 2009); Urbanz, "Die Gebetsschule des Jesus Sirach: Bemerkungen zu Inhalten, Subjekten und Methoden des Gebets im Sirachbuch," *PzB* 18 (2009): 31–48; cf. also Jan Liesen, *Full of Praise: An Exegetical Study of Sir 39,12–35*, JSJSup 64 (Leiden: Brill, 1999); Michael Reitemeyer, *Weisheitslehre als Gotteslob: Psalmentheologie im Buch Jesus Sirach*, BBB 127 (Berlin: Philo, 2000); Maurice Gilbert, "Prayer in the Book of Ben Sira: Function and Relevance," in *DCLY* 2004, 117–35; Palmisano, *Salvaci*; Palmisano, "La prière de Ben Sira dans les manuscrits Hébreux et dans les versions anciennes," in Joosten and Rey, *Texts and Versions of the Book of Ben Sira*, 281–96.

Westermann,[75] he identifies the basic forms of prayer in Ben Sira as lament and praise. The main body of the study is dedicated to the promotion of the terminological fields of these two basic forms, which culminate in the exhibition of the interdependence of lament and praise. Urbanz differentiates in detail between actual prayers, reflections on prayer, and instructions for prayer. In terms of groups supporting prayer, he first identifies humanity in general, second Ben Sira's students, and third the teacher of wisdom himself. The significant occasions for prayer are based in God himself and in special human situations, either in suffering or in joy. Urbanz highlights the lament in connection to the topic of sin, a characteristic topic for Ben Sira.

(5) The interest in the understanding *of wisdom* and its personification continues unbowed. In connection to the thesis of the sapientialization of Torah and the legalization of wisdom,[76] the question of the plurivalent understanding of תורה and νόμος in Ben Sira, the relationship of תורה and νόμος to חכמה and σοφία, as well as the relationship between universal and particular wisdom, or as the case may be, general and special revelation (cf. esp. Sir 17:1–10).[77]

(6) Finally, topics that are diversely discussed at present in the social sciences and humanities, the construction of identity versus otherness, of space and time, of ethnicity, of body and gender, the understanding of emotions and personhood and the use of language, especially metaphor, are reflected in the study of the book of Ben Sira. In this setting, scholarship on Ben Sira (like biblical studies in general) could benefit from the cultural studies definitions of structure and reference, methods, and theo-

75. Claus Westermann, *Lob und Klage in den Psalmen* (Göttingen: Vandenhoeck & Ruprecht, 1977).

76. See on this Bernd U. Schipper and D. Andrew Teeter, eds., *Wisdom and Torah: The Reception of 'Torah' in the Wisdom Literature of the Second Temple Period*, JSJSup 163 (Leiden: Brill, 2013).

77. Friedrich V. Reiterer, "Neue Akzente in der Gesetzesvorstellung: תורת חיים bei Ben Sira," in *Gott und Mensch im Dialog*, ed. M. Witte, BZAW 354.2 (Berlin: de Gruyter, 2004), 851–71; Reiterer, "Das Verhältnis der חכמה zur תורה im Buch Ben Sira: Kriterien zu gegenseitiger Bestimmung," in Xeravits and Zsengellér, *Studies in the Book of Ben Sira*, 97–133; Markus Witte, "'Das Gesetz des Lebens' (Sirach 17,11)," in *Lived Religion: Conceptual, Empirical and Practical-Theological Approaches*, ed. H. Streib et al. (Leiden: Brill, 2008), 71–87; Greg Schmidt Goering, *Wisdom's Root Revealed: Ben Sira and the Election of Israel*, JSJSup 139 (Leiden: Brill, 2009).

ries.[78] More recent contributions here include, for example, the studies on Ben Sira by Marko Marttila on the understanding of the nations (2012) and by Theresa Ann Ellis (2014) on the construction of gender.

Marttila works out how Ben Sira establishes Jewish identity in Hellenism by means of adaptation instead of isolation or assimilation.[79] Ben Sira thereby presents a differentiated view of the nations, classifying them in accordance with the exegesis of pertinent texts from the Torah and the Prophets into "anti-elect nations" (Canaanites, Amalekites, Midianites, and Philistines, who are subject to divine wrath),[80] "non-elect nations" (enemies of Israel, from whom blessing could be withheld if they do not come to terms with Israel), and the "elect nation" (Israel).[81] Marttila illustrates once again Ben Sira's role as an exegete.

The dissertation by Ellis at the Brite Divinity School, supervised by Leo G. Perdue, offers a semantic analysis of the conception of gender and gender formation in the Hebrew book of Ben Sira.[82] After a detailed methodological introduction, she analyzes Ben Sira's understanding of gender as it appears in his impersonal speech. This addresses not only classical form-critical questions (among others the recourse to Greek-Hellenistic genres), but also the historical contexts of the language (Hellenistic environment and life under Seleucid hegemony). The investigation focuses on linguistic analyses of the texts in which female figures appear in divine types (like personified wisdom) and human types (like mothers, daughters,

78. See Oda Wischmeyer in this volume.

79. Marko Marttila, *Foreign Nations in the Wisdom of Ben Sira: A Jewish Sage between Opposition and Assimilation*, DCLS 13 (Berlin: de Gruyter, 2012); cf. also Benjamin G. Wright, "'Put the Nations in Fear of You': Ben Sira and the Problem of Foreign Rule," in *Praise*, 127–46; Friedrich V. Reiterer, "Der Fremde bei Ben Sira: Die Spannungen zwischen der spätalttestamentlichen und hellenistischen Weltauffassung," in *The Stranger in Ancient and Mediaeval Jewish Tradition*, ed. G. G. Xeravits and J. Dušek, DCLS 4 (Berlin: de Gruyter, 2010), 64–83.

80. See Markus Witte, "'Barmherzigkeit und Zorn Gottes' im Alten Testament am Beispiel des Buchs Jesus Sirach," in *Divine Wrath and Divine Mercy in the World of Antiquity*, ed. R. G. Kratz and H. Spieckermann, FAT 2/33 (Tübingen: Mohr Siebeck, 2008), 176–202.

81. On Ben Sira's conception of Israel's and the nation's election, see also Schmidt Goering, *Wisdom's Root*.

82. Teresa Ann Ellis, *Gender in the Book of Ben Sira: Divine Wisdom, Erotic Poetry, and the Garden of Eden*, BZAW 453 (Berlin: de Gruyter, 2013); cf. also Ibolya Balla, *Ben Sira on Family, Gender, and Sexuality*, DCLS 8 (Berlin: de Gruyter, 2011).

and wives—always in juxtaposition to fathers, sons, and male friends). She analyzes in detail the Hebrew texts of Sir 4:11–19; 6:18–31; 7:18–26; 9:1–9; 9:10–16; 14:20–15:8; 22:9–15; 23:16–21; 23:22–27; 25:13–26:3; 26:13–17; 33:20–30; 36:18–26; 37:14–26; 40:18–27; 42:7–9; and 51:13–30. She only considers G when it is necessary to reconstruct a fragmentary Hebrew text. In addition, Ellis constantly looks beyond Sirach itself to comparative biblical texts (primarily Prov and Song), as well as the texts that Ben Sira has taken up from the Torah (i.e., Gen 1–4). She is able to show Ben Sira's semantic originality and gender discourse in contrast to the social role models of classical antiquity and Hellenism in a balanced manner. On the backdrop of a homo-social world, Ellis refutes the oft-presented position that Ben Sira was basically misogynist. Compared to the pagan world, Ben Sira is marked by according a high value to women and female sexuality, which is shown not least in the erotic metaphor of personified wisdom.

2.5. Reception History of the Book of Ben Sira

In this field as well, Ben Sira scholarship participates in a current trend within the scholarship of the humanities and social sciences, though comprehensive reception-historical scholarship in Sirach is only just beginning. Studies to date mostly concentrate on the modification of the figure of wisdom in the Wisdom of Solomon and citations in rabbinic literature.[83] The systematic investigation of Ben Sira's reception in early Jewish literature, including the writings of Philo and Qumran remains a lacuna. Such an investigation could be expected to provide further information about the textual and transmission history of Sirach as well as on the tradition-historical developments of conceptions of wisdom. Also lacking is a systematic investigation of Ben Sira in early Christian literature, particularly in the New Testament. The outstanding importance Sir 24, for example, has for John 1 and particular forms of wisdom Christology has long been known. A targeted review of the allusions and citations from Ben Sira in New Testament texts would afford a good starting point for the unfolding of a biblical theology.[84] The evaluation and classification of the Sirach texts

83. Martin Neher, *Wesen und Wirken der Weisheit in der Sapientia Salomonis*, BZAW 333 (Berlin: de Gruyter, 2004); Jenny R. Labendz, "The Book of Ben Sira in Rabbinic Literature," *AJSR* 30 (2006): 347–92; Benjamin G. Wright, "B. Sanhedrin 100b and Rabbinic Knowledge of Ben Sira," in *Praise*, 182–93.

84. See the preliminary study by Rosario Pistone, "Blessing of the Sage, Proph-

mentioned in the index of the *loci citati vel allegati* of the Novum Testamentum Graece (28th. ed., 2012) could form the point of departure.

As is the case with the other fields of study, the various versions of the book, each within its own community of transmission, should naturally be taken into account within the framework of the study of reception history. This is especially the case for the Jewish and Christian histories of reception with Sirach, given its divergent canonical value and the remarkable differences in the various forms, which diverge more significantly than for other biblical books

3. Outlook: Consensus and Disagreement

Perhaps more strongly than in other parts of Hebrew Bible studies, Ben Sira scholarship is marked by considerable consensus in important questions.

The authenticity of the Hebrew fragments found in the Cairo Genizah has been clear at least since the textual discoveries in Qumran and Masada, even when some details, especially in the Hebrew long version, suggest that one should reckon with reverse translations from G or Syr, meaning interdependency between the versions and their different textual histories.[85]

The date of Ben Sira in the first quarter of the second century BCE is likewise undisputed. Even if in detail it is discussed whether Ben Sira is more likely to be dated in the time around 190 or around 175 BCE, there is agreement that it arises before the Hasmonean period. The prayer for the deliverance of Zion in Sir 36:1–22 (G: 33:1–13a; 36:16b–22) can easily be read as a reflection on the time after the defeat of Antiochus III in 190 BCE by the Romans and the increasing pressure by the Seleucids upon Jerusalem that resulted.[86] The immediate temporal correlation of specific state-

---

ecy of the Scribe: From Ben Sira to Matthew," in *The Wisdom of Ben Sira: Studies on Tradition, Redaction, and Theology*, ed. A. Passaro and G. Bellia, DCLS 1 (Berlin: de Gruyter, 2008), 309–53; Marko Marttila, "Das Sirachbuch und das Neue Testament: Der Einfluss eines jüdischen Weisheitswerkes auf die frühchristlichen Autoren," *BN* 144 (2010): 95–116; Jeremy Corley, "Tracing Wisdom from Sirach to the Gospels," in *Weisheit als Lebensgrundlage*, ed. R. Egger-Wenzel et al., DCLS 15 (Berlin: de Gruyter, 2013), 27–46.

85. See the exemplary study by Reiterer, "Differenz," and Rey, "Feuillet," 421–22.

86. Johannes Marböck, "Das Gebet um die Rettung Zions in Sir 36,1–22 (G: 33,1–13a; 36,16b–22) im Zusammenhang der Geschichtsschau Ben Siras," in *Gottes*

ments, for example, the anti-Samaritan notes in 47:12–25 and 50:25–26, remain hypothetical, however.[87]

It is largely uncontested that the Greek short text, including the prologue, goes back to Ben Sira's grandson. The notion that this is secondary and arises first in the context of Christian reception of the book of Sirach, as argued by Bernd Jørg Diebner (1982) and Giuseppe Veltri (2006), dating the prologue to the first or second century CE is an outlying dissenting opinion.[88]

Throughout the scholarship, Ben Sira's systematizing force is recognized. The book forms a powerful synthesis of wisdom, priestly-cultic, legal, and historiographic or, as the case may be, prophetic traditions in ancient Judaism.

In the shadow of the correlation of wisdom and Torah—however the term of Torah is filled in detail and however the exact relationship between wisdom and Torah is determined in Sirach[89]—the book develops a completely individual form of speech about God that is of central importance for biblical theology. The character of the book of Ben Sira is increasingly recognized as a highly creative form of exegesis and viewed in light of the scribal processes in ancient Judaism.

Weisheit, 159. On the attempt to locate Sir 36 in the context of the Heliodor affair (cf. 2 Macc 3) and comparable events under Seleucus IV (187–175 BCE), see the comprehensive study by Palmisano, *Salvaci*, 305–14.

87. See Markus Witte, "'What Share Do We Have in David…?'—Ben Sira's Perspectives on 1 Kings 12," in *One God—One Cult—One Nation: Archaeological and Biblical Perspectives*, ed. R. G. Kratz and H. Spieckermann, BZAW 405 (Berlin: de Gruyter, 2010), 91–117.

88. Bernd Jørg Diebner, "Mein 'Großvater Jesus,'" *DBAT* 16 (1982): 1–37; Giuseppe Veltri, *Libraries, Translations, and 'Canonical' Texts: The Septuagint, Aquila and Ben Sira in the Jewish and Christian Traditions*, JSJSup 109 (Leiden: Brill, 2006), 196.

89. See Reiterer, "Akzente"; Reiterer, "Verhältnis"; Reiterer, "The Interpretation of Wisdom Tradition of the Torah within Ben Sira," in *The Wisdom of Ben Sira: Studies on Tradition, Redaction, and Theology*, ed. A. Passaro and G. Bellia, DCLS 1 (Berlin: de Gruyter, 2008), 209–31; Timo Veijola, "Law and Wisdom: The Deuteronomistic Heritage in Ben Sira's Teaching of Law," in *Leben nach der Weisung: Exegetisch-historische Studien zum Alten Testament*, ed. W. Dietrich and M. Marttila, FRLANT 224 (Göttingen: Vandenhoeck & Ruprecht, 2008), 144–64; Benjamin G. Wright, "Torah and Sapiential Pedagogy in the Book of Ben Sira," in *Wisdom and Torah: The Reception of 'Torah' in the Wisdom Literature of the Second Temple Period*, ed. B. U. Schipper and D. A. Teeter, JSJSup 163 (Leiden: Brill, 2013).

One remaining disagreement is found in the question of how to construct a commentary on the book. The models of a commentary on G as the oldest representative of the complete book (cf. most recently Marböck)[90] or a commentary on a mixed text, that is of H, where a Hebrew fragment is extant, and otherwise of G (cf. most recently Patrick Skehan and Alexander Di Lella; Sauer; Schreiner and Zapff; Corley)[91] are in competition. None of the newer commentaries follow the model of commenting on the text of a critical reverse translation of G into Hebrew (cf. Segal).[92] Also conceivable would be a synoptic commentary on G *and* H. Annotated running translations of the Hebrew fragments have been presented in recent years by Charles Mopsik (2003) and Víctor Morla (2012).[93] So far there are no modern commentaries from La and Syr. In the sense of a plural understanding of canon, which Sirach itself teaches, and of a truly ecumenical exegesis one may hope that this gap will soon be filled.

90. Marböck, *Jesus Sirach 1–23*.

91. Patrick W. Skehan and Alexander A. Di Lella, *The Wisdom of Ben Sira*, AB 39 (New York: Doubleday, 1987); Sauer, *ATD Apokryphen 1*; Josef Schreiner, *Jesus Sirach 1–24*, NEchtB AT 38 (Würzburg: Echter, 2002); Zapff, *Jesus Sirach*; Jeremy Corley, *Sirach*, New Collegeville Bible Commentary (Collegeville, MN: Liturgical Press, 2013).

92. See n. 16.

93. Charles Mopsik, *La Sagesse de ben Sira: Traduction de l'hébreu, introduction et annotation*, Collection "Le Dix Paroles" (Lagrasse: Verdier, 2003); Víctor Morla Asensio, *Los manuscritos hebreos de Ben Sira: Traducción y notas*, Asociación Bíblica Española 59 (Estella: Verbo Divino, 2012).

Der soziokulturelle Hintergrund des Sirachbuches

Siegfried Kreuzer

Das Sirachbuch entstand nicht nur in der Zeit des Hellenismus sondern im Hellenismus, wie auch immer man die Stellung Ben Siras und seines Enkels dazu im Einzelnen einschätzen mag. Sowohl Ben Sira in Jerusalem, als auch sein Enkel in Alexandrien partizipierten damit an der Stellung des Judentums insgesamt, das ebenfalls nicht nur in der Zeit des Hellenismus, sondern im Hellenismus lebte und darin seinen Weg gehen musste, was bekanntlich in durchaus unterschiedlicher Weise geschah.

Diese Situation war nicht völlig neu. Das Alte Israel hatte sich im Überschneidungsbereich der altorientalischen, der ägyptischen und der ostmediterranen Kultur herausgebildet und musste sich mit den verschiedenen Einflüssen auseinandersetzen. Dabei dominierten zeitweise die ägyptische und zeitweise die mesopotamische Welt. Insbesondere unter der Vorherrschaft der Assyrer und der Babylonier musste man sich nicht nur mit den Einflüssen, sondern auch mit den Forderungen fremder Herrscher und ihrer Kultur auseinandersetzen. Spätestens unter den Persern war die Welt nur mehr scheinbar jeweils monopolar (d.h. nur auf eine Großmacht ausgerichtet): Neben der persischen Vorherrschaft waren die Einflüsse Ägyptens, aber auch der griechischen Welt in vielfacher Hinsicht erkennbar.

Neu waren aber doch die Gleichzeitigkeit, die Vielfalt und die Vermischung der verschiedenen Einflüsse und die Intensität der Herausforderungen, die nicht nur die Küstenregion Palästinas prägten, sondern die ebenso auch die vergleichsweise abgelegenen Bergregionen um Jerusalem und in Samaria, ja sogar das noch entferntere Ostjordanland erfassten.

Der folgende Beitrag hat die Aufgabe, diesen soziokulturellen Hintergrund des Sirachbuches darzustellen. Angesichts der Weite und der Vielschichtigkeit dessen, was in die Zeit und die Kultur des Hellenismus gehört,[1] und angesichts des begrenzten Platzes ist es nur möglich—in durchaus subjektiver Auswahl—einige markante und typische und in dieser oder jener Weise für das Judentum bzw. das Sirachbuch relevante Aspekte darzustellen.

1. Politische Geschichte und Hellenismus: Zur zeitlichen Abgrenzung

Zunächst möchte ich kurz daran erinnern, dass die Epoche des Hellenismus zwar mit gewissen äußeren Daten zu verbinden ist, aber sowohl Anfang als auch Ende in unterschiedlicher Weise definiert werden können. Als gewissermaßen kalendarischer Anfang gilt der Eroberungszug von Alexander dem Großen mit der Schlacht von Issos 333 v.Chr. Aber so wie eine Jahreszeit manchmal etwas früher beginnt als im Kalender vermerkt ist, oder auch eine Nachgeschichte haben kann, so hat der Hellenismus im Orient zweifellos eine Vorgeschichte; und zwar in Form eines früh einsetzenden und weit reichenden Einflusses des Griechentums nach Ägypten

1. Zum Thema siehe u.a.: M. I. Rostovtzeff, *The Social and Economic History of the Hellenistic World*, 3 Bde. (Oxford: University Press, 1953); Claire Préaux, *Le monde hellenistic: La Grèce et l'orient de la morte d'Alexandre à la conquete romaine de la Grèce (323–146 av. J.-C.)*, 2 Bde. (Paris: Presses Universitaires de France, 1978); Frank W. Walbank, *The Hellenistic World* (Cambridge: Harvard University Press, 1992); Graham Shipley, *The Greek World after Alexander 323–30 BC* (London: Routledge, 2000); Hans-Joachim Gehrke, *Geschichte des Hellenismus*, 3. Aufl., Oldenbourg Grundriss der Geschichte 1A (Munich: Oldenbourg, 2003); Glenn R. Bugh, *The Cambridge Companion to the Hellenstic World* (Cambridge: University Press, 2006); Hans-Ulrich Cain et al., *Hellenismus: Eine Welt im Umbruch* (Darmstadt: Wissenschaftliche Buchgesellschaft, 2012); Hatto H. Schmitt and Ernst Vogt, Hrsg., *Lexikon des Hellenismus* (Wiesbaden: Harrassowitz, 2005).

Zu Ägypten siehe Günther Hölbl, *Geschichte des Ptolemäerreiches: Politik, Ideologie und religiöse Kultur von Alexander dem Großen bis zur römischen Eroberung*, 2. Aufl. (Stuttgart: Theiss, 2004).

Für die Weite des Phänomens Hellenismus siehe insbesondere die Vielfalt der Beiträge in Bernd Funck, Hrsg., *Hellenismus: Beiträge zur Erforschung von Akkulturation und politischer Ordnung in den Staaten des hellenistischen; Akten des Internationalen Hellenismus-Kolloquiums 9.–14. März 1994 in Berlin* (Tübingen: Mohr, 1996). Wie vielschichtig die Phänomene des Hellenismus allein schon in Relation zum Judentum sind, zeigen das bekannte Werk von Martin Hengel, *Judentum und Hellenismus: Studien zu ihrer Begegnung unter besonderer Berücksichtigung Palästinas bis zur Mitte des 2. Jh. v.Chr.*, WUNT 10 (Tübingen: Mohr, 1969), und die neueren Beiträge von Erich Gruen, etwa: *Heritage and Hellenism: The Reinvention of Jewish Tradition* (Oakland: University of California Press, 1998).

und Vorderasien und andererseits in Form der von dort her stammenden Einflüsse, die schon früh in der griechischen Welt zu finden sind.

In diesem Sinn des wechselseitigen Einflusses dieser beiden Welten hat auch Johann Gustav Droysen den Begriff Hellenismus geschaffen, wobei es ihm nicht zuletzt darum ging, diese Epoche nicht als Epigonentum nach dem klassischen Griechentum zu betrachten, sondern in ihrer eigenen Bedeutung und Kreativität wahrzunehmen. Dabei darf man für die griechische Welt nicht nur an Griechenland denken, sondern mindestens ebenso sind die griechischen Gebiete im Süden und Westen Kleinasiens mit zu beachten.

Zwei Beispiele mögen dies beleuchten: Der bekannte, rein oder in Abwandlungen bei praktisch allen hellenistischen Städten zu findende sog. Hippodamische Stadtplan mit seinen sich rechtwinkelig kreuzenden Straßen geht auf den gleichnamigen Architekten zurück, der diese Struktur im 5. Jh. für die Stadt Milet anwandte, wobei allerdings die Struktur als solche schon wesentlich älter ist. Ebenso eindrücklich ist, dass in dem berühmten Zug der Zehntausend, den Xenophon in seiner Anabasis dokumentierte, diese enorme Zahl griechischer Soldaten dem persischen Prinzen Kyros dem Jüngeren gefolgt war; und das nach bzw. neben den endlosen Perserkriegen des 5. Jh.s, die umgekehrt für die Perser natürlich Griechenkriege waren.

Nicht nur die Anfänge des Hellenismus sind fließend, auch das Ende ist eher eine Phase des Übergangs, ganz abgesehen von der weitreichenden Nachgeschichte des Hellenismus.

Die übliche Angabe ist, dass die Zeit des Hellenismus mit dem Beginn der römischen Herrschaft endet. Das wäre für Ägypten das Jahr 30 v.Chr. mit dem Ende der Ptolemäer in Person von Kleopatra VII., wobei allerdings Rom auch schon in den Jahrzehnten zuvor wesentlichen Einfluss auf Ägypten ausgeübt hatte.

Für Syrien liegt dieser Übergang etwas früher, mit dem Sieg des Pompeius über die Seleukiden im Jahr 64 v.Chr.; wonach Pompeius bekanntlich 62. v.Chr. Jerusalem einnahm. Im Großen und Ganzen ist somit die Übergangsphase im 1. Jh. v.Chr. anzusetzen.

Vor diesem Hintergrund nimmt man mit Verwunderung wahr, dass Hans-Joachim Gehrke in seiner Geschichte des Hellenismus[2] praktisch mit 200 v.Chr. endet. Dem Kapitel „Die Niederlagen gegen Rom (205–168)"

2. Gehrke, *Geschichte des Hellenismus*.

(S. 117) folgt im historischen Überblick als nächstes und letztes Kapitel bereits „Das lange Nachspiel" (S. 128). Hier wird somit die grundlegende und prägende Phase des Hellenismus auf das 3. Jh. eingeengt (allerdings bestimmt auch Gehrke die kulturelle Bedeutung des Hellenismus auf einen viel umfangreicheren Zeitraum.)

Es gibt auch andere Autoren, die ihre Darstellung nicht mit dem letzten Schritt der römischen Eroberung, d.h. dem Ende der Ptolemäer, sondern mit dem ersten, der Eroberung Griechenlands 146 v. Chr. enden lassen.[3] Die für unser Thema wichtige Wahrheit dieser Sicht ist, dass in der Tat die Römer auch schon lange vor Pompeius Einfluss auf die Geschichte des Judentums hatten, etwa indem die Hasmonäer die Römer zu Hilfe riefen. Zumindest indirekt von Bedeutung für Jerusalem ist die berühmte Anekdote, wie der römische Legat Popilius Laenas 168 v.Chr. bei der Unterredung in Eleusis im Sand einen Kreis um Antiochus IV. zog, ihn aufforderte, sich gegenüber dem römischen Ultimatum zu entscheiden, bevor er den Kreis verlasse, und ihn so zwang, sich aus Ägypten zurückzuziehen.[4]

2. Militärische und politische Prägungen des Hellenismus

Betrachten wir diesen Zeitraum, so ist er wesentlich geprägt von umfangreichen militärischen Auseinandersetzungen. In den einschlägigen Darstellungen reiht sich ein Krieg an den anderen. Die im Zusammenhang der Bibelwissenschaft am ehesten bekannten Syrischen Kriege sind nur ein Ausschnitt aus den zahlreichen Kriegen, die sich in Griechenland, Kleinasien und in Syrien bis nach Mesopotamien abspielten.

Zunächst rührten diese Konflikte aus der ungeklärten Nachfolgeregelung nach dem Tod Alexanders des Großen. Sie waren andererseits aber auch eine Fortsetzung des Gründungsgeschehens, denn das Alexanderreich war im Wesentlichen aus den Eroberungen entstanden und legitimiert. Die sog. Inbesitznahme mit dem Speer war die grundlegende Legitimation der Herrschaft. Dementsprechend waren die Herrscher auch nach der bis etwa 300 erfolgten Konsolidierung der Diadochenreiche laufend in Kämpfe verstrickt. Natürlich spielten dabei auch wirtschaftliche Gründe eine Rolle und nicht selten auch verwandtschaftliche Beziehungen und

---

3. So Max Cary, *The History of the Greek World 323–146 B.C.*, 2. Aufl. (London: Methuen, 1951). Ebenso Préaux, *Le monde hellenistic*, und Walbank, *Hellenistic World*.

4. Über diesen sog. Tag von Eleusis (in der Nähe von Alexandria) berichten Polybius 29.27; Livius 45.42 und Diodorus Siculus 31.2.

Rivalitäten. Aber es ist doch auffallend, in welcher Dichte und mit welcher zahlenmäßigen Stärke hier dauernd Kriege geführt wurden.

Wenn die Ptolemäer im 3. Syrischen Krieg ab ca. 246, nachdem Ptolemaios III. mit seinem Heer bis nach Babylon (!) vorgedrungen war und in der Heimat Unruhen ausgebrochen waren, etwas zurückhaltender wurden, so ist das nicht eine prinzipielle Änderung, sondern lag vor allem an der Erkenntnis der begrenzten Ressourcen des Landes.[5]

Für unseren Bereich kann man sich fragen, ob nicht auch die kriegerische Expansionspolitik der Hasmonäer diesem Schema der hellenistischen Königreiche folgt und welche wirtschaftlichen und ideologischen Faktoren zu einer solchen Entwicklung führen.

Bei den Kriegen der hellenistischen Zeit fällt auf, in welchem Ausmaß technische Neuerungen eine Rolle spielten. So wurden Geschütze entwickelt, die gleichzeitig eine große Zahl von Pfeilen abschießen oder Steine mit bis zu 75kg gegen die Stadtmauern schleudern konnten. Es wurden bewegliche Belagerungstürme entwickelt, die die Stadtmauern überragten und in deren Innerem auf mehreren Ebenen unterschiedlichste Geschütze untergebracht waren. Der größte dieser Türme soll bei der Belagerung von Rhodos verwendet worden sein. Er war über 30 m (nach anderen Berichten über 40m) hoch, hatte acht riesige Räder und soll von 3.400 Menschen bewegt worden sein.

Auf der anderen Seite wurden die Stadtmauern und die Befestigungsanlagen verbessert. Es kam für einige Jahrzehnte zu einem Wettrüsten ohnegleichen, in dem die Erfinder und Ingenieure ebenso große Bedeutung hatten wie die Generäle.

---

5. Dass Ptolemaios darüber hinaus noch Richtung oder bis Indien vorgedrungen sei, ist aber wohl nur Propaganda. Auch der Vorstoß bis Babylon blieb eine Episode, aber immerhin behielt Ptolemaios sogar die Hafenstadt Seleukia, die den Mittelmeerhafen für Antiochia darstellt. Auf dem Höhepunkt der Entwicklung beherrschten die Ptolemäer praktisch den ganzen Raum des östlichen Mittelmeeres, die Inseln aber auch die levantinische und die kleinasiatische Küste und übten ihren Einfluss auch in Athen aus. Zur Veranschaulichung könnte man sagen, dass im 3. Jh. außer dem im Inneren von Kleinasien gelegenen Galatien sowie Makedonien [von Philippi bis Beroia] praktisch alle Orte, die—viel später—Paulus auf seinen Missionsreisen aufsuchte, unter ptolemäischer Vorherrschaft oder zumindest ptolemäischem Einfluss standen.

Alexandria lag in dieser Zeit in der Tat nicht „in", sondern „bei" Ägypten, aber doch zugleich im Zentrum des ptolemäischen Herrschaftsgebietes.

Auch die Kriegsführung auf dem Meer wurde weiter entwickelt. Die wirtschaftliche und militärische Unterstützung auf dem Seeweg erhielt große Bedeutung. Der Zugang zu den Häfen wurde verteidigt bzw. blockiert. Seeschlachten mit größeren, besser bewaffneten Schiffen in großer Zahl wurden wichtig. Nach einigen Jahrzehnten stieß man allerdings an die Grenzen der Entwicklung und es kam auch zu einer gewissen Pattsituation.

Jener König, der sich auf dem Gebiet des Eroberns am meisten einen Namen gemacht hatte, war Demetrios Poliorketes von Makedonien. In seinem Auftrag wurden die erwähnten riesigen Belagerungstürme konstruiert, er konnte enorme Massen an Soldaten aufbieten und hatte zahlreiche Städte erobert. Selbst als er schließlich einige Misserfolge erlitt, blieb ihm sein Beiname Poliorketes, Stadteroberer.

Poliorketes gehörte zu denen, die es im Sinn des erwähnten prinzipiell aggressiven Königsverständnisses mit am weitesten gebracht hatten. Länder und Städte zu erobern galt als die höchste Leistung. Dass sich die Herrschaft an der Eroberung von Städten entschied, ist nichts Neues. Wir kennen die Geschichte von Abimelech, dessen Herrschaft an der Einnahme von Sichem scheiterte, wir kennen die Belagerung Jerusalems von 701 durch die Assyrer und die Einnahme Jerusalems durch die Babylonier, oder auch weiter zurück liegende Eroberungen wie die Einnahme von Mari durch Hammurapi im 18. Jh. v.Chr.

Dass die Fähigkeit, eine Stadt einzunehmen, als eine besondere Leistung galt, zeigt sich sprichwörtlich im Buch der Sprüche, wo dieser Großtat die Fähigkeit zur Selbstbeherrschung als die noch größere Leistung gegenübergestellt wird: „Besser ist es, sich selbst zu beherrschen, als Städte zu erobern" (Spr. 16,32). Wenn man daneben noch an die zahlreichen von Alexander dem Großen und seinen Nachfolgern erbauten Städte denkt und sich dazu an die kleine Notiz in Gen 10,8–12 über Nimrod, den Städteerbauer, erinnert, kann man sagen: Städte zu erbauen und Städte einzunehmen, war ein altes Thema für eine besondere Leistung, aber im Hellenismus wurde es noch bedeutsamer als zuvor.

Die Belagerung von Städten und die Kriegsführung zu Lande und zu Wasser versprachen zwar große Gewinne, sie waren aber auch riskant (man konnte unterliegen) und vor allem brauchte man zunächst viel Geld und viele Menschen.

Clemens Kühn formuliert dazu: „Charakteristisch für die Kriegsführung in hellenistischer Zeit waren nicht so sehr neuartige Taktiken oder Waffen, als vielmehr ein in allen Belangen gesteigerter Aufwand: an

Geld, an Menschen und an Material".[6] Allerdings würde ich sagen, dass der derart quantitativ gesteigerte Aufwand faktisch auch eine qualitative Steigerung bedeutete. Eine derartige Steigerung an Menschen bzw. Soldaten und an technischen Entwicklungen war etwas Neues, nicht zuletzt im Blick auf die Finanzierung diese Aufwands. Auseinandersetzungen dieser Art waren nicht mehr in der Dimension, die einzelne Städte oder kleine Gebiete leisten konnten, sondern nur die großen Königreiche: „Warfare in the Hellenistic period belonged primarily to the professionals and to the technical experts. And it was certainly the business of kings".[7]—Diese Entwicklung hatte schon in der Perserzeit und auch mit den Perserkriegen in Kleinasien, Griechenland und Ägypten eingesetzt, hatte sich aber nun ganz besonders gesteigert.

Diese Wendung ins Gigantische spiegelt sich im Alten Testament wohl in den großen Zahlen bei den in der Chronik erzählten Kriegen. Im Vergleich dazu ist es interessant, dass im Buch Jesus Sirach dieser kriegerische Aspekt m.W. nicht vorkommt. Für das Buch Jesus Sirach ist dagegen ein anderer Aspekt in hellenistischer Zeit sehr wichtig, nämlich die Bedeutung der Stadt zur Verbreitung und als Ort der Kultur.

Bevor wir uns diesem Aspekt zuwenden, zunächst aber noch ein kleiner *Exkurs zur Chronologie.*

Die Geschichte der hellenistischen Zeit ist von verschiedenen Autoren dargestellt, z.B. von Polybios. Dazu gibt es zahlreiche archäologische Funde und nicht zuletzt auch Münzen.[8]

Dabei besteht allerdings eine gewisse Diversität: Viele Ereignisse sind unterschiedlich dargestellt, oder zumindest unterschiedlich bewertet. Auch die Dichte der Überlieferung ist unterschiedlich: Über manche Ereignisse sind wir sehr gut informiert, über andere und auch über bestimmte Regionen liegen wenige Informationen vor. Nicht zuletzt auch bei der Chronologie gibt es erstaunliche Divergenzen. Manche Ereignisse sind auf den Tag

6. Clemens Kühn, "Ein Triumph neuer Techniken? Strategien der Kriegsführung," in Cain, *Hellenismus*, 57. Etwas anders, aber doch auch mit Betonung der Steigerung Glenn R. Bugh, "Hellenistic Military Developments": „For the most part, the Greeks continued traditions exiting in the Classical period but simply magnified them into what one scholar described as 'gigantism': Large professional (mercenary) armies, greater specialisation of arms and armor, terrifying machines of war, and huge ships" (265).

7. Bugh, "Hellenistic Military Developments," 265.

8. Zur Fülle aber auch zur Begrenzung des Quellenmaterials siehe Glenn R. Bugh, "Introduction," in Bugh, *Cambridge Companion to the Hellenistic World*, 3–5.

genau datierbar, etwa der Tod von bestimmten Personen. Bei anderen Ereignissen schwankt die Datierung um mehrere, wenn nicht bis zu 10 Jahren.

In unserem Zusammenhang ist die Datierung der im Rahmen des 5. Syrischen Krieges erfolgten Schlacht von Paneion bzw. Banjas (am Fuß des Hermon an einem der Quellflüsse des Jordan) interessant, mit der für Palästina die Vorherrschaft der Ptolemäer endete und die Vorherrschaft der Seleukiden begann. In unserer Literatur wird dabei häufig das Jahr 198 v.Chr. angegeben. In neuerer Zeit wird dafür auch oft das Jahr 200 genannt. Ist das eine neue Datierung? Oder hat jemand statt 198 die runde Zahl 200 genannt und wurde dann daraus versehentlich ein neues Datum? Unser Wuppertaler Historiker Wolfgang Orth, einer der besten Kenner der hellenistischen Zeit, hat mir dazu Folgendes geschrieben:

> Ich habe ... immer Sommer 200 als das Datum der Schlacht beim Paneion angenommen. Dann muss man freilich Eusebius Chronikon II 124f. verwerfen, bei dem man auf das Jahr 197 oder gar 196 kommt. Soweit ich die Sache überblicke, hat [Heinrich] Nissen im 19. Jhdt. („Kritische Untersuchungen", Berlin 1863, 142) die These zu begründen versucht, die Schlacht gehöre ins Jahr 198, weil er unter Hinweis auf Livius XXXI 43 annahm, die Auseinandersetzung sei später anzusetzen als die Werbungen eines gewissen Skopas im Jahre 199. Dem Polybios-Kommentar von [Frank J.] Walbank (Vol. II 523) entnehme ich, dass dem auch der große italienische Althistoriker [Francesco] De Sanctis gefolgt ist. Der von Nissen angenommene Zusammenhang ist freilich alles andere als klar.
>
> Mir scheint, dass die grundlegende Abhandlung dem französischen Historiker und Epigraphiker M[aurice] Holleaux verdankt wird: M. Holleaux, Etudes III, 317–335 (eingehende Rekonstruktion der Abfolge der Ereignisse des 5. Syrischen Krieges anhand der Interpretation der relevanten Polybios-Stellen). Auf ihn berufen sich dann alle, die für das Datum 200 plädieren (weiterführende Literatur: F. W. Walbank, *A Historical Commentary on Polybius*, vol. 2 [Oxford: Oxford University Press, 1967], 523; W. Huß, *Ägypten in hellenistischer Zeit* [Munich: Beck, 2001], 490–91).[9]

Das Beispiel zeigt, dass wir zwar eine relativ genaue Chronologie zur Verfügung haben, es im Einzelnen aber durchaus gewisse Diskrepanzen—und zwar auch für gewichtige Daten und Ereignisse—gibt.

9. Email vom 2.9.2014.

3. Stadtkultur und Königtum

Dass der Hellenismus im Wesentlichen Stadtkultur war, zeigt sich an vielen Aspekten.

Auch das hat seine Vorgeschichte bereits in der griechischen Welt. Die griechische Kultur war Stadtkultur. Genau genommen ging es immer um die Stadt und das dazugehörige Umfeld für die landwirtschaftliche Versorgung. Zwar hatte sich seit dem 6. Jh. in der griechischen Welt vieles geändert, aber die Städte waren der für die Entwicklung der Kultur bestimmende Faktor und Nährboden geblieben. Seit der Mitte des 5. Jh. gab es den Begriff der Demokratie und diese galt als die typische und auch ideale Organisationsform einer Stadt. Auch in der hellenistischen Zeit galt sie als das Ideal der politischen Organisation, wobei die Demokratie de facto immer schon eine Tendenz zur Oligarchie hatte; eine Tendenz, die sich dann in der hellenistischen Zeit zunehmend durchsetzte. Die Repräsentanz und das Handlungsorgan dieser Demokratie bzw. Oligarchie war die Boulé, der Rat der Stadt.

In Entsprechung dazu gab es in Jerusalem die Gerusia. Auch das erstmals in 1Makk 12,6 erwähnte Synhedrion ist nicht nur ein griechisches Wort, sondern eine typisch hellenistische Bezeichnung, die allerdings für sehr verschiedene Einrichtungen verwendet werden konnte.[10] Allerdings lag ein wesentlicher Unterschied darin, dass die Ämter in Jerusalem nicht regelmäßig neu gewählt wurden, sondern das Amt des Hohepriesters und des Tempelverwalters erblich waren und im Prinzip lebenslänglich ausgeübt wurden.

In seiner Beschreibung der Demokratie bzw. der Herrschaftsformen wendet sich Polybios ausdrücklich gegen einen Zustand, in dem eine beliebige Masse bestimmt, was zu tun ist, und lehnt eine solche Herrschaft der Menge (Ochlokratie) oder der Faust (Cheirokratie) ab.

„Wo man jedoch die Götter fürchtet, Vater und Mutter ehrt, den Gesetzen gehorcht, wenn sie [die Regierung] in einer solchen Staatsord-

---

10. Synhedrion (eigentlich „Rat der Zusammensitzenden") ist die „untechn[ische] und techn[ische] Bezeichnung für Beratungs- und Beschlussversammlungen verschiedener Art in Städten, Vereinen usw. S. heißen auch die Friedenskongresse der Landfriedensbünde und die Delegiertenversammlungen der Hellenenbünde.... Ferner der Kron- und Kriegsrat in hell[enistischen] Monarchien und der Ältestenrat von Jerusalem". Hatto H. Schmitt, "Synhedrion," in Schmitt and Vogt, *Lexikon des Hellenismus*, 1054.

nung durchsetzt, was der Mehrheit richtig scheint, dort ist die Bezeichnung Demokratie am Platz". Polybios grenzt diese Demokratie sowohl von der Tyrannis in Sparta als auch andererseits vom Königtum in Makedonien ab (6.43,4).[11]

Auf der anderen Seite waren Königtümer praktisch immer Flächenstaaten, wenn auch mit hervorragender Bedeutung der Hauptstadt. Das galt für die altorientalischen Reiche, für das Persische Reich und für Ägypten, und das galt auch für die Königreiche in der griechischen Welt, erst recht bei Alexander und in den Diadochenreichen. So wie innerhalb der Stadt, braucht es erst recht für diese Flächenstaaten eine weit reichende Administration, die den Willen des Herrschers durchsetzte und insbesondere auch die Steuern und sonstigen staatlichen Finanzen organisierte. Das galt im Prinzip auch für Jerusalem und Juda, sowohl für sich betrachtet, als auch im Rahmen der jeweiligen Oberherrschaft.

Ben Sira hat offensichtlich die Bildung dieser Führungsschicht vor Augen, allerdings auf dem Hintergrund der spezifisch jüdischen Traditionen.

Wie für die Demokratie gab es auch für das Königtum eine philosophische Rechtfertigung. Allerdings versuchten Philosophen, angehende Könige im Sinn ihrer philosophischen Vorstellungen zu erziehen oder regierende Herrscher diesbezüglich zu beeinflussen: Für Ersteres kann man an Aristoteles als Erzieher Alexanders des Großen denken, für Letzeres an die Beziehung der Ptolemäer zu den Gelehrten und insbesondere zu den Leitern der Alexandrinischen Bibliothek (jedenfalls bis zur Mitte des 2.Jh., wo es dann zu einer Krise in dieser Beziehung kam).

Dass es zur Herausbildung eines Herrscherideals kam und auch das Königtum idealisiert wurde, ist wenig überraschend. Interessant ist jedoch, wie diese Idealisierung zum Ausdruck kam. In der Realität gibt es ja zweifellos gute Könige und weniger gute Könige. In der Philosophie gibt es dagegen per definitionem nur gute Könige. Das geht ganz einfach: Ein schlechter König ist kein König mehr, sondern ein Tyrann. Man sieht auch hier die Ambivalenz: Einerseits wird dem König ein Leitbild geliefert, an das er sich halten soll, andererseits wird der König durch dieses legitimiert.[12] Markant und interessant ist dabei, in welchem Maß Philosophen (und Rhetoren)

11. Gauger, "Demokratie," in Schmitt and Vogt, *Lexikon des Hellenismus*, 239.

12. Dabei können natürlich die Gewichtungen unterschiedlich sein. Interessante Beispiele für diese Mischung aus Lobrede und Fürstenspiegel sind die um 370 v.Chr. geschriebenen Reden des Isokrates über bzw. an Euagoras und Nikokles.

an den Königshöfen als Erzieher und dann auch als Berater herangezogen wurden und welchen Einfluss sie dabei hatten bzw. haben konnten.[13]

Zum Herrscherideal gehört zunächst die schon erwähnte militärische Tüchtigkeit, die sich neben dem für die Dynastie anfänglichen und grundlegenden „Speergewinn" in Siegen und Rettungstaten konkretisiert. Ihren Ausdruck finden diese Aspekte in Beinamen wie „Nikator" und „Soter". Die entsprechenden Taten werden auf Siegesstelen, Münzen oder durch Siegesparaden dokumentiert und propagiert. Sehr wichtig ist aber auch das aus dem Wirken des Herrschers resultierende Wohlergehen des Landes und der Bewohner, zu dem nicht zuletzt auch gerechte Gesetze beitragen. Dieser Aspekt des Wohltäters und des Ernährers des Volkes findet seinen Ausdruck im Namen „Eumenes" sowie im Beinamen „Euergetes", und auf Münzen durch die Abbildung eines (mit dem königlichen Diadem geschmückten) Füllhorns. Nicht zuletzt sind die hellenistischen Herrscher Förderer sowohl der Kulte als auch der Kultur. Insbesondere die Ptolemäer haben sich in diesem Bereich durch Museion und Bibliothek(en) besonders hervorgetan.[14]

---

13. Siehe dazu Tessa Rajak, Sarah Pearce, James Aitken, and Jennifer Dines, *Jewish Perspectives on Hellenistic Rulers*, HCS 50 (Berkeley: University of California Press, 2007); inbesondere Oswyn Murray, "Philosophy and Monarchy in the Hellenistic World," 13–28: „Auch wenn die Behauptungen der Philosophen bezüglich ihrer Fähigkeiten manchmal etwas übertrieben wirken, muss man sich daran erinnern, dass jede Gesellschaft ihre Experten für die Regierungskunst hat.… In der hellenistischen Welt übte der Philosoph dieselbe Rolle aus wie der Arzt, der Priester oder der Prophet in anderen Gesellschaften, und—so mag man hinzufügen—machte es genauso gut. Er war das Gewissen des Königtums, der Prüfstein gegen Machtmissbrauch und der Protagonist korrekter Maßstäbe. Er besaß die Geheimnisse guter Regierung; er hatte dieselbe Position wie der Soziologe oder der Wirtschaftsexperte heute. Wie diese war er an den Königshöfen willkommen, bekam riesige Summen bezahlt, und man hörte ihm aufmerksam zu. Sein Ratschlag wurde zur Grundlage der Politik, sein Jargon dominierte die Administration. Und wer wollte behaupten, dass der Philosoph mit seiner Betonung der Tugend und moralisch gerechten Regierens im Sinn der Menschen mehr Schaden verursachte oder weniger effektiv war, als der politische Experte oder der Unternehmer? Jedenfalls konnte man den Philosophen, auch wenn seine Theorien oft wenig konkreten Inhalt hatten und praktische Überlegungen außer Acht ließen, nicht beschuldigen, das Elend und das Unglück der Untertanen vermehrt zu haben" (27; Übersetzung S.K.).

14. Siehe dazu u.a.: Hölbl, *Geschichte des Ptolemäerreiches*; zur Bedeutung des kulturellen Hintergrundes für die Entstehung und Bedeutung der Septuaginta siehe u.a. Siegfried Kreuzer, "Die Septuaginta im Kontext alexandrinischer Kultur und Bil-

Das Zentrum des Königreiches bildete die Basileia mit dem königlichen Palast, den Verwaltungsgebäuden, den Ministern und weiteren Bediensteten des Königs, aber auch dem Wohnort der Familie des Königs sowie des Hofpersonals und deren Angehörigen. Innerhalb dieser Residenzstadt war der Palastbereich abgegrenzt.

> Zwar sind die Paläste der Ptolemäer- und Seleukidenkönige in Alexandria, Antiochia und Seleukia archäologisch nicht faßbar, jedoch wird von Strabo überliefert, dass die Basileia in Alexandria ein Drittel bzw. ein Viertel des gesamten Stadtgebietes eingenommen habe.... Die Basileia bildete einerseits das Machtzentrum des Reiches, von dem alle politischen, militärischen und administrativen Entscheidungen ausgingen. Zugleich bildete der Palast aber auch den Bezugspunkt der herrschenden Gesellschaft; das Leben am Hof war für den einzelnen Philos der Ort der sozialen Identität und des sozialen Status.[15]

Das zentrale Ereignis des höfischen Lebens waren die königlichen Symposien. Das Symposion war der wesentliche „Ort der Prestigebildung und der Statusbestimmung".[16] Hier konnte man seinen Status gewinnen oder auch verlieren: „Die höfischen Symposien erfüllten in ihrer Prachtentfaltung, in der Bewirtung mit kostbaren Speisen und Getränken und in der reichen Ausstattung der Bankettträume zum einen sicherlich das Bedürfnis der herrschenden Gesellschaft nach Vergnügen und Unterhaltung. Zugleich war das Symposion aber auch der Ort der gesellschaftlichen Definition des einzelnen Philos, denn während des Gelages konzentrieren sich alle sozialen Beziehungen innerhalb der Institution des Hofes an einem Ort".[17]

---

dung," in *Studien zur Theologie, Anthropologie, Ekklesiologie, Eschatologie und Liturgie der Griechischen Bibel*, Bd. 3 von *Im Brennpunkt: Die Septuaginta; Studien zu Entstehung und Bedeutung der Griechischen Bibel*, hrsg. Heinz-Jozef Fabry und Dieter Böhler, BWANT 174 (Stuttgart: Kohlhammer, 2007), 28–56; cf. "Origin and Development of the Septuagint in the Context of Alexandrien and Early Jewish Culture and Learning," in Siegfried Kreuzer, *The Bible in Greek: Translation, Transmission, and Theology of the Septuagint*, SBLSCS 62 (Atlanta: SBL Press, 2015), 3–46.

15. Völcker-Janssen, Wilhelm, *Kunst und Gesellschaft an den Höfen Alexanders d.Gr. und seiner Nachfolger*, Quellen und Forschungen zur Antiken Welt 15 (Munich: Tuduv, 1993) 70–71.

16. Ibid., 78.

17. Ibid.

Im Blick auf unser Thema bzw. auf unsere Literatur passt das im Aristeasbrief beschriebene Symposion—auch wenn es fiktiv sein mag—bestens in diesen Kontext. Wichtig erscheint mir dabei auch, wie sehr die Fragen dieses Symposions auf das Herrscherbild konzentriert sind. M.E. ist diese Thematik des Symposions und die damit verbundene Intention des Autors des Aristeasbriefes noch zu wenig beachtet.

Im Vergleich dazu fehlt bei Ben Sira das Thema des Königtums, aber man kann sich fragen, ob nicht die großartige Beschreibung des Hohepriesters diese Funktion eines Ideal- und Leitbildes für den Herrscher ausfüllt, denn immerhin war zur Zeit Ben Siras der Hohepriester der in Jerusalem erlebbare Herrscher. Andererseits geht es auch bei Ben Sira um das rechte Verhalten bei einem Gastmahl. Gewiss waren Symposien in Jerusalem weit entfernt von den Symposien in Alexandrien oder Antiochia. Aber sie waren wohl doch auch in analoger Weise der „Ort der Prestigebildung und der Statusbestimmung", an dem man seinen Status gewinnen oder auch verlieren konnte. Von daher ist es nicht verwunderlich, dass Ben Sira bei seiner Unterweisung auch diesen Lebensbereich einbezieht.

Für den regionalen Bereich Palästinas ist noch darauf hinzuweisen, dass im Ostjordanland, am alten Sitz der Tobiaden, eine solche Basileia im Kleinen in archäologisch fassbaren Spuren erhalten blieb, nämlich in der Anlage von Iraq el-Amir. Diese Anlage, in deren Zentrum das berühmte und vieldiskutierte Qasr el 'Abd steht, hatte gewiss eine längere Geschichte. Insbesondere die Wohnhöhlen, von denen eine an ihrem Eingang mit dem Namen Tobija in hebräisch-aramäischer Schrift versehen ist, gehen wohl weiter zurück. Das Qasr aber wurde von Hyrkan, der in diesem Gebiet der letzte proptolemäische Herrscher war, erbaut. Es wurde zwar verschiedentlich als Tempel interpretiert, wobei man aber annehmen muss, dass Josephus, der die Anlage sehr genau beschreibt, die Funktion als Tempel verschwiegen habe. Auch wenn diese Interpretation auch heute noch gelegentlich unhinterfragt weitergegeben wird,[18] ist sie doch sehr

18. So z.B. bei Ernst Haag, *Das hellenistische Zeitalter: Israel und die Bibel im 4. bis 1. Jahrhundert v.Chr.*, BE 9 (Stuttgart: Kohlhammer, 2003), 50 und Fn. 28. Haag folgt hier der seinerzeitigen Position von Hengel, *Judentum und Hellenismus*, 496–503, der zwar die Forschungsgeschichte ausführlich darstellte, sich aber dann aus eher allgemeinen Erwägungen für einen Tempel entschied. Zu Recht wird diese Deutung bei Christian Frevel, "Gundriss Geschichte Israels," in *Einleitung in das Alte Testament*, hrsg. Erich Zenger and Christian Frevel, 8. Aufl., Kohlhammer-Studienbücher Theologie 1.1 (Stuttgart: Kohlhammer, 2012), 834, bestritten, der allerdings dann die

unwahrscheinlich. Zwar könnten bestimmte hellenistische Architekturelemente sowohl an einem Palast als auch an einem Tempel vorkommen, die Gesamtanlage des Gebäudes wie auch das Umfeld sprechen jedoch sehr deutlich für einen Palast,[19] gewissermaßen als Zentrum einer kleinen „Basilea" dieses ostjordanischen Herrschers. (Ich gestehe gerne, dass ich mir seit meinem ersten Besuch vor Ort nicht vorstellen konnte, dass dieses Gebäude ein Tempel, welcher Gottheit auch immer, hätte sein sollen).

Die Anlage von Iraq el-Amir ist nicht nur die zwar kleinste, aber einzige einigermaßen erhaltene Anlage dieser Art, sondern zugleich ein Beleg dafür, dass die großen Anlagen der Hauptstädte auch im regionalen Bereich ihre Nachahmung fanden. Dabei ging es sicher nicht nur um die Gebäude, sondern um das höfische Leben insgesamt. Dieses Anliegen wird auch für Jerusalem nicht ganz ohne Einfluss und Bedeutung geblieben sein.

4. Stadtkultur und Identität

In der Literatur wird verschiedentlich behauptet, dass mit dem Königtum und den Flächenstaaten der hellenistischen Zeit die Bedeutung der Polis zu Ende gegangen sei, jedenfalls sofern sie sich nicht zu großen Städtebünden zusammenschlossen. Das gilt allerdings nur für die sog. große Politik. Dagegen ist gerade die hellenistische Zeit eine Blütezeit der Stadtkultur.[20] Das zeigt sich alleine schon an der großen Zahl von Städtegründungen, die bekanntlich gerne mit dem Namen Alexanders oder zahlreicher weiterer hellenistischer Herrscher versehen wurden. Allerdings ist auch hier zu

---

ebenfalls fragliche Deutung als Festung vorträgt: „Die archäologischen Gebäudereste, die man in ʿIraq al-Emir aus dem 3./2. Jh. v. Chr. gefunden hat, wurden mehrfach als Sakralarchitektur interpretiert. Angemessener ist die Anlage als Festung zu deuten, so dass Hyrkan keinen Gegentempel zu Jerusalem bauen ließ". Allerdings ist das Gebäude mit seinen vergleichsweise dünnen Mauern und mit all seinen Dekorationen sowie seiner Lage im Tal als Festung ungeeignet und auch die Wasserversorgung der ganzen Anlage müsste für eine Festung anders konzipiert sein.

19. So nun auch neben vielen anderen Bürge, *Der Palast von Iraq al-Amir* (Vienna, University: Diplomarbeit Klassische Archäologie, 2011).

20. Zum Verhältnis von Königtum und Stadt siehe exemplarisch an Hand der Seleukiden und der kleinasiatischen Städte: W. Orth, *Königlicher Machtanspruch und städtische Freiheit: Untersuchungen zu den politischen Beziehungen zwischen den ersten Seleukidenherrschern (Seleukos I., Antiochos I., Antiochos II.) und den Städten des westlichen Kleinasien*, MBPF 71 (Munich: Beck, 1977).

differenzieren. Die meisten dieser Städte wurden zunächst nicht gegründet, um die griechische Kultur zu verbreiten, sondern aus militärischen Gründen und um die Wirtschaft zu kontrollieren, die wiederum für die Finanzierung des Heeres notwendig war. Bosworth hat das am Beispiel von Alexandria Eschate, dem äußersten Alexandrien, das im fernen Nordosten, nördlich des Hindukusch und des Pamirgebirges im heutigen Tadschikistan, gegründet wurde, gezeigt: Als die militärische Besatzung dieser und anderer weit im Nordosten gelegenen Städte sich nach Alexanders Tod in Richtung Heimat zurückziehen wollte, wurde sie in einer opferreichen Schlacht gezwungen, dort zu bleiben. Die Stationierung in einer dieser neugegründeten hellenistischen (= griechisch sprechenden) Städte war gewissermaßen ein Urteil zu lebenslänglicher Verbannung. Aber: Wenn man denn schon da bleiben musste, dann wollte man es sich auch etwas schöner machen, und zwar schöner im Sinn der gewohnten griechischen Kultur.[21] Dazu gehörten dann Bäder, Gymnasien und Theater.

Das heißt, der kulturelle Aspekt und die kulturelle Ausstrahlung kamen erst in einer zweiten Phase zum Tragen. Dann aber umso kräftiger.—Natürlich war diese Entwicklung in den verschiedenen Regionen unterschiedlich und natürlich knüpfte sie im Raum des östlichen Mittelmeeres an schon bestehende Traditionen und Tendenzen an.

Die Bedeutung der Stadt in der hellenistischen Zeit bringt Hatto H. Schmitt folgendermaßen sehr schön auf den Punkt:

> Sieht man von der ‚großen Politik' ab, in der die Städte—jedenfalls soweit sie sich nicht zu größeren politischen Gebilden zusammenschließen—in der Tat selten mehr als Objekte sind, so kann der Hell[enismus] geradezu als eine Blütezeit der griechischen Stadtkultur angesehen werden, sowohl quantitativ (Gründungen) wie inhaltlich. Insbesondere in den durch Alexanders Zug neuerschlossenen Räumen gewinnt die Stadt—in diesem Fall besonders die Neugründung, meist auf „barbarischem" Boden—neue Bedeutung als wichtigster Faktor der ethnischen, kulturellen und zivilisatorischen Hellenisierung. Die Stadt ist der Ort, an dem der Nichtgrieche den korrekten Gebrauch der griechischen Sprache erlernen …, zum Stadtbürger werden und damit eine wichtige Voraussetzung zum Aufstieg in die griechisch geprägte Oberschicht des Reichs erwerben kann; mit → Schule, → Gymnasion, → Theater, rechtlichen und politischen Institutionen bietet sie Einrichtungen zum Erwerb

21. Albert Brian Bosworth, "Alexander the Great and the Creation of the Hellenistic Age," in Bugh, *Cambridge Companion to the Hellenstic World*, 17–18.

> und zur Pflege jener Bildung, die nach damals vorgetragener Vorstellung den Hellenen ausmachen und ihn vom Barbaren unterscheiden.
>
> Die gemeinsamen Kulte und die immer zahlreicheren Feste schaffen und erhalten in den alten wie den neuen Städten durch gemeinsames Erleben ein Bürgerbewußtsein, das dem Zusammengehörigkeitsgefühl der Bürger in der klassischen Polis kaum nachgestanden haben dürfte.
>
> Durch (z.T. fiktive) Verwandtschaftsbeziehungen und ‚hellenische' Ausgestaltung ihrer Vergangenheit … rücken viele der Städte des Ostens in die geistige Nähe der alten Poleis.[22]

Die hier genannten Aspekte gelten m.E. mutatis mutandis auch für Jerusalem und Judäa und—nicht zu vergessen—gewiss auch für Samaria.

Aus den Makkabäerbüchern wissen wir, dass die sichtbaren Elemente der griechischen Kultur, vor allem ein Gymnasion, auch in Jerusalem eingeführt wurden; und die im 2. Jh. etablierte Akra hatte im Kleinen die Funktion, die ich vorher bei den Städtegründungen erwähnte, nämlich zunächst die militärische und wirtschaftliche Kontrolle.

Die weicheren Faktoren der Hellenisierung hatten sich in Jerusalem aber wohl schon früher und vermutlich eher schleichend eingestellt und etabliert: Die von Schmitt erwähnten Schulen hatten wohl schon im 3. Jh. einen wichtigen Einfluss ausgeübt. Gewiss gab es auch vorher schon eine Schreiberausbildung, und diese Ausbildung erfolgte nicht abstrakt, sondern an konkreten Texten, an Hand derer die Fähigkeiten trainiert und auch die alten Traditionen tradiert wurden. Die alte Diskussion um Schulen oder Famulussystem würde ich dahingehend beantworten, dass speziellere Kenntnisse und Fähigkeiten sicher in einem Famulussystem vermittelt wurden, aber dass sich wichtige Personen der Verwaltung oder auch ein Weisheitslehrer wie Ben Sira schwerlich mit „ABC-Schützen" abgeplagt haben. D.h. für die Anfänger und die breitere Basis gab es wohl eine Art Schulsystem, während die weiterführende Ausbildung in kleineren Kreisen und in einer Art Famulussystem erfolgte.[23]

---

22. Hatto H. Schmitt, "Stadt A–D," in Schmitt and Vogst, *Lexikon des Hellenismus*, 1023.

23. Bekanntlich ist eine Schule in Jerusalem bisher archäologisch nicht nachgewiesen. Das ist allerdings auch nicht zu erwarten. Denn im Prinzip konnten in jedem etwas größeren Wohnraum zehn bis zwanzig Kinder oder Jugendliche in Lesen und Schreiben unterrichtet werden. Wie problematisch es ist, aus dem Fehlen archäologischer Nachweise auf das Fehlen der Sache zu schließen, zeigt die oben erwähnte Tatsache, dass von den großen Palästen in den Hauptstädten keine archäologisch greifbaren

Wie auch immer dies im Einzelnen aussah—auf jeden Fall erhielt die Schule in der hellenistischen Zeit eine große und weiter gehende Bedeutung, nicht nur für praktische Zwecke, sondern als Schlüssel zu Kultur und Bildung und um dazu-zu-gehören.[24]

M.E. gab es vermutlich auch in Jerusalem, so wie in vielen hellenistischen Städten, einen Büchermarkt, auf dem man fremde aber auch einheimische Erzeugnisse erwerben konnte.

Das alles scheint mir dann auch der Hintergrund für das Lehrhaus und die Lehrtätigkeit Ben Siras zu sein.

Im obigen Zitat von Schmitt werden als ein weiterer Aspekt der hellenistischen Stadtkultur „die gemeinsamen Kulte und die immer zahlreicheren Feste" genannt, „die durch gemeinsames Erleben ein Bürgerbewußtsein schaffen und erhalten". Natürlich war der gemeinsame Kult für Jerusalem am Tempel auch in der älteren Zeit ein wichtiges Element der gemeinsamen Identität, aber dieser Aspekt bekommt nun nochmals eine neue und große Bedeutung. M.E. kann und muss man bereits die Bedeutung und auch die schönen Beschreibungen des Tempelkultes in Jerusalem im Buch der Chronik auch auf diesem Hintergrund sehen. Dabei hat nicht nur die weitere Umwelt einen Einfluss ausgeübt, sondern genauso und noch wichtiger auch das Nebeneinander und die Konkurrenz mit Samaria und dem Kult auf dem Garizim, der, wie die neueren Ausgrabungen zeigen, spätestens ab der Mitte des 5. Jh. existierte, und wo um 200 ein großartiges neues Tempelgebäude errichtet wurde.[25] M.E. ist dieses identitätsstiftende Element des gemeinsamen Kultes für die Polis Jerusalem und für das Judentum ein wichtiger Aspekt. Dabei sind übrigens auch die

---

Überreste erhalten sind, obwohl die betreffenden Paläste gewiss existierten. Solange es keine neuen Funde gibt, wird sich die Diskussion zwischen den beiden Polen, dass Schulen archäologisch nicht nachgewiesen sind und dass die in Wirtschaft, Verwaltung und Literatur zweifellos vorhandenen Lese- und Schreibkenntnisse irgendwie vermittelt werden mussten, bewegen. Im Übrigen sollte man sich bewusst machen, was man unter Schule versteht und erwartet.

24. Zu Schule und Bildung siehe Frank Ueberschaer, *Weisheit aus der Begegnung, Bildung nach dem Buch Ben Sira*, BZAW 379 (Berlin: de Gruyter, 2007).

25. Siehe dazu den Bericht über die Ausgrabungen auf dem Garizim in: Magen, Yitzhak, "Gerizim, Mount," *NEAEHL* 5:1742–48, sowie Siegfried Kreuzer, "Vom Garizim zum Ebal: Erwägungen zur Geschichte und Textgeschichte sowie zu einem neuen Qumran-Text," in *Juda und Jerusalem in der Seleukidenzeit: Herrschaft—Widerstand—Identität, FS Heinz-Josef Fabry*, hrsg. Ulrich Dahmen und Johannes Schnocks, BBB 159 (Göttingen: Vandenhoeck & Ruprecht, 2010), 31–42.

Ausstrahlung und das „Image“ des Jerusalemer Tempelkultes in die jüdische Diaspora von erheblicher Bedeutung.

Auch Schmitts Bemerkung über die immer zahlreicheren Feste ist interessant: Ist nicht das Purimfest ein solches neues Fest, das zwar auf einer älteren Überlieferung basierte, das aber vor allem als neues, identitätssteigerndes Fest eingeführt wurde und das man dann auch in die jüdische Diaspora nach Ägypten exportierte,[26] wohl nicht zuletzt auch im Sinn dieser gemeinsamen Identität? Auch das dann aus Anlass der Wiedereinweihung des Tempels im Jahr 164 v.Chr. eingeführte Chanukkafest passt in diesen Zusammenhang.

Zum Stichwort „Herstellung von Identität“ möchte ich auch noch kurz auf den Namen der Stadt Jerusalem selber eingehen. Bekanntlich wurden in der hellenistischen Zeit auch für die Juden Beziehungen mit der griechischen Welt konstruiert, z.B. mit Sparta, zu dem man sich als verwandt betrachtete (Josephus, Antiquitates 12.226–227; wo die Verbindung über Abraham als gemeinsamen Ahnherrn hergestellt wird). Griechische Wurzeln oder eine Verbindung zur griechischen Welt zu haben, war in der hellenistischen Welt ein wichtiger Pluspunkt für das Selbstverständnis und für die Wahrnehmung durch die anderen. Hierher ist gewiss auch die gräzisierte Form des Namens für Jerusalem, nämlich „Hierorsolyma“, zu rechnen. Der Name Hierosolyma findet sich seit dem 3. Jh. bei jüdischen, wie auch bei nichtjüdischen Autoren.[27] Von den Konsonanten her ist er mit dem Namen Jerusalem identisch, aber er bedeutet doch etwas anderes, nämlich ungefähr so viel wie „heiliges Solyma“.

Vor einigen Jahren machten wir eine Exkursion in die Türkei. Wir fuhren u.a. von der Südküste ein wenig hinauf ins Gebirge und besuchten die Ruinen der Stadt Solyma. Die Solymier verstanden sich als Nachfahren der Solymer, die aus Troja geflohen waren (Ilias 6.184. 204 und Odyssee 5.283). Damit hatten sie eine Verbindung mit der alten homerischen Welt, übrigens ganz ähnlich wie die Römer über den aus Troja geflohenen

---

26. Siehe dazu die diesbezügliche Notiz in der griechischen Übersetzung des Estherbuches.

27. Z.B. bei Polybius; Diodorus Siculus; Strabo, Cassius Dio. Siehe dazu Walter Bauer, Kurt Aland, und Barbara Aland, Hrsg., Griechisch-deutsches Wörterbuch zu den Schriften des Neuen Testaments und der frühchristlichen Literatur, 6. Aufl. (Berlin: de Gruyter, 1988), s.v. Für eine Diskussion der verschiedenen Belege siehe Martin Hengel, "Jerusalem als jüdische und hellenistische Stadt," in Funck, *Hellenismus*, 269–306.

Äneas. Als wir in Solyma standen, dachte ich an Hierosolyma. Mit dieser leicht variierten Lesung des Namens Jerusalem (die Konsonanten sind identisch, nur die Vokalisation bzw. Lesung ist anders) machte man sich zu einem Glied der homerischen Welt. Und zugleich zu etwas Besonderem: Man war nicht nur Solyma, sondern man war Hierosolyma, das heilige Solyma. M.E. ist diese Bezeichnung eine Selbstbezeichnung, mit der man sich in Jerusalem im 3.Jh. in die griechische Welt einreihte und zugleich als etwas Besonderes bezeichnete.—Es geht genau um jenes Phänomen, das Schmitt als hellenistische Ausgestaltung der Vergangenheit durch (z.T. fiktive) Verwandtschaftsbeziehungen bezeichnet hatte.

5. Die Schwierigkeit des Übersetzens? Ein hellenistisches Element im Prolog des Enkels

Machen wir zum Schluss noch einen Sprung in die Welt des Enkels von Ben Sira. Von der Bedeutung der hellenistischen Welt in der Kultur von Alexandrien werden wir gewiss noch hören, insbesondere auch von der Kenntnis und den Einflüssen der hellenistischen Literatur für die Septuaginta im Allgemeinen sowie für die Übersetzung des Sirachbuches im Besonderen.[28]

Ich möchte auf ein Element des Prologs des Sirachbuches eingehen, nämlich auf die bekannte Bemerkung des Enkels darüber, wie schwierig es sei, das Hebräische ins Griechische zu übersetzen.

> Darum bitte ich euch, das Buch freundlich aufzunehmen und aufmerksam zu lesen und dort Nachsicht zu üben, wo wir etwa einige Worte nicht recht getroffen haben, obwohl wir uns bemühten, gut zu übersetzen. Denn was in hebräischer Sprache geschrieben ist, verliert viel, wenn man es in einer anderen Sprache wiedergibt. Sogar das Gesetz selber und die Propheten und die übrigen Bücher lauten oft recht anders, wenn sie in ihrer eigenen Sprache gelesen werden. (Sirach, Prolog. 5–7)

---

28. Siehe dazu besonders den Beitrag von Knut Usener in diesem Band. Zum Hintergrund der Septuaginta siehe auch Siegfried Kreuzer, "Die Septuaginta im Kontext alexandrinischer Kultur und Bildung," sowie Kreuzer, "Entstehung und Entwicklung der Septuaginta im Kontext Alexandrinischer und Frühjüdischer Kultur und Bildung," in *Septuaginta-Deutsch: Erläuterungen und Kommentare* (Stuttgart: Kohlhammer, 2011), 1:3–39.

Diese Bemerkung hat sehr verschiedene Interpretationen erfahren, von Erörterungen über das Verhältnis von semitischen und indogermanischen Sprachen bis hin zur Interpretation, dass der Enkel hier vielleicht die eigene Unzulänglichkeit eingesteht.

Vor einigen Jahren habe ich mit unserem bereits genannten Wuppertaler Althistoriker Wolfgang Orth ein Seminar über Herrscherbilder abgehalten. Dabei lasen wir auch die Lobreden des Isokrates auf den zyprischen König Nikokles. Das für mich Erstaunlichste war die Einleitung dieser Lobrede. Der berühmte und geübte Rhetor Isokrates,[29] der mit solchen Lobreden schon einiges an Geld verdient hatte, beginnt mit endlosen Ausführungen über die Schwierigkeit, eine Lobrede zu verfassen, bis hin zur Behauptung, dass es schwieriger sei, eine solche Rede in Prosa zu schreiben als in Gedichtform, weil die Gedichtform über inhaltliche Schwächen hinwegtäuschen könne. Für unser Empfinden ist diese Einleitung der Rede schlicht peinlich, für Isokrates aber gehörte sie offensichtlich zum rhetorischen Inventar. Ich will nun nicht behaupten, dass der Enkel Ben Siras die Reden des Isokrates kannte, auch wenn es durchaus wahrscheinlich ist, weil sie zum hellenistischen Bildungskanon gehörten, aber der Enkel kannte gewiss die Stilmittel einer schönen Einleitungsrede.

Um die Worte des Prologs richtig zu verstehen, muss man sie im Horizont ihrer Gattung und ihrer Zeit interpretieren. M.E. ist die bekannte Bemerkung über die Schwierigkeit des Übersetzens keine sprachphilosophische Erörterung (auch wenn die Bemerkungen über die Differenzen zwischen der hebräischen und der griechischen Sprache gewiss zutreffen) und schon gar nicht ein Eingeständnis begrenzter Fähigkeiten, sondern der—im Vergleich zu Isokrates sehr bescheidene—aber doch klare Hinweis auf die in seiner Übersetzung steckende Leistung.[30]

---

29. Isokrates gehörte zum Kanon der ‚Zehn Attischen Redner', genauerhin zu deren drei besten (Demosthenes, Isokrates und Lysias). Zu Isokrates siehe die Beiträge in Wolfgang Orth, Hrsg., *Isokrates: Neue Ansätze zur Bewertung eines politischen Schriftstellers*, Europäische und Internationale Studien 2 (Trier: Wissenschaftlicher Verlag Trier, 2003).

30. Siehe dazu Siegfried Kreuzer, "Der Prolog des Buches Ben Sira (Weisheit des Jesus Sirach) im Horizont seiner Gattung," in *Geschehen und Gedächtnis: Die hellenistische Welt und ihre Wirkung, FS Wolfgang Orth*, hrsg. Jens-Frederik Eckholdt, Marcus Sigismund, and Susanne Sigismund, Antike Kultur und Geschichte 13 (Münster: LIT, 2009), 135–60; cf. "'Object of Great Care': The Prologue to the Wisdom of Jesus, Son of Sirach, in the Context of its Genre," in Kreuzer, *The Bible in Greek*, 94–109; dort auch Ausführungen und Literatur zur Gattung Prolog insgesamt.

Jesus Sirach:
Ein jüdischer Weisheitslehrer in hellenistischer Zeit

Otto Kaiser

1. Ben Sira, ein jüdischer Weiser in hellenistischer Zeit

1.1. Ben Sira und der Hellenismus

Martin Hengel hat seiner Behandlung des Buches Jesus Sirach in seinem 1969 veröffentlichten und mehrfach nachgedruckten Werk „Judentum und Hellenismus" die Überschrift „Ben Sira und die Auseinandersetzung mit dem hellenistischen Freigeist in Jerusalem" gegeben und damit die apologetische Tendenz des jüdischen Weisheitslehrers stärker betont, als es seine anschließende Darstellung rechtfertigt. Denn wie sich unschwer zeigen lässt, bediente sich Ben Sira in Anknüpfung und Widerspruch zahlreicher Motive griechischer Dichtung und hellenistischer Philosophie, besonders der stoischen; weil sie eine positive Theologie vertrat.[1] Dass bei ihm jüdische Weisheit und hellenistisches Bildungsstreben einander treffen, zeigt bereits die Rolle, die das Wort *mûsār* / *παιδεία*, „Erziehung" in seinen Lehrreden spielt.[2]

1. Vgl. dazu auch Otto Kaiser, "Anknüpfung und Widerspruch: Die Antwort der jüdischen Weisheit auf die Herausforderung durch den Hellenismus," in *Gottes und der Menschen Wahrheit: Gesammelte Aufsätze*, BZAW 261 (Berlin: de Gruyter, 1998), 201–16.

2. Vgl. Martin Hengel, *Judentum und Hellenismus: Studien zu ihrer Begegnung unter bessonderer Berücksichtigung Palästinas bis zur Mitte des 2. Jh. v. Chr*, WUNT 10 (Tübingen: Mohr Siebeck, 1969), 243 und dazu Sir 6,22a; 34,11c.17; 35,2c.14a; 37,31a; 47,14a.b; 42,5c.8a und 50,27a.

1.2. Ben Siras Zeitstellung

Seine ungefähre Zeitstellung geht aus dem Prolog seines Enkels zur griechischen Übersetzung des Weisheitsbuches seines Großvaters und aus Ben Siras Lob des Hohenpriesters Simon II. in Sir 50,1–24 hervor. Nach Sir.Prol 27–28 hat der Enkel das Buch seines Großvaters einige Jahre nach seiner Übersiedlung nach Ägypten im 38. Jahr des Königs Euergetes und d.h. Ptolemaios VII. Euergetes II. (170–116 v. Chr.) und d.h. im Jahr 132 und vermutlich nach dessen Tod im Jahr 116 v. Chr. verfasst,[3] indem er es „in relativ freier Weise ins Griechische übersetzt" hatte. Der volle Name seines Großvaters lautete nach Sir 50,27, korrigiert nach dem Prolog und der Überschrift des Buches in den griechischen Handschriften Jeschua Ben El´azar Ben Sira.[4] Die untere Grenze seiner Lebenszeit lässt sich aus seinem Lob des Hohenpriesters Simon II. in Sir 50,1–24 erschließen, der damals bereits gestorben war.[5] Simon amtierte nach Josesphus, *Ant.*

3. Zur Identifikation und Regierungszeit des Königs vgl. Werner Huß, *Ägypten in hellenistischer Zeit 332–30 v. Chr* (München: Beck, 2001), 596–625, bes. 624–25.

4. Zur Diskussion des Befundes vgl. Friedrich V. Reiterer, *Zählsynopse zum Buch Ben Sira*, FoSub 1 (Berlin: de Gruyter, 2003), 2, und Friedrich V. Reiterer, "Text und Buch Ben Sira in Tradition und Forschung. Eine Einführung," in *Bibliographie zu Ben Sira*, hrsg. Friedrich V. Reiterer, Núria Calduch-Benages, und Renate Egger-Wenzel, BZAW 266 (Berlin: de Gruyter, 1998), 1–10 bzw. Friedrich V. Reiterer, "Text und Buch Ben Sira in Tradition und Forschung: Eine Einführung," in *„Alle Weisheit stammt vom Herrn …": Gesammelte Studien zu Ben Sira*, von Friedrich V. Reiterer, hrsg. Renate Egger-Wenzel, BZAW 375 (Berlin: de Gruyter, 2007), 3–13. Er schlägt vor, den Verfasser als Jeschua/Jesus, Sohn des Simon und das Buch als „Weisheit des Ben Sira" zu bezeichnen. Zum Befund vgl. auch knapp Otto Kaiser, *Weisheit für das Leben: Das Buch Jesus Sirach; Übersetzt und eingeleitet* (Stuttgart: Radius, 2005), 129; und Johannes Marböck, *Jesus Sirach 1–23*, HThKAT (Freiburg: Herder, 2010), 48–49.

5. Vgl. dazu ausführlich Otto Mulder, *Simon the High Priest in Sirach 50: An Exegetical Study of the Significance of Simon the High Priest as Climax to the Praise of the Fathers in Ben Sira's Concept of the History of Isarel*, JSJSup 78 (Leiden: Brill, 2003), 102–259; und dazu Johannes Marböck, review of *Simon the High Priest in Sirach 50*, by Otto Mulder, *Bib* 86 (2005):276–79 = Johannes Marböck, review of *Simon the High Priest in Sirach 50*, by Otto Mulder, in *Weisheit und Frömmigkeit: Studien zur alttestamentlichen Literatur der Spätzeit*, hrsg. Johannes Marböck, ÖBSt 29 (Frankfurt am Main: Lang, 2006), 169–72; und zur liturgiegeschichtlichen Bedeutung des Textes Johannes Marböck, "Der Hohepriester Simon in Sir 50. Ein Beitrag zur Bedeutung von Priestertum und Kult im Sirachbuch," in *Treasures of Wisdom: Studies in Ben Sira and the Book of Wisdom; Festschrift M. Gilbert*, hrsg. Núria Calduch-Benages und Jacques Vermeylen, BETL 143 (Leuven: Peeters, 1999), 215–29 = Johannes Marböck,

12.223–224, vgl. 129–132, als der Seleukide Antiochos III. im Jahr 199/8 Jerusalem eroberte. Da Ben Sira jedoch die 175/4 erfolgte Absetzung seines Nachfolgers, des Hohenpriesters Onias III. durch den von Antiochos IV. bestätigten Hohenpriester Jason und die Einrichtung eines Gymnasiums in Jerusalem (vgl. II Macc 4,12–17) noch nicht voraussetzt,[6] dürfte er sein Buch zwischen 190 und 175 v. Chr. verfasst haben.

1.3. Ben Sira als „Schreiber"

Der Enkel rühmt ihn als einen Mann, der sich die Kenntnis des Gesetzes und der Propheten und der anderen Bücher der Väter erworben hatte und über Erziehung und Weisheit zu schreiben verstand (Sir.Prol 6–14). In unserer Sprache ausgedrückt handelt es sich bei ihm um einen „Schreiber" (*sôpēr*) und d.h. einen Schriftgelehrten und Weisheitslehrer, wie er ihn selbst in dem einschlägigen Lob in 38,24–39,11 beschrieben hat. Die Frage, ob man es autobiographisch oder typologisch auszulegen hat, lässt sich nicht sicher beantworten. Vermutlich deckt es beide Aspekte ab. Die Berufsbezeichnung des „Schreibers" deckt ein weites Aufgabenfeld ab, das von dem am Stadttor auf einen Kunden wartenden Briefschreiber bis zum Tempelschreiber und Hofbeamten reicht.[7] Ben Sira setzt ihn in den V. 25–34 scharf von allen handwerklichen Betätigungen ab; denn obwohl er den unentbehrlichen Beitrag der Handwerker für das Leben anerkennt, seien sie weder zum Richten noch zum Unterrichten in der Lage. Dagegen widme sich der Schreiber dem Studium der Gesetze des Höchsten, erforsche die Weisheit der Alten, erforsche und kenne die Reden berühmter Männer: Daher dürfe er vor Großen dienen und vor Fürsten erscheinen und in fremde Länder reisen, um zu erkunden, was dort als gut und böse bezeichnet würde. So sei er ein frommer Beter und Ratgeber, der von vielen gelobt und niemals vergessen würde (39,1–11).

"Der Hohepriester Simon in Sir 50: Ein Beitrag zur Bedeutung von Priesterum und Kult im Sirachbuch," in *Weisheit und Frömmigkeit: Studien zur alttestamentlichen Literatur der Spätzeit*, ÖBSt 29 (Frankfurt am Main: Lang, 2006), 155–72.

6. Vgl. dazu Klaus Bringmann, *Hellenistische Reform und Religionsverfolgung in Judäa* (Göttingen: Vandenhoeck & Ruprecht, 1983), 66–74; Bringmann, *Geschichte der Juden im Altertum: Vom babylonischen Exil bis zur arabischen Eroberung* (Stuttgart: Klett-Cotta, 2005), 101–11.

7. Vgl. dazu Herbert Niehr, "סוֹפֵר," *ThWAT* 5:921–29.

Außer dem Hinweis auf seine auf vielen Reisen erworbenen Kenntnisse und dabei dank Gottes Beistand überstandenen Gefahren in 34,9–20 hat Ben Sira in seinem Buch keine direkten Auskünfte über sein Leben erteilt. Aus dem Bericht über seine Reisen und Errettung aus Gefahren in 34,9–13 geht hervor, dass er viel gereist und dabei „mehr gelernt hat", als er sagen könne. Dabei dürfte es ihm wohl auch darum gegangen sein, die Sitten und Gebräuche fremder Völker zu erkunden. Verbindet man diese Auskunft mit dem, was er in 37,4 über den kundigen Schreiber sagt, der vor Großen stehen und vor Fürsten erscheinen dürfe, so könnten seine Reisen der Ausführung diplomatischer Aufträge gedient haben. Sollte er zu reinen Bildungsreisen in der Lage gewesen sein, müsste er aus einer reichen Familie stammen. Ob die von ihm auf seinen Reisen bestandenen Lebensgefahren durch Schiffbruch, Piraten oder Räuber verursacht worden sind,[8] muss mangels sachlicher Hinweise offen bleiben. Ausdrücklich angemerkt sei, dass die Bildungsreisen in fremde Länder bei den Griechen in Herodot[9] und Platon[10] große Vorbilder besessen haben. Sie wurden in hellenistischer Zeit durch einen regelrechten Bildungstourismus abgelöst.[11] Weil das Griechische im hellenistischen Zeitalter die *lingua franca* gewesen ist, muss Ben Sira über entsprechende Sprachkenntnisse verfügt haben, obwohl er sie in seinem Werk an keiner Stelle erwähnt: denn unter dieser Voraussetzung werden seine Kenntnisse griechischer Dichtung und Gnomik und nicht zuletzt die der stoischen Philosophie verständlich.

2. Nachklänge griechischer Dichtung bei Ben Sira

Ehe wir uns dem komplexen Thema der von Ben Sira neu in das biblische Weisheitsdenken aufgenommenen Themen und seinen Beziehungen zur Stoischen Philosophie zuwenden, sei in angebrachter Kürze an Motive in

---

8. Zu den Gefährdungen Reisender durch Räuber und Vagabunden vgl. Carl Schneider, *Die Welt des Hellenismus: Lebensformen in der spätgriechischen Antike*, Beck'sche Sonderausgaben (München: Beck, 1975), 281–83.

9. Vgl. z.B. Hdt.Hist. 2.99.1.

10. Vgl. Diog. Laert. 3.6–18.

11. Zum Bildungstourismus der Epoche vgl. Schneider, *Die Welt des Hellenismus*, 305–07; und zur Rezeption des Themas bei Ben Sira, Johannes Marböck, *Weisheit im Wandel: Untersuchungen zur Weisheitstheologie bei Ben Sira*, BBB 37 (Bonn: Hanstein, 1971), 161–62.

Ben Siras Lehrreden erinnert, die jedenfalls in älteren griechischen Dichtungen ihre Parallelen besitzen. Die Frage, ob Ben Sira Homers Ilias und Sophokles' König Ödipus als Ganze gelesen hatte oder er auf gnomische Florilegien zurückgriff, müssen wir offen lassen, weil wir über seine Vorbildung nur Vermutungen äußern könnten.[12]

Den Vergleich, dass Wolf und Lamm nicht zusammen leben, hat Ben Sira in seine Lehrrede über das Verhältnis zwischen Arm und Reich in Sir 13,1–14,2 in 13,17 als Illustration für seine vorausgehende Feststellung, dass alles Fleisch seine Art liebt, als bestätigenden Kontrast in Frageform eingefügt und dabei vermutlich auf das in Hom.Il. 22.261–266 breiter ausgestaltete Thema zurückgegriffen (Sir 13,17):[13]

> Verbindet sich etwa ein Wolf mit einem Lamm?
> So verhält sich der Sünder gegen den Frommen.

Hier könnte es sich um ein Echo auf den einschlägigen Vergleich in Hom. Il. 22.261–266 handeln, nach dem Wölfe und Schafe nie in Eintracht leben.

Eindrucksvoller ist freilich der Rat, vor dem Tode niemand glücklich zu preisen in Sir 11,27–28, mit dem er seine an den „Sohn" und d.h. den Schüler gerichtete Mahnrede beschließt, in der er ihn dazu auffordert, getrost seine Pflicht zu tun und sich nicht durch das vermeintliche Glück der Gottlosen verblenden zu lassen. Denn, so heißt die abschließende Begründung (Sir 11,27–28):

> Das heutige Unglück lässt das Glück vergessen,
> und das Ende des Menschen gibt über ihn Auskunft.
> Vor dem Ende preise keinen glücklich;
> denn an seinem Ende wird der Mensch erkannt.

Das Motiv des letzten Verses besitzt in Hdt.1.37.7; Eur.Andr.100–103 und Men.Mon.389, vor allem aber in den drei letzten Versen des Oedipus

12. Vgl. dazu Miriam Lichtheim, *Late Egyptian Wisdom Literature in the International Context: A Study of Demotic Instructions*, OBO 52 (Freiburg Schweiz: Universitätsverlag; Göttingen: Vandenhoeck & Ruprecht, 1983), 24–28.

13. Vgl. dazu Theophil Middendorp, *Die Stellung Jesu Ben Siras zwischen Judentum und Hellenismus* (Leiden: Brill, 1973), 9; und Hans V. Kieweler, *Ben Sira zwischen Judentum und Hellenismus: Eine Auseinandersetzung mit Th. Middendorp*, BEATAJ 30 (Frankfurt am Main: Lang, 1992), 94.

Rex des Sophokles (Soph.Oid.T. 1528–1530) seine Parallelen. Sie lauten in der Übertragung von Friedrich Hölderlin:[14]

Darum schauet hin auf jenen, der zuletzt erscheint, den Tag,
Wer da sterblich ist, und preiset glücklich keinen, eh denn er
An das Lebens Ziel gedrungen, Elend nicht erfahren hat.

Wieder zu Homer zurück führt der Vergleich der Hinfälligkeit menschlichen Daseins mit dem grünenden und welkenden Laub der Bäume in Sir 14,11–19. Hier heißt es nach der vorausgehenden Aufforderung, sich am erworbenen Besitz zu erfreuen und dem Freund soviel wie möglich Gutes zu tun, in V. 18:

Wie sprossendes Laub am grünenden Baum,
von dem eines fällt und anderes sprießt,
So ist der Menschen Geschlecht, dieses sprieß und jenes verwelkt.

Ben Sira hat den in Hom.Il. 6.146–149 (vgl. auch 21.462–466) breiter ausgeführten Vergleich auf das Wesentliche hin gekürzt; denn dort heißt es:[15]

Ganz wie der Blätter Geschlecht so sind die Geschlechter des Menschen,
Streut doch der Wind auf den Boden die einen Blätter, die andern
Treibt der grünende Wald zur Zeit des knospenden Frühlings.
So von der Menschen Geschlecht wächst eines, das andere schwindet.

4. Von Ben Sira in die biblische Weisheit eingeführte hellenistische Themen

Bedeutender als die erwähnten Anspielungen auf griechische Dichtungen sind für sein Lehr- und Lebensbuch die Themen, die er neu aus der griechisch-hellenistischen Welt aufgenommen und in seine Lehren inte-

14. Friedrich Hölderlin, *Werke, Briefe, Dokumente: Nach dem Text der von F. Beißner besorgten Kleinen Stuttgarter Hölderlin-Ausgabe; Ausgewählt und mit einem Nachwort versehen von P. Bertaux; Mit Anmerkungen und Literarturhinweisen von Chr. Prignitz*, hrsg. Pierre Bertaux, 4. Auf.., Winklers Weltliteratur (Munich: Winkler, 1990), 617.

15. Übertragung Th. von Scheffer, s. Homer, *Ilias: Verdeutscht von Thassilo von Scheffer*, Sammlung Dieterich 13 (Leipzig: Dietrich'sche Verlagsbuchandlung, 1938), 135.

griert hat. Johannes Marböck hat als erster darauf aufmerksam gemacht und dadurch zahlreiche Untersuchungen provoziert.[16] Es handelt sich nach ihm um die folgenden Themen: (1) das positive Verhältnis zum Arzt (Sir 38,1–15),[17] (2) das Benehmen bei einem Symposion, einem Gastmahl (31,12–32,13)[18] und (3) die Bildungsreise (34,9–13). Dazu würde ich auch (4) die Scham (4,21; 41,14–42,8) und (5) das jetzt mit einem ganz anderen Pathos als in der älteren biblischen Weisheit behandelte Thema der Freundschaft rechnen, dessen breite Entfaltung auf eine Lockerung der familiären und nachbarschaftlichen Bindung bei gleichzeitiger Individualisierung zurückweist.[19]

Thema 2 und 3: Sehen wir uns die einzelnen Themen etwas genauer an, so reicht es im Blick auf das zweite, das in Sir 31,12–32,13 verhandelte des Gastmahl, aus, auf die einschlägigen Anweisungen in der Theognidischen Sammlung zu verweisen[20] und zu seiner kulturellen Bedeutung an Platons und Xenophons Symposien zu erinnern.[21] Zu dem dritten, den Bildungsreisen, ist oben bereits das Nötige gesagt.

Thema 1: Was das in Sir 38,12–15 verhandelte erste Thema des Verhältnisses zum Arzt betrifft, so fällt der Unterschied zur strikten Ablehnung der Einschaltung eines Arztes in Krankheitsfall in 2 Chr 16,12–13 auf: Denn während dort König Asa nach dem chronistischen Bericht sterben musste, weil er sich in seinem Leiden an einen Arzt gewandt hatte, fordert Ben Sira seine Schüler und Leser dazu auf, sich rechtzeitig mit einem Arzt anzufreunden, weil Gott ihn ebenso erschaffen hätte wie die aus der Erde sprossenden Heilkräuter, deren er sich bedient. Im Fall ihrer

16. Vgl. dazu Marböck, *Weisheit im Wandel*, 154–73.

17. Ibid., 154–60.

18. Ibid., 162–64; vgl. z.B. Phokylides 14; Theogn. 1.309–312; 467–510.563–566.627–628 und dazu Schneider, *Die Welt des Hellenismus*, 156–74.

19. D. Kellermann, "רֵעַ," *ThWAT* 7:549: „*rea*ʿ bezeichnet im AT ursprünglich den Stammverwandten, den Bundesgenossen (vgl. 1 Sam 30,26), den Freund (vgl. a. II.6. den ‚Freund des Königs' und die Parallele ʾohe<u>b</u>, z.B. Ps 88,19), der wie ein Bruder ist (Ps 122,8; Spr 17,17), den Bekannten, mit dem man den Friedensgruß wechselt (Ps 28,3;122,8, Spr 27,14). Er ist der Nächste als Nachbar (Spr 25,17), auch über die Grenzen des Volkes Israel hinaus (vgl. Ex 3,22)".

20. Vgl. z.B. Theog. 1.309–312; 467–510.563–566.627–628, dazu Schneider, *Die Welt des Hellenismus*, 156–74, und Marböck, *Weisheit im Wandel*, 162–64.

21. Zur Symposion-Literatur vgl. H. Görgemanns, "Symposion-Literatur," *DNP* 11:1138–41.

Erkrankung aber sollten sie allerdings auch nicht vergessen, zu Gott als dem eigentlichen Helfer zu beten (38,9–15):[22]

9 Mein Sohn, in Krankheit zögere nicht
Und bete zu Gott, denn er ist es, der heilt.
10 Fliehe vor Unrecht und Parteilichkeit
und reinige dein Herz von Sünden.
11 Bringe Wohlgeruch und Weihrauch das
und reichliche Opfer nach deinem Vermögen.
12 Dann aber gib dem Arzte Raum,
er gehe nicht fort, denn du brauchst auch ihn.
13 Denn es gibt Zeiten, da liegt die Hilfe bei ihm;
14 denn auch er betet zu Gott,
dass ihm die Diagnose gelingt
und seine Behandlung Leben erhält.
15 An seinem Schöpfer versündigt sich,
wer den Arzt stolz von sich weist.

Möglicherweise hängt dieses veränderte Denken über das ärztliche Wirken mit der Einsetzung von Amtsärzten in den Kernländern der Ptolemäer und Seleukiden und in den von ihnen annektierten Gebieten zusammen, so dass sie auch in Jerusalem anzutreffen waren.[23]

Das der Scham (*bôš* / *αἰσχύνη* bzw. *αἰδώς*) gewidmete Thema 4 behandelt Ben Sira in 4,21 und 41,14–42,8. In 4,21 weist er auf ihren doppelten Aspekt hin: Sie könne ebenso zur Sünde führen wie Achtung verdienen. Entsprechend unterscheidet er in 41,14–42,8 zwischen wahrer, berechtigter und falscher, unberechtigter Scham. Zur ersten gehört es zum Beispiel, sich vor den Eltern wegen Unzucht, vor den Herrschenden wegen Lügen, vor dem eigenen Herrn wegen Empörung, vor der Volksversammlung wegen Sünden, vor Genossen wegen Treulosigkeit sowie wegen Diebstahl, Eidbruch und Gier bei Tisch, wegen des Beischlafes mit einer Sklavin oder der Schmähung der Freunde zu schämen (41,17–42,1).[24] Dagegen solle

---

22. Dabei dürfte Ben Sira nicht nur an jüdische, sondern auch an nichtjüdische Ärzte denken, vgl. dazu Burkhard M. Zapff, "Sir 38,1–15 als Beispiel der Verknüfpung von Tradition und Innovation bei Jesus Sirach," *Bib* 92 (2001): 365–66.

23. Vgl. dazu Michael I. Rostovtzeff, *Gesellschafts- und Wirtschaftsgeschichte der hellenistischen Welt*, 3 Bde. (Darmstadt: Wissenschaftliche Buchgesellschaft, 1984), 2:866–870.

24. Vgl. auch P.Ins. 9,6–8 und dazu Lichtheim, *Late Egyptian Wisdom Literature in the International Context*, 159.

man sich nicht wegen des Einhaltens der Thora, gerechter gerichtlicher Urteile, sachgemäßer Abrechnung mit Freunden und Reisegefährten oder Teilung des Erbes, der Benutzung sauberer Waagen und gereinigter Maße und Gewichte und dergleichen schämen (42,2–8). Bei der Scham handelte es sich mithin um einen das sittliche und religiöse Verhalten begleitenden Affekt, der auf das gemeinschaftsgerechte Handeln des Einzelnen abzielt.

In der griechischen Literatur lässt sich das Thema der Scham bis zu Homer zurückverfolgen.[25] Danach war sie zunächst ein Gefühl der Verpflichtung des adligen Kriegers und mithin Ausdruck seines Ehrgefühls gegenüber Königen, Mitstreitern und Freunden. So spornte Ajas in Hom. Il. 15.559–565 die Mitkämpfer an, von Scham (αἰδώς) erfüllt einander im Kampf zu achten und den Tod nicht zu scheuen. In der Polisethik wurde sie zu einem Gefühl für Recht und Anstand. So wird das Schamgefühl in Eur. Supp. 911–917 als Anleitung zu einem tugendhaften Leben gepriesen:[26]

> Die gute Zucht erweckt das Ehrgefühl (αἰδώς),
> Wer Edles übt, will nie ein Feigling sein.
> Die Tugend wird erlernt, so wie ein Kind
> Das Unbekannte hört und sagt und weiß.
> Was Knaben lernen, bleibt den Greisen treu.
> So sorgt, dass ihr die Kinder recht belehrt![27]

Das 5. Thema der Freundschaft hat Ben Sira in sieben Texten umfassend behandelt (6,5–15; 9,10; 12,8–12; 19,13–17; 22,19–26; 27,16–21 und 37,1–6).[28] Die Parallelen in der antiken Literatur sind so zahlreich, dass sie hier nur in einer repräsentativen Auswahl berücksichtigt werden können. So entspricht dem Rat in Sir 6,7–8, nur einem erprobten Freund zu vertrauen, der Senecas an seinen Freund Lucilius (Sen.Epist. 1.3.2):

---

25. Vgl. dazu J. Ruhnau, "Scham, 1–2 a," *HWPh* 8:1208–11.

26. Übersetzung E. Buschor in *Euripides Sämtliche Tragödien und Fragmente: Griechisch-Deutsch*, hrsg. Gustav A. Seeck, übers. Ernst Buschor, 6 Bde., STusc (Munich: Heimeran Verlag, 1972), 3:69.

27. Nach Aristoteles Eth.Nic. 2.7.1108a30–35 ist die Scham zwar keine Tugend, wird der Schamhafte aber trotzdem gelobt, weil er die Mitte zwischen Blödigkeit und Unverschämtheit einhält Vgl. dazu J. Ruhnau, "Scham, 1–2 a," *HWPh* 8.

28. Vgl. dazu die Beiträge in dem, Friedrich V. Reiterer, Hrsg., *Freundschaft bei Ben Sira: Beiträge des Symposions zu Ben Sira, Salzburg, 1995*, BZAW 244 (Berlin: de Gruyter, 1996); und umfassend Jeremy Corley, *Ben Sira's Teaching on Friendship*, BJS 316 (Providence: Brown Judaic Studies, 2002).

Tu vero omnia cum amico delibera, sed de ipso prius: post amicitiam credendum est, ante amicitiam iudicandum.

Ja, in allem berate dich mit deinem Freund, aber über ihn vorher: nachdem eine Freundschaft geschlossen, muss man vertrauen, vorher urteilen.

Weitere Parallelen liegen in Theogn. 1.79–82 (Wenige Freunde wirst du finden, Polypaïde, die sich/ als vertrauenswürdig erweisen unter widrigen Umständen,/ die den Mut haben, mit einmütigem Sinn/ gleichermaßen an Gutem und Schlechtem Anteil zu haben);[29] vgl. auch Theogn. 1.857–860; Anchschechonqi 14,8 (Wenn du einen Weisen zu deinem Freund machst, über dessen Herz du dir nicht im klaren bist, öffne ihm nicht dein Herz.)[30] und Papyrus Insinger 11,23 (Vertraue nicht auf den, den du nicht kennst.) und 12,18 (Man entdeckt nicht das Herz eines Freundes, wenn man ihn nicht in Not um Rat gefragt hat)[31] vor.

Zu Sir 6,14: Dem Lob des Freundes als einem starken Schutz in Sir 6,14 sei Eur.Or. 676–678 an die Seite gestellt:

Im schlimmsten Unglück hilft der Freund dem Freund!
Wem schon sein Dämon hilft, braucht keinen sonst.
Der Gott, der Glück bringt, ist schon Freund genug.[32]

Vgl. auch Men.Sent. 214:

In Notlagen ist ein Freund besser als Reichtümer.

Men.Sent. 575:

Es gibt keinen besseren Besitz als einen Freund.

Und weiterhin Anch. 21.6:

---

29. Übersetzung D. U. Hansen, "Theognis; Mimnermos; Phokylides," 49 in *Frühe griechische Elegien: Griechisch und deutsch*, Edition Antike (Darmstadt: Wissenschaftliche Buchgesellschaft, 2005), 49.

30. Übersetzung H. J. Thissen, "Die Lehre des Anchscheschonqi," *TUAT* 3.2:264.

31. Übersetzung H. J. Thissen, "Die Lehre des P. Insinger," *TUAT* 3.2:293 und 294.

32. Übertragung E. Buschor, *Euripides Sämtliche Tragödien und Fragmente: Griechisch-Deutsch*, 6 Bde, STusc (Munich: Heimeran Verlag, 1972), 5:53.

Kein Freund geht allein dahin (stirbt allein).[33]

Zu Sir 9,10: Zu dem Rat in Sir 9,10, einen alten Freund nicht zu verwerfen, vgl. Theogn. 1.1151–1152:

Verlasse nicht den Freund, den du hast, und suche einen andren
nur weil du den Worten schlechter Menschen vertraust.

Zu Sir 12,8–9: Zur Warnung vor dem Opportunismus falscher Freunde in Sir 12,8–9 vgl. Theogn. 1.78–80:[34]

Wenige Freunde wirst du finden, Polypaïde, die sich
als vertrauenswürdig erweisen unter widrigen Umständen
die den Mut haben, mit einmütigem Sinn
gleichermaßen an Gutem und Schlechtem Anteil zu haben.

Vgl. auch Eur.Or. 454–455:[35]

Wer sich im Unglück nicht als Freund bewährt,
Trägt nur den Namen, aber ist es nicht.

Zu Sir 22,19–26: Zum Thema des Streits mit einem Freund in Sir 22,19–26 vgl. Hes.op.707–712:

Stelle den Gefährten nicht dem leiblichen Bruder gleich.
Wenn du es aber getan, erweise ihm nicht Böses zuerst!
Lüge auch nicht der Zunge zuliebe, doch wenn er als erster
dir ein hässliches Wort sagt, vielleicht sogar etwas antut,
doppelt lass ihn dann büßen, das merk dir! Will er dann wieder
dich zum Freunde gewinnen und will die Sühne er leisten,
nimm es an! Denn schlecht ist der Mann, der bald diesen, bald jenen
sich zum Freunde macht, dich soll der Schein nicht berücken.

Vgl. auch P.Ins. 26.27,12–15:

Pflege keinen Umgang mit jemandem, in dessen Herz Hass herrscht.
Der Dummkopf mit seinem bösen Charakter hört nicht zu hassen auf.

---

33. Übersetzung Thissen, *TUAT* 3.2 (1991):270.
34. Theognis wird durchgehend nach der Übersetzung von D.U. Hansen zitiert.
35. *Euripides Sämtliche Tragödien und Fragmente*, 5:37.

Bitte nicht um eine Gabe von einem bösen Bruder in der Familie. Es gibt keinen Bruder in der Familie außer dem, der barmherzig ist.[36]

Zu Sir 27,16–21: Zur Pflicht, dem Freunde treu zu sein und sein Geheimnis nicht zu verraten, vgl. immer Theogn.1.529–530:

Keinen Freund und keinen verlässlichen Gefährten habe ich je preisgegeben, und in meiner Seele wohnt kein sklavischer Sinn.

Zu Sir 37,1–6: Zur Warnung vor einem untreuen Freund in Sir 37,1–6 vgl. Theogn.1.115–124:

Gefährten beim Essen und Trinken gibt es natürlich viele,
weniger aber in ernster Angelegenheit.
Nichts ist schwerer zu erkennen als ein falscher Mann,
Kyrnos, und nichts wichtiger als Vorsicht.
Täuschung durch falsches Gold und Silber ist nicht sehr schlimm
Kyrnos, und für einen klugen Mann leicht aufzudecken;
wenn sich aber im Herzen eines befreundeten Mannes
ein betrügerischer Sinn versteckt, und er einen tückischen Geist im Herzen trägt,
hat dies ein Gott zur größten Täuschung unter den Menschen gemacht,
und es ist schmerzlicher als alles andere zu erkennen.

Vgl. auch Men.Sent. 49:

Ein undankbarer Mann soll nicht für einen Freund gehalten werden.

Und Anch.21.10:

Es gibt keinen, der seinen Reisegefährten verstieße, ohne dass Gott mit ihm abrechnete.[37]

Zusammenfassung: Dass zu den angeführten Parallelen auch solche aus den demotischen Lehren des Anchscheschonqi und des Pap. Insin-

36. Übersetzung Thissen, *TUAT* 3.2:309.
37. Übersetzung ibid, 271.

ger gehören, hat als erster Jack T. Sanders[38] beobachtet. Miriam Lichtheim hat daraus den Schluss gezogen, dass es in hellenistischer Zeit eine von Griechenland bis Ägypten reichende gnomische Koine gegeben hat, in deren Rahmen zwischen der Lehre des Pap.Insinger und der Weisheit Ben Siras besonders enge Beziehungen nachweisbar sind: Bei beiden ist der Weise zu einem Vorbild geworden, der gelassen lebt, anderen mit ruhiger Zurückhaltung, Freundlichkeit, Großzügigkeit und zugleich einem gewissen Misstrauen begegnet. Er nimmt Unglücksfälle mit Geduld und Hoffnung an, weil er auf Gott vertraut. Geistig ist er dem stoischen Weisen verwandt, der eher selbstgenügsam als gesellig ist und dessen Weg ‚der Weg Gottes' ist.[39]

Soziologisch weist die breite Rezeption des Themas der Freundschaft bei Ben Sira darauf hin, dass der Individualisierungsprozess zumindest die jüdische Oberschicht erreicht hat.[40] Als Zeuge für diesen in der griechischen Welt des Mutterlandes bereits im ausgehenden 6. Jh. v. Chr. einsetzenden Prozess können wir auf die elegischen Ratschläge des Theognis aus Megara an seinen Liebling Kyrnos[41] und für seine hellenistische Ausformung auf die später erweiterten Sentenzen des Komödiendichters Menanders verweisen, der von 342/41–293/92 ebenfalls in Megara lebte.[42] Dieser mithin im griechischen Mutterland früher einsetzende Prozess der Isolierung des Einzelnen und der von ihr erzwungenen Individualisierung seiner persönlichen Beziehungen hatte in hellenistischer Zeit auch die demotische und jüdische Oberschicht erreicht, so dass die frei gewählte Freundschaft unentbehrlich geworden war. Dieser Prozess spiegelt sich in

---

38. Vgl. Jack T. Sanders, *Ben Sira and Demotic Wisdom*, SBLMS 28 (Chico, CA: Scholars Press, 1983), 103–6.

39. Vgl. Lichtheim, *Late Egyptian Wisdom Literature in the International Context*, 184–85.

40. Zum sozialgeschichtlichen und philosophischen Aspekt der Freundschaft in der Antike vgl. H. J. Gehrke, "Freundschaft I: Sozialgeschichtlich," *DNP* 4:669–71; zum philosophischen B. von Reibnitz, "Freundschaft II: Philosophisch," *DNP* 4:671–74 bzw. Hans-Georg Gadamer, "Freundschaft und Selbsterkenntnis: Zur Rolle der Freundschaft in der griechischen Ethik (1985)," in *Gesammelte Werke VII*, von Hans-Georg Gadamer (Tübingen: Mohr, 1991), 396–406; und umfassend David Konstan, *Friendship in the Classical World*, Key Themes in Ancient History (Cambridge: Cambridge University Press, 1997).

41. Vgl. zu ihm Ewen Bowie, "Theognis (Θέογνις)," *DNP* 12.1:351–54.

42. Vgl. zu ihm Heinz-Günther Nesselrath, "Menander, 4: der bedeutendste Dichter der Neuen Komödie in Athen," *DNP* 7:1215–19.

dem Rat, den Euripides (485/480–406 v. Chr.) in seinem „Orest“ Pylades dem Titelhelden erteilen lässt (Eur.Or.804–806):[43]

Wieder zeigt sich: Habe Freunde,
Nicht verwandtes Blut allein!
Wer mit meinem Sinn verbunden,
Sei er auch von fremdem Stamm.
Wiegt mir tausend Blutsverwandte
Durch seine treue Liebe auf.

Diese Hochschätzung der Freundschaft war bei den Epikuräern geradezu zum Programm geworden; denn sie lebten nach dem Rat ihres Begründers in engen Hausgemeinschaften als Freunde zusammen. Dem lag Epikurs Sentenz (Diog. Laert. X. Rat.Sent.XXVII) zugrunde:[44]

> Von allem was die Weisheit zur Glückseligkeit des ganzen Lebens in Bereitschaft hält, ist weitaus das wichtigste der Besitz der Freundschaft.

5. Stoische Elemente in Ben Siras Lehren

5.1. Die Identifikation der Weltvernunft mit der Weisheit Gottes des Schöpfers

Dass Ben Siras Denken in Anknüpfung und Widerspruch durch die stoische Philosophie beeinflusst war, hat Ursel Wicke in ihrer Dissertation „Göttliche Providenz und menschliche Verantwortung bei Ben Sira und in der Frühen Stoa“ umfassend nachgewiesen. Daher sei im vorliegenden Zusammenhang nur hervorgehoben, dass seine Identifikation der stoischen Weltvernunft mit der Weisheit in Sir 1,1–10 ihr Ziel in V. 10 besitzt, nach dem Gott sie denen reichlich gibt, die ihn lieben. Dass Weisheit und das Halten der Thora eine Einheit bilden, ist das Thema der Benediktion in Sir 14,20–15,10. Weisheit, Furcht des Herrn und

43. Übersetzung Buschor, in *Euripides Sämtliche Tragödien und Fragmente*, 5:63.

44. Übersetzung Diogenes Laertius, *Buch VII–X: Aus dem Griechischen übersetzt von O. Apelt. Unter Mitarbeit von H. G. Zekl neu hg. und mit Vorwort, Einleitung und neuen Anmerkungen vers. von K. Reich*, Bd. 2 von *Leben und Meinungen berühmter Philosophen*, PhB 54 (Hamburg: Meiner, 1967), 292; zu seinem Leben, seinen Werken, seiner Lehre und seiner Nachwirkung vgl. Michael Erler, “Epikuros (Ἐπίκουρος),” *DNP* 3:1130–40.

Halten des Gesetzes gehören auch nach Sir 19,20–30 zusammen. In Sir 24,1–34 rühmt sich die Weisheit dessen, dass sie auf dem Zion ihre Ruhestatt gefunden hat und die, die auf sie hören, nicht zu Schanden werden. Dann aber meldet sich Ben Sira selbst zu Wort, um zu versichern, dass diese unausschöpfliche Weisheit im Bundesbuch des Höchsten enthalten ist und er selbst sich darum bemüht, allen, die nach ihr suchen, zu ihr zu verhelfen. Am Ende des Buches aber steht in 42,15–43,33 der große Hymnus auf Gott den Schöpfer, der größer als alle seine Werke ist, und den zu ergründen, die Möglichkeiten des Menschen übersteigt, der aber trotzdem den Frommen Weisheit verleiht. Die Übertragung des stoischen Logos, der Weltvernunft, auf die Weisheit Gottes des Schöpfers und die sich im Gehorsam zur Thora erweisende Liebe zu ihm bilden den großen Rahmen für die praktischen Lehren Ben Siras.

5.2. Die stoische Lehre von der Notwendigkeit alles Geschehens und das Problem der Verantwortlichkeit des Menschen nach Sir 15,11–17

Vermutlich konnte das Gerücht von der stoischen Lehre über den kausalen Ablauf alles Geschehens jüdische Libertinisten zur Selbstrechtfertigung ihres Verhaltens veranlassen. Dagegen hat sich Ben Sira in Sir 15,11–17(20) gewandt. Wenden wir uns dem Problem der Verantwortlichkeit des Menschen für sein Tun zu, so sprechen wir in der Regel von seinem freien Willen. Doch so schwer es uns dank langer Gewohnheit auch fallen mag, müssen wir im Folgenden den Begriff der Willensfreiheit vermeiden, weil die Vorstellung vom Willen ein römisches Erbe ist, dem in der griechisch-hellenistischen Welt die Wahlfreiheit entsprach.[45] Auf dem Hintergrund der stoischen Lehre vom notwendigen Zusammenhang aller Dinge unterschied Chrysipp in seinem berühmten Walzengleichnis zwischen vollkommenen Haupt- und mithelfenden Nebenursachen (Cic. Fat. 39–43; Gell. 7.2.1–15): Setze ich eine Walze auf eine schiefe Ebene, so rollt sie dank ihrer Gestalt als vollkommener Hauptursache abwärts. Der äußere Anstoß ist dabei nur eine mithelfende Nebenursache. Übertrage man das auf eine menschliche Handlung, so wäre die Situation die mithelfende Nebenursache, während die die Handlung auslösende Zustimmung die Hauptursache sei. Da diese scheinbare Freiheit der Wahl

45. Vgl. dazu Albrecht Dihle, *Die Vorstellung vom Willen in der Antike*, Sammlung Vandenhoeck (Göttingen: Vandenhoeck & Ruprecht, 1985), 31–38.

ihrerseits eine Folge des angeborenen und erworbenen Charakters des Handelnden und damit der Notwendigkeit ist,[46] können wir das Problem auf die Formel bringen, dass sich jeder seiner schicksalhaften Eigenart gemäß verhalten muss, wobei er für sich selbst, sein Schicksal und also für sein Handeln verantwortlich ist. Seine Freiheit (so fügen wir hinzu) besteht mithin in der entschlossenen Selbstübernahme seines Daseins und Soseins. Diese Lehre könnte bei philosophisch ungebildeten Juden die Reaktion ausgelöst haben, ihre eigene sittliche Verantwortung zu leugnen und in frevelhafter Weise die Schuld an ihrem Sosein Gott zuzuschreiben. Hören wir also Ben Siras Einspruch (Sir 15,11–17):

> 11 Sage nicht: „Von Gott stammt meine Sünde."
> Denn was er hasst, bewirkt er nicht.
> 12 Sage nicht: „Er führte mich irre!"
> Denn an Ungerechten hat er keinen Bedarf,
> 13 Böses und Gräuel hasst der Herr,
> er lässt sie nicht treffen, die ihn fürchten.
> 14 Als Gott am Anfang den Menschen schuf,
> gab er ihn in die Hand seines Triebes.
> 15 Wenn es dir gefällt, hältst du das Gebot,
> und Einsicht ist es, nach seinem Gefallen zu handeln.
> 16 Feuer und Wasser sind vor dir ausgeschüttet,
> strecke deine Hand nach dem aus, was dir gefällt.
> 17 Vor dem Menschen liegen Leben und Tod,
> was ihm gefällt, wird ihm gegeben.

Die Aussage in V. 14, dass Gott den Menschen als sein Geschöpft in die Hand seines Triebes gegeben habe und er daher für seine Taten verantwortlich ist, ist nur sinnvoll, wenn es sich bei ihm um die ὁρμὴ λογιστική, den vernünftigen Trieb als die Kontrollinstanz des Urteilsvermögens handelt, womit wir wieder bei den Stoikern und genauer ihrer Oikeiosislehre angekommen sind, die zwischen den angeborenen und vernünftigen sittlichen Handlungen des Menschen unterschied. Noch in der Verteidigung der biblischen Anthropologie bediente sich Ben Sira mithin stoischer Argumente.[47] Sollen wir also dem biblischen Theologen Inkonsequenz

46. Vgl. dazu Josiah B. Gould, *The Philosophy of Chrysippus*, PhA 17 (Leiden: Brill, 1971), 137–52; und Anthony A. Long, *Hellenistic Philosophy: Stoics, Epicureans, Sceptics*, Classical Life and Letters (London: Duckworth, 1974), 163–70.

47. Vgl. dazu Otto Kaiser, "Die stoische Oikeiosis-Lehre und die Anthropologie

vorwerfen? Ich schlage vor, ihn stattdessen (neben Philo) als ein Urbild denkenden Glaubens zu verstehen, der sich philosophischer Gedanken bediente, um der biblischen Botschaft in einer veränderten Welt Gehör zu verschaffen. Wie viel Menschenkenntnis in seinen konkreten Lehren zu Worte kommt, brauche ich Ihnen als Sirachforschern kaum zu versichern. So lassen Sie mich meinen Vortrag mit Sir 1,1–10 als Zusammenfassung seiner Weisheit beschließen:

> 1 Alle Weisheit kommt vom Herrn
> und ist bei ihm in Ewigkeit.[48]
> 2 Der Sand des Meeres, die Tropfen des Wassers
> und die Tage der Ewigkeit—wer kann sie zählen?
> 3 Die Höhe des Himmels und die Breite der Erde
> und das Urmeer—wer kann sie erforschen?
> 4 Vor allen Dingen wurde die Weisheit erschaffen
> und verständige Einsicht von Ewigkeit her.[49]
> 6 Die Wurzel der Weisheit—wem wurde sie offenbart?
> und ihre Geheimnisse—wer hat sie erkannt?[50]
> 8 Einer ist weise und sehr zu fürchten,
> er sitzt auf seinem Thron:
> 9 Der Herr selbst hat sie erschaffen[51]
> und über alle seine Werke ausgegossen.
> 10 Sie ist bei allem Fleisch nach seiner Gabe,
> aber am meisten gab er sie denen, die ihn lieben.[52]

---

des Jesus Sirach," in *Vom offenbaren und verborgenen Gott: Studien zur spätbiblischen Weisheit und Hermeneutik*, BZAW 392 (Berlin: de Gruyter, 2008), 60–77.

48. S: "von Ewigkeit," vgl. V.5b. und zur Diskussion Martin Neher, *Wesen und Wirken der Weisheit in der Sapientia Salomonis*, BZAW 333 (Berlin: de Gruyter, 2004), 71, Anm.1.

49. Einfügung G II V. 5: „Und der Quell der Weisheit ist Gottes Wort in der Höhe // und ihre Pfade sind die ewigen Gebote".

50. Einfügung G II V.6c–d: „Die Kenntnis der Weisheit—wem wurde sie kundgetan? // und ihre reiche Erfahrung—wer hat sie verstanden?„

51. Einfügung G II V.9b: „und sie gesehen und gezählt".

52. Einfügung G II: V.10 c–d: „Die Liebe des Herrn ist herrliche Weisheit; // denen er erscheint, teilt er sie zu, damit sie ihn schauen".

Die Konstruktion von Kultur im Sirachbuch

Oda Wischmeyer

Vor zwanzig Jahren habe ich eine Rekonstruktion der Kultur des Sirachbuches veröffentlicht und den Versuch unternommen, ein Gesamtbild der Kultur Jerusalem-Judäas vor der Makkabäerzeit aus der Sicht des Siraciden zu entwerfen.[1] Der Kulturbegriff, der dieser Studie zugrunde liegt, beruht auf Konzepten aus der vorletzten Generation. Inzwischen ist nicht nur der Kultur*begriff* neu bestimmt worden, sondern auch der *wissenschaftliche Zugang* zu dem, was wir heute Kultur nennen. Es erscheint daher lohnend, diesen Wandel zum Anlass zu nehmen, die Verflechtung von Studien zur frühjüdischen Kultur und speziell zu Jesus Sirach mit allgemeinen Kulturkonzepten und -theorien zu reflektieren. Dabei sind für mich verschiedene Aspekte von Interesse. *Erstens* werde ich am Leitfaden meiner eigenen Monographie ältere Beiträge zum Sirachbuch im Hinblick auf folgende Fragen vorstellen: Mit welchen unterschiedlichen Paradigmen von Kultur arbeiteten die Verfasser? Wie wirkte sich ihr Verständnis auf ihre Rekonstruktion der Kultur der Sirachzeit aus? Wie nahmen sich die unterschiedlichen Paradigmen gegenseitig wahr? Diese Fragen werde ich nicht der Reihe nach abarbeiten, sondern jeweils zur Klärung heranziehen. *Zweitens* werde ich in Kürze versuchen, die Dynamik in der Veränderung des Kulturbegriffs seit den 20er Jahren des letzten Jahrhunderts nachzuzeichnen und neue Konzepte des Kulturbegriffs vorzustellen. Außerdem werde ich *drittens* diskutieren, wie die Sirachforschung Themen aufgreifen kann, die an kulturwissenschaftliche Fragestellungen anschließen.

Mein Beitrag ist keine forschungsgeschichtliche Darstellung zum Sirachbuch im engeren Sinne, sondern dient der Eröffnung der histori-

Dem Andenken an Georg Sauer gewidmet († 2012).

1. Oda Wischmeyer, *Die Kultur des Buches Jesus Sirach*, BZNW 77 (Berlin: de Gruyter, 1995).

schen und der aktuellen Horizonte der Forschung zur Kultur Ben Siras und seiner Zeit. Besonderen Wert lege ich auf die kulturellen und religiösen Prägungen wichtiger Vertreter der Sirachforschung, da diese Prägungen die jeweiligen Konzepte von Kultur bestimmt haben und bestimmen.

1. „Die Kultur des Buches Jesus Sirach" im Rahmen der älteren Sirachforschung

Ich beginne bei meiner eigenen Studie, die—soweit ich sehe—noch nicht durch eine neuere thematische Untersuchung ersetzt worden ist. Wenn man eine exegetische Studie zwanzig Jahre nach ihrem ersten Erscheinen noch einmal liest—nicht „benutzt" im Sinne einer kurzen Information, sondern im Zusammenhang liest und die Fragestellung, die Analyse und die Ergebnisse überprüft, stellen sich bei der kritischen *rélecture* geradezu selbstverständlich eine Reihe von Fragen: (1) Was führte zu der *Fragestellung* der Untersuchung? (2) Welcher *Ansatz* wurde gewählt? (3) Ist das *Ergebnis* heute noch wichtig? Und speziell in Verbindung mit der Konstruktion von Kultur: (4) Welches *Konzept von Kultur* unterlag der Untersuchung? Welche Aspekte lassen sich mit diesem Modell darstellen, und welche Aspekte fehlen?

1.1. Themenwahl und Grundlagen

Es liegt auf der Hand und erscheint selbstverständlich, dass Sirach die Kultur Jerusalem-Judäas mit seiner Lehre und seinem Weisheitsbuch einerseits mit geprägt hat und andererseits wohl der schärfste zeitgenössische Beobachter dieser Kultur war, wie ich formulierte:

> Die Untersuchung geht davon aus, daß Sirach ein bedeutender Faktor im Gesamtgefüge seiner Kultur Jerusalem-Judäas nach 200 v. Chr. war. Zugleich war er als Weiser ein geübter Beobachter des Lebens seines Volkes und ist daher ein hervorragender Zeuge der Kultur, in der er lebte und die ihn genauso prägte, wie er sie beeinflußte.[2]

Es war aber keineswegs selbstverständlich, aus dieser *Beobachtung* die *Frage* nach der Kultur des Sirachbuches zu entwickeln und diesem *Thema*

2. Ibid., 18.

eine monographische Untersuchung zu widmen.[3] Was bedeutete es Anfang der 90er Jahre des letzten Jahrhunderts forschungsgeschichtlich, Jesus ben Sira,[4] den großen *Weisheits*lehrer, als Vertreter der Jerusalemer *Kultur* nach 200 v.Chr. zu verstehen?

Die Themenwahl war in mehrfacher Hinsicht ein *Novum*. Was damals an Interpretationsvorschlägen zum Sirachbuch vorlag, waren neben philologischen Studien zwei große Interpretationsmodelle: *weisheitliche Theologie* einerseits und Geschichte des Judentums im Hellenismus andererseits. Der theologischen Thematik waren vor allem die wichtigen Monographien zur frühjüdischen und speziell zur siracidischen sog. Weisheitstheologie von Josef Haspecker,[5] Johannes Marböck,[6] Otto Rickenbacher,[7] Theophil Middendorp,[8] Martin Löhr,[9] Helge Stadelmann[10] und anderen Exegeten gewidmet. Gewichtige Beiträge stammten von katholischen Gelehrten, für die die frühjüdische—damals teilweise noch spätjüdisch genannte—Literatur, soweit sie zur Septuaginta gehörte, als Teil der Vulgata kanonischen Status hatte und damit nicht nur ein eigener Bestandteil der Theologie des Alten Testaments war, sondern auch als ethischer Wegweiser und als frömmigkeitsbildendes Werk verstanden wurde.[11] Auf protestantischer Seite wurde die Forschung an

3. Vgl. dazu unten Anm. 28: Victor Tcherikover geht über das Thema „Kultur des Sirachbuches und der Sirachzeit" mit einem Satz hinweg.

4. Zum Namen vgl. Martin Hengel, *Judentum und Hellenismus: Studien zu ihrer Begegnung unter besonderer Berücksichtigung Palästinas bis zur Mitte des 2. Jh.s v. Chr.*, WUNT 10, 3. Aufl. (Tübingen: Mohr, 1988), 241.

5. Josef Haspecker, *Gottesfurcht bei Jesus Sirach: Ihre religiöse Struktur und ihre literarische und doktrinäre Bedeutung*, AnBib 30 (Rome: Päpstliches Bibelinstitut, 1967).

6. Johannes Marböck, *Weisheit im Wandel: Untersuchungen zur Weisheitstheologie bei Ben Sira*, BBB 37 (Bonn: Hanstein, 1971; Abdr., Berlin: de Gruyter, 1999).

7. Otto Rickenbacher, *Weisheitsperikopen bei Ben Sira* (Fribourg: Universitätsverlag, 1973).

8. Theophil Middendorp, *Die Stellung Jesu Ben Siras zwischen Judentum und Hellenismus* (Leiden: Brill, 1973); dazu Hans Volker Kieweler, *Ben Sira zwischen Judentum und Hellenismus: Eine kritische Auseinandersetzung mit Th. Middendorp*, BEAT 30 (Frankfurt am Main: Lang, 1992).

9. Martin Löhr, "Bildung aus dem Glauben" (Diss. Bonn, Friedrich Wilhelms-Universität, 1975).

10. Helge Stadelmann, *Ben Sira als Schriftgelehrter*, WUNT 2/6 (Tübingen: Mohr, 1980).

11. Die katholische Sirachforschung ist weiterhin äußerst aktiv und hat eine eigene exegetische Literatur hervorgebracht. Schwerpunkte setzten Maurice Gilbert

der frühjüdischen Weisheitsliteratur besonders von den grundlegenden Arbeiten Gerhard von Rads zur theologisch-ethischen Dimension alttestamentlicher Weisheit beeinflusst.[12] Otto Kaiser und sein Schülerkreis haben dann protestantischerseits die Sirachforschung ebenfalls im Rahmen von Ethos und Frömmigkeit verortet und konnten dabei auch an die Hochschätzung des Sirachbuches im älteren Protestantismus anknüpfen.[13] Die Ergebnisse dieser primär theologisch interessierten und mindestens teilweise konfessionellen theologischen Sichtweisen verpflichteten Arbeiten flossen in die Kommentare von Georg Sauer[14] einerseits und den großen Anchor Bible Commentary[15] von Patrick W. Skehan und Alexander A. di Lella andererseits.[16] In allen diesen Arbeiten stehen die theologisch-religiösen Aspekte des Sirachbuches im Vordergrund: Gesetz, Frömmigkeit, Weisheit, Geschichte Israels. Ich habe die Forschungssituation folgendermaßen beschrieben:

> Die Grundlagen dieser [der Kultur Sirachs] Kultur, Frömmigkeit („Gottesfurcht") und Pädagogik („Weisheit", „Erziehung"), sind weitgehend in der Forschung dargestellt. Nun kann die Kultur selbst in ihren verschiedenen Aspekten rekonstruiert werden.[17]

(bes. die großen Art. "Jesus Sirach," *RAC* 17:878–906; und "Siracide," *Supplement de la Dictionnaire de la Bible* 12:1399–1437), die Arbeiten von P. C. Beentjes sowie die zahlreichen Veröffentlichungen von Friedrich Vinzenz Reiterer (vgl. nur den ausgezeichneten Einführungsartikel "Jesus Sirach/Jesus Sirachbuch," *WiBiLex* [2006], http://tinyurl.com/SBL0467a), Renate Egger-Wenzel u.a. in dem Sirachzentrum in Salzburg.

12. Gerhard von Rad, *Weisheit in Israel* (Neukirchen-Vluyn: Neukirchener Verlag, 1970).

13. Vgl. dazu einführend E.-M. Becker, "Jesus Sirach und das Luthertum des 16. Jahrhunderts: Über Inhalt und Funktion eines schlesischen Katechismus von 1561," in *Ben Sira's God*, hrsg. Renate Egger-Wenzel, BZAW 321 (Berlin: de Gruyter, 2002), 352–60.

14. Georg Sauer, *Jesus Sirach (Ben Sira)*, JSHRZ 3.5 (Gütersloh: Gütersloher, 1981; Abdr., Göttingen: Vandenhoeck & Ruprecht, 2000); Sauer, *Studien zu Ben Sira: Redigiert und mit einem Vorwort versehen von S. Kreuzer*, BZAW 440, Berlin: de Gruyter, 2013).

15. Patrick W. Skehan and Alexander A. di Lella, *The Wisdom of Ben Sira*, AB 39 (New York: Doubleday, 1987).

16. Jetzt auch Josef Schreiner, *Jesus Sirach 1–24*, NEchtB 38 (Würzburg: Echter 2002); und Burkard M. Zapff, *Jesus Sirach 25–51*, NEchtB 39 (Würzburg: Echter, 2010).

17. Wischmeyer, *Sirach*, 15.

Bei diesem Urteil bezog ich mich auf die bereits erwähnte theologische Weisheitsforschung vor allem des *deutschsprachigen* Raums. Für mein eigenes Thema, die Kultur des Siraciden, konnte ich an eine andere Forschungslandschaft anknüpfen. Das Thema der frühjüdischen Kultur ist in der zweiten Hälfte des letzten Jahrhunderts mehrfach im Zusammenhang großer *englischsprachiger* Monographien behandelt worden. Die bedeutendsten Darstellungen der frühjüdischen Kultur stammten und stammen aus amerikanischer Feder: von Moses Hadas, Victor Tcherikover und Elias Bickerman.[18] Im weiteren Umfeld sind die Althistoriker Michael Rostovtzeff und Arnaldo Momigliano zu nennen.[19] Bestimmte

---

18. Moses Hadas (1900–1966), klassischer Philologe. Hadas hatte den Lehrstuhl für Griechisch an der Columbia University inne. Zugleich hatte er eine Rabbinerausbildung. Seine wichtigen Werke für unser Thema: *Hellenistic Culture: Fusion and Diffusion* (New York: Norton, 1959); Hadas, *Die Kultur des Hellenismus: Werden und Wirkung* (Stuttgart: Klett, 1963); Hadas, *The Letter of Aristeas to Philocrates* (New York: Wipf & Stock, 1951).

Victor Tcherikover (1894–1958), russischer Althistoriker. Studium in Berlin, bereits 1925 nach Palästina ausgewandert. Professor an der Hebrew University, Jerusalem. Vgl. Art. John J. Collins, "Tcherikover, Victor (Avigdor)," in *The Eerdmans Dictionary of Early Judaism* (Grand Rapids: Eerdmans, 2010), 1281. Sein wichtigstes Werk für unser Thema: *Hellenistic Civilization and the Jews*, mit einem Vorwort von John J. Collins (Philadelphia: The Jewish Publication Society of America, 1959; Abdr., Peabody, MA: Hendrickson, 1999). Schon der Titel macht deutlich, dass Tcherikovers Kulturkonzept ausschließlich griechisch, d.h. hellenistisch ist. Es gibt kein Äquivalent für „die Juden".

Elias Bickerman (1897–1981) Russischer Althistoriker. Studium bei M. Rostovtzeff in St. Petersburg. Nach der kommunistischen Revolution seit 1922 in Berlin. Habilitation 1930 in Berlin, 1933 Emigration. Professor für Alte Geschichte an der Columbia University. Vgl. Art. A. I. Baumgarten, "Bickerman, Elias," in *The Eerdmans Dictionary of Early Judaism* (Grand Rapids: Eerdmans, 2010), 442–43. Ausführlich: A. I. Baumgarten, *Elias Bickerman as a Historian of the Jews: A Twentieth Century Tale*, TSAJ 131 (Tübingen: Mohr Siebeck, 2010). Bickermans wichtigstes Werk für unser Thema: *The Jews in the Greek Age* (Cambridge: Harvard University Press, 1988).

19. Michael Rostovtzeff (1870–1952), russischer Althistoriker. Studium und Promotion an russischen, deutschen und österreichischen Universitäten, Professor für Alte Geschichte in St. Petersburg, nach der kommunistischen Revolution Professor in Madison, Wisconsin und Yale. Für unser Thema besonders wichtig: *A Social and Economic History of the Hellenistic World* (New Haven: Yale University Press, 1941); Rostovtzeff, *Gesellschafts- und Wirtschaftsgeschichte der hellenistischen Welt*, 3. Aufl. (Darmstadt 1955).

Arnaldo Momigliano (1908–1987), italienischer Althistoriker. 1938 von seiner Professur in Turin aufgrund der antijüdischen Gesetzgebung vertrieben, Professor für

Plätze wurden—vor allem durch jüdische Gelehrte, die während der nationalsozialistischen Herrschaft aus Deutschland vertrieben wurden—zu Zentren der Erforschung des hellenistisch-römischen Judentums im Zusammenhang der Altertumswissenschaften, einerseits Yale und die Columbia University, andererseits Jerusalem. Alle diese hervorragenden Gelehrten waren in der einen oder anderen Weise durch das Studium der Alten Geschichte und der Klassischen Philologie an den großen deutschsprachigen Universitäten der vornationalsozialistischen Zeit geprägt. Sie waren ausgezeichnete Althistoriker und Altphilologen, die darüber hinaus die ganze Breite der damaligen Altertumswissenschaften im Blick hatten: Archäologie, Epigraphik, Papyrologie und—besonders von Georg Wissowa und Eduard Norden vermittelt—Religionsgeschichte.[20] Sie waren keineswegs Vertreter der Judaistik bzw. der Jewish Studies,[21] wohl aber waren sie—mit Ausnahme von Rostovtzeff—Juden[22] und dem Schicksal des Judentums tief verbunden. Sie dachten allgemeinhistorisch, und ihr Kulturbegriff war historisch-literarischer Art,[23] was besonders

---

Alte Geschichte in London, Pisa, Chicago. Verschiedene Bücher und Aufsätze zum antiken Judentum. Für unser Thema besonders wichtig: *Alien Wisdom: The Limits of Hellenization* (Cambridge: Cambridge University Press, 1975) (*Hochkulturen im Hellenismus: Die Begegnung der Griechen mit Kelten, Juden, Römern und Persern*, Beck'sche schwarze Reihe 190 [Munich: Beck, 1979]); Momigliano, *Die Juden in der Alten Welt* (Berlin: Wagenbach, 1988); Prolog in Deutschland, in: *Ausgewählte Schriften zur Geschichte und Geschichtsschreibung*. Bd. 3: *Die moderne Geschichtsschreibung der Alten Welt*, hrsg. Glenn Most (Berlin: Springer, 2000), 367–92.

20. Tcherikover studierte Alte Geschichte bei Eduard Meyer (der den Deutschnationalen nahestand) in Berlin; Bickerman studierte Altertumswissenschaften bei Eduard Norden (der aus einer jüdischen Familie stammte und nach seiner Emeritierung 1933 sukzessiv alle akademischen Ämter und Mitgliedschaften verlor und 1939 Deutschland verlassen musste) und Ulrich Wilcken in Berlin, promovierte und habilitierte sich dort. Rostovtzeff studierte Altertumswissenschaften in Wien und Berlin, promovierte in Halle bei Georg Wissowa und wurde Professor in St. Petersburg. Nach der kommunistischen Revolution emigrierte er zunächst nach Großbritannien und dann nach USA.

21. Vgl. unten Anm. 37.

22. Rostovtzeff setzte sich persönlich sehr für die verfolgten Juden ein. R. wurde in Großbritannien und den USA teilweise für jüdisch (und kommunistisch) gehalten und daher zunächst nicht berufen. Vgl. zu weiteren Gelehrten: Hans Peter Obermayer, *Deutsche Altertumswissenschaftler im amerikanischen Exil. Eine Rekonstruktion* (Berlin: de Gruyter, 2014).

23. Das schließt natürlich Interessen auf dem Gebiet von Archäologie und Papyrologie etc. nicht aus, sondern gerade ein. Rostovtzeff war Mitglied des Deutschen

dem Überlieferungsstand jüdischer kultureller Erzeugnisse hellenistischer Zeit entspricht: Die architektonischen Überreste aus hellenistischer Zeit sind eher gering, bildende Kunst aus diesem Zeitraum fehlt ganz, die Literatur dagegen ist reich, und die Geschichte der Juden im Mutterland und in der Diaspora ist Teil der hellenistisch-römischen Geschichte. Mit Josephus hat das Judentum zudem einen der großen Historiker der Antike hervorgebracht.

Jeder dieser Gelehrten untersuchte das Judentum der ptolemäisch-seleukidischen und der römischen Epoche als Teil der allgemeinen politischen, sozialen, wirtschaftlichen und kulturellen Geschichte der Zeit. Das Sirachbuch fungiert in diesem Kontext als wesentliche Quelle für diesen Abschnitt der Alten Geschichte. So zeichnet Victor Tcherikover Jesus ben Sira in die hellenistische *civilization*, d.h. Kultur, ein, die für ihn durch politische, wirtschaftliche und soziale Determinanten bestimmt ist. Aus dieser Perspektive ist die hellenistische Stadt die wichtigste Hervorbringung der hellenistischen *civilization*. Tcherikover betont Sirachs Reiseerfahrungen—das heißt: seine Kenntnis der Jerusalem umgebenden hellenistischen Reichs- und Städtekultur, um dann Sirachs konservativ-jüdische Haltung diesem Typ von Kultur gegenüber herauszustellen:

> Ben Sira returned to Jerusalem the orthodox Jew he had been before and in vain do we seek in his book symptoms of Greek culture.[24]

Für Tcherikover ist Sirachs konservative Kultur die Weisheit. Die übrigen Aspekte der Kultur Sirachs erwähnt Tcherikover nur mit einem einzigen Satz:

> Rich and colorful material of the life of the period prior to the efflorencense of Hellenism in Jerusalem is furnished by the great book of Ben Sira.[25]

Archäologischen Instituts und wurde Leiter der Yale-Grabungskampagne in Dura Europos (Synagoge und älteste christliche Hauskirche, vorausgehende Grabungen unter Leitung von Franz Cumont). Tcherikovers Hauptwerk (zusammen mit A. Fuks) war die Herausgabe der jüdischen Papyri aus dem hellenistisch-römischen Ägypten. Alexander Fuks (1917–1978) stammte aus Breslau, wanderte früh nach Palästina aus, promovierte 1946 an der Hebrew University und wurde dort Professor für Altertumswissenschaften. Schwerpunkte seiner wissenschaftlichen Arbeit: Athenische Geschichte und Jüdische Papyri.

24. Tcherikover, *Hellenistic civilization*, 143–44.

25. Ibid., 142.

Dies *material*, nämlich die Kultur in ihren verschiedenen Erscheinungsformen, als eigenen Forschungsgegenstand zu verstehen und darzustellen, hat Tcherikover nicht unternommen.

Eine *theologische* Dimension im Sirachbuch zu finden, gehörte ebenfalls nicht zu den wissenschaftlichen Fragestellungen dieser Gelehrten. Das Sirachbuch ist nicht Teil der „Schriften" des Judentums. Und es lag diesen Gelehrten begreiflicherweise fern, Beziehungen zur christlichen Theologie und ihren textlich schmalen Disziplinen Altes und Neues Testament herzustellen. Ebenso wenig hatten sie als Altertumswissenschaftler überhaupt mit Bibelstudien zu tun.[26] Zwischen „Alter Geschichte" und „Theologie" verlief eine unsichtbare Trennlinie. Es gab von beiden Seiten weder eine detailliertere Kenntnisnahme noch einen Austausch. Es ist ebenfalls nicht überflüssig zu erwähnen, dass den amerikanischen Althistorikern auch ein nachhistorischer theoretischer Kulturbegriff, der unabhängig von den primären Gegenständen ihrer altertumswissenschaftlichen Forschungen konzipiert wurde, noch ganz fern lag. Sie waren alle von dem großen deutschen Paradigma des späten Historismus geprägt, der programmatisch theoriefern war. Das ist umso wichtiger, als gerade in den Vereinigten Staaten schon früh an der Entwicklung eines neuen Kultur- und Kunstbegriffs auf der Basis der symbolischen Logik gearbeitet wurde.[27] Ich komme erst später darauf zurück, da dies philosophisch basierte Paradigma noch nicht zu den Voraussetzungen meiner Arbeit gehörte.

Wie wurde diese zweigeteilte Forschungslandschaft, zwischen deren unterschiedlichen Wissenschaftskulturen wenig Austausch bestand, für die deutschsprachige theologisch basierte Wissenschaft vom frühen Judentum und vom Neuen Testament vermittelt? Es war Martin Hengel,[28] der diese Vermittlungstätigkeit mit großem und bleibendem Erfolg unternahm.[29]

---

26. Eine Ausnahme bildet E. Norden wegen seines religionsgeschichtlichen Interesses und der Mitgliedschaft in der Kirchenväterkommission, die ihn in enge Berührung mit der Patristik brachte.—Als Altertumswissenschaftlern, die durch die Traditionen des Judentums geprägt waren, mussten ihnen die Bibelstudien in der Gestalt der alt- und neutestamentlichen Wissenschaft fremd bleiben, da diese Disziplinen Resultat einer Selbstaufklärung der *christlichen* Theologie waren.

27. Siehe das unten zu Cassirer Gesagte.

28. Martin Hengel; Professor für Neues Testament und Antikes Judentum in Tübingen (1926–2009). Wichtigstes Werk für unser Thema: *Judentum und Hellenismus*. Die erste Auflage erschien zwischen den Monographien von Haspecker und Marböck.

29. Einen guten Einblick in seine Sicht auf das Frühe Judentum und das Neue

Er brachte mit seiner Habilitationsschrift „Judentum und Hellenismus" die Perspektive vor allem Victor Tcherikovers und Elias Bickermans in die deutschsprachige Erforschung des antiken Judentums, die durch das Dritte Reich in der Wurzel getroffen war.[30] Hengel sorgte damit in gewisser Weise für die Rückkehr wesentlicher Stimmen derjenigen deutschen Altertumswissenschaftler nach Deutschland, die von ihren Universitäten nicht geschützt und aus dem Land vertrieben worden waren. Hengel selbst konzentrierte sich in seinem *opus magnum* auf das Verhältnis zwischen Judentum und Hellenismus in Palästina bis zur Mitte des 2. Jahrhunderts v.Chr. Mit Jesus Sirach beschäftigte er sich ausführlich.[31]

Hengel interpretiert die hebräische Weisheitsschrift in ihrem historischen Kontext, der Seleukidenherrschaft „zwischen 190 und 175 v. Chr.",[32] und ordnet sie zugleich als religiöse Schrift in die „Auseinandersetzung mit dem jüdischen Freigeist in Jerusalem"[33] ein. Sirachs Weisheitslehre wird von Hengel als Dokument der Auseinandersetzung mit Einflüssen griechischer Aufklärung—gab es die?—gelesen und ist nach seiner Meinung zugleich durch eine gewisse Nähe zu stoischen Gedanken gekennzeichnet.[34] Wenn in Hengels Darstellung auch ein Schwerpunkt auf der

---

Testament findet sich bei: M. Hengel, "Die Aufgaben der neutestamentlichen Wissenschaft," *NTS 40* (1994): 321–57; und Hengel, "Eine junge theologische Disziplin in der Krise," in *Neutestamentliche Wissenschaft*, hrsg. Eve-Marie Becker, UTB 2475 (Tübingen: Francke, 2003), 18–29.

30. Dasselbe gilt für die benachbarten Disziplinen der antiken, speziell der spätantiken und byzantinischen Kunstgeschichte: besonders bedeutend die deutschen Emigranten Richard Krautheimer (1897–1994), Habilitation in Marburg, 1933 emigriert, New York University; Kurt Weitzmann (1904–1993), Angestellter des Deutschen Archäologischen Instituts, 1935 emigriert, Princeton; Ernst Kitzinger (1912–2003), 1934 emigriert, Dumbarton Oaks, Harvard; Erwin Panofsky (1892–1968), Professor für Kunstgeschichte in Hamburg, 1933 emigriert, Princeton.

31. Hengel, *Judentum*, 241–74: „Ben Sira und die Beschäftigung mit dem hellenistischen Freigeist in Jerusalem". Weiter: "Die »Weisheit« bei Ben Sira," 284–92. Die Forderung Hengels nach einer dreisprachigen Ausgabe des Sirachbuches mit Kommentar (Hengel, *Eine junge theologische Disziplin*, 26) ist noch nicht erfüllt.

32. Hengel, *Judentum*, 268.

33. Vielleicht eine etwas unglückliche Übersetzung von V. Tcherikovers „spirit of free Hellenism", Tcherikover, *Hellenistic civilization*, 143.

34. Hengel, *Judentum*, 265ff. Diese Interpretationslinie hat Otto Kaiser weitergeführt: siehe seinen Beitrag in diesem Band. Weiter: Otto Kaiser, "Athen und Jerusalem: Die Begegnung des spätbiblischen Judentums mit dem griechischen Geist, ihre Voraussetzungen und ihre Folgen," in *Die Griechen und der Vordere Orient*, hrsg. Markus

Einordnung der Weisheit in die umfangreiche altorientalische Weisheitsliteratur liegt und hier eher theologiegeschichtlich in deutlicher Nähe zur deutschsprachigen alttestamentlichen Wissenschaft gearbeitet wird, ist das Werk doch weitgehend aus der Perspektive der großen amerikanischen Darstellungen verfasst, die die jüdischen literarischen Werke stets als Zeugnisse ihrer Zeit und deren politischer und wirtschaftlich-sozialer Konstellationen, eben des ptolemäischen Hellenismus in Ägypten und des seleukidischen Hellenismus in Palästina, beschreiben. Hengels Werk liegt damit auf der Schnittlinie zwischen amerikanischen und deutschen Perspektiven auf das antike Judentum, d.h. sein Interesse gilt einerseits der historischen Darstellung[35] und andererseits der theologischen Interpretation. „Kultur" allerdings wird—wie bei den beiden dargestellten Paradigmen, die sich im mangelnden Interesse an der Wahrnehmung einer eigenen Kultur Jerusalem-Judäas einig waren—auch bei Hengel nicht als selbständige Größe thematisiert, sondern im Sinne Tcherikovers unter „Zivilisation"[36] (politischer und wirtschaftlicher Aspekt) und „Der Hellenismus in Palästina als kulturelle Macht"[37] rubriziert. Eine eigene Kultur Sirachs kann nicht in den Blick kommen, da wie bei Tcherikover der Kulturbegriff der hellenistischen Kultur vorbehalten bleibt. Trotzdem hat Hengel die Perspektive auf das Sirachbuch und verwandte Schriften grundsätzlich erweitert. Er gab den entscheidenden Impuls, nicht bei der theologiegeschichtlich orientierten Sirachforschung stehenzubleiben, sondern daneben ein neues Untersuchungsfeld, die Kultur des Sirachbuches und Jerusalem-Judäas darzustellen. Äußerst wichtig ist im deutschsprachigen Forschungskontext Hengels strikte Einbindung der jüdischen Literatur in Palästina in ihre politisch-wirtschaftlichen Rahmenbedingungen, d.h. die weite historische Perspektive jenseits der notwendigen philologischen und theologiegeschichtlichen Detailarbeit.

Witte und Stefan Alkier, OBO 191 (Fribourg: Vandenhoeck & Ruprecht; Göttingen: Universitätsverlag, 2003), 87–120; monographisch: Ursel Wicke-Reuter, *Göttliche Providenz und menschliche Verantwortung bei Ben Sira und in der Frühen Stoa*, BZAW 298 (Berlin: de Gruyter, 2000).

35. Vgl. besonders das Vorwort zur 3. Auflage von "*Judentum und Hellenismus*". Hengel wirbt hier überzeugend für sein Verständnis „der jüdischen Geschichte in der Antike" als von einer „elementare[n] Bedeutung der religiösen Überzeugung" geprägt (xiii).

36. Hengel, *Judentum und Hellenismus*, 8–107.

37. Ibid., 108–95.

Die ebenso ausgezeichnete wie besondere Wissenschaftslandschaft englischsprachiger Studien zum antiken Judentum bildete in doppelter Hinsicht, in ihrer Abständigkeit von der deutschsprachigen Sirachforschung *und* in ihrer Adaption durch Martin Hengel, den Hintergrund für meine eigene Untersuchung. Hier fand ich die Basis für ein Verständnis des Sirachbuches, das die Beschränkung auf eine vornehmlich religiös-theologische Perspektive ausgleichen konnte. Ein Rückblick macht Dreierlei deutlich: *Erstens* setzten die amerikanischen Werke hohe Maßstäbe, da sie jeweils Epochendarstellungen gaben, die auf den umfassenden Quellenkenntnissen und der historischen Rekonstruktions- und Darstellungskraft der genannten Gelehrten beruhten. Es ging immer um die große historische Perspektive: um die Rekonstruktion der Geschichte der hellenistischen Reiche und der Einzeichnung der Geschichte Jerusalem-Judäas und der alexandrinischen Diaspora in diesen Rahmen. Das gilt auch für Martin Hengels Werk.

Zweitens haben die genannten englischsprachigen Arbeiten ein verhältnismäßig einheitliches Profil. Sie verstehen die frühjüdische Literatur sehr unbefangen als das, was sie ist: als „ihre" Literatur. Das heißt: sie lesen sie im Zusammenhang der griechischen und römischen Literatur vor allem als Quellen des hellenistischen Judentums und damit als die Quellen der Geschichte ihres Volkes. Weder theologisieren sie, noch widmen sie sich Detailstudien zu einzelnen sprachlichen Fragestellungen, Motiven, Gattungen, Textstellen und Themen, sondern schreiben *Geschichte* des Hellenismus und des Judentums in hellenistischer Zeit und damit auch ihre eigene Geschichte. Das Judentum wird als eigenes Subjekt von Geschichte und damit zugleich als Objekt von Geschichtsschreibung verstanden. Letztere ist der Gegenstand, dem sich die genannte Gruppe von Gelehrten widmete.[38] Diese Optik kann eine nichtjüdische Darstellung nicht einnehmen.

Nun ergeben sich aber gerade aus dieser notwendigen Optik *drittens* auch bestimmte eigene Einseitigkeiten, die Neuansätze ermöglichen und erfordern. Die Texte der frühjüdischen Autoren—seien sie Hebräisch oder

38. Besonders deutlich bei Salo W. Baron, Studium in Krakau und Wien, daneben Rabbinerausbildung (wie M. Hadas), Lehrer am Jüdischen Pädagogium in Wien. Baron zog schon 1927 in die USA, seit 1930 Professor für jüdische Geschichte an der Columbia University, Gründer der Jewish Studies in den Vereinigten Staaten (1895–1989). Sein großes Werk: *A Social and Religious History of the Jews*, 2. Aufl., 8 Bde. (New York: Columbia University Press, 1952–1960).

Griechisch—werden in den amerikanischen Darstellungen vornehmlich aus der Perspektive althistorischen Interesses gelesen. Hengels Analysen fügen den theologie- und philosophiegeschichtlichen Aspekt hinzu. Das *literarische Eigenprofil* und die *literarische Qualität* von so ausgezeichneten Texten wie dem Prediger Salomo, der Weisheit Salomos, dem Aristeasbrief oder eben dem Sirachbuch treten demgegenüber ganz zurück. Entsprechendes gilt für die siracidische Pädagogik, die nicht als eigener kultureller Typus von *Paideia* neben dem griechischen Typus und als große selbständige Leistung wie auch als kulturelles Programm erkannt wird.[39] Die Texte werden als historische oder religiöse *Quellen* der *Geschichte* des Judentums, nicht aber als eigenwertige kulturelle Hervorbringungen, eben als *Literatur* und als Zeugnisse eigener *jüdischer Kultur*, gelesen. Eine gewisse Ausnahme stellt—wie schon erwähnt—Moses Hadas dar, der in seiner „Hellenistischen Kultur" jüdische Schriften in die griechisch-hellenistische Literaturgeschichte einbezieht und umgekehrt vom Einfluss der hellenistischen Literatur auf die jüdische Literatur ausgeht.[40] Hadas hat noch mehr getan, indem er Sprache, Ethos, Erziehung und Liebe als eigene Bereiche der hellenistischen und auch der frühjüdischen Kultur thematisierte, ohne dies aber im Einzelnen auszuarbeiten.[41] Gerade an diese Linie konnte meine Untersuchung anknüpfen.

1.2. Ansatz

Aus dieser ebenso besonderen wie in mehrfacher Hinsicht jeweils einseitigen Forschungslage ergab sich folgerichtig der *Ansatz* meiner eigenen Untersuchung, so wie ich ihn in Kürze definiert habe:

---

39. Klassisch ausgearbeitet von Werner Jäger: Werner Jäger, *Paideia: Die Formung des griechischen Menschen*, 3 Bde. (Berlin: de Gruyter, 1934–1947). Jäger war Klassischer Philologe und wurde 1921 Nachfolger Ulrich von Wilamowitz-Moellendorffs in Berlin. Er emigrierte 1936 mit seiner jüdischen Frau in die USA. Professor für Classical Studies in Chicago und Harvard.

40. In seiner kommentierten Ausgabe des Aristeasbriefes: 'Letter of Aristeas' in: "The Dropsie College Edition of the Jewish Apocryphal Literature from 1951," schreibt Hadas: "Aristeas is neither a translation from a Semitic original, nor does it follow the forms of Semitic writings. The prime factor in the criticism of Aristeas is that, to a unique degree in the literature with which it has been associated, *it is a Greek book*" (55, Hervorhebung von mir).

41. Hadas, *Hellenistische Kultur*, passim.

> Die Frage nach der Kultur Sirachs verhält sich … sowohl alternativ als auch komplementär zur vorliegenden Sirachforschung, deren Interesse vornehmlich Sirachs Theologie und seiner theologiegeschichtlichen Einordnung ins Frühjudentum galt. Das Buch Jesus Sirach wird unter dieser Fragestellung nicht primär als ein Zeugnis der Religion des Judentums des Zweiten Tempels gelesen, sondern als ein Dokument frühjüdischer Kultur interpretiert. Daraus ergibt sich dann aber auch eine neue Definition des Ortes der Religion und Theologie im kulturellen Gesamtgefüge Sirachs und seiner kulturellen Welt.[42]

Aus heutiger Sicht zusammengefasst: Das Sirachbuch lässt sich aus unterschiedlichen Perspektiven lesen. Es ist ein Dokument frühjüdisch-weisheitlicher Frömmigkeit und damit eine religiöse Urkunde im Kontext des hebräischsprachigen Jerusalemer Judentums und der Adaption in der griechischsprachigen Judenschaft Alexandrias. In den Kanones von Septuaginta und Vulgata wird es darüber hinaus für eine relativ kurze Zeit zu einem Teil der fundierenden Schriften des griechischsprachigen Judentums und—langfristig—des Christentums. Das Sirachbuch ist zugleich eine wichtige Quelle für die Geschichte des Frühjudentums in ptolemäisch-seleukidischer Zeit. Darüber hinaus aber ist das Sirachbuch ein literarisches Werk und als solches ein wesentlicher Teil frühjüdischer Kultur. Außerdem ist es das Ergebnis eines pädagogischen Programms und fungiert als Werkzeug der pädagogisch-psychologischen Weisheitserziehung des Siraciden. Diesem Aspekt bin ich in meiner Studie besonders nachgegangen.

1.3. Ergebnisse

Nun zu den *Ergebnissen* meiner Studie. Sie betreffen zwei Bereiche. *Erstens* geht es um die *Rekonstruktion der Kultur* Jerusalem-*Judäas* nach 200 v. Chr. oder um Jesus Sirach als Kulturbeobachter. Das Sirachbuch gewährt umfangreiche Einblicke in das, was Tcherikover *material* nannte: in die materielle Kultur der Zeit, von einfachen Wohnbedingungen bis zum Palast, von Alltagskleidung bis zum priesterlichen Gewand, von Wasser und Brot bis zum eleganten Symposion, vom Sklaven bis zum Luxus liebenden Grundherrn und zu den Fürstensitzen, vom einfachen Haus bis zum Tempel. Weiter lassen sich Wirtschafts- und Rechtswesen

42. Wischmeyer, *Sirach*, 18.

sowie Gesellschafts-, Verwaltungs- und Herrschaftsstrukturen, wie sie sich Sirach in Beobachtung und in Kritik darstellten—und wie er sie sich wünschte—rekonstruieren. So lässt sich aus dem Sirachbuch ein dichtes Bild der materiellen und institutionellen Kultur seiner Zeit entwerfen. Jesus ben Sira beobachtet die kleinsten Details des alltäglichen und festlichen Lebens seiner Umgebung. Häufig finden wir diese Details in Vergleichen, die der moralischen Erfahrungs- und Erziehungsweisheit dienen.[43] Die Ergebnisse meiner Analyse zu den entsprechenden Themen können von althistorischer Seite in eine Wirtschafts-, Sozial- und Kulturgeschichte des Zeitraums eingezeichnet werden.

Ben Sira ist aber nicht einfach Protokollant, sondern hat seine eigene Perspektive *und* seine eigene Agenda. Sein Verständnis der Kultur seines Volkes ist die eines Vertreters der religiösen gebildeten Oberschichten, der auf die breite agrarisch-handwerkliche Basis der Gesellschaft blickt, in der er in herausgehobener Position lebt. Er kannte und beobachtete die Welt der Bauern, Handwerker und Kaufleute, die die übergroße Mehrheit der Bürger Jerusalems darstellte, und schätzte ihre Tätigkeit und deren Erzeugnisse, ohne ihnen aber *Bildung* vermitteln zu wollen—das galt übrigens auch und besonders für die Frauen:

> Unterricht für die große Mehrheit der Juden gab es von seiner Seite nicht. Er intendierte weder Volksbildung noch Volksfrömmigkeit aus der Tora noch autochthon juristische Belehrung aus der Tora. Ein Wertgefühl vermittelte er den jüdischen Handwerkern und Bauern nicht.[44]

Sirach ist weder ein Volkserzieher, noch vertritt er eine Luxuskultur. Er ist der Vertreter einer pädagogischen Elitekultur. Dem Luxus aller Art steht er skeptisch bis ablehnend gegenüber.[45] Luxus und Alltagsgüter, Verhalten der Reichen und der Armen: All das war für ihn (nur) Anschauungsmaterial, das seiner eigentlichen Aufgabe diente: der Erziehung der gebildeten jungen Männer in Jerusalem-Judäa. Wirkliche

---

43. Georg Sauer hat in einer kleinen Studie auf bestimmte Veränderungen hingewiesen, die der Enkel bei seiner Übersetzung am hebräischen Text vorgenommen hat und die auf den Wechsel von der mindestens teilweise agrarisch vor-städtisch geprägten Kultur des Großvaters zu seiner eigenen, bereits durch die hellenistische Großstadt Alexandria bestimmte Kultur bedingt sind: G. Sauer, "Ben Sira in Jerusalem und sein Enkel in Alexandria," in Sauer, *Studien zu Ben Sira*, 25–34.

44. Wischmeyer, *Sirach*, 298.

45. Ibid., 116–19.

Kultur findet Jesus Sirach im Weisheitsstudium, d.h. bei sich selbst, bei seiner „Schule" und bei Männern, die wie er Erziehung und Bildung in Jerusalem verkörpern.

Deshalb bildet *zweitens* die *innere* Kultur, die Jesus ben Sira selbst vermittelt und der er verpflichtet ist, den Schwerpunkt meiner Studie. Denn hier ist der Siracide selbst Akteur. Damit kommen wir zur tätigen Formung der Kultur Jerusalem-Judäas durch den Siraciden. Ich habe diesen Bereich unter der Überschrift „Sirachs fromme Kultur" folgendermaßen beschrieben:

> Sirachs Schrift „Über die Erziehung und Weisheit" (Prolog 12) zeigt den Prozess der Etablierung einer Kultur als Größe sui generis im Rahmen der Religion Israels. Diese Kultur empfängt aber ihre Strukturen, ihre Gegenstände, ihre Bedeutung und ihre Reichweite von der Religion, ohne mit dieser zusammenzufallen. Tradition, d.h. Anknüpfung an die vorgegebenen Koordinaten der überkommenen Religion Israels, und Innovation in Form einer neuen Rollenbestimmung der „Weisheit" stehen nebeneinander.[46]

Ohne auf die Einzelheiten von Sprache und Literatur, beobachtender Psychologie, vor allem aber Erziehung, Bildung und Seelenleitung einzugehen, komme ich gleich zu meiner Auswertung, die sich in der These zusammenfassen lässt, Sirach habe mit seinen Lehrvorträgen eine *eigene Kultur* für Jerusalem-Judäa geschaffen:

> Die(se) oral-literarische Arbeit an der Tora, die über das bloße Studium zu eigener Gestaltung in Form steter Neufassung der Gesamtheit der Theologie, Ethik, Anthropologie und der Geschichte des Gottesvolkes gelangt, ermöglicht einen kulturellen Freiraum, der aus der Religion erwächst und von Sirach positiv qualifiziert und erweitert wird. Der Vorgang der Ausgestaltung und Qualifikation des Raumes der Kultur läßt sich an den Themen der pädagogischen und psychischen Kultur genauer darstellen.... Denn die oral-literarische Kultur ist zugleich eine pädagogisch-psychische Elitekultur. Ihr Freiraum gilt einer bestimmten Menschengruppe, nicht dem *kahal Israel*, sondern den gebildeten Jünglingen in Israel und den weisen älteren Männern. Der pädagogische Eros, den Sirach als exemplarischer Weisheitslehrer in seiner Beziehung zur Weisheit den Schülern vorlebt, geht weit über alles hinaus,

46. Ibid., 294.

> was pragmatisch zum Lernen der Tora notwendig ist. Dieser Eros ist eine Form der Steigerung der Bedeutsamkeit der eigenen Tätigkeit ins Religiöse hinein, das im Israel der Sirachzeit höchste Wertpriorität genießt. Der Weise erlebt und versteht sich in seiner Tätigkeit als genauso wertvoll und führend wie die Priesterschaft, deren Wert durch ihre primäre Verbindung zur Religion definiert ist. Also definiert auch der Weise seine Bedeutung in der ihm zur Verfügung stehenden Erlebnis- und Wertesprache: der religiösen. Denn der selbständige Raum der Kultur hat noch keine eigene Wertesprache, die gesellschaftlich anerkannt wäre.[47]

Im Zentrum von Sirachs Interesse steht „die Kultivierung der Person“: Sie „dominiert … die gesamte Kultur“.[48]

1.4. Kulturbegriff

Welches *Konzept* von Kultur lag meiner Rekonstruktion zugrunde? Mein Ausgangspunkt war eine sehr einfache Definition:

> Konsensfähig ist ein Begriff von Kultur, der „die Gesamtheit derjenigen Leistungen und Orientierungen des Menschen, die seine ‘bloße’ Natur fortentwickeln und überschreiten, meint“.[49]

Damit habe ich mich dem vortheoretischen, stark historisch geprägten und praktikablen Kulturbegriff der damaligen Archäologen und Althistoriker unter Einbeziehung von Motiven der Schule der *Annales* angeschlossen, die nicht nur Hochkultur und Alltagskultur gleichermaßen untersuchten, sondern neben den Artefakten auch institutionelle Strukturen und Mentalitäten bzw. innere Dispositionen und Erziehungsprozesse als wesentliche Aspekte von Kultur verstanden.[50] Auf letzteren lag der Schwerpunkt meiner Untersuchung, denn in dem Feld von Erziehung und innerer Kultivierung

47. Ibid., 295.

48. Ibid., 21.

49. Ibid., 20, Zitat von Art. O. Schwemmer, “Kultur,” *Enzyklopädie Philosophie und Wissenschaftstheorie* 2:507–11, dort 507.

50. Einführend J. Revel, “Die Annales,” in *Kompass der Geschichtswissenschaft*, hrsg. J. Eibach und G. Lottes (Göttingen: Vandenhoeck & Ruprecht, 2002), 23–37. Wesentliche Elemente der Schule der *Annales* wie die Beobachtung langer Zeiträume und die Quantifizierbarkeit von sozialgeschichtlich relevanten Ergebnissen ließen sich für die „Kultur Sirachs“ nicht übernehmen.

liegt der eigene Beitrag Sirachs zur Kultur Jerusalem-Judäas nach 200 v.Ch. Ich habe damit einen möglichst weiten, hierarchisch flachen, heuristisch arbeitenden und nicht-theoretischen Meta-Begriff von Kultur verwendet, der auch die religiösen Symbolsysteme einschließt, ohne diese doktrinär auf ihre kulturelle Dimension zu reduzieren.

Das Sirachbuch und seinen Verfasser wird man weder mit einem holistischen Religions-, noch einem entsprechenden Kulturbegriff interpretieren können. Die eigenständige Kultur Sirachs entsteht vielmehr gerade in dem *Freiraum*, der sich neben der dominierenden Religion mit ihren eigenen kulturellen Aspekten von Liturgie, priesterlichem Ornat und religiöser Sprache für die sich institutionell selbständig etablierende pädagogisch-psychologische Kultur des siracidischen Lehrhauses öffnet. So konnte ich einerseits in Übereinstimmung mit Tcherikover und Hengel die grundlegende Dominanz des Religiösen bei Sirach festhalten. Aber als erster orthonym schreibender jüdischer Weisheitslehrer erlaubt sich Sirach andererseits, über Gesetz und Propheten und die anderen Schriften hinaus „*auch selbst* etwas Einschlägiges zur Erziehung und Weisheit zu schreiben" (Prolog 12).[51] In diesem „Auch selbst" und der Angabe seiner *Verfasserschaft*, die vom Enkel mit Stolz wiederholt und in einen autobiographischen Rahmen gestellt wird[52], liegt die Ansage der eigenen kulturellen Aufgabe Jesus Sirachs und seines Selbstverständnisses als Weisheitslehrer und Erzieher in Jerusalem. Er formuliert diese Ansage in dem akrostichischen Schlusstext 51,13–30 im Stil eines nicht pseudepigraph auf Salomon bezogenen, sondern autobiographisch[53] perspektivierten Lobliedes auf die Weisheit:

> Ich habe Freude an meinem Lehrhaus,
> und auch ihr werdet euch nicht schämen über mein Loblied. (51,29)

---

51. Übersetzung nach Otto Kaiser, *Weisheit für das Leben: Das Buch Jesus Sirach; Übersetzt und eingeleitet* (Stuttgart: Radius, 2005), 7.

52. Dieser Rahmen ist dem griechisch-hellenistischen autobiographischen Interesse angepasst. Dabei fehlt allerdings der Name des Enkels, ein hebräisches Erbe, das leicht übersehen wird.

53. Kap. 51,13–30 ist das Äquivalent zum Prolog. Ben Sira schreibt im topischen Stil des Lobpsalms und bringt doch seine eigene Person ins Spiel (Zapff, *Jesus Sirach*, 394). Der Enkel schreibt in hellenistischer autobiographischer Prosa.

2. Weiterentwicklung des Kulturbegriffs

Ich lenke nun den Blick auf die Entwicklung des *Kulturbegriffs* vor allem in der amerikanischen Anthropologie und Soziologie des letzten Jahrhunderts. Hier zeigt sich, in welcher Weise auch mein eigener Ansatz, obgleich er bewusst über Tcherikover, Hadas und Hengel hinausging, die Fragmentierung der verschiedenen Paradigmen der Sirachforschung nur teilweise überwand und seinerseits forschungsgeschichtlich determiniert und begrenzt war. Ich befand mich mit der Wahl dieses Kulturbegriffs nicht nur—wie dargestellt—im *mainstream* damaliger Altertumswissenschaften unter Einbeziehung wichtiger Fragestellungen der französischen Historikerschule der *Annales* und der Mentalitätsgeschichte, sondern auch, da ich sehr detailliert nach den *Erzeugnissen* und der Gestalt einer bestimmten historischen Kulturepoche fragte, in einer gewissen Kontinuität zu vortheoretischen *kulturgeschichtlich* arbeitenden Paradigmen, die unter anderem mit den großen Namen von Jakob Burckhardt, Karl Lamprecht und Johan Huizinga verbunden sind.[54]

Neben dieser kulturgeschichtlichen Fragestellung, die eine strenge historische und gegenstandsbezogene Dimension hat und damit zugleich an Differenzierung und Modellierung von Details interessiert ist, wurden aber ohne gegenseitige Beziehungnahme schon lange explizit theoriebasierte Zugänge zum Thema „Kultur“ entwickelt. Spätestens seit dem großen Werk von Ernst Cassirer: „Philosophie der symbolischen Formen“,

54. Vgl. besonders den kulturgeschichtlichen Ansatz von Karl Lamprecht (1856–1915, Geschichtsprofessor in Leipzig), der in mehreren Aspekten ein Vorläufer der *Annales* war, und das grundlegende Werk Jakob Burckhardts (1818–1897, Professor für Geschichte und Kunstgeschichte in Basel). Weiter Johan Huizinga (1872–1945, Professor für Geschichte in Leiden, 1942 von den nationalsozialistischen Behörden interniert). Huizingas These, die Kultur sei im Spiel entstanden, bietet eine Möglichkeit, die Emanzipation der Kultur von der Religion zu beschreiben. Zu Huizingas Kulturbegriff vgl. bes. Johan Huizinga, Verratene Welt. Eine Betrachtung über die Wiederherstellung unserer Kultur, in: ders., *Kultur- und zeitkritische Schriften*, herausgegeben und mit einem Nachwort versehen von Thomas Macho (Paderborn: Wilhelm Fink, 2014) 133–282. — Zur älteren Kulturgeschichte Karl Lamprechts und Burckhardts vgl. den guten Beitrag von H. Böhme, P. Matussek, and L. Müller, “Kulturgeschichtsschreibung,” in *Orientierung Kulturwissenschaft: Was sie kann, was sie will*, RE 55608 (Reinbek bei Hamburg: Rowohlt Taschenbuch, 2000), 44–56.—Vgl. auch die Realiensammlungen von G. H. Dalmann, *Arbeit und Sitte in Palästina*, Bde. 1–7 (Berlin: de Gruyter 1928–1942), Bd. 8 (Berlin: de Gruyter, 2001).

das bereits in den zwanziger Jahren des letzten Jahrhunderts erschien,[55] wurde an allgemeinen Kulturtheorien gearbeitet, die die Welt der kulturellen Erscheinungsformen ordnen und systemisch und funktional beschreiben wollten. In den Mittelpunkt des Interesses amerikanischer, angelsächsischer, französischer und deutscher Kulturtheoretiker rückte die Frage nach dem Wesen und der Funktion von Kultur überhaupt. Der Literaturwissenschaftler Claus-Michael Ort betont in seiner Einführung in die Entstehung und in die unterschiedlichen Typen der modernen Kulturtheorien besonders die Bedeutung Cassirers und seines zeichentheoretischen Ansatzes, weist aber auch darauf hin, dass es eine Generation dauerte, bis es zu einer Wahrnehmung von Seiten der Fachwissenschaften kam:

> Als Forschungsprogramm setzt sich diese [Cassirers] Tendenz jedoch erst in den 1960er und 1970er Jahren durch, nachdem sozialtheoretische und zeichentheoretische ... Kulturdefinitionen ihre einzelwissenschaftlich getrennten Wege verlassen haben und sich dank eines *cultural* und *interpretive turn* in den Sozialwissenschaften und dank der Soziologisierung der hermeneutischen (›geisteswissenschaftlichen‹) Disziplinen wieder anzunähern beginnen. Symboliken, Semantiken, Diskursstrukturen und ihre jeweiligen narrativen oder rhetorischen Medien rücken nun als handlungsleitende oder verhaltensmodellierende Sinnsysteme, als Ordnungsmuster sozialen Wissens und als Voraussetzung der Wahrnehmung, Deutung und Konstruktion sozialer ›Realität‹ in den Mittelpunkt sozialwissenschaftlichen Interesses.[56]

Um die Funktion und die Reichweite von Kultur zu bestimmen, wurde seit der Aufklärung mit großen Gegensatzpaaren gearbeitet. Die Diskussionen um die Definitionsfragen der Gegensatzpaare „Kultur *versus* Natur"[57] und „Kultur *versus* Zivilisation"[58] konnte ich für meine Studie voraussetzen. Die gegenseitige Abgrenzung von Kultur und Gesell-

55. Ernst Cassirer, *Philosophie der symbolischen Formen*, 3 Bde. (Berlin: Cassirer, 1923–1929; Neuaufl., Hamburg: Meiner, 2002, 2003). Ernst Cassirer (1874–1945), Philosophieprofessor in Hamburg. Seit 1933 als Jude im Exil. Professor in Göteborg, Yale und New York an der Columbia University.

56. Claus-Michael Ort, "Kulturbegriffe: Ich füge nicht nur im Hinblick auf das Handbuch religionswissenschaftlicher Grundbegriffe," in *Handbuch religionswissenschaftlicher Grundbegriffe*, hrsg. H. Cancik et al. (Stuttgart: Kohlhammer, 1988), 1:24.

57. Vgl. dazu oben meine eigene Definition.

58. Diese oft mit dem Unterschied zwischen deutschem und angelsächsischem Kulturbegriff (Polemiken im 1. Weltkrieg) belastete, von Kant geprägte Unterschei-

schaft, also „Kultur *versus* Gesellschaft" stand dagegen erst in den beiden letzten Forschergenerationen im Zentrum des Interesses und war zur Zeit der Entstehung meiner Studie ganz offen. Besonders umstritten war das Begriffspaar „Religion *versus* Kultur"—ein Thema, das für die Sirachinterpretation entscheidend ist.[59] Ein Verständnis von Kultur, das die „Auflösung des Religionsbegriffs im Kulturbegriff"[60] zum Ziel hat, wie es programmatisch in dem „Handbuch religionswissenschaftlicher Grundbegriffe" vertreten wird, habe ich kritisch diskutiert.[61] Gerade für das Sirachbuch macht die nivellierende Subsumierung von Religion unter Kultur unmöglich, die kulturelle Leistung ben Siras zu beschreiben, der *in und neben* der Religion eine pädagogische Kultur formiert.

Die Kulturtheorie fragt stets nach der Reichweite und dem Gegenüber des Kulturbegriffs. Neue Vorschläge zum Verständnis von Kultur und ihrer Funktion in der Gesellschaft wurden vor allem von der Seite der Kulturanthropologie gemacht. Ich nenne besonders die Kulturrelativisten Franz Boas, Ruth Fulton Benedict, Alfred L. Kroeber und Margaret Mead[62]. Die *cultural anthropology* arbeitet mit den *materials* der von

---

dung ist für das Verständnis von Tcherikovers „Hellenistic civilization" wichtig und erschien mir für meine Fragestellung ungeeignet.

59. Die drei komplementären Ordnungsfragen nach Ort, "Kulturbegriffe." Ich füge nicht nur im Hinblick auf das Handbuch religionswissenschaftlicher Grundbegriffe (Cancik, *Handbuch religionswissenschaftlicher Grundbegriffe*), sondern vor allem auf Niklas Luhmann das vierte Paar „Kultur versus Religion" hinzu. Vgl. Niklas Luhmann, *Die Religion der Gesellschaft: Herausgegeben von A. Kieserling* (Frankfurt am Main: Suhrkamp, 2000). Diese grundlegende Monographie wurde erst nach dem Erscheinen meiner Sirachstudie veröffentlicht.

60. Zum Thema vgl. Wischmeyer, *Sirach*, 250–54, Zitat von: D. Sabbatucci, "Kultur und Religion," in Cancik, *Handbuch religionswissenschaftlicher Grundbegriffe*, 43–58, darin 55.

61. Die Tendenz des „Handbuchs religionswissenschaftlicher Grundbegriffe" ist durch die aktuellen Entwicklungen im Islam und im Hinduismus überholt worden. Religion tritt gegenwärtig global als eigener starker Akteur hervor: Friedrich Wilhelm Graf, *Götter global: Wie die Welt zum Supermarkt der Religionen wird* (Munich: Beck, 2014). Wichtige Beiträge zum Thema „Religion" sind gesammelt in: *Was ist Religion? Texte von Cicero bis Luhmann; herausgegeben von J. Schlieter*, RUB 18785 (Stuttgart: Reclam, 2010).

62. Franz Boas: 1858–1942, Professor an der Columbia University New York; Ruth Fulton Benedict: 1887–1948, Columbia University New York; Alfred L. Kroeber: 1876–1960, Professor in Berkeley; Margaret Mead: 1901–1978, Professorin des American Museum of Natural History New York.

ihr untersuchten Kulturen, um dann aber ebenfalls die gesellschaftlichen Strukturen und Funktionen von Kultur als Muster zu erschließen. Einen anderen Weg ging die systemtheoretische Kultur- und Wissenssoziologie, wie sie Talcott Parsons[63] und in Deutschland Niklas Luhmann geprägt haben. Diese Richtung entfernt sich besonders weit vom gegenständlichen Bereich der Kultur und sucht nach möglichst allgemeinen Definitionen von Kultur im Blick auf die Gesellschaft.[64] Der weitere Verlauf der Ausdifferenzierung der Kulturtheorien im Kontext von Anthropologie, Soziologie, Systemtheorie, Semiotik und Literaturwissenschaft kann hier nicht dargestellt werden.[65] Grundsätzlich verbindet die genannten kulturtheoretischen Richtungen die Frage nach den gesellschaftlichen Funktionen von Kultur,[66] die die Beschäftigung mit den kulturellen Artefakten ablöst.

Für das Sirachbuch können diejenigen Theorien interessant sein, die Kultur als Sprache, einfach als Abstraktion oder allgemein als symbolisches Zeichensystem verstehen. Ein wesentlicher Faktor war und bleibt in diesem Zusammenhang die kulturwissenschaftliche Perspektive der Literaturwissenschaft,

> literarische Texte als Medien gesellschaftlicher Selbstbeobachtung zu interpretieren und ihnen Beobachtungs- und Unterscheidungssemantiken zuzuschreiben, die ›Realität‹ als soziales Konstrukt überhaupt erst wahrnehmbar und kommunizierbar machen.[67]

Dass Literatur perspektivisch konzipiert wird und dem Leser nicht einfach ein „Realitäts"-Protokoll, sondern *gedeutete* Realität vermittelt und damit eigenen Zwecken dient, wusste man schon immer.[68] Aber kultur- bzw. literaturwissenschaftliche Theorien, die Kulturen als „Texte"

63. 1902–1979, Professor in Harvard.

64. Ort, "Kulturbegriffe," 28–30.

65. Vgl. Roland Borgards, *Texte zur Kulturtheorie und Kulturwissenschaft*, RUB 18715 (Stuttgart: Reclam, 2010).

66. Ort, "Kulturbegriffe," 25–28. Ort nennt Max Weber, Alfred Weber und Karl Mannheim, weiter die angelsächsischen *cultural studies* (deren Neuheitswert aber m.E. angesichts der Breite des Kulturbegriffs der älteren Kulturgeschichte überschätzt wird: Alle Archäologie hat stets die materielle Kultur eingeschlossen. So bin ich auch in meiner Studie vorgegangen).

67. Ort, "Kulturbegriffe," 34.

68. Darauf beruht die antike Rhetorik.

lesen,[69] weisen darauf hin, in welch hohem Maß Literatur erst Realität in einem allgemeineren Sinn aussagbar und erfahrbar macht—kurz „konstruiert". Und dabei sind wir bei dem Titel meines Beitrags angekommen. Der Gedanke literarischer *Konstruktion* von Kultur ist äußerst hilfreich für die Interpretation der Kultur des Sirachbuches—in der doppelten Bedeutung des Begriffs, *einmal* jener Kultur, die durch den literarischen Wurf des Buches überhaupt erst einmal artikuliert und damit auch konstituiert wird,[70] das zum *anderen* selbst ein kulturelles Artefakt darstellt. Dass Jesus ben Sira die Kultur seiner Lebenswelt durch sein Werk erst einmal ins Bewusstsein gehoben und gleichsam festgeschrieben habe, lässt sich mit der literatur- und kulturwissenschaftlichen Metapher von der Kultur als Text darstellen. Weder eine weisheitstheologische noch eine althistorische Perspektive kann diese besondere Leistung des Siraciden erfassen. Das Ergebnis meines eigenen kulturgeschichtlich-mentalitätsgeschichtlichen Zugangs wird durch diese theoretische Beschreibung an andere kulturwissenschaftliche Fragestellungen vermittelbar.

Das bringt mich zu der Frage, wie diese allgemeinen Kulturtheorien mit der Arbeit an den kulturellen Artefakten zu verbinden seien—eine Frage, die immer wieder mit skeptischem Unterton von den philologischen und historischen Einzelfächern gestellt wird. Claus-Michael Ort hat folgendermaßen darauf geantwortet:

> Solche Definitionen [wie z.B. Max Weber: „Kultur ist das von den Mitgliedern einer Kultur selbstgesponnene ›Bedeutungsgewebe‹"] treffen zwar zu, sind aber einzelwissenschaftlich nicht anwendbar, ohne entweder die sozial- oder die zeichentheoretische Dimension von ›Kultur‹ metaphorisch zu verabsolutieren und auf den anderen Bereich zu übertragen.[71]

Richtig ist, dass die Theoriediskussion nicht methodisch umgesetzt werden kann—was sie ja auch gar nicht beabsichtigt. Die Arbeit der Einzelwissenschaften bleibt im rekonstruierenden Bereich, der von der Handschriftenkonservierung[72] bis zu komplizierten architektonischen Rekons-

69. Besonders Doris Bachmann-Medick, *Kultur als Text: Die anthropologische Wende in der Literaturwissenschaft*, 2 Aufl. (Tübingen: Francke, 2004).

70. Es geht um die Festschreibung und allgemeine sichere Kommunikation der vorangegangenen mündlichen Lehre, die sachlich gesehen ebenfalls schon kulturelle Realität konstruierte.

71. Ort, "Kulturbegriffe," 34.

72. Beispiel: Derveni-Papyrus, Pyapyrusrollen von Herculaneum.

truktionen[73] reicht, ebenso unersetzbar wie in der Interpretation. Sie gilt nach wie vor den materiellen und immateriellen Artefakten der menschlichen Kulturen und ist in ihren Methoden ihren jeweiligen Gegenständen—Architektur, Texte etc.—verpflichtet. Das haben die verschiedenen Spielarten der Anthropologie, besonders die *cultural anthropology*, die eng mit der Museumsarbeit verbunden ist,[74] noch einmal von einer anderen Seite her deutlich gemacht. In dieser Hinsicht veralten Einzelergebnisse, die aus historisch-philologischen Analysen stammen, auch nicht, sondern werden innerhalb des historisch-philologischen Methodensets immer wieder geprüft und gegebenenfalls korrigiert. Andererseits hat sich durch die allgemeinen Theorien auch die Wahrnehmung des Begriffs der Kultur verändert, und neue Fragen haben neue Themenstellungen generiert. Dadurch können alte Ergebnisse an Relevanz und an Aussagekraft gewinnen. Eine genaue Wahrnehmung der Kulturtheorien kann den Fachwissenschaften, die an Einzelaspekten der „Kultur" arbeiten, nur nützen.

3. Der cultural turn und das Sirachbuch

In der praktischen Forschungsarbeit bleibt das Verhältnis von Kulturtheorie und Einzelfächern schwierig. Die Gießener Anglisten und Kulturwissenschaftler Ansgar und Vera Nünning, die sich in besonderer Weise um die Dokumentation und fachwissenschaftliche Umsetzung von Kulturtheorien verdient gemacht haben,[75] zitieren im Einleitungsbeitrag ihres Sammelbandes „Konzepte der Kulturwissenschaften"[76] eine Polemik der Kulturwissenschaftler Bernd Henningsen und Stefan Michael Schröder gegen die Vertreter der klassischen Fächer der Philosophischen Fakultät bzw. der Geisteswissenschaften, die als symptomatisch für die Friktionen zwischen den etablierten Fächern und den neuen kulturwissenschaftlichen Fragestellungen und ihrem Führungsanspruch gelten mag: Die Philolo-

---

73. Ein heute durch die computerbasierten Rekonstruktionsmodelle besonders wichtiger Bereich wissenschaftlicher Arbeit.

74. Frans Boas, Margaret Mead.

75. Vgl. auch das einflussreiche Werk von Ansgar Nünning, hrsg. *Metzler Lexikon Literatur- und Kulturtheorie*, 5. Aufl. (Stuttgart: Metzler, 2103).

76. Kulturwissenschaften: Eine multiperspektivische Einführung in einen interdisziplinären Diskussionszusammenhang in: Ansgar Nünning und Vera Nünning, Hrsg., *Konzepte der Kulturwissenschaften* (Stuttgart: Metzler, 2003), 1–18, Zitat 1. Das Zitat ist entnommen: Bernd Henningsen, ed., *Das Ende der Humboldt-Kosmen: Konturen von Kulturwissenschaft* (Baden-Baden: Nomos, 1997), 6.

gien agierten oder agitierten „aus der saturierten Perspektive des fachdisziplinären Schrebergartens heraus" gegen theoriebasierte Kulturwissenschaften. Der Vorwurf der „Schrebergarten-Mentalität" lässt sich aus einer Außenperspektive tatsächlich trefflich allen Philologien, besonders solchen, die alte orientalische Sprachen mit einer umfangmäßig geringen Literaturproduktion und teilweise desolater Textüberlieferung betreffen, machen, etwa unter der gönnerhaft-kritischen Frage: „Lesen sie immer noch ihre alten Texte, ohne einmal fertig zu werden?" Solche—bewusst und strategisch gezielte—polemische Angriffe auf die klassischen geisteswissenschaftlichen Fächer sind wissenschaftlich ebenso kontraproduktiv wie eine *a limine* Ablehnung kulturtheoretischer Fragestellungen. Auch das Sirachbuch ist ein—großer—Schrebergarten, dessen verschiedene Pflanzen, hebräische, griechische, syrische, lateinische Manuskripte im unterschiedlichsten Erhaltungszustand, kultiviert und zu *edierten Texten* gemacht werden müssen, wenn überhaupt Forschung zum Sirachbuch stattfinden soll. Perspektiven des *cultural turn*[77] können dann zu einer *Gesamtsicht* auf das Buch Jesus Sirach führen, die die kulturgeschichtliche Rekonstruktion auch im Rahmen dieses neuen Paradigmas darstellt: Jesus Sirach als Teil der literarischen Kultur Jerusalem-Judäas, sein Verfasser und dessen Übersetzer als kulturelle Akteure in Jerusalem und Alexandria, die Arbeit der vielen Gelehrten als Teil der Rezeption des Werkes durch die verschiedenen Sprachen, Kulturen und Religionen bis zur gegenwärtigen historischen und philologischen Forschung.

Ich nenne abschließend vier Themen, die im Zusammenhang des *cultural turn* für die Sirachinterpretation verstärkte Bedeutung gewinnen können: Überwindung von Fragmentierung—Übersetzung und Kulturtransfer—Bedeutung der Autorschaft—Rezeption.[78]

3.1. Fragmentierungen und ihre Überwindung

Wir sahen, wie grundsätzlich *fragmentiert* die Forschungsgeschichte in Bezug auf das Sirachbuch war und ist. Diese Fragmentierung hat wissen-

77. Doris Bachmann-Medick, *Cultural Turns: Neuorientierung in den Kulturwissenschaften*, 5. Aufl. (Reinbek bei Hamburg: Rowohlt-Taschenbuch, 2014).

78. Zu den neuen kulturwissenschaftlichen Themen gehören Fragestellungen wie Identität und Alterität, Scham und Schande, Körper, *gender*, *ethnicity*, Zeit und Raum, Macht u.a., die alle für das Sirachbuch von Interesse sind, die ich hier aber nicht einzeln kommentiere.

schaftsgeschichtliche, biographische,[79] religiös-konfessionelle und nationale Gründe,[80] die meist unausgesprochen bleiben und deren Bedeutung für die wissenschaftliche Arbeit nicht reflektiert oder ganz geleugnet wird. Der Leugnung liegt eine eindimensionale Hermeneutik zugrunde, die von der wissenschaftlichen „Unvoreingenommenheit" bzw. Objektivität der Wissenschaftler ausgeht und eigene religiös-kulturell-nationale Prägungen mit fehlender Objektivität gleichsetzt. Ich habe gezeigt, dass diese Fragmentierungen oder Prägungen Teil des Interpretationsprozesses sind und als solche nicht nur hermeneutisch wahrgenommen werden müssen, sondern selbst zu dem Sirachbuch gehören. *Erstens* sind die Biographien der Wissenschaftler Teil des wissenschaftlichen Interpretationsprozesses, *zweitens* ist die wissenschaftliche Rekonstruktion Teil des nach vorn offenen Prozesses der *Rezeption*, und *drittens* ist die Rekonstruktion sachlich stets auch eine eigene Konstruktion.

Zum *ersten* Aspekt: Biographische Faktoren beeinflussen die interpretatorische Perspektive. Die jüdischen Althistoriker beabsichtigten in der ersten Phase ihrer wissenschaftlichen Laufbahn nicht, Erzeugnisse frühjüdischer Literatur zu untersuchen. Sie waren hochqualifizierte Altertumswissenschaftler. Ihr persönliches Schicksal war der Grund für ihre vertiefte Beschäftigung mit dem hellenistischen Judentum, das sie aber gemäß ihrer fachlichen Bildung stets im Rahmen der Alten Geschichte behandelten. Sehr anders die katholischen und evangelischen Theologen: Sie untersuchten im Zusammenhang des theologischen Paradigmas die Weisheitstheologie und die damit verbundene Ethik der frühjüdischen Schriften. Der Wahrnehmung der selbständigen pädagogischen Kultur des Sirachbuches standen entsprechende Gründe entgegen: Die amerikanischen Althistoriker gingen davon aus, dass es eine hellenistische Kultur (*civilization*) gegeben habe, der die Juden letzten Endes fremd gegenübergestanden hätten. Die theologischen Interpreten ihrerseits lasen die frühjüdischen Schriften gerade als kanonische und damit theologische Texte, nicht als Zeugnisse einer frühjüdischen Kultur. Die Eröffnung der kultu-

79. Dieser Aspekt ist für das Sirachbuch wie für andere frühjüdische Schriften so bedeutend, dass ich Grunddaten der an der Sirachforschung und ihrem weiteren Umfeld beteiligten Wissenschaftler mitgeteilt habe.

80. Letzteres ist ebenfalls sehr wichtig. Ein Beispiel: die amerikanischen Arbeiten von Tcherikover etc. blieben stark durch ältere deutsche altertumswissenschaftliche Paradigmen geprägt und öffneten sich weniger den amerikanischen Ansätzen der *cultural anthropology*.

rellen Dimension des Sirachbuches setzt dagegen eine literarisch und pädagogisch gebildete Biographie voraus.

Zum *zweiten* Aspekt: Gerade die Sirachforschung ist ein beredtes Beispiel für die Dynamik der Abfolge und Überschneidung wissenschaftlicher Paradigmen, die in ihrem Zusammenhang die Geschichte der Rezeption des Sirachbuches seit den hebräischen Textfunden in der Geniza der Kairoer Esra-Synagoge[81] sowie den Funden in Qumran und Masada darstellen und nur aus der ursprünglichen Multiperspektivität des Buches zu erklären sind. Hier wird an einem der umfangreichen und bedeutenden späten hebräischen Texte Jerusalem-Judäas textkritisch und textrekonstruierend im Verbund mit der griechischen und der syrischen Übersetzung sowie den lateinischen Übersetzungen gearbeitet. Die Philologie bildet die unverzichtbare Grundlage aller Interpretationsarbeit, sei sie historisch, theologisch oder kulturfokussiert. Diese Interpretationen stellen das Sirachbuch nicht nur der hebräischen, griechischen und lateinischen Philologie zur Verfügung, sondern auch der Judaistik, der alttestamentlichen und neutestamentlichen Wissenschaft und den Spezialdisziplinen der Septuaginta-, Vulgata- und Peschittaforschung sowie der Alten Geschichte. Hier ergibt sich eine fächerübergreifende Zusammenarbeit, die die Barrieren der einzelnen Sprachen überschreitet. Das gilt besonders für die äußerst dynamische Septuagintaforschung, die *per se* mehrsprachig ist und mit drei eng miteinander verbundenen Religions- und Kultursystemen arbeitet: dem hebräischsprachigen antiken Judentum, der griechischsprachigen Diaspora und dem entstehenden Christentum.

Zum *dritten* Aspekt: Dass jede Rekonstruktion zugleich als Konstruktion fungiert, ist spätestens seit dem Konstruktivismus wissenschaftliches Gemeingut. Um ein letztes Mal auf meine eigene Studie zurückzukommen: Alle Details meiner Rekonstruktion der äußeren und inneren Kultur, die das Sirachbuch spiegelt, sind der genauen Textanalyse entnommen und gemäß den thematischen Schwerpunkten, die der Text anbietet, zusammengeordnet. Sie sind das Ergebnis einer Rekonstruktion. Zugleich stellen sie aber meine eigene interpretatorische Konstruktion dar. Der Jerusalemer Lehrer selbst schrieb keine „Kultur Jerusalem-Judäas", sondern stellte seine Lehrsprüche und Lehrgedichte zusammen. Es bleibt der späteren Interpretation überlassen, hier ein kulturelles Manifest zu finden. *Die Interpretation konstruiert.*

81. Von Solomon Schechter (1847–1915) seit 1896 gesammelt und bearbeitet.

Die *Zusammenschau* der genannten Aspekte ermöglicht es, das Buch Jesus Sirach als Teil der Kultur Israels in seiner letzten Epoche zu verstehen. Das bedeutet Überwindung der Fragmentierungen, ohne dass die einzelnen fachspezifischen Analysen und die biographischen Zugänge überflüssig oder weniger wichtig würden.

3.2. Übersetzung und Kulturtransfer

Für Jesus Sirach ist die Übersetzung von zentraler Bedeutung. Es ist stets vermerkt worden, dass das Sirachbuch das erste Werk der hebräischen Literatur mit einer orthonymen Verfasserangabe ist. Hinzugefügt sei, dass dieser Autor mehrfach autobiographische Angaben über seine Tätigkeit als Weisheitsschriftsteller macht und dass der Enkel daran anknüpft. Hier liegt also hebräische *Literatur* im Sinne des griechisch-römischen Literaturbetriebes (*literary activity*) mit einer Selbstvorstellung des Autors vor. Dieser Spur muss weiter nachgegangen werden. Damit verbunden ist der Umstand, dass wir auch den Übersetzer durch seine Selbstvorstellung persönlich kennen.[82] Der Prolog ist ein Schlüsseltext für die Septuagintaforschung und steht trotz seiner Kürze ebenbürtig neben dem Aristeasbrief.[83] Die griechische Übersetzung des Enkels ist die wichtigste Urkunde für den direkten Kulturtransfer, der von Jerusalem nach Alexandria stattfindet. Die Übersetzung ist Ausdruck der Überzeugung, dass die hellenistische—d.h. zunächst einmal griechischsprachige—jüdische Gemeinde Alexandrias aus dem hebräischen Werk des in Jerusalem beheimateten Großvaters Erziehung und Bildung gewinnen könne. Denselben Kulturtransfer, der als großes Übersetzungswerk stattfindet, stellt ausführlich der Aristeasbrief dar. Diese Übersetzungsarbeit, die zugleich als Kulturtransfer verstanden wird, lässt sich am ehesten mit der Arbeit Ciceros vergleichen und muss in diese Dimension gestellt werden.

3.3. Rezeption

Die Kategorie der *Rezeption* erschließt die Phänomene der Fragmentierung und des Kulturtransfers von einer anderen Seite: einmal von der Geschichte der Texte und ihrer stetigen Neubewertung als kanonisch

82. S.o. Anm. 52 und 53.

83. Vgl. auch die späteren Äußerungen des Josephus zum Verhältnis der hebräischen und griechischen Sprache.

oder nicht-kanonisch oder semikanonisch—d.h. deuterokanonisch oder apokryph—und der damit verbundenen größeren oder kleineren theologischen und ethischen Autorität sowie dem damit verbundenen Bekanntheitsgrad her. Andererseits treten die Interpreten selbst in die Interpretationsgeschichte, die ein Teil der Rezeptionsgeschichte ist, ein und bestimmen diese ebenso mit, wie sie von ihr bestimmt sind.

3.4. Autorschaft

Schließlich die *Autorschaft*: die Autorschaft des Siraciden habe ich schon mehrfach betont. Ihre Bedeutung für die These, Jesus ben Sira habe sich als selbständiger kultureller Akteur verstanden, ist offensichtlich. Unter gegenwärtigen literaturwissenschaftlichen Gesichtspunkten wie *self fashioning* erhält sie noch einmal mehr Gewicht. Ben Sira ist damit der erste uns historisch bekannte jüdische Schriftsteller, der sich als Schriftsteller versteht („Ich habe selbst etwas Einschlägiges schreiben wollen") und von seinem Enkel als Autor in Alexandria eingeführt wird. Damit ist Jesus ben Sira der Erste in der nicht langen, aber illustren Reihe antiker jüdischer Schriftsteller, die außer ihm Philon, Paulus und Josephus umfasst, um mit diesem ans Ende zu kommen.[84]

84. An diese Fragestellung schließen sich die Themen von Schulbetrieb, Kanon, Schriftauslegung und Zitat sowie Autorisierung an, die aus der Perspektive der Autorschaft neu bedacht werden müssen.

Scribal Practices in the Ben Sira Hebrew Manuscript A and Codicological Remarks

Jean-Sébastien Rey

This paper stems from the production of a new critical edition of the Hebrew manuscripts—the Genizah, Qumran, and Masada fragments—of Ben Sira, coauthored with Jan Joosten and Eric Reymond. To summarize briefly the characteristics of this edition, each Hebrew manuscript is edited and translated independently, as it has been preserved, avoiding any correction, even if we are convinced that this text is not the "original" and that it has undergone many transformations through the ages. A first apparatus presents paleographical notes. A second apparatus gives the variant readings of other Hebrew witnesses. Finally, a third apparatus provides a philological commentary, to explain the preserved Hebrew text, or, when the Hebrew is incomprehensible, to produce a possible reconstruction.

It seems clear to us that each Hebrew manuscript of Ben Sira needs to be considered by itself, as it has been preserved, with no attempt to reconstruct a possible original by comparison or retroversion via ancient translations. The multifarious textual witnesses testify to the vitality and richness of the Ben Sira tradition through time, reflect scribal activity in textual transmission, and may even furnish evidence of the development of the Hebrew language from the second century BC to the tenth century CE.

In scholarship history, the material characteristics of Hebrew manuscripts—the corrections or marginal readings, for instance—have been used primarily to build a hypothetical original Hebrew text of Ben Sira.

I wish to thank G. Gordon-Bournique for her English translation, Prof. C. Martone for our rich discussions and his help in searching bibliographic references during my stay in Torino, as well as Dr. B. Outhwaite and Dr. R. Shoshany for their help on the Babylonian accentuation. I would like also to thank the MSH Lorraine and my laboratory "Ecritures" at the University of Lorraine for their support.

Following this scientific paradigm, textual variants have been considered alterations and sentenced to oblivion. I intend to assume a different attitude and concentrate not on a reconstructed text but on the text as it stands in the witnesses available to us. I wish to examine and compare the scribal practices evident in the different Hebrew manuscripts from the Cairo Genizah. In reality significant attention has not been paid to this question in the previous editions of the text, neither in the preliminary publications of the late nineteenth century nor in the more recent editions of Ze'ev Ben-Ḥayyim or Pancratius C. Beentjes.[1] In this paper, a preliminary effort, I will limit myself to manuscript A and try to reach some conclusions on the basis of our observations.

1. Marginal Corrections

Since the marginal inscriptions of the Ben Sira manuscript B are clearly alternative readings,[2] we can safely assume as a first observation that in manuscript A all marginal or interlinear notations will be correctives. They are in fact written in the same hand as the plain text and treat systematically what the scribe himself recognized as an erroneous word or sentence.

The manner of indicating mistakes is far from systematic. One word or letter may be crossed out (see the dittography of יגלה in Sir 3:20 or תבואה in Sir 15:3 [see plate 1 below]), marked with a cancellation dot over the

1. Ze'ev Ben Ḥayyim, *The Book of Ben Sira: Text, Concordance and Analysis of the Vocabulary* (Jerusalem: The Academy of the Hebrew Language and the Shrine of the Book), 1973; Pancratius C. Beentjes, *The Book of Ben Sira in Hebrew: A Text Edition of All Extant Hebrew Manuscripts and a Synopsis of All Parallel Hebrew Ben Sira Texts*, VTSup 68 (Leiden: Brill), 1997. See, however, Saloman Schechter and Charles Taylor, *The Wisdom of Ben Sira: Portions of the Book Ecclesiasticus from Hebrew Manuscript in the Cairo Genizah Collection Presented to the University of Cambridge by the Editors* (Cambridge: Cambridge University Press, 1899), 7–10; and Israel Lévi, *L'Ecclésiastique, ou la Sagesse de Jésus, fils de Sira: Texte original hébreu édité, traduit et commenté; Deuxième partie* (Paris: Ernest Leroux, 1901), vi–viii.

2. See Jean-Sébastien Rey, "Scribal Practices in Ben Sira's Manuscript B from the Cairo Genizah," in *Discovering, Deciphering and Dissenting: Ben Sira's Hebrew Text, 1896–2016*, ed. J. Aitken, R. Egger-Wenzel, and S. Reif; DCLS (Berlin: de Gruyter, forthcoming); Rey, "Transmission textuelle et sacralisation: Quelques caractéristiques de la pratique des copistes des ms. A et B du texte hébreu de Ben Sira," in *Littérature et sacré*, ed. Valentina Litvan, Recherche en Littérature et Spiritualité (Frankfurt am Main: Lang, 2016), 163–77.

letter (see ורשִׁיש in Sir 4:30 or the *circellus* on לא in Sir 8:2 [and see *infra* §5 on the use of *ketiv* and *qere*]) or with two cancellation dots over and/or under the letter (see טמֿטם in Sir 10:16 with three dots in the margin; סרײדה in Sir 10,1 also with three dots in the margin; על in Sir 15:19 with two dots over and under the letter), or marked with a reversed *segol* over the word (see תנתע in Sir 3:14, with a marginal correction given the same sign).[3] We have also found two cases where a letter seems to have been erased {ב}{ל}דלותו) in Sir 10:31 and perhaps {ם}כל in Sir 15:18).

Three dots in the margin generally indicate a mistake somewhere in the line. Most of the time, the word has been corrected by the scribe, usually by vocalizing a miswritten word (see הא > הֵ'א in 6:10; כנים > כְּנִיּום in 10:11; מופין > מ־ופין in 13:22; ותין > וְתֵן in 14:16[4] [see plate 1]; etc.). In a few instances, the scribe just indicated that the text is corrupt, without offering any rectification. For instance, in Sir 10:16, the word טִמְטֵם seems to have been considered erroneous, for the scribe marked it with a double dot and three dots are in the margin. But טִמְטֵם is well attested in Rabbinic Hebrew, with the meaning "to thicken, to obstruct," and especially "to blunt the understanding."[5] The meaning of the sentence is not impossible: עקבת גֵוִים טִמְטֵם אלהים "God made the guile of the proud stupid."[6] 
Nevertheless, most commentators suggest correcting טִמְטֵם to טֵאטֵא "to sweep away."[7] This correction is purely conjectural, and neither the Greek

---

3. In Sir 4:2, the *segol* under the double *waw* of ד/רווח would indicate the dittography of the *waw* rather than its vocalization.

4. Here the sign could also indicate a dittography.

5. See Marcus Jastrow, *Dictionary of the Targumim, Talmud Bavli, Talmud Yerushalmi and Midrashic Literature* (New York: Judaica Treasury, 2004), 532; Jacob Levy, *Neuhebräisches und Chaldäisches Wörterbuch über die Talmudim und Midraschim* (Leipzig: Brockhaus, 1879), 165.

6. The translation of the sentence is difficult. We took עקבה in the sense of "guile," as in 2 Kgs 10:19, while Rudolf Smend and Israel Lévi prefer the meaning "trace," "sign," as understood by the Syriac. For the Hebrew גוים, the Greek ἐθνῶν clearly requires the vocalization גּוֹיִם, but the Syriac "proud" implies reading גֵּוִים, a defective writing of גאוים, which vocalization would give better meaning to the context. The spelling of גאה is highly variable (גאי, גא, גאוה, גאות, גוה), and it would not be the only case of confusion with גוים; see Zeph 3:6, where the Greek translates the consonantal Hebrew גוים by ὑπερηφάνους "proud," see also Sir 35:22 where, perhaps, גֵּוִים would be expected.

7. See, for example, Israel Lévi, "Notes sur les ch. VII.29–XII.1 de Ben Sira édités par M. Elkan N. Adler," *JQR* 13 (1901): 11 n. 2; Alexander A. Di Lella and Patrick W. Skehan, *The Wisdom of Ben Sira: A New Translation with Notes*, AB 39 (New York: Doubleday, 1987), 222.

καραστρέφω "to turn over, to turn under" nor the Syriac ܚܡܐ "to uproot, to pull out" support it. Therefore the question arises concerning the reason the scribe held טְמְטֵם to be mistaken, since the text is understandable. Was it on the basis of some ancient translations? Or was it on the basis of another copy? In any event he did not suggest any replacement.

In a few other places where the text is almost incomprehensible and certainly corrupt, the scribe put three dots in the margin without localizing the mistake nor providing any solution (see, for instance, Sir 7:3[8] or Sir 11:18b[9]). It is possible that the scribe simply did not know what correction to make, but this restraint also shows that he maintained a critical attitude towards the text. He avoided correcting it on his own authority; he respected the text he had and did not provide an alternative reading based on another copy or by retroversion via the Greek or the Syriac.[10]

But here again the scribe is not really consistent: we have found a few cases not pointed by the scribe, yet where the Hebrew is quite incomprehensible and definitely corrupt,[11] as, for instance, is the case in Sir 4:14.[12]

---

8. אל תדע חרושי על אח. Greek and Syriac translations would suggest a *Vorlage* אל תזרע על חרושי עולה "Sow not in the furrows of unrighteousness" (see G. H. Box and W. O. E. Oesterley, "Sirach," in *Apocrypha*, vol. 1 of *The Apocrypha and Pseudepigrapha of the Old Testament in English*, ed. R. H. Charles [Oxford: Clarendon, 1913], 268–517; Lévi, *L'ecclésiastique*, 39; Moshe Z. Segal, ספר בן סירא השלם [*The Complete Book of Ben Sira*] [Jerusalem: Bialik Institute, 1958], 44).

9. וי[ש] יְחיב שכרו "There are who make his reward guilty." The scribe put three dots in the margin to indicate a mistake but without showing where in the line the mistake is situated. It could concern the use of the verb חוב, only attested in Biblical Hebrew in the *piel* in Deut 1:10 with the meaning "to make guilty." The sentence would then speak of one whose pay has been wrongly acquired.

10. The scribe has also put three dots in the margin of Sir 4:18, although the text seems quite correct.

11. I am not convinced that one should interpret such erroneous verses as the sign of scribal negligence or incompetence as suggested by Schechter and Taylor: "He must be described as a very careless copyist. For not only may he be fairly suspected of having corrupted many words and even omitted whole verses, but it can hardly be doubted that he was not always competent to read the MS. from which our copy was prepared" (*Wisdom of Ben Sira*, 9) or Lévi: "L'exemplaire … est malheureusement l'œuvre d'un scribe qui n'a pas toujours compris ce qu'il copiait; il a commis les fautes les plus grossières, mal coupé certains versets; parfois il n'a pas craint d'écrire ou de transcrire des passages entiers absolument inintelligibles" (*L'ecclésiastique*, viii).

12. וא'הו במא ויהא is incomprehensible and is probably a corruption of ואל אוהב מאהביה "And God loves them that love her" (see Schechter and Taylor, Lévi, Segal, Box, and Oesterley).

Conversely, in Sir 8:7, the copyist pointed the *waw* of גוע and put three dots in the margin, although it agrees with the Greek and the Syriac.

Corrections are generally written in the margins,[13] but sometimes they figure interlinearly (see, for instance, Sir 15:9, added between Sir 15:8 and 15:10 [see plate 1]). The latter clearly indicates that the scribe has corrected his own copying errors on the basis of his parent text. For instance, in Sir 3:14, צדקת אב לא תמחה ותמור חטאת היא תנ̊תע, in the second sentence, the word תנתע, "it will be crushed," with three dots over the *tav* is corrected in the margin by תנטע with *ṭet*, "it will be planted," which agrees with the Greek and the Syriac. Another significant example is in Sir 14:18, where verse 19 is added in the margin [see plate 1]. This verse was missing by *homoioteleuton*: at the end of verse 18, the scribe had erroneously ended the sentence with ואחר גומל, which corresponds to the end of verse 19, and continued with verse 20. The scribe crossed out the גומל at the end of verse 18, inserted the reading צומח between two lines and added the complete verse 19 in the margin.

2. Corrective Vocalizations

Another characteristic of this manuscript is the sporadic use of vocalizations, some of which try to rectify an erroneous consonantal text, usually with three dots in the margin (see *infra*). For instance, in Sir 14:11, the form שרות is vocalized שֶׁרֵ(ו)ת, which requires the *waw* either to be ignored or read as a *yod*. Another example, in Sir 6:22, is even more complex and interesting.

כי המוסר כשמה כן הוא
ולא לרבים היא נְכוֹחָה:

For discipline, is like its name, so it (is)
It is not obvious to many[14]

13. In Sir 12:13, it is not really clear where the marginal correction עז is to apply (replacing שן?), in addition, the *'aïn* bears a double dot, which could indicate the reversal of the correction.

14. This sentence presents a number of difficulties (מוסר as feminine, the use of the masculine pronoun הוא), see Eric Reymond, "Wordplay in the Hebrew to Ben Sira," in *The Texts and Versions of the Book of Ben Sira: Transmission and Interpreta-*

As in the preceding example, the scribal vocalization does not fit the consonantal text. It presupposes a case of metathesis between *kaf* and *waw* and implies interpreting the form as a *niphal* feminine participle of יכח[15] with a meaning close to the *hiphil* "to appoint, to assign" (cf. Gen 24:14.44 "It is not appointed to many").[16] The *niphal* of יכח is rare in biblical Hebrew, although it is more frequent in medieval times. What is intriguing is that the consonantal text נְכוֹחָה has a perfectly legitimate spelling and meaning, "straight forwardness, honesty," also well attested in *piyyutim*.[17] The last two letters preserved in the tiny Qumran fragment 2Q18 3 8, כח[, are not really helpful, as they could represent the defective writing either of נָכֹחַ, נֹכַח, or נוֹכַח.[18] In any event, what is remarkable is that the scribe considered the consonantal text so sacred that he did not choose to modify it and preferred to use a vocalization to correct the text.[19] This practice is well attested in the Masoretic tradition.[20]

Some vocalizations are epexegetic and aim at clarifying an ambiguous consonantal word; for instance, אל תמצא in Sir 3:18 should be understood as אֵל תמצא "Before God, you will find." Some vocalizations seem to set the pronunciation or the meaning of rare words, as עשְׁתון in Sir 3:24 or מִמְדֻכְדָּךְ in Sir 4:8.

---

tion, ed. Jan Joosten and Jean-Sébastien Rey, JSJSup 150 (Leiden: Brill, 2010), 37–53, esp. 42, nn. 19 and 20.

15. Lévi suggests understanding the form as the substantive or the preposition נֹכַח "opposite," "in front" (Si 8:14^{A}; 31:16^{Bmg}; and 33:14^{E}), but it is difficult to explain the final *he* in this case.

16. See already W. Bacher, "Notes on the Cambridge fragments of Ecclesiasticus," *JQR* 12 (1900): 277.

17. See BDB, 647; and KBL, 660.

18. This masculine form imposes restoring in the lacuna a masculine pronoun, ולא לרבים הוא נ]כח, in agreement with the masculine pronoun of the preceding sentence, as suggested by Émile Puech, "Ben Sira and Qumran," in *The Wisdom of Ben Sira: Studies on Tradition, Redaction, and Theology*, ed. A. Passaro and G. Bellia (Berlin: de Gruyter, 2008), 81–82.

19. See also the case of בשְׁאֹתֿ in Sir 4:21. The dot on and under the *aleph* seems to indicate an erroneous letter, perhaps a scribal mistake under the influence of the following word משאת. But how to explain the dot on the *šin*? The *rafe* on the *tav* indicates the spirantization of the letter.

20. See, for instance, in Jos 10:1 the vocalization יְרוּשָׁלַםִ, which supposes ירושלים in the consonantal text, or the famous feminine pronoun הוא vocalized הִוא in the book of Genesis.

3. Vocalization and Accentuation

Sometimes the scribe put vocalization and accentuation on a whole verse for reasons we do not grasp, for instance, in Sir 9:3–4; Sir 10:2; Sir 11:6–8. Why these verses and not others? While vocalization is not limited to the biblical text in the Cairo Genizah manuscripts, we are yet justified in interpreting this practice as an indication of willingness to imitate the Masoretic text. It would seem to indicate a process of sacralization of the book of Ben Sira in the medieval period. The reality of this phenomenon may also find confirmation in a short note of Saadiah Gaon in the *Sepher Hagaluy*, where he defends himself against attacks by Karaites:[21]

> And when these wicked people saw that I had composed a book in Hebrew, divided into verses and provided with vowels and accents, they denounced me with mean slander, and said that this is pretension to prophecy (that is, they accused him to the ambition to imitate the Scriptures).... But this is only their folly, ... for these things (the dividing of a Hebrew book into verses and providing it with vowels and accents) any man can do, as, indeed, Ben Sira did, Ben Iri, the sons of the Hasmonaeans, and the Bene Africa, but none of them pretended to prophecy.[22]

This controversy states clearly that the text of Ben Sira existed already, with vocalization and accentuation, outside Karaite circles, and shows also that, in this period, vocalization was felt to be linked to imitation of Scriptures and ambition towards prophecy.

Concerning the use of *ṭeʿamim*, the signs employed are close to the Masoretic punctuation, but the scribe does not seem to have followed exactly the same rules. He basically used the *atnaḥ* and two accents drawn in the form of an arc of a circle, or simply a line slanted to the right or the left, either over (*pašṭa, azla, gereš*) or under the letter (*tifha, mereka*). This arc is sometimes angular, resembling a *munaḥ* when it precedes the *atnaḥ*. In 11:6–8, the scribe also used a vertical line similar to the *meteg* or to the *silluq*, but which does not seem to have the same functions. Finally, some letters have a *rafé* over the *begadkefat* and the final quiescent *he*.

---

21. S. ben Josef, *Sefer Ha-galuy*, ed. A. E. Harkavy (St. Petersburg: Berlin, 1891).

22. Quoted by Solomon Schechter, "A Fragment of the Original Text of Ecclesiasticus," *The Expositor* 4 (1900): 3.

The use of Masoretic punctuation in this text is quite characteristic insofar as it is usually limited to the biblical text, to Targum manuscripts, especially Targum Onqelos, and to some manuscripts of the Mishnah and of other rabbinic literature. Accents are also used occasionally in *piyyuṭim* texts.[23]

In addition to the Tiberian accentuation, on two occasions, Sir 11:25 and 15:14, the text presents intriguing superscript letters. In Sir 11:25, four letters are written in superscript:

טובַ[ת] יום[ט] תְשַׁכַּח רעׄהׄ[ה]
ורעת עׄתׄ תשׁׄכח טובׄהׄ
ואחרית אד[ד]ם תהיה עליו:

A day of happiness makes misfortune be forgotten
And a time of misfortune makes happiness be forgotten
but the end of a man will be upon him.

The *tav* on טוב might, of course, be a correction for טובת יום to conform to רעת עת in the second sentence, and the *he* on רעה might be a correction for the article, but how could one understand the *ṭet* on יום, or the *dalet* on אדם? The same problem is found in Sir 15:14, where it is hard to explain the *ṭet* on מבראשית and the *ḥet* on אדם (see plate 1):

אלהים מבראשׁית[ט] ברא אד[ח]ם

It seems probable that these signs reflect Babylonian accentuation,[24] but the scribe seems not to have understood this system fully.[25] They all correspond to Babylonian accents, except the *he* of רעה, which could translate

23. Israel Yeivin, *Introduction to the Tiberian Masorah*, trans. and ed. E. J. Revell, MasS 5 (Missoula: Scholars Press, 1980), §180.

24. I wish to thank B. Outhwaite, who first suggested this type of answer to me, as well as Ronit Shoshany for her help. I am entirely indebted to them for this solution.

25. On the Babylonian accentuation see Ronit Shoshany, "Biblical Accents: Babylonian," in *Encyclopedia of Hebrew Language and Linguisticsm*, ed. G. Khan (Leiden: Brill, 2013), 268–75; Shoshany, "Babylonian Accentuation System: Rules Of Division and Accentuation, Stages of Development, and Relationship to the Tiberian System" [Hebrew] (PhD diss.; Tel-Aviv University, 2003); Israel Yeivin, "The Accentuation of Texts of the Oral Law" [Hebrew], *Leshonenu* 24 (1960): 47–69, 167–78, 207–31.

a *mappiq* in the Babylonian vocalization,[26] although that is not adapted to the present case, or to a supra-linear correction for the article. This sort of mix of Tiberian vocalization and accentuation with Babylonian accentuation is also attested in some biblical manuscripts of the Cairo Genizah (see, e.g., most of the fragments catalogued in the T-S AS 62 binder, as 62.240; 62.243; 62.259).[27] Here again, this trait seems to indicate that the copyist regarded the text of Ben Sira as sacred as the biblical text.

4. Punctuation

The scribe used several systems of punctuation: two super-posited dots (*sof passuq*), a suspended dot, some *vacat* (see 4:11, which indicates the beginning of the passage 4:11–19 concerning wisdom), one or another indentation: Sir 6:1; 11:31; 13:2 (following an empty end-of-line). Although the first *vacat* does, in fact, correspond to the beginning of a passage, that is not true of the following two.[28] It is hard to find coherence or hierarchy among these various systems of punctuation. It is also noteworthy that several times this punctuation is badly placed (see 12:14; 12:15; 13:18; 14:16; 16:16).

5. *Ketiv* and *Qere*

Another indication of this sacralization of the text could be found in Sir 8:2, where the marginal note fits the Masoretic *ketiv* and *qere* precisely: a circellus on the *ketiv* (לא), and the *qere* (לו) written in the margin. This practice demonstrates the scribe's desire not to modify the consonantal text he is copying, considering this text sacred and immutable, even though it is found erroneous.[29] The use of *ketiv* and *qere* illustrates perfectly the will to imitate the biblical text.

26. Geoffrey Kahn, "Vocalization, Babylonian," in *Encyclopedia of Hebrew Language and Linguistics*, ed. G. Khan (Leiden: Brill, 2013), 953–63, esp. 956.

27. See Malcolm C. Davis and Ben Outhwaite, *Taylor-Schechter Additional Series 32-255 with Addenda to Previous Volumes*, vol. 4 of *Hebrew Bible Manuscripts in the Cambridge Genizah Collections* (Cambridge: Cambridge University Press, 2003), ix, 406ss.

28. See Schechter and Taylor, *Wisdom of Ben Sira*, 10.

29. Lévi does not attribute this phenomenon to a process of sacralization but to the willingness of the scribe to show his erudition: "le scribe peut avoir voulu simplement faire admirer son érudition en se servant, pour cette correction, de la lettre qui

6. Dating and Identification of the Scribe

The last point I want to consider is the paleographical dating of the manuscript and the identification of the scribe. When consulting the catalogue of dated manuscripts from the Cairo Genizah published by Malachi Beit-Arié, Colette Sirat and Mordechai Glatzer,[30] I was pleasantly surprised to notice that the square or semi-square oriental script of this manuscript was quite similar to at least two other manuscripts of the Genizah (T.S. F3.29 and EBP.-AP. I 2889).[31] These latter each have a colophon with the date (1089/90 and 1091 respectively) and the name of the scribe or the person for whom the copy was made, that is, Abraham ben Rabbi Shabbetaï.

Colophon T-S F3.29 (1089/90) (see plate 2)

נשלם זה הדיפתר לאברהם ברבי שבתי תֹנֹצֹבֹהֹ בשנת דֹתֹתֹנֹ
הֹקֹבֹהֹ יזכהו ללמוד וללמד לשמור ולעשות ויזכה לשמוח בשמחת ביאת
הגוׄא ויתן חלקו עם מצוקי ארץ וינחילהו שני עולמות כדכתֹ
כי בי ירמו[32] ימיך ויוסיפו לך שנות חיים:

This book [*diftar*] has been completed for Abraham b. R. Shabbetaï—may his life be bound in the bundle of the living (1 Sam 25:29)!—in the year 4850 (of the creation of the world). May the Holy One—Blessed be He—give him the merit to learn, teach, fulfill, and execute [the commandments], may He give him the merit to rejoice in the joy of the coming of the Liberator, may He give him his share with the pillars of the earth and may He grant him both worlds as inheritance, as it is said:

---

justement accompagne une faute du même genre dans la Bible (voir, entre autre, Isaïe, 63, 9)" (Lévi, *L'Ecclésiastique*, vii), while in the next paragraph he understands the vocalization and punctuation as an imitation of the Bible by what he calls a "pseudo-Massoret."

30. Colette Sirat, Mordechai Glatzer, Malachi Beit-Arié, eds., *Codices Hebraicis litteris exarati quo tempore scripti fuerint exhibentes, Tome III de 1085 à 1140* (Turnhout: Brepols, 2002).

31. The codicological description of both witnesses is provided by Sirat, Glatzer, Beit-Arié, *Codices Hebraicis*, 32; 42; see also Malachi Beit-Arié, ed., *Oriental and Yemenite Scripts*, vol. 1 of *Specimens of Mediaeval Hebrew scripts*, in collaboration with Edna Engel and Ada Yardeni (Jerusalem: The Israel Academy of Sciences and Humanities, 1987), pl. xxxiv. The attribution of these three manuscripts to a same scribe was already noticed, independently, by Engel (*Codices Hebraicis litteris Exarati*, 32).

32. Correct in ירבו.

"For through me, your days will be increased and years be added to your life" (Pr 9,11).[33]

Colophon EBP.-AP. I 2889, f. 12r (1091)

אני אברהם ברבי שבתי תֹּנֹצֹבֹהֹ כתבתי זה האגרון
לעצמי בצור מדינתא המקום בֹהֹ ישימהו עלי סימן טוב
סימן ברכה וחיסנא ויקירא ורחמי מן קדם שמייא ויתן
וימלא שאלותי ברצון ונשלם האות העשירי ~~בשנת~~
שהוא אות י׳ בשנת דֹתֹתֹנֹאֹ לביריתיה דעלמא בירח אדר הרחמן
אדר ראשון בכ֗ז יום בו
ישמור צאתי ובואי ויצילני מבני אדם הרעים ומאורב בדרך
וכן יהי רצון:

I, Abraham b. R. Shabbetaï,—May my life be bound in the bundle of the living (1 Sam 25:29)—, wrote this book Agron for my personal use in the city of Tyre. May God (ha-Maqom)—Blessed be He!—place on me a favourable sign, a sign of benediction, protection, wealth and divine mercy, may He give and accomplish with favour my requests. [Here] ends the letter 10 which is the letter *yod* of the year 4851 of the creation of the world, in the first month of Adar, the 27th of the month. May the Merciful One keep me in my going out and in my coming in, and may He protect me from evil people and from the dangers of highway thieves. May that be His will.[34]

The colophon of T-S F3.29 gives Abraham b. R. Shabbetaï as he for whom the copy was made, without naming the scribe; however, the following colophon (EBP.-AP. I 2889 f12r), which is written by the same hand, says that Abraham copied the manuscript for his own use. However, the manuscript T-S F3.29 presents two different hands. The first hand (see the first folio) seems to be the same as the two letters written by Abraham ben R. Shabbetaï (see T-S. 32.8 ; T-S. 13J13.20), while the last folio (with the colophon) is not by the same hand, which shows that he employed a scribe for one or the other of the documents (or for both).

33. Trans. from *Codices Hebraicis litteris Exarati*, 32.
34. Trans. from *Codices Hebraicis litteris Exarati*, 42.

This identification is especially interesting in that this Abraham b. R. Shabbetaï is also known by at least two letters (T-S 32.8 and T-S 13J13.20).[35] The data allow us to form an idea of this rabbanite who must have studied at the Palestinian Academy in Tyre, where there was a dynamic Jewish community.[36] He would have received the title of *ḥaver*, before going to Egypt and becoming *dayyan*, judge, in the city of Minyat Zifta.[37] This information lets us place the copy of manuscript A with precision and certainty at the end of the eleventh or the beginning of the twelfth century. In addition, it clearly shows how important the book of Ben Sira and its transmission were in rabbanite, and not (only) in Karaite, circles in Palestine and Egypt at that time

7. Conclusion

The unusual presence at both Qumran and the Genizah of the Damascus Document, Ben Sira, the Aramaic Testament of Levi, and the Hebrew text of Tobit has induced researchers to try to explicate the links between the two sites. Using the letter from the Patriarch Timothy I to Sergius the

---

35. See Jacob Mann, *The Jewish in Egypt and in Palestine under the Fāṭimid Caliphs: A Contribution to Their Political and Communal History Based Chiefly on Genizah Material Hitherto Unpublished*, 2 vols. (Oxford: Oxford University Press, 1970), 1:212–13 and 2:258–59. Mann also found Abraham ben Shabbetaï's signature on a bifolio (T-S 10J27.3) mentioning the engagement of Joseph Hallevi ben Berakot to a young lady from Cairo in the month of Sivan 1418 Sel. (= 1107). Finally, Mann also mentions a contract dated in the month of Av 1465 Sel. (= 1154) in Minyat Zifta and signed by the son of Abraham ben Shabbetaï (Bodl. 2874.22). See also Jacob Mann, *Texts and Studies in Jewish History and Literature*, 2 vols. (Cincinnati: Hebrew Union College; Philadelphia: Jewish Publication Society of America, 1935), 446–47; see also the rich description of Abraham ben Shabbetaï by Shlomo D. Goitein, *The Community*, vol. 2 of *A Mediterranean Society: The Jewish Communities of the World as Portrayed in the Documents of the Cairo Geniza* (Berkley: University of California Press, 1971), 47–48.

36. This explains the relatively high number of documents from Tyre preserved in the Cairo Genizah (see Moshe Gil, *A History of Palestine, 634–1099* [Cambridge: Cambridge University Press, 1992], §298, 186–88). These same documents show that although inferior in numbers to the rabbanites, the Karaite community was active and politically important (Judith Olszowy-Schlanger, *Karaite Marriage Documents from the Cairo Geniza: Legal Tradition and Community Life in Mediaeval Egypt and Palestine*, [Leiden: Brill, 1998], 56).

37. Mann, *Jewish in Egypt and in Palestine*, 1:212–13 and 2:258–59.

Metropolite of Elam, Paul Kahle and others following him[38] framed the hypothesis that the texts in the Genizah came from manuscripts found in the beginning of the ninth century in a cave near Jericho, probably at Qumran. According to Kahle they would have been collected by the Jerusalem Karaites—which would be confirmed among others by the testimony of the Karaite *Jaʿaqūb al Qirqisāni*—who would have copied and circulated them within their movement, landing them finally in the Cairo Genizah. This hypothesis was warmly received by the research community,[39] although it was criticized by some.[40] Stefan C. Reif justifiably maintains that there is no special reason for the Karaites to have had more interest than the rabbanites for these texts that are not directly tied to the Torah. Reif considers it quite possible that these texts were transmitted without interruption, within minority Jewish groups, from the Hellenistic period to the Middle Ages, when they were consigned to the Genizah.[41] In any case, the attribution of this manuscript to Abraham Ben R. Shabbetaï

38. Several studies appeared at more or less the same time. The first one who made the connection between Eusebius, the letter of Timothy I and the caves of Qumran was Otto Eissfeld, "Der gegenwärtige Stand der Erforschung der in Palästina neu gefundenen hebräischen Handschriften," *TLZ* 74 (1949): 595–600. The next year, following Eissfeld, Roland de Vaux, "À propos des manuscrits de la mer Morte," *RB* 57 (1950): 417–29, made the connection that he owes to one of his student, Dominique Barthélémy, "Notes en marge de publications récentes sur les Manuscrits de Qumrân," *RB* 59 (1952): 187–218, with Qirqisāni and Al-Biruni. The next year, in 1951, Paul Kahle made the link between the discoveries of the Qumran Scrolls, the Karaites and the Cairo Genizah,"The Age of the Scrolls," *VT* 1 (1951):38–48; and Kahle, *The Cairo Geniza*, 2nd ed. (Oxford: Blackwell, 1959), 13–18. After him, see especially Naphtali Wieder, *The Judean Scrolls and Karaism*, 2nd ed. (Jerusalem: Ben-Zvi Institute, 2005); André Paul, *Ecrits de Qumran et sectes juives aux premiers siècles de l'Islam: Recherches sur l'origine du Qaraïsme* (Paris: Letouzey et Ané, 1969); Yoram Erder, "When Did the Karaites First Encounter Apocryphic Literature Akin to the Dead Sea Scrolls?" [Hebrew], *Cathedra* 42 (1987): 54–68 and 85–86. Erder, *The Karaite Mourners of Zion and the Qumran Scrolls: On the History of an Alternative to Rabbinic Judaism* [Hebrew] (Tel Aviv: Hakibbutz Hameuchad, 2004).

39. See especially Alexander A. Di Lella, *The Hebrew Text of Sirach: A Text-Critical and Historical Study* (The Hague: Mouton, 1966).

40. H. Ben-Shammai, "Some Methodological Notes concerning the Relationship between the Karaites and Ancient Jewish Sects" [Hebrew], *Cathedra* 42 (1987): 69–84.

41. Stefan C. Reif, "The Genizah and the Dead Sea Scrolls: How Important and Direct Is the Connection?," in *The Dead Sea Scrolls in Context: Integrating the Dead Sea Scrolls in the Study of Ancient Texts, Languages, and Cultures*, ed. A. Lange, E. Tov, and M. Weigold, VTSup 140 (Leiden: Brill, 2011), 673–91, esp. 691.

leaves no doubt that the text of Ben Sira circulated in rabbanite circles in the eleventh–twelfth centuries, as does also the interest that Saadiah Gaon, and before him the rabbinic tradition, had for it. These objective data let us affirm that, in the current state of our knowledge, the diffusion of the book of Ben Sira is in fact more evident in rabbanite circles than in Karaite ones. If, however, one accepts the hypothesis of manuscripts found in the time of Timothy I, it is still possible to suggest that they may just as well have been preserved and copied by rabbanites, who found in them an important testimony to rabbinic tradition, rather than by Karaites. In addition, our analysis of the scribal practices shows that the Ben Sira text, in spite of being noncanonical, seems to have undergone in medieval times a real process of sacralization. The scribe of manuscript A paid special attention to the text he was transmitting, and many signs indicate that he tended to consider it on the same level as the biblical text, in particular, the refusal to modify an erroneous consonantal text, corrected by vocalization or by using *ketiv* and *qerê*, and the use of Tiberian and also Babylonian vocalization and punctuation. There remains however an important question: if the book of Ben Sira elicited such interest, how can one explain why the Hebrew text again disappeared from circulation after the twelfth century, though it remained a major element of later traditions.

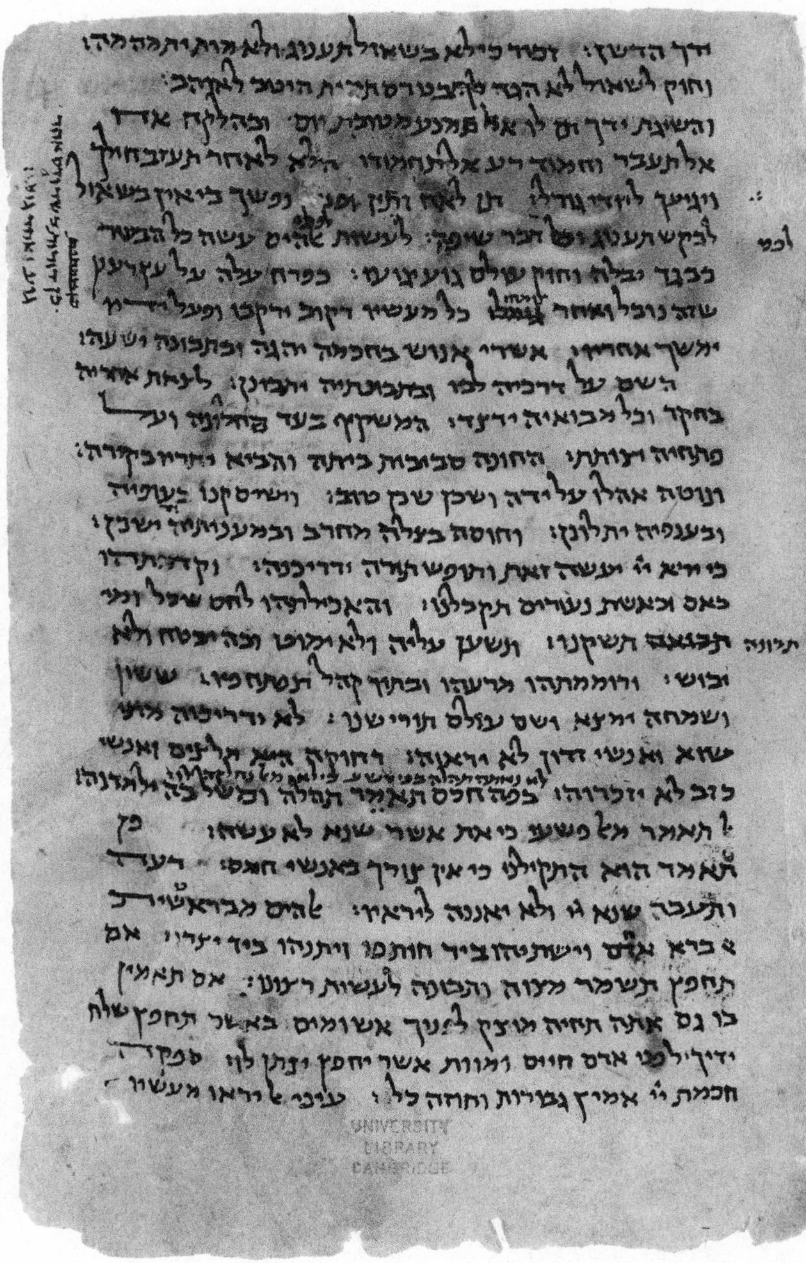

Plate 1. TS 12.863 recto. MS A. Sir 14:11–15:19. With the kind permission of the Taylor-Schechter Genizah Research Unit and the Syndics of Cambridge University Library.

שעה שבאו ואמרו לך משבאן מת מצוה נטרפה דעתי ואמרתי
עכשיו ועמד מר ואמר עכשיו יעמוד מר אמ׳ לו תן דעתך ואשנה
לך שנה לו ארבע מאות פעמ׳ אחרות ולמד יצתה בת קול ואמרה
לו פרידא ארבע מאות שנים נוסיף על חייך או תרצה שתזכה
אתה ודורך לעולם הבא אמ׳ להן נבקש שנזכה אני ודורי לעולם
הבא אמ׳ להם הקב״ה תנו לו זו וזו אמ׳ ר׳ חסדא אין התורה
נקנית אלא בסימנין שנ׳ ולמדה את בני יש׳ שימה בפיהם אל
תיקרא ושימה אלא וסימנה בפיהם שמע רב תחליפא בר
מערבא ואמרה לפני ר׳ אבהו אמ׳ אנו מן המקרא הזה נלמד
אתו הציבי לך ציונים עשה לך ציונים לתורה ומנין שציון הזה
סימן הוא שנ׳ וראה עצם אדם ובנה אצלו ציון ר׳ אלעזר אומ׳ מן
המקרא הזה אמור לחכמה אחתי את ומודע לבינה תיקרא עשה
רבא אמ׳ עשאום מועדים לתורה
לך מועדים לתורה רבא היה לו קפידה עם רבא בר רב יוסף בר
חמא כשבא ערב יום הכפורים אמ׳ נלך לפייסו הלך ומצא שמש
שלו שהיה מוזג לו את הכוס אמ׳ לו תן לי שאמזגיהו לו מזג ונתן לו
כשטעמו אמ׳ מזיגה זו דומה למזיגה של רבא בר רב יוסף בר חמא
אומ׳ לו הוא הוא אמ׳ לו אל תשב עד שתפרש לי המקראות האלה
מאי דכת׳ וממדבר מתנה וממתנה נחליאל ומנחליאל במות ומבמות
הגיא אמ׳ לו כשעשה אדם את עצמו כמדבר הזה שהכל דשין אותו
תורה ניתנה לו במתנה שנ׳ וממדבר מתנה וכיון שנתנה לו במתנה
נחלו אל שנ׳ וממתנה נחליאל וכיון שנחלו אל עולה לגדולה שנ׳
ומבמות הגיא ומנחליאל במות ואם הגיס דעתו עליו הקב״ה
משפילו שנ׳ ומבמות הגיא וג׳ אם חוזר בתשובה הקב״ה מגביהו
שנ׳ ונשקפה על פני הישימון:

נשלם זה הדיפתר לאברהם בירבי שבתי תנצב״ה בשנת דתתנ״ג
הקב״ה יזכהו ללמוד וללמד לשמור ולעשות ויזכה לשמוח בשמחת ביאת
הגואל ויתן חלקו עם מצוקי ארץ וינחילהו שני עולמות כדכת׳
כי בי ירבו ימיך ויוסיפו לך שנות חיים:

Plate 2. TS F3.29 verso. With the kind permission of the Taylor-Schechter Genizah Research Unit and the Syndics of Cambridge University Library.

The Literary and Linguistic Subtlety of the Greek Version of Sirach

James K. Aitken

The Greek version of Sirach is a complex work. Henry St.-J. Thackeray originally classified the translation as reflecting "indifferent Greek,"[1] perhaps acknowledging both the style of the Greek and the translation technique. In addition, the now standard study of Benjamin G. Wright established the high degree of consistency in the translation.[2] Despite this, there is subtlety and elegance in the Greek that suggest an experienced translator,[3] and within the consistency there can be detected occasional modifications and reordering of words in the book.[4] For the most part, the translator was consistent in segmentation and quantitative representation of elements in the Hebrew, following the word order of the Hebrew as far as possible. We can use as an example of this Sir 3:30:

אש לוהטת יכבו מים כן צדקה תכפר חטאת:

1. Henry St.-J. Thackeray, *Introduction, Orthography and Accidence*, vol. 1 of *A Grammar of the Old Testament in Greek according to the Septuagint* (Cambridge: Cambridge University Press, 1909), §2.

2. Benjamin G. Wright, *No Small Difference: Sirach's Relationship to its Hebrew Parent Text*, SCS 26 (Atlanta: Scholars Press, 1989).

3. James K. Aitken, "The Literary Attainment of the Translator of Greek Sirach," in *The Texts and Versions of the Book of Ben Sira: Transmission and Interpretation*, ed. Jan Joosten and Jean-Sébastien Rey, JSJSup 150 (Leiden: Brill, 2011), 95–126. Wright, *No Small Difference*, also recognized that there was variety in the choice of equivalents.

4. Cf. A. Minisalle, *La versione greca del Siracide: Confronto con il testo ebraico alla luce dell'attività midrascica e del metodo targumico*, AB 133 (Rome: Pontifical Biblical Institute, 1995).

πῦρ φλογιζόμενον ἀποσβέσει ὕδωρ, καὶ ἐλεημοσύνη ἐξιλάσεται ἁμαρτίας.

A blazing fire water will extinguish, and charity will atone for sins.[5]

The Greek equivalents are what might be expected for the Hebrew words, especially when compared to the other Septuagint translations. Significantly the word order follows precisely that of the Hebrew, and each element in Hebrew has an equivalent element in Greek, without any addition of an article or particle. The translation thus maintains strict equivalence in this verse. The one minor unexpected element is the choice of *καί* for כן "thus," but this is a tolerable translation even if we do not presume the *Vorlage* contained a *waw*. It is also an equivalent that still maintains the one-to-one word correspondence.

Wright demonstrated the consistency in word order and quantitative elements through a statistical analysis using the CATSS database.[6] He also was able to show that the translator was largely independent of the translations of other books in the Septuagint and did not make explicit allusions to biblical books through the use of their Septuagint versions.[7] Overall, Wright's assessment is that the value of the Greek for reconstructing the Hebrew is fairly low, since there are moments when the translator is independent both in his departure from standard Septuagint equivalents and in his varying in his rendering of his Hebrew *Vorlage*.[8] Therefore, for Wright the consistency does not represent reliability for Hebrew reconstruction. As a result the Greek text cannot be reduced to simple classification or description.

Our appreciation of the Greek of Sirach has perhaps been unduly influenced by Thackeray's classification. The heading "Indifferent Greek" (group 2) in his *Septuagint Grammar* classifies Sirach along with the Minor

5. All English translations of Greek Sirach are taken from the NETS translation, produced by Benjamin G. Wright for Sirach.

6. Wright, *No Small Difference*.

7. Ibid., 119–230.

8. Benjamin G. Wright, "Preliminary Thoughts about Preparing the Text of Ben Sira for a Commentary," in *Die Septuaginta—Text, Wirkung, Rezeption, 4. Internationale Fachtagung veranstaltet von Septuaginta Deutsch (LXX.D), Wuppertal, 19–22 Juli 2012*, ed. W. Kraus and S. Kreuzer, WUNT 325 (Tübingen: Mohr Siebeck, 2014), 100–104.

Prophets, Chronicles, Psalms, and Judith, and OG portions of Kingdoms, Jeremiah, and Ezekiel.[9] For Thackeray the translation is not as extreme as the *kaige* group, but it does not have the literary quality of the Pentateuch, Isaiah, or Joshua. The problem with Thackeray's classifications are that they are based on the imprecise term "style," which he specifies as the literary quality of the Greek combined with the degree of faithfulness to the Hebrew.[10] When he classes books as heading in the direction of pedantic literalism, he is focusing on translation technique and not the literary quality of the Greek. That the two can be separated—translation technique from literary style—shall be seen below. The problem is that we can be blinded by the translation technique to evaluate the literary nature of the Greek negatively, and certain aspects of translation technique can then obscure other aspects. There are undoubtedly oddities pertaining to the translation method, but these should not obscure the literary elements and sophistication within the translation.[11] Accordingly, the Greek version of Sirach offers a challenge to traditional interpretations of translation method and invites us to reconsider our categories of the conceptualisation of books.[12]

In an earlier study I drew attention to the literary features of the Greek Sirach, which revealed both the register in which he chose to compose his translation and the sophistication of his translation methods.[13] These indicated that the translator's proficiency in Greek was high and that his intended style of translation should not to be reduced to the relation to the *Vorlage* alone. In other words, there are assessments to be made of his Greek that are independent of the translation technique itself. Building upon this work, I shall examine some additional features of the translation that demonstrate the complexity of the translation and illuminate its literary qualities. From this, some further observations may be made regarding the social status of the translator himself.

9. Thackeray, *Grammar*, §2.

10. Ibid., §2, pp. 6, 9.

11. Wright tends to prioritize translation features and the degree of interference from the source text in his descriptions of the translation. See his "Translation Greek in Sirach in Light of the Grandson's Prologue," in Joosten and Rey, *Texts and Versions of the Book of Ben Sira*, 90–93.

12. For criticisms of Thackeray's classification of Sirach, see Aitken, "Literary Attainment," 113; and (on the classification of LXX Isaiah) John A. L. Lee, "The Literary Greek of Septuagint Isaiah," *Semitica et Classica* 7 (2014): 135–46.

13. Aitken, "Literary Attainment."

1. Variation

We saw above in the example of Sir 3:30 that the translation can follow closely the Hebrew structure of the verses. At the same time consistency can incorporate within it lexical variation. For, in the very next verse, Sir 3:31, we find this translation:

פועל טוב יקראנו בדרכיו ובעת מוׄטו ימצא משען:

ὁ ἀνταποδιδοὺς χάριτας μέμνηται εἰς τὰ μετὰ ταῦτα
καὶ ἐν καιρῷ πτώσεως εὑρήσει στήριγμα.

He who repays favors gives thought to what comes after,
and at the moment of a fall he will find support. (Sir 3:31)

Once more word order and quantitative equivalence are maintained, but almost every word is translated by a surprising or nonstandard equivalent. Listed below are the Greek equivalents to the Hebrew from this verse, along with the equivalents to the same Hebrew lexemes as they appear elsewhere in Sirach. Except for the unsurprising מצא~ εὑρίσκω, the equivalents in 3:31 are unique within Sirach.

- פעל ~ ἀνταποδιδοὺς: ἐργάτης (19:1); ποιέω (32:19); σύγκειμαι (43:26)
- טוב ~ χάριτας: ἀγαθός (7:19; 10:27; 11:12, 14, 31; 13:24, 25, 26; 14:25; 16:3; 20:31; 26:1, 3; 30:14, 17; 25; 33:14, 22; 37:18; 39:25, 33; 40:28; 41:15; 42:14; 51:21); εὖ (12:1); εὐσεβής (12:4; 33:14; 39:27); κάλος (39:16; 41:2; 46:10); λαμπρός (31:23); πιστός (33:3); φίλος (37:5); ἀρεστός (48:2)
- קרא ~ μέμνηται: εἰμί (4:10); καλέω (5:14; 36:11); ὑπαντάω (12:17); ἐπικαλέω (46:5; 47:5, 18)
- דרך ~ τὰ μετὰ ταῦτα: ἀτραπός (5:9); ὁδός (6:26; 14:21; 16:20; 32:20, 21; 33:11; 37:9; 48:22; 49:9); ἔρημον (8:16); ἔργον (10:6; 32:23); ταραχή (11:34); τελευτή (46:20)
- מוט ~ πτώσεως: ἐκκλίνω (12:15); κλίνω (15:4); σαλεύω (13:21a); πίπτω (13:2b); ὑποκρίνομαι (33:2)
- מצא ~ εὑρίσκω: γινώσκω (6:27); εὑρίσκω (3:18; 6:14, 28; 11:19; 12:2, 16, 17; 15:6; 31[34]:8; 40:18; 42:1, 17, 20, 23; 51:16, 20, 27); καταλαμβάνω (11:10); κληρονομέω (4:13); παραμένω (6:10)

► משען ~ στήριγμα: ἀνάπαυσις (36:29[24]); βοήθεια (40:26)

The example of this one verse, coming as it does after a verse that maintains regular and quantitative equivalence, demonstrates the surprising inconsistency in the translation. The translator drew on a wide range of options for translating each of the Hebrew words and did not maintain a regular consistency in his choice of equivalences. Thus, while consistency on the level of word order and quantity are maintained, consistency in the choice of equivalence is not, and one aspect of so-called literalism is not maintained. Nevertheless, such variation is counterbalanced by a frequent repetition of translation equivalents. For example, in the twelve appearances of *καὶ γάρ* as a conjunction, it seems to render no less than six different Hebrew conjunctions: וגם (49:9, 19; 38:12?), גם כי (37:8[?]; 38:12, 14), גם כי (38:1), כי (32:23), כי (8:6), and אשר (8:9). It is possible that in some cases the *Vorlage* for the translator was the same, since the addition of a *waw* or the reversal of the order of the pair גם כי is the sort of variation that would occur in the manuscript tradition.[14] Even so, the variety of the Hebrew is significant enough that we can assume some repetition on the part of the translator is likely. The many cases of variation can be said to arise from the literary sensitivity of the translator who seems to have displayed a level of literary education higher than many of the translators.

2. Prepositive Enclitic Pronouns

This view of the literary sophistication of the translator can be confirmed by a grammatical feature. In Hebrew grammar object pronouns and possessive pronouns are indicated by pronominal suffixes. This generates in the Septuagint a standard translation whereby the pronoun follows the verb or the noun. Thus, we commonly see examples such as this:

> ἐὰν ἀποπλανηθῇ, ἐγκαταλείψει αὐτὸν
> καὶ παραδώσει αὐτὸν εἰς χεῖρας πτώσεως αὐτοῦ.

> If he goes astray, she will abandon him
> and hand him over to the grip of his fall. (Sir 4:19)

14. For the problem of appearance or not of the *waw* in similar constructions, see James K. Aitken, "The Origins of *καί γε*," in *Biblical Greek in Context*, ed. J. K. Aitken and T. V. Evans, BiTS (Leuven: Peeters, 2015), 25–26.

The presence of pronominal suffixes in the Hebrew (אשליכנו ואסגירנו לשדדים) results in the postpositive pronouns after the verb and the genitive after the noun, since the translation technique preserves word order.[15] The technique also leads to the unnecessary repetition of the object pronoun after each verb. Understandably this is a typical feature of those translations that adhere closely to their Hebrew source text (those in the *kaige* tradition).[16] In ancient Greek, however, it was standard to place the enclitic pronouns before the relevant verb or noun, and (following Wackernagel's Law) even to position it second in the clause where the opening word is heavily accented.[17] It has been shown that this tendency to using postpositive pronouns is a feature not unique to the Septuagint, but more common in vernacular Greek.[18] Therefore, not only is it a sign of the vernacular in the Septuagint, but it is brought into prominence by Septuagint translation technique, corresponding as it does to Hebrew suffixation. Consequently Mark Janse has drawn attention to the importance of prepositive enclitic pronouns, noting how significant it is that they appear at all in the Septuagint.[19] The translator had to choose the idiomatic word order and manage the subtleties of Greek grammar to implement Wackernagel's Law. In the case of Sirach we find many examples of prepositive enclitic pronouns. The following is illustrative of a fairly frequent phenomenon (e.g., Sir 5:10; 11:23; 13:29; 21:8; 27:3; 30:4; 46:11):

μήποτε ἀντιστήσῃ σου τὴν ὁλκήν·

lest he counter your weight (Sir 8:2)

The tendency to place the pronoun after the noun corresponding to the Hebrew suffix (מחירך) has been avoided, and we find instead a prepositive

15. Discussed by A. Wifstrand, "Die Stellung der enklitischen Personalpronomen bei den Septuaginta," *Årsberättelse, Kungl. Humanistiska Vetenskapssamfundet i Lund* (1949–1950): 44–70; Mark Janse, "Aspects of Bilingualism in the History of the Greek Language," in *Bilingualism in Ancient Society: Language Contact and the Written Text*, ed. J. N. Adams, M. Janse and S. Swain (Oxford: Oxford University Press, 2002), 379–83.

16. Wifstrand, "Die Stellung," 44–45.

17. Janse, "Aspects of Bilingualism," 380–81.

18. Ibid., 380.

19. Ibid., 381.

pronoun. In another example the prepositive pronoun comes second in the clause:

> *εἶπα Ποτιῶ μου τὸν κῆπον*
> *καὶ μεθύσω μου τὴν πρασιάν·*
>
> I said, "I will water my garden,
> and I will drench my flower bed." (Sir 24:31)

Although there is no Hebrew version preserved for this passage, it must have contained suffixes on the nouns and the pronouns are positioned before their governed nouns. It may be chance that the enclitics come second in the clause, but elsewhere the operation of Wackernagel's Law seems likely:

> *καὶ μὴ εἴπῃς Τίς με δυναστεύσει;*
> *ὁ γὰρ κύριος ἐκδικῶν ἐκδικήσει.*
> *μὴ εἴπῃς Ἥμαρτον, καὶ τί μοι ἐγένετο;*
> *ὁ γὰρ κύριός ἐστιν μακρόθυμος.*
>
> And do not say, "Who shall hold power over me?"
> For the Lord, when he punishes, will punish.
> Do not say, "I sinned, and what has happened to me?"
> For the Lord is longsuffering. (Sir 5:3–4)
>
> *μὴ εἴπῃς ὅτι Αὐτός με ἐπλάνησεν*
>
> Do not say, "It was he who led me astray" (Sir 15:12)

In this second example the emphatic pronoun *αὐτός* at the head of the clause has encouraged the positioning of the enclitic noun second. In Genesis it has been calculated that there are 65 examples of prepositive enclitic pronouns compared to 850 postpositives.[20] Janse suggests that this is indicative of the Pentateuch translators being native koine Greek speakers. One can compare this to one of the most literary translations of the Septuagint, the book of Job, where it has recently been shown that

---

20. Wifstrand, "Die Stellung," 50; Janse, "Aspects of Bilingualism," 380.

this translation with high literary pretensions avoids vernacular forms and seeks a higher register by using more prepositive enclitics.[21] The ratio in that translation of postpositive to prepositives is 665 to 210. For Sirach, A. Wifstrand has calculated that the ratio is similar to that of Isaiah and closer to Proverbs and Job than to the Pentateuch.[22] Therefore this high number of examples in Sirach indicate that the translator, despite aiming to preserve the word order of the Hebrew, has allowed his natural Greek usage to come through. In sum, this small grammatical feature can be used as an indicator of the Sirach translator's ease in Greek, a possible indication of his native language and certainly evidence of his sensitivity to the register of the language.[23]

3. Literary Awareness

Key to understanding Sirach is the prologue attached to the Greek. Wright has insightfully noted that the prologue is written in elegant Greek and therefore concluded that the apology "things translated do not sound the same" is for his translation Greek that follows.[24] Wright is quite correct that the prologue is in literary Greek, although to my mind the apology remains one for the modification of Hebrew into Greek, not for an internal Greek comparison, and is to be seen as a literary trope. Much of the prologue is rhetorical in intent and aimed at elevating the status of the translation rather than drawing attention to its deficiencies.[25] For as far as possible within the translation the translator has undertaken to produce Greek in as literary a fashion as the prologue; this can be seen if we identify the lexical choice, word-play and some rhetorical features, and if we distinguish these from the lexical consistency, word order and certain syntactic forms.

---

21. M. Dhont, "The Language and Style of Old Greek Job in Context" (PhD diss., Université catholique de Louvain and KU Leuven, 2016), 109.

22. Wifstrand, "Die Stellung," 56–58.

23. In a multilingual environment a native language need not indicate only one language and does not preclude fluency in other languages as well. A bilingual could have more than one native language.

24. Benjamin G. Wright, "Why a Prologue? Ben Sira's Grandson and His Translation," in *Emanuel: Studies in Hebrew Bible, Septuagint and Dead Sea Scrolls in Honor of Emanuel Tov*, ed. S. Paul, R. A. Kraft, L. H. Schiffman, W. Fields, VTSup 72 (Leiden: Brill, 2003), 633–44; Wright, "Translation Greek in Sirach," 76–83.

25. See Aitken, "Literary Attainment," 101–8.

The translator's intent and literary aspirations are highlighted from the opening of the prologue itself:

> Πολλῶν καὶ μεγάλων ἡμῖν διὰ τοῦ νόμου καὶ τῶν προφητῶν ...
>
> Many and great teachings [have been given to us] through the law and the prophets

The Greek rhetorical use of πολύς and its derivatives, providing both an emphasis on the importance of the topic and a pleasing alliteration on the letter *pi*, was a popular device in ancient Greek.[26] It would have been learned in any school room of antiquity. A comparable example with the same two adjectives πολύς and μέγας can been found in Demosthenes (fourth century BCE) in the opening of his second oration against Aphobus:

> Πολλὰ καὶ μεγάλ' ἐψευσμένου πρὸς ὑμᾶς Ἀφόβου ....
>
> Regarding the many and great lies that Aphobus made against you ... (2 *Aphob.* 1.1)

Closer to home we find a similar effect in the recently discovered Heliodorus stele from Maresha, a Seleucid decree regarding governance of temples in the province. The composer chose an opening to the decree that again emphasizes the importance of the topic through emphasis on the labour involved but also plays on the pleasing alliterative effect with the letter *pi*:

> πλείστην πρόνοιαν ποιούμενοι ...
>
> Taking the utmost consideration (l.14)[27]

---

26. For similar examples of openings, see Eduard Fraenkel, "Eine Anfangsformel attischer Reden," *Glotta* 29 (1961): 1–5; Loveday Alexander, *The Preface to Luke's Gospel: Literary Convention and Social Context in Luke 1.1–4 and Acts 1.1*, SNTSMS 78 (Cambridge: Cambridge University Press, 1993), 109.

27. Published in Hannah M. Cotton and Michael Wörrle, "Seleukos IV to Heliodoros: A New Dossier of Royal Correspondence from Israel," *ZPE* 159 (2007): 191–205.

This same phrase reappears in a number of other documents, indicating that it was a set expression taught in schools (e.g., *IG* 9.2.507 [ca. 130 BCE]; ID 1501 [148/7 BCE]; *IG* 12.5.653). The popularity of openings with words beginning with *pi* and the appearance of the same word combination in Sirach's prologue and in other literature, also suggest that his opening arises from school education.

The prologue of Sirach, after this emphatic opening, continues by using a range of terms typical of prologues, from the lovers of learning to the sleeplessness of production that place this within a literary rather than a factual tradition.[28] All these features serve to indicate that the prologue has a highly rhetorical stance; indeed the very existence of a prologue would imply this as it is a literary choice to include one. The features also show that the translator was familiar with the canons of Alexandrian literary style, and we should not take the self-effacement of the prologue too seriously as genuine concern but a typical literary conceit.

The translator's educational background is revealed not only in his careful choice of vocabulary but also in some surprising literary allusions too. One that has not been noted before is his translation from the Hebrew of the famous Homeric allusion. It is well-known that Ben Sira 14:18 (MS A) contains a proverb that seems to derive from Homer:[29]

כפרח עלה על עץ רענן / שזה נובל ואחר גומל {צומח}
כן דורות בשר ודם אחד גוע ואחד גומל

As leaves grow upon a green tree, Whereof one withereth, and another springeth up;
So of the generations of flesh and blood, One perisheth, and another ripeneth.[30]

The image is derived from a passage in Homer's *Iliad*:

28. Aitken, "Literary Attainment," 105–6.

29. Jack T. Sanders, *Ben Sira and Demotic Wisdom*, SBLMS 28 (Chico, CA: Scholars Press, 1983), 39.

30. Translation: S. Schechter and C. Taylor, *The Wisdom of Ben Sira: Portions of the Book Ecclesiasticus from Hebrew Manuscripts in the Cairo Genizah Fragments Presented to the University of Cambridge by the Editors* (Cambridge: University Press, 1899), xxx.

οἵη περ φύλλων γενεὴ τοίη δὲ καὶ ἀνδρῶν.
φύλλα τὰ μέν τ' ἄνεμος χαμάδις χέει, ἄλλα δέ θ' ὕλη
τηλεθόωσα φύει, ἔαρος δ' ἐπιγίνεται ὥρη:
ὣς ἀνδρῶν γενεὴ ἣ μὲν φύει ἣ δ' ἀπολήγει.

As is the generation of leaves, so is that of humanity.
The wind scatters the leaves on the ground, but the live timber
burgeons with leaves again in the season of spring returning.
So one generation of men will grow while another dies.[31] (*Il.* 6.146–149; cf. 21.463–466)

The precise history of transmission from *Il.* 6 to Ben Sira is no doubt complex, and we have no other evidence that the Hebrew author Ben Sira knew the text of Homer himself. Similar sentiments are already found in Job 14:7–10 where the dead are contrasted to trees planted by water. Jack Sanders was one who thought that there was a genetic relationship between the two texts, noting that "the manner of expression and the movement of thought in these two passages is strikingly similar."[32] He points to specific verbal connections, such as: פרח/φύλλον; עלה/τηλεθάω /φύω; צומח/φύω; דור/γενεά. It is true that, unlike Job, Ben Sira is similar in sentiment and phraseology to the Homeric passage, but that does not mean there has been a direct descent. It could have been a proverb widely circulating. It is intriguing, nonetheless, when we come to the Greek translation of this passage how it has been rendered.

ὡς φύλλον θάλλον ἐπὶ δένδρου δασέος,
τὰ μὲν καταβάλλει, ἄλλα δὲ φύει,
οὕτως γενεὰ σαρκὸς καὶ αἵματος,
ἡ μὲν τελευτᾷ, ἑτέρα δὲ γεννᾶται.

Like a sprouting leaf on a thickly leaved tree,
some it sheds, but others it puts forth;
so is a generation of flesh and blood,
the one dies and the other is born.

31. Translation: R. Lattimore, *The Iliad* (Chicago: University of Chicago Press, 1962).

32. Sanders, *Ben Sira and Demotic Wisdom*, 39.

In the translation there is both convergence and divergence regarding the words from the Homeric text. The words φύλλον, γενεά, and φύει agree with Homer, but δένδρον, δασύς, and καταβάλλω are different. What is most striking though is the second line: τὰ μὲν καταβάλλει, ἄλλα δὲ φύει. The Hebrew זה and אחר, singular as the rest of the verse, become plural in the Greek in the same manner as Homer, where the plural is demanded by the context. This is also one of only three places in the whole translation where the translator has used the contrastive μέν/δέ (elsewhere in 23:23 and 48:16), also a feature of the Homeric verse. The use of μέν/δέ is rare in post-classical Greek and especially so in the Septuagint since there is no equivalent in Hebrew for it (other than a simple *waw*).[33] Although it is not an unusual contrast, it does not conform to the grammar of the Hebrew at this point but is a feature of the Homeric verses. Indeed the Greek translation is closer to the sense of the Homeric passage too, turning the growth imagery into death and birth.

It is perhaps no surprise that this simile was known in antiquity since these Homeric lines did have some popularity in antiquity. They are paraphrased, for example, in one Attic inscription (*IG* 2.2.13147 = SEG 30.301) as an epitaph on a grave from the second or third century CE:

1 [ἀθάνατοι μὲν] ἔχουσιν ἀγήρα[τον βίον αἰεί],
[ὄλλυνται δ]ένδρων ὀλλυμ[ένων Δρυάδες]·
[οἷα δὲ φύλλα ζ]ῶσι βροτῶν [γενεαὶ ταχυπότμων]·
[κάτθαν᾽ Ἀλεξ]άνδραι ξυν[ὸς ὁ παῖς nomen]·
5 [ὤλετο πᾶσα ἐλ]πὶς καὶ ἐβλ[ήθη πᾶς κάτω οἶκος]·
[πᾶσαν γὰρ δ]αίμων ὤλ[εσεν εὐτυχίαν].

While immortals for ever have unaging life
The Dryads die when the trees die
Just as leaves so live generations of short-lived mortals
The boy PN died along with Alexandra
All hope is lost and the whole household is cast below
Since a spirit has destroyed all fortune

33. John A. L. Lee, "Some Features of the Speech of Jesus in Mark's Gospel," *NovT* 27 (1985): 1–13; James K. Aitken, "The Characterisation of Speech in the Septuagint Pentateuch," in *The Reception of the Hebrew Bible in the Septuagint and the New Testament: Essays in Memory of Aileen Guilding*, ed. D. J. A. Clines and J. C. Exum (Sheffield: Sheffield Phoenix, 2013), 28–29.

Book 6 of the *Iliad* was one of the more popular books to be read in the educational system, along with the other opening books of the Iliad and therefore would have been known to many literate Greeks.[34] These particular lines are quoted in a number of ancient writers and seem to have become popular as a proverb as the inscription attests. It is most often used as a source of the changeability of nature (Theophrastus, *Physicorum opinions* 12; Philo, *Aet.* 132; Marcus Aurelius, *Med.* 10.34). Allusions in other authors can also be identified.[35] One of the earliest uses of the Homeric lines as a simile on death appears to be in the sixth-century BCE poet Simonides (frag. 19; preserved by Stobaeus),[36] which has now also been preserved as a fragment in POxy 3965 frag. 26.[37]

> and one thing the Chian poet said that was finest of all:
> οἵη περ φύλλων γενεὴ τοίηδε καὶ ἀνδρῶν.
> Few men have taken that properly to heart,
> for they have (false) expectations,
> that grow naturally in the breasts of the young.[38]

It is likely that the translator knew something of this popular verse and at least had its ring in his ears if not the text of Homer himself.

A comparable example of how popular expressions can appear in translations is found in the Greek translation of Ecclesiastes, where a proverbial expression in Hebrew has brought to mind a Greek popular proverb. The translation of the biblical *hapax legomenon* שַׁחֲרוּת might generate some surprise for the reader:

כי־הילדות והשחרות הבל

for youth and youthfulness are vanity

---

34. See Teresa Morgan, *Literate Education in the Hellenistic and Roman Worlds* (Cambridge: Cambridge University Press, 1998), 308 (table 11), 320 (table 21).

35. David Sider, "As Is the Generation of Leaves in Homer, Simonides, Horace, and Stobaios," *Arethusa* 29 (1996): 263–82.

36. Martin L. West, "Simonides Redivivus," *ZPE* 98 (1993): 10–11.

37. On the debate regarding the identification of the author, see Thomas K. Hubbard, "'New Simonides' or Old Semonides? Second Thoughts on POxy 3965, FR. 26," *Arethusa* 29 (1996): 255–62.

38. Stobaeus, *Anth.* 19.1. Translation from West, "Simonides Redivivus," 11.

ὅτι ἡ νεότης καὶ ἡ ἄνοια ματαιότης

for youth and ignorance are vanity. (Eccl 11:10b)

The Hebrew noun is usually understood to denote young age,[39] especially given its pairing here with ילדות. On this understanding, the noun is a derivative of "black," denoting the colour of a young person's hair before the grey takes hold. Such is the understanding in rabbinic Hebrew (m. Ned. 3:8; Gen. Rab. 59), and accordingly adopted by Rashi.[40] The translator's choice of ἄνοια "ignorance" could be attributed to his own ignorance of the rare Hebrew term and his resorting to a conjecture in the context of a passage on vanity.[41] However, the pairing of νεότης and ἄνοια appears frequently enough in Greek literature that we might deem the pair proverbial. Thucydides was the first to speak of it, placing in the mouth of Alcibiades self-deprecation regarding his youthful enthusiasm:

> Καὶ ταῦτα ἡ ἐμὴ νεότης καὶ ἄνοια παρὰ φύσιν δοκοῦσα εἶναι ἐς τὴν Πελοποννησίων δύναμιν λόγοις τε πρέπουσιν ὡμίλησε καὶ ὀργῇ πίστιν παρασχομένη ἔπεισεν.
>
> So, in my youth and with this folly of mine which is supposed to be so prodigious, I found the right arguments for dealing with the power of the Peloponnesians, and the energy which I displayed made them trust me. (*P.W.* 6.17)[42]

Similar sentiments are expressed by Plato (*Leg.* 716a; cf. 934a) and Andocides (*On His Return* 7.2):[43]

---

39. For alternative interpretations, see Antoon Schoors, *The Preacher Sought to Find Pleasing Words: A Study of the Language of Qoheleth*, 2 vols. (Leuven: Peeters, 1992–2004), 2:468–69.

40. Rashi on Qoheleth. For scholarship, see Schoors, *Preacher*.

41. So Françoise Vinel, *L'Ecclésiaste: Traduction du texte grec de la Sepante, introduction et notes*, BA 18 (Paris: Cerf, 2002), 168.

42. Translation: Rex Warner, *Thucydides: History of the Peloponnesian War*, with an introduction and notes by M. I. Finley (London: Penguin, 1972), 420.

43. Cf. the comment in Sophocles, frag. 583.5: τερπνῶς γὰρ ἀεὶ παῖδας ἀνοία τρέφει.

> ὁ δέ τις ἐξαρθεὶς ὑπὸ μεγαλαυχίας, ἢ χρήμασιν ἐπαιρόμενος ἢ τιμαῖς, ἢ καὶ σώματος εὐμορφίᾳ ἅμα νεότητι καὶ ἀνοίᾳ φλέγεται τὴν ψυχὴν μεθ' ὕβρεως
>
> But anyone who is puffed up with boastfulness, or who feels exalted because of riches or honors or good bodily form accompanied by youth and mindlessness, anyone whose soul burns with insolence. (Plato, *Lrg.* 716a)[44]

Such sentiments become familiar enough in the post-classical period that the expression is used not only by those citing Plato (e.g., Plutarch, *Is. Os.* 360c) but by writers independently (Dionysius of Halicarnassus, *Ant. rom.* 2.26.3).

Therefore, rather than a mistranslation or conjecture, we have in the Greek of Ecclesiastes a fitting proverbial pairing. There is no semantic loss since the poetic and emphatic repetition in Hebrew of youth as a type of vanity is brought out all the more sharply in Greek, where youth is associated with ignorance and thereby the reason for its being vain is underscored. This suggests a translator fully aware of the meaning of the Hebrew but adept enough in Greek to produce a translation that draws out the meaning of the Hebrew clearly for a Greek audience and in a manner that would resonate on the literary level in the Greek ear. The same can be said for the translator of Sirach, who drew out the original allusion in Hebrew and made it more familiar for a Greek audience.

4. Rhetorical Features

In my earlier study I drew attention to some sophisticated word choices (such as the pun on εὐδία in Sir 3:15) and rhetorical features.[45] We find a further example of possible wordplay in a passage where the Hebrew is no longer extant, but where the prepositional prefixes in Greek draw attention to a word association that would not have been possible in Hebrew. In the midst of a section advising proper treatment to the oppressed and low in society, the widows are recalled:

---

44. Translation: Thomas L. Pangle, *The Laws of Plato* (Chicago: University of Chicago Press, 1988), 102.

45. Aitken, "Literary Attainment," 115–16, 118–21.

οὐχὶ δάκρυα χήρας ἐπὶ σιαγόνα καταβαίνει
καὶ ἡ καταβόησις ἐπὶ τῷ καταγαγόντι αὐτά;

Do not a widow's tears run down upon her cheek,
and is not her cry against the one who drew them down? (Sir 32[35]:18–19)

There is a phonetic similarity between the verb καταβαίνει and the rare noun (unique in the LXX here) καταβόησις "outcry," both sharing the same prefix and the letter *beta*. This play is strengthened by the following verb κατάγω "to draw down" that also includes the same prefix "down." Whether or not the translator was implying that the significance of crying is that things go down (tears and oneself), the associations unite the verse and tie together the two hemistichs.

The second topic of rhetoric has recently been the focus of much discussion in LXX studies,[46] and it can now be largely accepted as a recognized feature in Septuagint translations. Nevertheless, care needs to be exercised in its application. On the level of identifying tropes, it has to be shown that the Greek has not arisen by chance from choosing the standard translation equivalents to the Hebrew.[47] Once identified, the type and extent of rhetorical features need to be assessed. Some features are little more than euphony that represent the careful attention to sound of any native author. Other features, however, can be viewed as deliberate if they are of a more extensive nature and if they reflect known techniques in antiquity.

As an example of a significant rhetorical device, alliteration on the letter *pi* was a standard device in Greek writers, as was observed above. A passage from Pindar is one of the best illustrations of this:

ὃς Πριάμοιο πόλιν πέρσεν ,τελεύτασέν τε πόνους Δαναοῖς

who sacked the city of Priam and brought an end to the toils of the Danaans (Pindar, *Pyth.* 1.54)

46. See, for example, the essays in Eberhard Bons and Thomas J. Kraus, eds., *Et Sapienter et Eloquenter: Studies on Rhetorical and Stylistic Features of the Septuagint*, FRLANT 241 (Göttingen: Vandenhoeck & Ruprecht, 2011).

47. See the discussion in James K. Aitken, "Rhetoric and Poetry in Greek Ecclesiastes," *BIOSCS* 38 (2006): 58–61.

Greek Sirach, who already demonstrated his preference for *pi* alliteration in the opening of his prologue, opts for the alliteration in a popular fashion of a tricolon:

> ἔστιν ἀνὴρ πανοῦργος πολλῶν παιδευτής,
> καὶ τῇ ἰδίᾳ ψυχῇ ἐστιν ἄχρηστος.
>
> There exists a clever man who is an instructor of many,
> and to his own soul he is useless. (Sir 37:19)

The intentionality here is visible when the Hebrew of the first hemistich is compared:

> יש חכם לרבים נחכם
>
> There is a wise person who offers his wisdom to many

The rendering πανοῦργος, which has a negative sense of "crafty," is used as a translation for ערום elsewhere in the LXX (e.g., Prov 13:16; Job 5:12), while at Sir 22:17 it translates the verb ערם, the one other place where we have a Hebrew text preserved. Here in 37:19 by contrast it renders the positive חכם. It is possible that we reconstruct the Hebrew *Vorlage* of the Greek to read ערום, but the presence of the alliterative device in the Greek makes one consider differently, especially as the Hebrew text is confirmed by three witnesses among the Genizah manuscripts—manuscripts B, C, and D. Unable to render successfully the Hebrew wordplay on חכם into Greek, the translator produced a compensating equivalent of alliteration. Indeed the device leads to a modified sense in the Greek by comparison with the Hebrew. The Hebrew text contrasts a wise person who only appears wise in public but is a fool to himself, while the Greek contrasts a crafty individual that instructs many but who is unable to help himself. The nuance is different but in each case the meaning is clear.

There may be a similar alliteration on the letter *pi* at 21:12, but no Hebrew text is extant with which to compare.

> οὐ παιδευθήσεται ὃς οὐκ ἔστιν πανοῦργος,
> ἔστιν δὲ πανουργία πληθύνουσα πικρίαν.

He who is not clever shall not be instructed,
but there is a cleverness that increases bitterness. (Sir 21:12)

Once more in the second half of the verse there is a tricolon with alliteration on *pi*, which has been prepared for by two other words beginning with the letter in the first half of the verse.

The same passage in chapter 37 that contains the *pi* alliteration also displays other devices. In this same passage there are a number of sayings that begin with יש חכם "There is a wise man," and each appearance of חכם in succession is rendered in Greek differently: πανοῦργος, σοφιζόμενος, and σοφός (37:19, 20, 22). Such variation is a popular device in Greek and is found commonly in Greek Sirach. Thus, the Hebrew עבד "slave" in 33:26 is rendered by παῖς but then in the next verse, verse 27, by οἰκέτης. Features such as this are unsurprising but they are characteristic of the translator and represent the lack of a simple consistency in his translation method. That these features are well established in Greek compositions outside of the Septuagint supports the likelihood that this was an intentional literary device by the translator of Sirach.

5. Attention to Particles

Particles are an important indicator of a translator's method. The choice of particles in Hebrew are few, especially as much Hebrew coordination and subordination is marked by a simple *waw*. Greek has a far wider choice of particles and connectors so that even when Hebrew does use a specific particle other than *waw*, there are still more options available to a translator. Some particles will be of a decidedly literary nature and a sign of writing in a higher register too. Thus, in my earlier study I drew attention to the emphatic particle τοιγαροῦν, which is found once in Sirach (41:16) and only appears to be the equivalent of the Hebrew *waw* (MS B; reconstructed in Mas).[48] As a particle τοιγαροῦν is favoured amongst late Hellenistic writers, owing to a weakening in its strength, as seen in its placement second in the sentence (e.g., 4 Macc 9:7; 13:16; 17:4) or in its repetition in close succession (Prov 1:26, 31; cf. SEG 26.821). Its distribution in the Septuagint only in writings or translations of a higher literary level (2 Maccabees,

48. Aitken, "Literary Attainment," 113–14.

4 Maccabees, Proverbs, Job, and Isaiah) is evidence of Sirach's attempt at literary Greek.

Other examples were noted in that study of complex particles where a simpler one might have been chosen. For example, εἴτε in Sir 41:4 (*tris*) is striking since it is only found elsewhere in the Septuagint in the books of Joshua (24:15 *bis*), Job (9:21), and Isaiah (30:21 *bis*). The emphatic negative μηδέποτε appearing in Sir 19:7 is only attested elsewhere in the Septuagint in 3 Maccabees (3:16; 7:4, 11). More significant still is the LXX *hapax legomenon* μήπως (Sir 28:26), a particle that seems to have an epic flavour to it, since it is common in Homer, Hesiod, and Aesop, although occasional too in Plato. It is notable that it is taken up by Apollonius Rhodius in the Hellenistic period in his attempt to imitate Homeric epic style. Whether or not it was distinctly epic, it was rare in prose and therefore would have been marked. The same may be said for the introduction of the particle γε at Sir 34(31):12, for which there is no equivalent in Hebrew.

One oversight was my statement that the translator did not use the forward-pointing particle τε "both."[49] It does in fact appear first in his prologue, where we might expect more natural literary Greek (Sir Prol. 7–9):

> ὁ πάππος μου Ἰησοῦς ἐπὶ πλεῖον ἑαυτὸν δοὺς [8] εἴς τε τὴν τοῦ νόμου [9] καὶ τῶν προφητῶν [10] καὶ τῶν ἄλλων πατρίων βιβλίων ἀνάγνωσιν
> Iesous, my grandfather, since he had given himself increasingly both to the reading of the Law and the Prophets and the other ancestral books

He then employs it again elsewhere as a neat method to correlate the pairing in Hebrew of לו ולזרעו "to him and to his seed":

> καὶ γὰρ θυσίας κυρίου φάγονται,
> ἃς ἔδωκεν αὐτῷ τε καὶ τῷ σπέρματι αὐτοῦ.
>
> For also they shall eat sacrifices of the Lord,
> which he gave both to him and to his seed. (Sir 45:21)

This liking for correlation can also be seen in his choosing the forward-pointing particle μέν, already discussed above in relation to the

49. Ibid., 115.

Homeric allusion. In the two other appearances of *μέν* in Sirach coordination between two elements is strongly marked. Thus at Sir 23:23 the topic is identified by the spelling out of "first" and "second," which are then coordinated by *μέν*:

> *πρῶτον μὲν γὰρ ἐν νόμῳ ὑψίστου ἠπείθησεν,*
> *καὶ δεύτερον εἰς ἄνδρα αὐτῆς ἐπλημμέλησεν*
>
> Now, first, she disobeyed the law of the Most High,
> and second, she committed a wrong against her husband, (Sir 23:23)

In the second example, there is a classic contrast between two groups of people:

> *τινὲς μὲν αὐτῶν ἐποίησαν τὸ ἀρεστόν,*
> *τινὲς δὲ ἐπλήθυναν ἁμαρτίας.*
>
> Some of them did what was pleasing,
> but others multiplied sins. (Sir 48:16)

While there is a decline in the use of particles in the late Hellenistic and Roman periods, writers could choose to use these forward-pointing particles when they wished to mark correlation between clauses. It can be seen as a particular preference of some writers in documentary papyri, notable especially when the particles are initially omitted but added later above the line.[50] It is a deliberate stylistic choice and all the more so for a translator when there is nothing in Hebrew that can be equivalent to the Greek to stimulate it.

Most interesting is one other appearance of the particle τε, this time in a set phrase:

> לב אנוש ישנא פניו אם לטוב ואם לרע:

50. Examples of this in Roman papyri are noted by Rafaella Luiselli, "Authorial Revision of Linguistic Style in Greek Papyrus Letters and Petitions (AD i–iv)," in *The Language of the Papyri*, ed. T. V. Evans and D. D. Obbink (Oxford: Oxford University Press, 2010), 93–94.

> Καρδία ἀνθρώπου ἀλλοιοῖ τὸ πρόσωπον αὐτοῦ,
> ἐάν τε εἰς ἀγαθὰ ἐάν τε εἰς κακά.
>
> A person's heart changes his face,
> whether for good things or bad. (Sir 13:25)

The translator has rendered Hebrew אם by the expression ἐάν τε, which in the second case provides a quantitative equivalence at least to the two elements of the Hebrew ואם. The pairing ἐάν τε appears to be a literary means of coordination as it does not appear once in papyri but is known in classical authors:

> ἐάν τε οἱ τετρακόσιοι κρατήσωσιν ἐάν τε οἱ ἐκ Μιλήτου πολέμιοι, διαφθαρήσεσθαι
>
> should either The Four Hundred prevail or the enemy stationed at Miletus, they were doomed to utter destruction. (Thucydides, *P.W.* 8.75.3)[51]
>
> ὡς ἅπανθ' ὑμῖν τυραννίς ἐστι καὶ ξυνωμόται,
> ἤν τε μεῖζον ἤν τ' ἔλαττον πρᾶγμά τις κατηγορῇ.
>
> How you see tyranny and conspirators everywhere, as soon as anyone voices a criticism large or small. (Aristophanes, *Vesp.* 488–89)[52]

6. Word Order

We have already had call to refer to change in word order, which may be instigated by the use of a postpositive particle or notably enclitic pronouns. There seems to be a deliberate intent on the part of the translator to vary word order, especially when it has the benefit of bringing emphasis to a passage.

---

51. Translation: Charles Forster Smith, *Thucydides, with an English Translation*, 4 vols., LCL 108–110, 169 (Cambridge: Harvard University Press, 1919–1923), 4:323.

52. Translation: Jeffrey Henderson, *Aristophanes: Clouds, Wasps, Peace*, LCL 488 (Cambridge, MA: Harvard University Press, 1998), 283.

היה כאב ליתומים ותמור בעל לאלמנות:

γίνου ὀρφανοῖς ὡς πατὴρ
καὶ ἀντὶ ἀνδρὸς τῇ μητρὶ αὐτῶν

Be like a father to orphans
and instead of a husband to their mother (Sir 4:10)

In the example of 4:10 the topic of the verse is fronted, "Be to orphans," when in the Hebrew these words appear at the end of the clause. This emphasis in Greek is not represented in the NETS translation quoted above. The result is a chiasm within the verse in which the comparatives "Like a father" and "in the place of a husband" are joined in the center. A similar reordering is seen in Sir 4:1–3 where the effect is visible across the verses. In 4:1 the topic of the verse is once again fronted:

בני אל תלעג לחיי עני ואל תדאיב נפש עני ומר נפש

Τέκνον, τὴν ζωὴν τοῦ πτωχοῦ μὴ ἀποστερήσῃς
καὶ μὴ παρελκύσῃς ὀφθαλμοὺς ἐπιδεεῖς.

Child, the life of the poor do not defraud,
and do not put off needy eyes (Sir 4:1)

Although the Hebrew differs from the Greek in the second half of the verse, the word order of the first half is clear and unproblematic. The new order of the Greek (represented well in NETS) results in another chiasm with the two prohibitions falling in the center. The second verse has a similar structure, although in this case it matches the word order of the Hebrew:

ψυχὴν πεινῶσαν μὴ λυπήσῃς
καὶ μὴ παροργίσῃς ἄνδρα ἐν ἀπορίᾳ αὐτοῦ.

A hungry soul do not grieve,
and do not anger a man in his difficulty. (Sir 4:2)

In verse 3 we once more see the same word order with the prohibitions in the center of a chiasm, and the topic at the front.

אל [תחמיר] מעי דך וקרב עני אל תכאיב:

καρδίαν παρωργισμένην μὴ προσταράξῃς
καὶ μὴ παρελκύσῃς δόσιν προσδεομένου.

An angry heart do not trouble,
and do not delay giving to one in need. (Sir 4:3)

Here again the translator has reordered the clauses and produced the same structure as the other two verses. In these three verses, then, the translator has rearranged verses 1 and 3 to ensure all three verses have the topic fronted and a chiasm with prohibitions as the central pairing. The existence of this change in word across three verses and the coordination through the similar structure suggest that the reordering is intentional on the part of the translator.

7. Conclusions

This paper has shown a number of features that the translator employs in his rendering of the Hebrew source text. Despite an appearance of a regular quantitative representation of the source, there is much variation and subtle modification. He aims for a Greek that reflects a higher register and chooses a range of rare or literary words. This is supported by word plays and rhetorical devices that contribute to the literary effect of the text. Such evidence confirms Wright's observation that the Greek is not a sure guide for reconstruction of the Hebrew where the text is missing or damaged.[53]

The following passage illustrates this problem of Hebrew reconstruction once one is aware of the translator's preference for literary devices. The translator ends the section on dreams, where we no longer have the Hebrew text preserved, with the warning:

7 πολλοὺς γὰρ ἐπλάνησεν τὰ ἐνύπνια,
καὶ ἐξέπεσαν ἐλπίζοντες ἐπ' αὐτοῖς.
8 ἄνευ ψεύδους συντελεσθήσεται νόμος,
καὶ σοφία στόματι πιστῷ τελείωσις.

---

53. Wright, "Preliminary Thoughts," 101.

7 For dreams have deceived many,
and persons who hope in them have fallen.
8 Without falsehood the law will be accomplished,
and wisdom in a trustworthy mouth is completeness. (Sir 31[34]:7–8)

There is a possible alliteration on the letter *pi* once again, which we are now attuned to as one of the translator's favourite devices. The next section, an "autobiographical" pericope on the benefits of travel, opens with yet more alliteration on the letter *pi*:

9 Ἀνὴρ πεπλανημένος ἔγνω πολλά,
καὶ ὁ πολύπειρος ἐκδιηγήσεται σύνεσιν·
10 ὃς οὐκ ἐπειράθη, ὀλίγα οἶδεν,
11 ὁ δὲ πεπλανημένος πληθυνεῖ πανουργίαν.
12 πολλὰ ἑόρακα ἐν τῇ ἀποπλανήσει μου,
καὶ πλείονα τῶν λόγων μου σύνεσίς μου·

Since a man roamed, he knew many things
and he who is experienced will tell with understanding.
He who had no experience knows few things,
But he who has roamed will increase cleverness.
I have seen many things in my wandering,
and more than my words is my understanding. (Sir 31[34]:9–12)

There are several aspects here that suggest these words are those of the translator rather than a standard rendering of the Hebrew. First there is the continuance from the previous pericope of the verb πλανάω, where it firstly denoted "to deceive" and now is used of the "wandering" scribe. It has become a leitmotif (see vv. 9, 11 and 12) and the sense has been transformed from the first pericope to the second. Typical vocabulary of the translator is apparent here too, when he opts for rare words that are not used by other translators of sapiential literature. The rare adjective πολύπειρος "with much experience" reflects his penchant for compounds.[54] It appears also in Sir 21:22 but there is no obvious equivalent in the preserved Hebrew there. Another compound πανουργία "clever-

54. Cf. Aitken, "Literary Attainment," 109.

ness" is also a rare word, appearing in Sirach four times (elsewhere at 19:23, 25; 21:12), but in no instance with a Hebrew text preserved. In Proverbs the noun is the equivalent of ערמה "craftiness" (Prov 1:4; 8:5) and yet, given the discussion above of πανοῦργος and its equivalents, it cannot be assumed the equivalents are the same as in Proverbs. Finally, the frequency of words beginning with the letter *pi* is not accidental if verse 11 is an indication. There we find another example of a tricolon with alliteration on *pi* that seems to be a deliberate rhetorical device. Words beginning with *pi* also open verses 12, 13, and 14 so that there is a strong sense of this sound throughout this passage and continuing after the section quoted.

It is a reasonable assumption that the Hebrew verb behind Greek πλανάω is תעה, which has the same double meaning of "to mislead" (e.g., Jer 23:13) as well as "to wander" (e.g., Gen 21:14). This would have been the basis for the translator's choice of the verb πλανάω, but caution should be exercised in retroverting other words. It has been seen that where the translator sees the opportunity for alliteration or a rhetorical device he will not always opt for the most obvious equivalent. This passage rather is a further example of the translator's command of Greek and enjoyment of such rhetorical devices.

The evidence of the translator's ability leads to some final reflections on his socio-historical position. We have no reason to doubt the testimony of the translator in the prologue that he relocated to Egypt (Sir Prol. 27–28), presumably from Judah, the home of his grandfather. Previously I have focused on the use of Greek in Egypt and place of the translator within Egyptian society.[55] However, as he presumably moved to Egypt as an adult, his translation testifies to Greek education in Judah and the knowledge of Greek there, too. As multilingualism was common in antiquity and as there is no need to presume knowledge of one language precludes knowledge of another,[56] it can be expected that the translator grew up speaking Hebrew or Aramaic and yet also knowing Greek. The use of Greek by

55. Ibid., 98–100.

56. Scholarship in this area is now extensive. For antiquity, see for example: James N. Adams, Mark Janse, Simon Swain, eds., *Bilingualism in Ancient Society: Language Contact and the Written Text* (Oxford: Oxford University Press, 2002); Arietta Papaconstantinou, ed., *The Multilingual Experience in Egypt, from the Ptolemies to the ʿAbbāsids* (Farnham: Ashgate, 2010); Alex Mullen and Patrick James, eds., *Multilingualism in the Graeco-Roman Worlds* (Cambridge: Cambridge University Press, 2012).

Jews in Judah for official business is attested as early as the third century BCE when Toubias sent gifts to Ptolemy, accompanied by letters in Greek (P.Cair.Zen. I.59076; P.Cair.Zen.I.59075). The Dead Sea Scrolls also witness to the use of Greek for documentary purposes even where Hebrew was preferred for literary purposes.[57] By the late second century, the time of the Greek translator of Sirach, there is the example of Eupolemus, who was an ambassador at the time of the Maccabees and may have been the same person who composed a historical narrative in Greek. Although his Greek has been unfairly dismissed as poor,[58] he represents an interest in Greek composition in Judah, something that might have been positively promoted by the Hasmoneans as they modelled themselves on the tradition of Greek courts. In such a climate the translator would have gained proficiency in Greek and be fully equipped once in Egypt to produce such an elegant and intriguing translation.

57. Matthew Richey, "The Use of Greek at Qumran: Manuscript and Epigraphic Evidence for a Marginalized Language," *DSD* 19 (2012): 177–97.

58. E.g., Ben Zion Wacholder, *Eupolemus: A Study of Judaeo-Greek Literature*, HUCM 3 (Cincinnati: Hebrew Union College-Jewish Institute of Religion, 1974), 169.

Das Griechisch des Jesus Sirach

Knut Usener

1. Hinführung

Wenn es im Folgenden um das *Griechische* Sirach-Buch geht, so sind zwei Fragestellungen zu bedenken, die nicht unabhängig voneinander behandelt werden können:

1. In welchem Gattungshorizont steht das LXX-Sirach-Buch?
2. Wie sieht vor diesem Hintergrund seine sprachliche Gestaltung aus? Dabei ist die Verortung der Sprache im Rahmen der pagangriechischen Literatur einerseits und im Rahmen von Übersetzungsliteratur andererseits in den Horizont der nachfolgenden Betrachtungen einzubeziehen.

Im Folgenden wird es nicht hauptsächlich um die Diskussion *einzelner Beispiele* sprachlicher Beobachtungen gehen—dies ist Gegenstand anderer Beiträge.[1] Vielmehr soll aus einer *übergreifenden* und zugleich *externen* Perspektive heraus das Spezifikum des LXX-Sirach erfragt werden, indem der Text im Zusammenhang seiner Gattung und aus altphilologischer Perspektive betrachtet wird.

2. Gattungsfragen

Zwei Themenbereiche sind hier zu besprechen: (1) der Prolog, (2) die Weisheitsschrift selbst. Im Hintergrund erhebt sich dabei die Frage, welche

1. James K. Aitken, "The Literary and Linguistic Subtlety of the Greek Version of Sirach," und Anthony J. Forte, "Plerique codices, nonnulli codices: Ambrose's Biblical Text; The Case of Ben Sirach and the Canticum Canticorum," in diesem Band.

Referenztexte aus der paganen griechischen Literatur benannt werden können, auf die Sir Bezug genommen haben kann.[2]

1. Der Prolog *als gesondertes literarisches Element* eines größeren Textganzen sowie als literarischer Terminus, der als solcher in der Textüberlieferung zu Sirach wohl erst später hinzugekommen sein dürfte und überdies nicht einheitlich ist (πρόλογος, προοίμιον jeweils mit Varianten im Umfang der Zusätze), ist erst sekundär in Prosa-Texten vorfindlich:[3] zunächst war er ein Spezifikum der *dramatischen* Literatur insbesondere mit der Funktion der Handlungs-Exposition oder der Angabe der Begleitumstände, die zur Aufführung des jeweiligen Stückes geführt haben.[4] Das erste Aufkommen des Prologs als eines fest abgegrenzten Abschnitts innerhalb eines heterogenen Textsystems lässt sich spätestens in das Jahr 478 oder 476 v. Chr. datieren,[5] und diese Form der „Einleitung“ bleibt

2. Otto Kaiser, *Weisheit für das Leben: Das Buch Jesus Sirach; Übersetzt und eingeleitet* (Stuttgart: Radius, 2005), bietet S. 157–94 einen recht umfangreichen Index der möglichen Parallelen, die Sir zu Passagen des AT sowie zu außerbiblischer Literatur hat. Insbesondere listet er zahlreiche Parallelen zur griechischen Literatur auf, die hier aus Raumgründen nicht vorgelegt oder überprüft werden können. Eine Überprüfung aber ist auf der Basis einer methodischen Reflexion erforderlich, die klärt, welche inhaltlichen und sprachlichen Rahmenbedingungen erfüllt sein müssen, damit man von einer Parallele sprechen kann. Eine solche Untersuchung scheint geboten, da Kaiser diese Stellen ohne weitere Erläuterung benennt.

3. Pherekydes von Syros (Mitte 6. Jh.) soll nach einer antiken Nachricht (erhalten in der byzantinischen Suda; VS 7A2 DK) der Verfasser des ersten attischen Prosabuches gewesen sein; seine darin entwickelte Theologie und Kosmogonie war möglicherweise orphisch beeinflusst. Dass dieses Werk einen Prolog hatte, ist denkbar, aber nicht nachweisbar, da zu wenig erhalten ist. Vgl. Anne Schlichtmann und Bernhard Zimmermann, Hrsg., *Die Literatur der archaischen und klassischen Zeit*, Bd. 1 von *Handbuch der griechischen Literatur der Antike*, Handbuch der Altertumswissenschaft 7.1 (München: Beck, 2011), 260–61, 293–94.

4. Die in der Antike generell akzeptierte Definition des Prologs findet sich bei Aristoteles (*Ars poetica* 1.12, 1452b19–20).

5. Auf Thespis oder Phrynichos dürfte die Etablierung des Prologs als eines Bestandteils der Tragödie zurückgehen. Aristoteles weiß bereits nicht mehr zu berichten, wer den Prolog eingeführt habe (Aristoteles, *Ars poetica* 1449b4–5). Nach einer späten Notiz bei Themistios aus dem 4. Jh. n. Chr. (*Oratio* 26.316d) habe Thespis, der im 6. Jh. v. Chr. gewirkt hat und der seit der Antike überwiegend als Schöpfer der Gattung „Tragödie“ gilt, den Prolog „erfunden“ (ἐξεῦρεν, schreibt Themistios). Vgl. hierzu Albin Lesky, *Die tragische Dichtung der Hellenen*, 3. Aufl., Studienhefte zur Altertumswissenschaft 2 (Göttingen: Vandenhoeck & Ruprecht, 1972), 52–53. Die „Phönissen“ des Phrynichos, die 478 oder 476 aufgeführt wurden, hatten nachweislich

lange Zeit dem Drama als „erstem Erfinder“ vorbehalten. Dieser Prolog ist in gebundener, also metrischer Form gestaltet, nicht wie bei Sirach in Prosa. Der literarisch-beschreibende *Terminus* πρόλογος wird erstmals von Aristoteles verwendet.[6]

Der zweite, in den Hss zu Sirach überlieferte Begriff, das προοίμιον,[7] wird sowohl in epischer und lyrischer Dichtung als auch in der vorwiegend *forensischen* performativen Literatur und somit in Prosaschriften verwendet. Das Prooimion kann in der Dichtung verschiedene Elemente enthalten wie den Musenanruf, die Bitte um Inspiration, die Sphragis (also die Autorinformation) oder die Themenangabe. In Prosa-Reden finden sich als Elemente des Prooimion etwa die thematische Hinführung, eine *captatio benevolentiae* oder auch die Rechtfertigung des eigenen rhetorischen Vorgehens.[8]

Wenn also die griechische Übersetzung des Sirach-Buchs mit einem Prosa-„Prolog“ beginnt,[9] den sie auch (möglicherweise in einem späteren Zusatz) terminologisch so benennt, mit einem „Prolog“ also, in dem das Vorhaben des Textes skizziert, die Entstehungsbedingungen von Quelltext und Übersetzung genannt, eine *adhortatio* an den Leser gerichtet sowie methodologische Fragen wie etwa die Reflexion der Sprachdifferenzen (Prol. 19–22) und das als Topos lesbare „große Problem des Übersetzens“ (Sir Prol. 15–26) angerissen werden, ohne dass diese Differenzen im hebräischen Prätext begründet sind, so verweist diese literarische Vorgehensweise in den Gattungshorizont der *Rede*. Insofern ist die ebenfalls überlieferte Bezeichnung der Eingangspassage als „Prooimion“ sachlich

einen Prolog. Vgl. hierzu Joachim Latacz, *Einführung in die griechische Tragödie*, 2. Aufl., UTB 1745 (Göttingen: Vandenhoeck & Ruprecht, 2003), 83–85, 391.

6. Vgl. Anm. 4.

7. Der erst Beleg für den Begriff προοίμιον findet sich bei Pindar, *Pythie* 1.4–5.

8. Vgl. bereits Aristoteles, *Rhet.* 3.14, 1414b19–1416a3 mit einer funktionalen Definition des Prooimion. Die antike Theorie der Rhetorik behandelt das Prooimion/Prooemium/Exordium/Principium ausführlich, wie aus den verschiedenen Zugriffen bei Quintilian erhellt. Die Passagen sind leicht auffindbar über Eckart Zundel, *Clavis Quintilianae: Quintilians “Institutio oratoria” aufgeschlüsselt nach rhetorischen Begriffen* (Darmstadt: Wissenschaftliche Buchgesellschaft, 1989), 78, s v „prooemium“.

9. Vgl. zum Sirach-Prolog bes. Benjamin G. Wright, “Translation Greek in Sirach in Light of the Grandson’s Prologue,” in *The Texts and Versions of the Book of Ben Sira: Transmission and Interpretation*, hrsg. Jan Joosten und Jean-Sébastien Rey, JSJSup 150 (Leiden: Brill, 2011), 75–94.

zu bevorzugen.[10] Das Prooimion (oder lat. *exordium*) übernimmt im Gattungskontext der *Rede* insbesondere und hauptsächlich die Funktion der Hörer- (oder Leser-) Steuerung, indem es die für die eigene Sache erforderliche Aufmerksamkeit und Gewogenheit herzustellen versucht: Im Sirach-Prooimion werden diese Funktionen so auch eindeutig in Z. 15–20 umgesetzt:

> Παρακέκλησθε οὖν μετ᾽ εὐνοίας καὶ προσοχῆς τὴν ἀνάγνωσιν ποιεῖσθαι καὶ συγγνώμην ἔχειν ἐφ᾽ οἷς ἂν δοκῶμεν τῶν κατὰ τὴν ἑρμηνείαν πεφιλοπονημένων τισὶν τῶν λέξεων ἀδυναμεῖν·
>
> Lasst euch also ermahnen, mit Wohlwollen und Aufmerksamkeit die Lektüre zu betreiben und Nachsicht zu haben in den (Fällen), bei denen wir versagt zu haben scheinen, obwohl wir uns gemäß der Übersetzungskunst um (bestimmte) Redewendungen für einige (Leser) emsig bemüht haben. (Sir Prol. 15–20 [Übers. LXX.D])

Schlüsselbegriffe wie εὔνοια („Wohlwollen“) und συγγνώμη („Nachsicht“) begegnen regelmäßig in markanten Abschnitten von Reden in der griechischen Literatur, insbesondere aber auch in den ersten Worten an die Zuhörer.[11] Προσοχή („Aufmerksamkeit“) hingegen kommt in der griechischen Literatur erst später und auch dann nur selten vor.[12] Eine knappe Inhaltsskizze und die Benennung der Intention des Autors sowie die *captatio benevolentiae* sind im Sirach-„Prolog“ somit als Elemente vertreten, die so auch in rhetorisch ausgefeilten Reden paganer Schriftsteller begegnen. Die sprachliche Gestaltung entspricht insgesamt ebenso den Gewohnheiten antiker Redepraxis.

2. Nun soll der Gattungshorizont des zentralen Textes des Sirach-Buches, der Weisheitstext erhellt werden. Die Weisheitsliteratur stellt eine alte orientalische Textgattung dar, die in der originären griechischen Literatur in dieser Form nicht existiert. Ohne hier auf die Spezifika der orientalischen Weisheitsliteratur einzugehen, soll hier nur ein skizzenhafter

10. Aristoteles, *Rhet.* 1414b19–20, analogisiert die Begriffe von Prolog, Prooimion und Proaulion (πρόλογος, προοίμιον, προαύλιον), weist sie aber eindeutig dem jeweiligen Gattungshorizont zu.

11. Vgl. z.B. Demosthenes, *De corona* 1 (εὔνοιαν); Demosthenes, *Philippica* 1.1.7 (συγγνώμη).

12. Προσοχή liest man z.B. bei Dionysios v. Halikarnass (1. Jh. v. Chr.) im Kontext einer Rede, 6.85.3.

Überblick über vergleichbare Erscheinungen in der griechischen Kultur erfolgen.

Die Gemeinsamkeiten der Belehrung, der (zumindest bei den Griechen) anonymen oder namentlichen Adressierung an einen fiktionalen oder realen Adressaten, der als Schüler des Autors gedacht sein kann, die in älteren (archaischen) Texten anonym gehaltene Verfasserschaft, die kurze Belehrung in Form von Frage, Beispiel oder Aufforderung, die bisweilen persönliche oder auktoriale Haltung und Färbung der Aussagen, die bisweilen gnomische Allgemeingültigkeit oder auch z.B. die Vorstellung von einer allmählichen Deprivation des Menschen bzw. der jeweiligen Gesellschaft sind einige zentrale Themenbereiche und Topoi der orientalischen Weisheitsliteratur:[13] Ob es allerdings überhaupt angemessen ist, alle entsprechenden Texte aus verschiedenen Epochen und Kulturen in einem Atemzug zu nennen, mag hier offen bleiben.[14]

Wie sieht es aber mit der griechischen Kultur aus? Auch sie kennt die literarische Belehrung seit ihren Anfängen, geht aber eigene Wege in der inhaltlichen und formalen Ausgestaltung. Auch sie kennt in diesem Kontext die Adressaten-Anrede, verwendet Gleichnisse oder Vergleiche und formuliert sentenzenhafte Aussagen, Mahnungen oder Gewissheiten. Aber in der paganen griechischen Literatur bildet die Weisheitsliteratur keine eigene Gattung aus, wie dies andere Themenbereiche getan haben. Weisheitsliteratur ist somit in der originären griechischen Literatur keine

13. Im AT ist besonders auf Dan 2,39–40 zu verweisen. Vgl. hierzu dann die Kulturentstehungslehre bzw. den Zeitaltermythos bei Hesiod, *Opera et dies* 106–201, dem von anderen griechischen Autoren ähnliche oder auch gegenteilige Vorstellungen (Aszendenz-Theorie, Fortschrittsgedanke) entgegengestellt worden sind. Vgl. hierzu einführend Schlichtmann und Zimmermann, *Die Literatur der archaischen und klassischen Zeit*, 91 (oben Anm. 3), mit weiterer Literatur. Insbesondere ist zu verweisen auf Eric R. Dodds, *Der Fortschrittsgedanke in der Antike und andere Aufsätze zu Literatur und Glauben der Griechen* (Zürich: Artemis, 1977), 10–19; Bodo Gatz, *Weltalter, goldene Zeit und sinnverwandte Vorstellungen*, Spudasmata 16 (Hildesheim: Olms, 1967), 146–49 und passim; Klaus Kubusch, *Aurea saecula, Mythos und Geschichte: Untersuchung eines Motivs in der antiken Literatur bis Ovid*, Studien zur klassischen Philologie 28 (Frankfurt am Main: Lang, 1986); Hesiodus, *Works and Days*, hrsg. Martin L. West (Oxford: Clarendon, 1978), 172–75.

14. Zu den Verbindungen und Differenzen orientalischer Weisheitsliteratur und den hiervon wahrscheinlich in gewissem Umfang beeinflussten griechischen Texten vgl. u.a. Martin L. West, *The East Face of Helicon: West Asiatic Elements in Greek Poetry and Myth* (Oxford: Clarendon, 1997), 76–78, 94–95, 306–7.

eigenständige Gattung: Vielmehr verteilen sich im Griechischen einzelne Elemente derjenigen Erscheinung, die in der orientalischen Literatur in den Gattungsbereich der Weisheitsliteratur gehören, auf heterogene *didaktische* ebenso wie *erzählende* Gattungen. Insbesondere ist hier natürlich das *Lehrgedicht* anzuführen, doch kommen weitere Textgattungen hinzu, in der Dichtung ebenso wie in der Prosa.

Hesiod gilt als der erste Verfasser und somit als literarischer Archeget des *Lehrgedichts*. Er hat möglicherweise bereits im späten 8., vielleicht aber auch erst im 7. Jh. v. Chr. die „Abstammung der Götter" (θεογονία) sowie einen „Bauernkalender" (ἔργα καὶ ἡμέραι, „Werke und Tage") in epischer Form, also in hexametrischem Versmaß mit 1022 bzw. 828 Versen verfasst. Er verfährt dabei jeweils nicht streng nach dem Prinzip, dass ein abgeschlossener Aussagebereich zwei, drei oder geringfügig mehr Verse umfasst, wie dies etwa bei Sirach der Fall ist: Beide Lehrgedichte von Hesiod haben trotz ihrer Besonderheiten stilistische ebenso wie sprachliche Elemente wie Metrik, formelhafte Wendungen und Kompositionsprinzipien aufzuweisen, die in vergleichbarer Form aus dem griechischen Heldenepos vertraut sind.[15] Mit Themen der Weisheitsliteratur haben dennoch insbesondere Hesiods „Werke und Tage" durchaus Berührungspunkte, etwa in der Vermittlung moralischer Erfahrung bzw. Anleitung, in Sentenzen und Sprichworten, in Rätseln, in direkten Apostrophen an den Adressaten oder auch in Anleitungen zur landwirtschaftlichen Arbeit.[16]

Neben dem Lehrgedicht können—ebenso bedingt—auch noch weitere Texte zur Weisheitsliteratur zählen, so etwa die aus ursprünglich anderen Werken oder Rede-Zusammenhängen zusammengestellten *Spruchsammlung*, zu denen etwa die „Sprüche der Sieben Weisen",[17] aber auch spe-

15. Die Frage der zeitlichen Priorität von Homer und Hesiod bleibt hier unberücksichtigt. Schlichtmann und Zimmermann, *Die Literatur der archaischen und klassischen Zeit*, 78–94 (oben Anm. 3).

16. Für Hesiods Ausführungen zu landwirtschaftlichen Aufgaben wurde nicht das Sirach-Buch, wohl aber bedingt Jesaia 28,23–28 zum Vergleich herangezogen, was aber nur sehr bedingt seine Berechtigung hat, da der jeweilige Kontext differiert und keine direkten sprachlichen Parallelen vorliegen. In diesem Sinne vgl. ibid., 88 und 91–92. (oben Anm. 3). Zu Jesaia und Hesiod vgl. ibid., 91–92, sowie West, *East Face of Helicon*, 228–32 (oben Anm. 14). Zu weiteren Parallelen wie etwa der jeweils mehrfachen Themenbearbeitungen innerhalb desselben Werkes etc. vgl. Schlichtmann und Zimmermann, *Die Literatur der archaischen und klassischen Zeit*, 93–94. (oben Anm. 3).

17. Zu den Sprüchen der Sieben Weisen (deren Gruppe je nach Autor verschieden zusammengesetzt ist) vgl. Jochen Althoff, Dieter Zeller, und Markus Asper, hrsg.,

zielle Sammlungen wie die späteren κύριαι δόξαι (oder *ratae sententiae*) von Epikur oder auch die Sentenzen Menanders zu rechnen sind. Bei jeder der genannten Texturen sind wiederum jeweils Besonderheiten zu nennen, die eine klare Abgrenzung von der Weisheitsliteratur empfehlen. Im Falle Epikurs etwa ist es der unter ethischen Aspekten geformte philosophische Diskurs einer speziellen hellenistischen Denkrichtung, der die Texte prägt.[18] Bei Menander ist der Hintergrund der ethisierten Komödie zu beachten.[19] Dass es in dem Vorsokratiker Heraklit auch für prägnante Allgemeinaussagen Vorgänger gibt, die bewusst knappe und sentenzenhafte, zugleich aber auch schwer verständliche Aussprüche in den Kontext philosophischer Reflexionen stellen, sei nur am Rande erwähnt: Heraklit „der Dunkle"[20] hat bereits Sprüche verfasst, die inhaltlich fast das Gegenteil von Weisheitsliteratur im Sinne einer lebenspraktischen Hilfestellung oder Hinführung zur Weisheit im Horizont der Gottgefälligkeit sein wollen: Heraklit wollte provozieren; er war bewusst unbequem und kantig. Damit steht er in starkem Kontrast zu Sirach.

Die Existenz von Spruchsammlungen einerseits des Komödiendichters Menander,[21] andererseits der Sieben Weisen[22] oder Epikurs (und

---

Die Worte der Sieben Weisen, Texte zur Forschung 89 (Darmstadt: Wissenschaftliche Buchgesellschaft, 2006).

18. Eine Auswahl übersetzter und kommentierter Texte von Epikur, speziell auch der κύριαι δόξαι (*ratae sententiae*, „Hauptlehrsätze") bietet u.a. Arthur A. Long, D. N. Sedley, und Karlheinz Hülser, *Die hellenistischen Philosophen: Texte und Kommentare* (Stuttgart: Metzler, 2006), passim. Vgl. insbesondere die Darstellung der Lehre Epikurs (mit ausführlicher Bibliographie) bei Michael Erler, Hellmut Flashar, und Friedrich Ueberweg, *Die hellenistische Philosophie*, Philosophie der Antike 4.1 (Basel: Schwalbe, 1994), 29–490.

19. Vgl. insbesondere Eckard Lefèvre, "Menander," in *Das griechische Drama*, hrsg. Gustav A. Seeck, Grundriss der Literaturgeschichten nach Gattungen (Darmstadt: Wissenschaftliche Buchgesellschaft, 1979), 307–53.

20. Als σκοτεινός hatte man Heraklit in der Antike bereits vor der Entstehung der unter Aristoteles' Namen überlieferten Schrift *De mundo* 396b20 (Über die Welt) aufgrund der oft kryptischen Ausdrucksweisen bezeichnet.

21. Zu den jeweils aus einem Vers bestehenden Gnomen Menanders (γνῶμαι μονόστιχοι), die ab dem 3. Jh. n. Chr. in verschiedenen Sammlungen anzutreffen sind, die aber großenteils lediglich Menander zugeschreiben worden sind, vgl. Bernhard Zimmermann et al., Hrsg., *Die Literatur der klassischen und hellenistischen Zeit*, Bd. 2 von *Handbuch der Griechischen Literatur der Antike*, Handbuch der Altertumswissenschaft 7.2 (München: Beck, 2014), 1084–87 mit weiterer Literatur.

22. Vgl. oben Anm. 17.

bedingt auch etwa die Sammlung von Apophthegmata bei Plutarch) zeigen allerdings, dass die Griechen an allgemeingültigen Aussagen oder Empfehlungen ein großes Interesse hatten: Kluge Aussprüche finden sich nahezu in allen Werken und Gattungen der griechischen Literatur, und vielleicht kommt daher auch das allmähliche Ausdifferenzieren von verschiedenen Bezeichnungen wie etwa ἀπόφθεγμα (Ausspruch, Bon mot), γνώμη (Lebensweisheit), παροιμία (Maxime, Sentenz) oder ὑποθήκη (Mahnspruch).[23] All diesen Sammlungen ist gemeinsam der unmittelbare Bezug zur jeweiligen Gesellschaft und deren Lebensbedingungen. Die Mentalität ist dabei die gemeinsame Schnittstelle. In diesem Bezug besteht die deutlichste Parallele zum Sirach-Buch.

Es ist—um hier einen Blick auf die sprachliche Realisierung zu werfen—kaum Zufall, dass es im Griechischen, greifbar seit Homer, *Ilias* 1.218,[24] den sogenannten „gnomischen Aorist" gibt: Eine Aorist-Form, die auch im Falle der Augmentierung keinen temporalen Vergangenheitsverweis formuliert, sondern den Abschluss eines Handlungsvollzugs (*konfektiv*) markiert und so die aus der Erfahrung der Vergangenheit begründete Allgemeingültigkeit einer Aussage bezeichnen kann.[25]

Als Exkurs ein Beispiel: Hesiod mahnt seinen Bruder Perses, auf die Gerechtigkeit zu hören und nicht die Gewalt zu mehren (ἄκουε δίκης, μηδ᾽ ὕβριν ὄφελλε, Hesiod, *Opera et dies* 213). Nachdem er dargelegt hat, wozu ὕβρις führt, schließt er mit der allgemeinen Lebensweisheit παθὼν δέ τε νήπιος ἔγνω—„wenn er es erst einmal so erfahren hat, kapiert es auch ein Dummkopf". Παθών und ἔγνω sind Aoristformen, wobei das Partizip durchaus zwingend als Voraussetzung für das Prädikat ἔγνω zu verstehen ist: Das Partizip ist vorzeitig zum Prädikat, das seinerseits hier aber trotz Augment *keine* Vergangenheit ausdrückt sondern Allgemeingültigkeit—die Form wird somit als „gnomisch" bezeichnet, weil sie insbesondere in

23. Vgl. Steven Scully, "Weisheitsliteratur III: Klassische Antike," *DNP* 12.2:448–451. Die Griechen haben bereits in der Antike begonnen, das Wesen von Spruchweisheiten unter den Aspekten insbesondere der philosophischen Inhalte und der stilistischen Gestaltung zu reflektieren. Hierzu vgl. grundlegend Jan F. Kindstrand, "The Greek Concept of Proverbs," *Eranos* 76 (1978): 71–85.

24. Homer, *Ilias* 1,218: ὅς κε θεοῖς ἐπιπείθηται μάλα τ' ἔκλυον αὐτοῦ (Wer den Göttern gehorcht, den haben sie immer schon erhört).

25. Vgl. zu Erklärung und Diskussion des gnomischen Aorist Eduard Schwyzer et al., eds., *Syntax Und Syntaktische Stilistik*, 5. Aufl., Handbuch der Altertumswissenschaft. Griechische Grammatik, auf der Grundlage von Karl Brugmanns Griechischer Grammatik 2 (München: Beck, 1988), 285–86.

derartigen Spruchweisheiten Verwendung findet. Eine direkt parallele Formulierung verwendet etwa auch Homer: „Wenn es geschehen ist, kapiert es auch ein Dummkopf", ῥεχθὲν δέ τε νήπιος ἔγνω (Homer, *Ilias* 17.32). Dass diese Aussage als Weisheitsspruch galt und Erziehungs-Charakter hatte, bezeugen die Scholien zu dieser Homerstelle, in denen zugleich ein Verweis auf eine ähnlich formulierte Gedankenfügung bei Platon erfolgt.[26]

Auch Sirach verwendet den gnomischen Aorist öfter. Beispielsweise wird er in Sir 1,6 in einer rhetorischen Frage formuliert:

ῥίζα σοφίας τίνι ἀπεκαλύφθη; | καὶ τὰ πανουργεύματα αὐτῆς τίς ἔγνω;

Die Wurzel der Weisheit—wem *wurde* sie offenbart? | Und ihre Raffinesse—wer *erkannte* sie? (LXX.D; Hervorhebung vom Verf.)

Die Tempuswahl der *deutschen* Übersetzung ist allerdings eher ungewöhnlich, da im Deutschen bei Sentenzen bevorzugt das Präsens oder (eher selten) das Perfekt gewählt wird.[27] So sagen wir gewöhnlich unter Verwendung des Präsens „das weiß doch jedes Kind". Im Rheinischen Dialekt sagt man „Et hät noch immer jot jejange"—„Es ist noch immer gut gegangen". Hier wird das Perfekt gewählt.[28]

Sir 3,28 verwendet in einem weiteren Spruch hingegen das *gnomische* Präsens und kombiniert dieses im Begründungsnachsatz mit einem Perfekt:

ἐπαγωγῇ ὑπερηφάνου οὐκ ἔστιν ἴασις·| φυτὸν γὰρ πονηρίας ἐρρίζωκεν ἐν αὐτῷ—

26. Scholion A zu Homer, *Ilias* 17,31: φιλόσοφος ἡ γνώμη … ex. <ῥεχθὲν δέ τε νήπιος ἔγνω:> πιστὸν τὸ παίδευμα καὶ πολλῆς ὠφελείας περιεκτικόν. Der Verweis betrifft Platon, *Symposion* 222b4.

27. Im Deutschen ist der Tempusgebrauch, der regionale Unterschiede aufweist, im Zusammenspiel von Aktionsart und Aspekt sowie in Abhängigkeit der Semantik des Verbalstammes nach wie vor Gegenstand wissenschaftlicher Reflexionen, und verschiedene Sichtweisen stehen oft thesenhaft einander gegenüber. Einen umfassenden und doch knappen Überblick bietet Björn Rothstein, *Tempus*, Kurze Einführungen in die germanistische Linguistik 5 (Heidelberg: Winter, 2007).

28. Das Präteritum ist in Sentenzen in der deutschen Sprache deswegen eher ungebräuchlich, weil Sprichworte bevorzugt nicht-dynamische Sachverhalte wie etwa Erzählungen formulieren, die in den Augen des Sprechenden als in der Erfahrung begründet und somit täglich sich wiederholend wahrnehmbar sind.

Für die Verlockung des Hochmütigen gibt es keine Heilung, | denn ein schlechter Sprössling hat in ihm Wurzel geschlagen. (LXX.D)

In Sentenzen können neben dem Aorist genauso das Präsens und das Futur Verwendung finden. Dies ist dem Sirach-Übersetzer offensichtlich gut bekannt. In der Spruchsammlung in Sir 20,27[29]–31[33] finden sich nur Präsens- und Futur-Formen.

Viele weitere Passagen bei Sir belegen den Gebrauch des gnomischen Aorist. So gestaltet etwa Sir 14,12 eine *Aussage* mit zwei Aorist-Formen:

μακάριος ἀνήρ, ὃς οὐκ ὠλίσθησεν ἐν τῷ στόματι αὐτοῦ | καὶ οὐ κατενύγη ἐν λύπῃ ἁμαρτιῶν·

Selig [ist] der Mann, der nicht verdorben wurde durch seinen Mund | und (der) nicht gepeinigt wurde in Betrübnis über (seine) Sünden. (Übers. LXX.D; Ergänzung vom Verf.)

Auch Sir 18,28 könnte neben vielen weiteren Beispielen herangezogen werden. Dabei ist noch die Beobachtung hinzuzufügen, dass Sirach unmittelbar neben einem gnomischen Aorist auch das Futur verwendet, wie etwa in Sir 18,28:

πᾶς συνετὸς ἔγνω σοφίαν | καὶ τῷ εὑρόντι αὐτὴν δώσει ἐξομολόγησιν

Jeder Verständige hat die Weisheit erkannt, | und dem, der sie findet, wird sie (ihre) Anerkennung geben. (Übers. LXX.D)

Dass neben dem Aorist ἔγνω auch das Futur δώσει steht, eröffnet die Perspektive auf die Semantik der Verbalformen in Sentenzen: Das Futur kann die Gewissheit des zu Erwartenden mitformulieren, wie der Aorist die Erfahrung aus der Vergangenheit *mitformuliert*, ohne die Handlung als solche dadurch aus dem Gegenwartshorizont des Sprechers zu entfernen. Denselben Befund bietet auch der noch vorzustellende griechische Spruch-Dichter Ps.-Phokylides.[29]

29. Vgl. etwa Ps.-Phokylides 23, wo Aorist und Futur in einem Vers nebeneinander stehen: πληρώσει σέο χεῖρ'. ἔλεον χρηίζοντι παράσχου „Er wird deine Hände [gr.: Sg.] füllen—[sc. daher] hab jetzt Mitleid mit dem Bedürftigen." Das Futur πληρώσει verweist auf erwartbare Zukunft, der Imperativ Aorist hingegen (παράσχου) formu-

Doch zurück zum griechischen Gattungshorizont der Weisheitsliteratur. Neben Hesiods „Werken und Tagen" und anderen, bereits kurz erwähnten Texten sind weitere Werke bezeugt, die insbesondere sentenzenhaften Charakter haben wie etwa die nur in Fragmenten erhaltenen, Hesiod zugeschriebenen „Mahnenden Sprüche des Chiron" (Χείρωνος ὑποθῆκαι, Frg. 283–285 West) und die „Großen Werke" (Μεγάλα ἔργα, Frg. 286–287 West). Hesiod hat in Form von umfangreichen „Katalogen" (wie den Frauen-Katalogen oder der Liste der Helena-Freier) Informationen aus der Sagenwelt zusammengetragen und gleichsam als poetische Auflistung konserviert—eher eine Form von *Wissens*literatur, nicht von *Weisheits*literatur. In denselben Grenzbereich gehört wohl auch seine „Astronomia" (Frg. 288–293 West). Im Artikel über Weisheitsliteratur von Scully aus dem Jahr 2002 werden dennoch Werke genannt, die bei genauerer Betrachtung aufgrund ihrer andersartigen Gestaltung hier nicht verortet sind.[30]

Mit den „Werken und Tagen" setzt bei den Griechen bereits früh die Tradition des Lehrgedichts ein, für das bis in die byzantinische Zeit hinein immer wieder neue Wissensgebiete erschlossen werden: Hier hat sich schnell die Abspaltung der ursprünglichen Weisheitsliteratur hin zur Wissens- oder sogar Wissenschafts-Literatur vollzogen.

In der späten Klassik und sodann wesenhaft verstärkt im Hellenismus sind prominente Lehrtexte vor allem in *Prosa* entstanden: Isokrates' Rede an Nikokles kann als „Fürstenspiegel" verstanden werden.[31] Xenophon hat z.T. philosophisch getränkte Spezialliteratur zur Jagd, zur privaten Haushaltsführung, zum staatlichen Finanzwesen sowie über die Pferdezucht verfasst (Κυνηγετικός, Οἰκονομικός, Πόροι, Περὶ Ἱππικῆς).[32] Die Liste könnte leicht fortgeführt werden—Fachliteratur entsteht im Hellenismus erstmals systematisch und in inhaltlich sehr breit gefächerten Ausrichtungen.[33] Hinzu kommen sodann im Hellenismus erneut kunstvolle Lehr*gedichte* wie etwa die „Himmelserscheinungen" (Φαινόμενα) von Arat aus Soloi in Kilikien oder auch die „Alexipharmaka" und die „Theriaka" des

liert eine Aufforderung, die aktuell im Moment der Formulierung, nicht also generell oder allgemein erfüllt werden soll.

30. Vgl. zur Literaturangabe oben Anm. 23.

31. Vgl. in diesem Sinne Zimmermann et al., *Die Literatur der klassischen und hellenistischen Zeit*, 787–88 (oben Anm. 21) mit weiterer Literatur.

32. Vgl. ibid., 287–88, 586–589 (oben Anm. 21).

33. Vgl. den derzeit aktuellen Überblick ibid., 453–583 (oben Anm. 21).

Nikander von Kolophon.[34] Arat schrieb im frühen 3. Jh. v. Chr., erhalten sind aber nur die Φαινόμενα, das Werk über Sternbilder und die mit ihnen verbundenen Sagen sowie über die Wetterzeichen. Arat verwebt die Lehre, die Bauern und Seeleute betreffen, im Horizont der stoischen Darstellung des Kosmos mit dem spröden Stoff der Astronomie, geht also ergänzend und unter einer anderen thematischen Gewichtung über das hinaus, was Hesiod bereits geleistet hatte. Nikander, der seine naturwissenschaftlichen Lehrgedichte etwas später als Arat schreibt, verleiht sehr detailliertem Fachwissen u.a. über Vergiftungen durch Tierverletzungen, deren Prävention und deren Gegenmitteln eine sehr ausgefeilte poetische Gestalt. Überdies bietet das Werk Beschreibungen und aitiologische Hintergründe der gefährlichen Tiere: So überführt er einen hoch komplexen Sachverhalt in eine ebenso hoch komplexe dichterische Form.[35]

Ohne weitere Lehrgedichte etwa aus dem Bereich der Geographie (Kallimachos oder auch Alexander von Ephesos), der Mythologie oder der Geschichte aufzulisten, sei hier nur festgehalten, dass diese Texte eine immense Beliebtheit und Wirkung hatten—das Wirkpotenzial bei den Römern ist bedeutend und reicht insbesondere durch die Anverwandlung zahlreicher hellenistischer Lehrgedichte in der römischen und lateinischen Literatur über die Renaissance hinaus.[36] Doch hat sich in der Nachfolge von Hesiod das neue, spezialisierte Lehrgedicht bereits erheblich von dem entfernt, was Weisheitsliteratur leisten kann und will: Es geht in ihnen überhaupt nicht mehr um allgemeine Lebensweisheiten, sondern darum, poetische Finesse auf höchstem Niveau mit Details aus dem aktuellen oder auch abgelegenen philosophischen Diskurs auf ebenso hohem Niveau zu verknüpfen. Die sprachliche Form hat sich entsprechend verfeinert und wartet mit dem für den hellenistischen Literaturbetrieb üblichen Kunstanspruch auf. Insofern ist ein Vergleich derartiger Texte mit dem Sirach-Buch aus der Gattungsperspektive kaum sinnvoll: Diese Form der

34. Ibid., 126–40 (oben Anm. 21), mit weiterführender Literatur.

35. Vgl. neben der in Anm. 34 genannten Literatur auch insbesondere Hatto H. Schmitt und Ernst Vogt, Hrsg., *Kleines Wörterbuch des Hellenismus* (Wiesbaden: Harrassowitz, 1988), 409–16.

36. Zur Rezeption von Lehrdichtung vgl. Christine Walde, Hrsg., *Die Rezeption der antiken Literatur: Kulturhistorisches Werklexikon*, Bd. 7 von *Der Neue Pauly: Supplemente*, hrsg. Hubert Cancik (Stuttgart: Metzler, 2010), 69–76 (zu Arat), 295–322 (zu Hesiod), 300 (zu Nikander). Einzelnachweise finden sich auch in Zimmermann et al., *Die Literatur der klassischen und hellenistischen Zeit*, 123–40 (oben Anm. 21).

Lehrdichtung ist nicht auf ihre Alltagstauglichkeit ausgelegt. Überdies gibt es keine überzeugenden sprachlichen Parallelen.[37]

In den affinen Bereich der Weisheitsliteratur gehören ferner die nach Hesiod entstandenen Verse des Phokylides (wohl 5. Jh. v. Chr.). Hier gibt es zwar nur bedingte Parallelen zum Sirach-Buch wie etwa den bereits erwähnten Tempus-Wechsel von finiten Verbalformen. Allerdings verwendet Phokylides den gnomischen Aorist erstaunlich selten. Er macht dafür weit mehr Gebrauch vom Infinitiv, der dann Ge- oder Verbotsfunktion hat, wie etwa Phokylides, V. 8 zeigt:

> πρῶτα θεὸν τιμᾶν, μετέπειτα δὲ σεῖο γονῆας
>
> Zunächst Gott ehren, dann deine Eltern!

Auch Sir 1,14 formuliert ebenso unter Verwendung des Gebots-Infinitivs:

> Ἀρχὴ σοφίας· φοβεῖσθαι τὸν κύριον,
>
> Anfang der Weisheit: den Herrn fürchten, …[38]

Hesiod hatte in den „Mahnenden Sprüchen des Chiron" (Χείρωνος ὑποθῆκαι) gesagt:

> Εὖ νῦν μοι τάδ' ἕκαστα μετὰ φρεσὶ πευκαλίμῃσι
> φράζεσθαι· πρῶτον μέν, ὅτ' ἂν δόμον εἰσαφίκηαι,
> ἔρδειν ἱερὰ καλὰ θεοῖς αἰειγενέτῃσιν
>
> Gut nun merke dir all dies in deinem klugen Verstand: Zu allererst, wenn du dein Haus betrittst, schöne heilige Handlungen zu vollführen für die ewiggeborenen Götter. (Frg. 283 West)

Die inhaltlichen Parallelen und Differenzen sind deutlich—bei Hesiod steht die Ermahnung zur heiligen Handlung am Anfang, wenn man heim kommt. Sie bezieht sich aber natürlich auf alle Götter. Phokylides formuliert viel prägnanter eine Spruchweisheit, formuliert also nicht „episch" wie Hesiod. Der Befehles-Infinitiv unterstützt die Knappheit der Aussage. Doch

37. Vgl. hierzu oben Anm. 2.

38. Änderungen der Interpunktion und der Übersetzung im Vergleich zu LXX.D vom Verf.

bei Phokylides wird eine Reihung vorgenommen—erst den Gott zu ehren, dann die Eltern. Sirach spricht von „fürchten", nicht von „ehren" oder „heilige Handlung vollziehen"—das gleiche Thema wird also inhaltlich und semantisch jeweils ganz unterschiedlich, formal aber vergleichbar durchgeführt. Die Differenzen sind erkennbar, gehören aber in den Bereich der auktorialen Formulierungsfreiheit. „Einfluss oder Rezeption?"—Diese Frage führt hier nicht weiter.

Phokylides verwendet auch häufig Nominalsätze; vgl. etwa V. 42: ἡ φιλοχρημοσύνη μήτηρ κακότητος ἁπάσης—„die Habsucht ist Mutter allen Übels".

Sodann begegnet mahnend-lehrhafte Dichtung nicht nur in den erwähnten ὑποθῆκαι des mythischen Helden-Erziehers Chiron, sondern auch in der griechischen *Elegie* (die nicht zu verwechseln ist mit der völlig eigenen Inhalten und Formprinzipien verpflichteten *römischen* Form der Liebes-Elegie):[39] Mimnermos, Solon und Theognis sind deren bekannteste Vertreter, von denen insbesondere Theognis (wohl 6./5. Jh.) rasch im 5. Jh. zu einem vielbehandelten Schulautor avanciert ist.[40] Der bisweilen melancholische (und so wohl auch namengebende) Tenor dieser Elegien, die sympotischen Charakter mit deutlichen Zügen der Knabenliebe[41] tragen und die sprachlich-formal aus der Abfolge von Hexameter und Pentameter bestehen, ist ein besonderer Zug dieser Dichtung: Die Vergänglichkeit des Lebens steht im Zentrum zusammen mit der Aufforderung, den Tag zu nutzen und das Leben zu genießen, solange dies möglich ist. Der bedeutende Redner, Zeitgenosse und Konkurrent Platons, Isokrates, würdigt die Werke von Hesiod, Phokylides und Theognis ausdrücklich wegen ihrer Beliebtheit und oft hilfreichen Verhaltens-Anleitungen.[42] Wegen ihrer gesellschaftsbezogenen Prägung ist ein Vergleich mit dem Sirach-Buch zumindest im Falle von Theognis eher irreführend: Die Basis der griechischen und der jüdischen Kultur ist jeweils in diesem Aspekt zu verschieden.

39. Vgl. hierzu Niklas Holzberg, *Die römische Liebeselegie: Eine Einführung*, 5. Aufl., Einführung: Klassische Philologie (Darmstadt: Wissenschaftliche Buchgesellschaft, 2012).

40. Vgl. Scully, *DNP* 12.2:448 (oben Anm. 23); Schlichtmann und Zimmermann, *Die Literatur der archaischen und klassischen Zeit*, 176–79 (oben Anm. 3).

41. Kyrnos wird von Theognis als dessen Geliebter häufig angesprochen.

42. Dies betont im 4. Jh. v. Chr. etwa der Redner Isokrates, Ad Nicoclem (*Oratio* 2), 43.2. Vgl. Scully, *DNP* 12.2:448 (oben Anm. 23).

Wenn sich die prägnanten Sprüche der seit Platon (Protagoras 343a) sogenannten Sieben Weisen, deren Namen unter insgesamt 22 Aspiranten bereits in der Antike nicht einheitlich überliefert sind,[43] unter Weisheitsliteratur einreihen lassen, dann zeigt sich hier die Tendenz einer späteren Kanon-Bildung von aphoristischen Texten oder Einzelaussagen, die (jeweils für sich betrachtet) keinen in sich geschlossenen Kontext bilden, wohl aber wegen ihrer Sentenzenhaftigkeit beliebt und verbreitet waren.[44] Die sprachliche Gestaltung dieser Sentenzen oder Gnomai impliziert eine jeweils zugrunde gelegte Fragestellung, die mit Burkert treffend als τί-μάλιστα-Fragen bezeichnet werden können, also als die der Spruch-Antwort vorausgehende, nicht aber explizit gestellte Frage „was am ehesten …": *Was ist am ehesten zu erstreben* oder *zu vermeiden* usf.[45] Die Auskünfte der Sieben Weisen haben gemeinsam die Tendenz, lebenspraktische Fragen vor dem Hintergrund eines σοφία-Begriffs zu vermitteln, der insbesondere mit den diversen τέχναι verknüpft, also noch nicht theoretisch oder noetisch orientiert ist. Die Sprüche wollen daher nicht primär philosophisches oder theologisches Wissen tradieren, sondern sie sprechen eher ein Gemeinschaft stiftendes oder sich der Gemeinschaft vergewisserndes „collective statement" aus.[46] Auch hierin liegt ein gewisser Unterschied zu Sirach.

Somit kann zunächst zusammenfassend gesagt werden, dass sich in Hinblick auf den Gattungshorizont das Phänomen der Weisheitsliteratur bei den Griechen nur in Ansätzen mit der orientalischen Literatur oder im speziellen Fall mit Sirach vergleichen lässt: Ähnliche Ansätze führen zu einer Auseinander- oder Weiterentwicklung im Kontext der jeweils kulturbedingten Fragestellungen einer Gesellschaft, deren religiöses und philosophisches Weltkonzept nicht zuletzt durch den Polytheismus und durch eine andersartige Entwicklung der Lebensstruktur eine eigene Entwicklung erfahren hat. Vor dem Hintergrund einer differenten

43. Vgl. Althoff, Zeller, und Asper, *Die Worte der Sieben Weisen*, bes. 5–24 (oben Anm. 17).

44. So die Einschätzung von Scully, *DNP* 12.2:449 (oben Anm. 23).

45. Walter Burkert, *Weisheit und Wissenschaft: Studien zu Pythagoras, Philolaos und Platon*, Erlanger Beiträge zur Sprach- und Kunstwissenschaft 10 (Nürnberg: Carl, 1962), 153. Die Frageform begegnet im Zusammenhang mit den *Akusmata* bei Imablich (vgl. ibid., 150ff.).

46. So Markus Asper, "'Literatursoziologisches' zu den Sprüchen der Sieben Weisen," in Althoff, Zeller, und Asper, *Die Worte der Sieben Weisen*, 85–103, Zitat S.87 (oben Anm. 17).

Gattungsentfaltung wird nun das damit eng verknüpfte Phänomen der sprachlichen Gestaltung bei Sirach zu sehen sein.

3. Sprachliche Gestaltung

3.1. Prolog und übersetzter Text

Der Hauptprolog—nur er, nicht der nur in der Minuskelhandschrift 248 überlieferte alternative Prolog wird hier herangezogen,[47]—ist eine eigenständige Textur ohne hebräischen Quelltext. Sein Verfasser ist nach eigener Aussage (Prol 7) der Enkel dessen, der die *Sophia Sirach* auf Hebräisch verfasst hat. Somit ist der Prolog nicht nur in Hinblick auf seine Gattung, sondern auch hinsichtlich seiner Originalität anders zu betrachten als der griechische *Übersetzungstext* der hebräischen Weisheitsschrift.

Für die Übersetzung sind als Parameter heranzuziehen: (1) der bereits dargelegte Gattungshorizont des Weisheitstextes, (2) die Übersetzung des Pentateuch als Rahmen oder Muster für nahezu alle nach dem Pentateuch entstandenen LXX-Übersetzungen, (3) die persönliche Vorgehensweise des Sirach-Übersetzers.

Reiterer betont zurecht,[48] dass der Sirach-Text, den die Göttinger Ausgabe von Ziegler präsentiert, nicht den ursprünglichen und somit ältesten Übersetzungstext des Enkels (G I) oder die später entstandene Version G II bietet: Auf diese Schwierigkeiten sei hier nur vorab hingewiesen: Im Folgenden wird, sofern es nicht ausdrücklich erwähnt wird, von der Ziegler-Ausgabe ausgegangen.

Zunächst kann generell festgestellt werden, dass die Sprachgestaltung im Sirach-Buch ein sehr gut verständliches literarisches Griechisch verwendet, das somit dem griechischen Sprachsystem sehr entgegen kommt. Es weist kaum befremdliche Erscheinungen auf, die auf eine dem hebräischen Prätext geschuldete Oberflächenübersetzung *ad verbum* zurückzuführen wären. Dennoch finden sich Passagen, in denen die Textstruktur näher an der hebräischen Wortstellung orientiert ist als an anderen Stellen: Hier ist zu prüfen, unter welchen Bedingungen sich die Stilistik und

47. Vgl. Joseph Ziegler, ed., *Sapientia Iesu Filii Sirach*, 2. Aufl. (Göttingen: Vandenhoeck & Ruprecht, 1980), 66.

48. Friedrich V. Reiterer, *"Die Vollendung der Gottesfurcht ist Weisheit" (Sir 21,11): Studien zum Buch Ben Sira (Jesus Sirach)*, SBAB 50 (Stuttgart: Katholisches Bibelwerk, 2011), 21.

die Wortwahl ändern. Besonders gut greifbar wird die Differenz zwischen Prätext und Übersetzung in Passagen, in denen der Übersetzer, anders noch als sein Großvater, in einen bereits stärker hellenistisch geprägten Kultur- und Lebenskontext eingebunden ist und somit bisweilen nicht mehr alle Inhalte des hebräischen Prätextes nachvollziehen kann.[49]

Gleichsam eine „Visitenkarte" für die griechische Textur ist die korrekte Verwendung der bereits oben erwähnten Tempora oder auch der Umgang mit den Syntagmen der Nominalformen. Diese Phänomene sollen hier als Spezimina im folgenden skizziert werden:

3.2. Tempus-Gebrauch und Nominalformen

Der Tempusgebrauch ist von Vornherein bei dieser Textgattung insofern erwartbar unproblematisch, da kein erzählender oder prophetischer Text vorliegt. Insbesondere aber fällt die Variations-Bereitschaft im Tempusgebrauch dort auf, wo der gnomische Aorist verwendet bzw. vermieden wird: Statt einer auf Sicherheit bedachten Stereotypie zu verfallen, beherrscht der Autor die Zielsprache so gut, dass er zwischen dem bei Weisheitssprüchen generell anzutreffenden Präsens, dem Gewissheit signalisierenden Futur und dem im Horizont dieser Textsorte entstandenen gnomischen Aorist frei wechseln kann. Dabei ist die Tendenz zu beobachten, dass auch innerhalb eines gedanklichen Zusammenhangs über mehrere Kola der Tempusgebrauch nicht zwingend einheitlich ist. Als repräsentatives Beispiel sei Kap. 1 vorgeführt. Dabei werden das jeweilige Tempus sowie dessen Funktion im Kontext notiert:

1	Πᾶσα σοφία παρὰ κυρίου	Nominalsatz
	καὶ μετ' αὐτοῦ ἐστιν εἰς τὸν αἰῶνα.	gnomisches Präsens
2	ἄμμον θαλασσῶν καὶ σταγόνας ὑετοῦ	
	καὶ ἡμέρας αἰῶνος τίς ἐξαριθμήσει;	Futur (als Folge v.V. 1)
3	ὕψος οὐρανοῦ καὶ πλάτος γῆς	
4	καὶ ἄβυσσον καὶ σοφίαν τίς ἐξιχνιάσει;	Futur (als Folge v.V. 1)
5	προτέρα πάντων ἔκτισται σοφία	Perfekt (konstatierend, resultativ)
	καὶ σύνεσις φρονήσεως ἐξ αἰῶνος.	
6	(πηγὴ σοφίας λόγος θεοῦ ἐν ὑψίστοις,	(Nominalsatz)
	καὶ αἱ πορεῖαι αὐτῆς ἐντολαὶ αἰώνιοι.)	(Nominalsatz)

49. Vgl. Georg Sauer, *Studien zu Ben Sira*, BZAW 440 (Berlin: de Gruyter, 2013), 25–34.

7	ῥίζα σοφίας τίνι ἀπεκαλύφθη;	gnom. Aorist
	καὶ τὰ πανουργεύματα αὐτῆς τίς ἔγνω;	gnom. Aorist
8	(ἐπιστήμη σοφίας τίνι ἐφανερώθη;	(gnom. Aorist)
	καὶ τὴν πολυπειρίαν αὐτῆς τίς συνῆκεν;)	(gnom. Aorist)
9	εἷς ἐστιν σοφός, φοβερὸς σφόδρα,	gnom. Präsens
	καθήμενος ἐπὶ τοῦ θρόνου αὐτοῦ.	[Part. Präsens]
10	κύριος αὐτὸς ἔκτισεν αὐτὴν	Aoristus narrans
	καὶ εἶδεν καὶ ἐξηρίθμησεν αὐτὴν	Aoristus narrans
	καὶ ἐξέχεεν αὐτὴν ἐπὶ πάντα τὰ ἔργα αὐτοῦ,	Aoristus narrans
11	μετὰ πάσης σαρκὸς κατὰ τὴν δόσιν αὐτοῦ,	
	καὶ ἐχορήγησεν αὐτὴν τοῖς ἀγαπῶσιν αὐτόν.[50]	Aoristus narrans

Die freie, aber eben sehr angemessene und sinnvolle Tempus-Gebung zeugt davon, dass der Übersetzer sprachlich gleichsam griechisch denkt. Dort, wo eine Eingangstatsache formuliert wird wie in V. 1, wird erst ein Nominalsatz gebildet—damit erfolgt das Signal, den Satz möge man bitte als Weisheitsspruch mit genereller Gültigkeit als Tatsachenaussage verstehen. Im zweiten Kolon wird hingegen das Prädikat ἐστιν gesetzt, und zwar im Präsens: Eine *variatio per amplificationem* gegenüber der Sprachgestaltung im 1. Kolon.

---

50. 1 Alle Weisheit (ist) vom Herrn
und mit ihm ist sie in Ewigkeit.
2 [2ab] Den Sand der Meere und die Tropfen des Regens
und die Tage der Ewigkeit—wer wird (sie) auszählen?
3 [2cd] Die Höhe des Himmels und die Breite der Erde
und den Abgrund und die Weisheit—wer wird sie ausspüren?
4 Früher als alle (Dinge) ist die Weisheit geschaffen worden,
und die Einsicht der Vernunft (ist) von Ewigkeit her.
5 | Die Quelle der Weisheit (ist) Gottes Wort in den Höhen,
| und ihre Wege (sind) ewige Gebote.
6 Die Wurzel der Weisheit—wem wurde sie offenbart?
Und ihre Raffinesse—wer erkannte sie?
7 | Das Verstehen von Weisheit—wem wurde es offenbart?
| Und ihre umfassende Erfahrung—wer kennt sie?
8 Einer ist weise, sehr furchterregend,
(und) sitzt auf seinem Thron.
9 [9–10a] Der Herr selbst schuf sie,
und er kannte und zählte sie
und goss sie über alle seine Werke aus.
10 Unter allem Fleisch (ist sie) gemäß seiner Gabe,
und er gewährte sie denen, die ihn lieben. (LXX.D)

Vers 2 und 3 bestehen nun nicht mehr aus zwei einzelnen Kola, sondern aus jeweils *einer Einheit* mit jeweils nur einem Prädikat (ἐξαριθμήσει, ἐξιχνιάσει), das im Futur steht und jeweils als Folge der Grundaussage verstehbar ist. Dabei wird als Form die rhetorische Frage gewählt, womit im Vergleich zu Vers 1 eine *variatio per orationem* erfolgt.

Vers 4 besteht wiederum aus einem Bikolon, dessen erstes ein Prädikat im konstatierend-resultativen Perfekt hat (ἔκτισται), während Kolon 2 dieses Prädikat ungesagt „mitbenutzt". Der Satzbau stellt auch hier wiederum durch die Platzierung des Prädikats in der ersten Hälfte eine *variatio per ordinem* dar.

Das nominale Bikolon in V. 5 ist nicht überall überliefert und bleibt daher hier unbeachtet.

V. 6 sowie das nicht überall bezeugte Bikolon 7 ist jeweils parallel als rhetorische Frage mit gnomischem Aorist (ἀπεκαλύφθη, ἔγνω, ἐφανερώθη, συνῆκεν) gebildet.

Mit dem Bikolon 8 kann man einen neuen, den Beginn vertiefenden Absatz erkennen: εἷς „einer" betont exkludierend die Aussage von V. 1: Die Aussparung des Gottesnamens in diesem erneut mit dem gnomischen und somit eine Grundwahrheit feststellenden Präsens (ἐστιν) formulierten Abschnitt bereitet das folgende Trikolon vor (V. 9), in dem der Herr—bezeichnet als κύριος αὐτός (der Herr selbst) nun wieder mit Prädikaten im Aorist (ἔκτισεν, ἐξηρίθμησεν, ἐξέχεεν) versehen ist—allerdings diesmal in einer *narrativen* Funktion: Auch auf dieser Ebene weist der Text innerhalb einer kurzen Reichweite das Prinzip der Variatio auf—die Variatio hat hier jedoch nicht die Satzordnung oder Wortstellung oder den Tempus-Stamm zum Gegenstand, sondern sie betrifft hier die *Funktion* des jeweiligen Tempus-Stammes.

Das letzte vorgelegte Bikolon in V. 10 setzt das vorangehende Trikolon zwar abschließend fort, bietet aber noch einen neuen Gedanken—daher kann die Interpunktion etwas variiert werden, und daher kann καί in Sir 1,10.2 auch mit fortführendem „aber" wiedergegeben werden. Beim Aoristus narrans (ἐχορήγησεν, 1,10.2) ist eine gegenüber LXX.D andere Übersetzung zu erwägen:

(1,9) κύριος αὐτὸς ἔκτισεν αὐτὴν
καὶ εἶδεν καὶ ἐξηρίθμησεν αὐτὴν
καὶ ἐξέχεεν αὐτὴν ἐπὶ πάντα τὰ ἔργα αὐτοῦ[·]
(1,10) μετὰ πάσης σαρκὸς κατὰ τὴν δόσιν αὐτοῦ
καὶ ἐχορήγησεν αὐτὴν τοῖς ἀγαπῶσιν αὐτόν.

(1,9) Der Herr selbst *hat* sie erschaffen,
und er hat sie in den Blick genommen und vollständig ermessen,
und er hat sie über all seine Werke *ausströmen lassen[;]*
(1,10) mit all ihrer Leiblichkeit nach seiner Gabe aber
hat er sie *ausgestattet*[51] für diejenigen, die ihn lieben.[52]

Neben dieser durchaus feinsinnig gehandhabten Sprachgestaltung sind noch zahlreiche weitere Beobachtungen (wie etwa die bereitwillige Verwendung des Partizips) möglich, die hier nicht im Detail vorgestellt werden können. Vielmehr ist festzustellen, dass der Übersetzer im Übersetzungstext den Prinzipien der griechischen Sprachgestaltung in sehr hohem Maße verpflichtet ist. Sein Wortschatz ist der eines hochgebildeten Griechen, der in der Kultur des Hellenismus heimisch ist.[53] Im Prolog

51. LXX.D übersetzt ἐχορήγησεν mit „gewährte". Die Bedeutung von χορηγέω (in LXX nur hier und in 1 Makk 14,10—ein Hinweis auf die gute Vertrautheit beider Verfasser mit der attischen Kultur) verweist zunächst auf die Bühnensprache und bedeutet zunächst „Chorführer sein"; daraus entwickelt sich sodann im Attischen die Sonderbedeutung „einen Theater-Chor finanzieren", „einen Theater-Chor finanziell ausstatten". Diese Bedeutung erweitert sich sodann allgemein darauf, dass eine Person die „Ausstattung" von XY im öffentlichen Interesse übernimmt. Diese Bedeutung scheint im vorliegenden Kontext durchaus angemessen. Da nun bei den vorangehenden Verben in Sir 1,9–10 im Deutschen der Aspekt (im Griechischen liegt jeweils ein Aorist vor) durch Wortwahl und Tempus (Perfekt) in der hier angebotenen Übersetzung dem griechischen Prätext etwas näher kommt, ist es konsequent, auch in Sir 1,10.2 statt des Präteritum, das hier durchaus im Deutschen verwendbar ist, ebenfalls das Perfekt zu wählen.

52. Kursiv: Änderungen des Verf. LXX.D: „Unter allem Fleisch (ist sie) gemäß seiner Gabe, und er gewährte sie denen, die ihn lieben." Vgl. Kaiser (2005) (oben Anm. 2), 9: „Sie ist bei allem Fleisch nach seiner Gabe, | aber am meisten gab er sie denen, die ihn lieben." Beide Versionen gehen von einem elliptischen Nominalsatz im Griechischen aus, der parallel zu den anderen Sätzen des Abschnitts gedacht wird. Die hier vorgeschlagene Übersetzung hingegen macht dadurch, dass Sir 1,10.1 mit dem folgenden Vers verbunden wird, diese Ergänzung überflüssig.

53. Insbesondere fallen die ausgesprochen zahlreichen Hapaxlegomena auf, die deutlich zeigen, wie groß die literarische Bildung und wie frei die Wortwahl des Übersetzers ist. Hierzu vgl. die einschlägige und methodisch umfassend reflektierte Darstellung bei Christian Wagner, *Die Septuaginta-Hapaxlegomena im Buch Jesus Sirach: Untersuchungen zu Wortwahl und Wortbildung unter besonderer Berücksichtigung des textkritischen und übersetzungstechnischen Aspekts*, BZAW 282 (Berlin: de Gruyter, 1999), 91–101 und passim. Weiterhin kann auf die insbesondere durch den hellenistischen Lebenskontext begründbaren Änderungen gegenüber dem hebräischen Prätext hingewiesen werden. Hierzu vgl. Georg Sauer, "Ben Sira in Jerusalem und sein Enkel

geht der Autor noch einen Schritt weiter, indem er den komplexen Periodenbau griechischer Prosa gleichsam als Bravourstück vorlegt und ihn so stilisiert, wie dies auch ein griechischer Redner tun könnte. Längere Sätze mit Hyperbaton und Partizipialstruktur finden sich sonst in den Übersetzungstexten der LXX und auch speziell bei Sir nicht—hier aber gibt es keinen Prätext, und somit kann sich der Autor sozusagen sprachlich-stilistisch austoben.

4. Bündelung und Ausblick

Einer Übersetzung einen Prolog voranzustellen ist dann angemessen, wenn es mit der Übersetzung etwas Besonderes auf sich hat. Sirach hat sich also *sehr angemessen* an seine Arbeit gesetzt. Dass der Prolog sich sprachlich klar von der Übersetzung abhebt, liegt zum einen an der Entscheidung, den Prolog in Prosa zu gestalten und damit deutlich vom Weisheitsbuch abzusetzen. Zum anderen hatte der Übersetzer keine Vorlage oder Vorgabe dafür: Er hält es aus eigener Überzeugung für notwendig, sein Tun zu begründen und das Publikum auf das vorzubereiten, was es vorfinden wird. Dabei kann der Übersetzer den mit den thematischen Schlüsselworten der *σοφία*, der *παιδεία* und der *ἐπιστήμονες* im ersten Satz in das Thema einleiten und somit zugleich denjenigen Hintergrund anklingen lassen, der auch für ihn selbst bestimmend war: Weisheit, Bildung und Tradierung. Dies sind zugleich Schlüsselbegriffe, die die Bildungselite im Hellenismus sowohl charakterisieren als auch zur Lektüre (*ἀναγιγνώσκοντας* im 1. Satz des Prologs) einladen. Insofern wird nicht allein die Diasporagemeinde in Alexandria der *intendierte* Leser sein.

Insgesamt finden sich in der *Übersetzung* viele Elemente, die aus sentenzenhaften Sätzen der nur bedingt vergleichbaren originären griechischen Literatur bekannt sind, in der es Weisheitsliteratur nicht in dem Umfang und in der qualitativen Durchdringung gibt wie im Orient: Hier sind die Griechen völlig eigene Wege gegangen, die zur Ausprägung einer anders diversifizierten Gattungsvielfalt geführt haben.

---

in Alexandria," in *Studien zu Ben Sira*, von Georg Sauer, BZAW 440 (Berlin: de Gruyter, 2013), 25–34 (oben Anm. 49). Vgl. ferner auch zu einzelnen Aspekten der Sprache wie Wortbedeutung und Wortwahl Friedrich V. Reiterer, *"Alle Weisheit stammt vom Herrn…": Gesammelte Studien zu Ben Sira*, hrsg. Renate Egger-Wenzel, BZAW 375 (Berlin: de Gruyter, 2007), 278–305 und passim.

Im Sirach-Buch werden dort also, wo gattungsbedingt Parallelen zu erwarten sind, diese souverän gehandhabt und im Rahmen der Vorliebe für Variationen zu einer eigenständigen Übersetzungsliteratur um- und weitergestaltet.[54]

54. Dass Sir zwar deutlich in hebräischer Tradition steht, aber dennoch einen ebenso deutlichen griechischen Einfluss zeigt, betont West, *East Face of Helicon*, 95. Obwohl hier von West keine detaillierten Beobachtungen mitgeteilt werden, ist dies dennoch deswegen zu erwähnen, weil Sir in den meisten altphilologischen Abhandlungen zur hellenistischen Literatur kaum Erwähnung findet. Zu weiteren Beobachtungen zur sprachlich-kulturellen Bildung und Eigenständigkeit vgl. Anm. 53.

Sirach 10:1–18: Some Observations on the Work of the Translator

Benjamin G. Wright

Introduction

For most of the transmission history of the Wisdom of Ben Sira, the Greek translation (henceforth Sirach) constituted its primary textual form, with other important witnesses to the text in Latin and Syriac.[1] As important as these latter two translations are for the textual history of Ben Sira, however, the Greek text is the oldest complete version and was translated within a generation or so of its composition.[2] It also was the only one of the three to translate the Hebrew before it had been expanded with additional proverbs. With the discovery and identification of six fragmentary Hebrew manuscripts in the Cairo Geniza (MSS A–F) along with 2Q18, 11Q5, and the Masada manuscript from the Judean Desert, a great deal

1. The Latin was made from the expanded GK II text and the Syriac from HB II. A number of scholars maintain that the Syriac translator consulted the Greek as well. See, for example, Conleth Kearns, *The Expanded Text of Ecclesiasticus: Its Teaching on the Future Life as a Clue to Its Origin*, ed. Pancratius C. Beentjes, DCLS 11 (Berlin: de Gruyter, 2011), 57–58 and Moshe Z. Segal, ספר בן סירא השלם [*The Complete Book of Ben Sira*] (Jerusalem: Bialik Foundation, 1958), 61–62. W. Th. van Peursen has questioned this conclusion. See his monograph, *Language and Interpretation in the Syriac Text of Ben Sira: A Comparative Linguistic and Literary Study*, MPIL 16 (Leiden: Brill, 2007), ch. 2. See the chart on 38. I extend thanks to Brad Gregory and Jeremy Corley for their comments on an earlier version of this paper, all of which served to make it better.

2. Although even by that time some corruptions had entered the Hebrew text used by the translator. See, for instance, the examples in Yigael Yadin, *The Ben Sira Scroll from Masada* (Jerusalem: The Israel Exploration Society and The Shrine of the Book, 1965), 9 (English Introduction).

of scholarly interest and energy was directed toward the possibility of recovering Ben Sira's Hebrew text, and although we now have Hebrew that covers approximately seventy percent of the book, the extant manuscripts are replete with textual difficulties of their own. This situation presents the scholar with a complicated and sometimes bewildering textual morass through which to wade.

Essentially two approaches have been taken to recovering the Hebrew text of Ben Sira. First, scholars have engaged in text-critical research on the Hebrew manuscripts to determine, if possible, where the surviving Hebrew manuscripts preserve what looks like the best text available. Second, scholars have looked to the translated versions, primarily the Greek and Syriac, to attempt to reconstruct the Hebrew parent text on which the translations were made, but the possibility of recovering the parent text of the translations depends on close examination of their translation technique(s).[3] In my earliest work on the Greek of Ben Sira in my PhD dissertation, I argued that on the basis of the approach taken by the translator, who claims to be the author's grandson, the Greek held only limited value for recovering the Hebrew parent in those places where Hebrew did not survive.[4] In my subsequent work, I remain convinced that my conclusions in that study still hold true.

The relationship between a Hebrew text and its translation might be studied for any number of reasons besides the reconstruction of the parent text, however. One might examine the Greek translation of Ben Sira, among other reasons, in order to arrive at a satisfactory description of the translation itself, to assess the kind of Greek it exhibits, to determine the educational level of the translator, to understand the development of the Greek language in the period the translation was made, or to discover the exegetical or theological ideas that the translator brought to his work. As a percentage of the growing mountain of scholarship on Ben Sira, relatively little attention has been paid to the Greek translation on its own and for its habits and character.[5]

---

3. See, for example, Antonino Minissale, *La versione greca del Siracide: Contfronto con il testo ebraica alla lucedell' attività midrascica e del metodo targumico*, AnBib 133 (Rome: Pontifical Biblical Institute, 1995).

4. Benjamin G. Wright, *No Small Difference: Sirach's Relationship to Its Hebrew Parent Text*, SCS 26 (Atlanta: Scholars Press, 1989), ch. 4.

5. See, for example, Wright, *No Small Difference*; Wright, "Translation Greek in Sirach in Light of the Grandson's Prologue," in *The Texts and Versions of the Book of Ben*

One specific issue that has roiled Septuagint Studies in recent years also compels comprehensive examination of the translation, that is, the problem of when translators are engaging in deliberate exegesis of their source texts and the extent to which we can identify theology in the LXX/OG translations. As part of the work that led to *A New English Translation of the Septuagint* (NETS), Albert Pietersma argued that when looking at these translations, scholars needed to distinguish what the translator was doing at the translation's point of production and what subsequent readers did with the text in its reception history.[6] So, for example, what looks like theology or exegesis to a later reader might not have been what the translator was trying to accomplish in the translation process. In order to identify a translator's exegetical proclivities, if he indeed had any—whether of a general sort or of theological ideas imposed on any specific passage—a detailed knowledge of any translator's work is required.

In this paper, then, I will examine the Greek translation of Sir 10:1–18, focusing specifically on the translation at its point of production, in order to try to understand how the grandson/translator approached his parent text. I selected this passage for several reasons. As might be expected, some of the most interesting passages in a text are those that might be inherently loaded theologically, where the author or translator potentially might be

---

Sira: Transmission and Interpretation, ed. Jan Joosten and Jean-Sébastien Rey, JSJSup 150 (Leiden: Brill), 75–94; several articles by James K. Aitken, including "The Literary Attainment of the Translator of Greek Sirach," in Joosten and Rey, *Texts and Versions*, 95–126; several articles by Anssi Voitila, including "Transposed Items between Sentences, Lines, and Verses, in the Sapientia Iesu Filii Sirach," *BIOSCS* 40 (2007): 1–10; Christian Wagner, *Die Septuaginta-Hapaxlegomena im Buch Jesus Sirach*, BZAW 282 (Berlin: de Gruyter, 1999).

6. NETS = Albert Pietersma and Benjamin G. Wright, eds., *A New English Translation of the Septuagint and the Other Greek Translations Traditionally Included under That Title* (New York: Oxford University Press, 2007). See Albert Pietersma, "LXX and DTS: A New Archimedean Point for Septuagint Studies?," *BIOSCS* 39 (2006): 1–11; Pietersma, "A New Paradigm for Addressing Old Questions: The Relevance of the Interlinear Model for the Study of the Septuagint," in *Bible and Computer: The Stellenbosch AIBI-6 Conference; Proceedings of the Association Internationale Bible et Informatique "From Alpha to Byte"; University of Stellenbosch 17–21 July 2000*, ed. Johann Cook (Leiden: Brill, 2002), 337–64; Cameron Boyd-Taylor, *Reading between the Lines: The Interlinear Paradigm for Septuagint Studies*, BTS 8 (Leuven: Peeters, 2011); Benjamin G. Wright, "The Septuagint and Its Modern Translators," in *Die Septuaginta—Texte, Kontexte, Lebenswelten*, ed. Martin Karrer and Wolfgang Kraus with Martin Meiser, WUNT 219 (Tübingen: Mohr Siebeck, 2008), 103–14.

expected to work out some theological point. Chapter 24 on Wisdom or the Praise of the Ancestors in chapters 44–50 immediately come to mind as prime examples in Ben Sira. Yet, if we want to get a good sense of how a translator works, we might be better served to pay attention to places where this kind of theological or exegetical activity does not appear as likely, where the translator might not have as much at stake—that is, looking at the translator's "normal" or "usual" approach in a less theologically charged section. Sirach 10:1–18 looks to be just that kind of a passage. Although it deals with rulers and purveys some more general wisdom teaching about pride, on the surface nothing in these verses immediately jumps out as obviously theologically fraught.

Moreover, when working with Ben Sira, one has to take into consideration all of the Hebrew manuscript evidence, which can get quite complex at times. In the case of 10:1–18, only one manuscript is extant, MS A from the Geniza, and in these verses there are few textual issues that have to be negotiated in the Hebrew text.[7] Thus, we have a relatively uncomplicated Hebrew text that can be compared with the Greek and that, for the purposes of this exercise at least, we can consider the putative parent text of the Greek to serve as a basis for comparison. So, as an overall approach, I will take the Hebrew of MS A as the parent text of the Greek unless there is good reason to abandon that text for a different parent. Of course, this is essentially how Septuagint scholars work with the MT, regarding it as the *putative* parent text, even though we know that in places the Greek translators had before them texts that were not identical to the MT. Examining these verses, then, allows us to focus on the Greek translation rather than on the complex textual situation that we encounter elsewhere in the Hebrew manuscripts. This approach will not eliminate the difficulties, but as an exercise in examining the Greek translation, it will make them manageable.

In general I will concentrate on the differences between the Greek and the Hebrew texts. If the translator has rendered the Hebrew adequately without difficulty, I will not comment much, if at all. These are not the most interesting passages. When the translation does differ from the Hebrew, we have to ask what the reason for that difference is, and several are possible. For example, the translator might have had a different parent text; he

7. On the Hebrew of MS A for about half of this section and chapter 11, see Jean-Sébastien Rey, "Si 10,12–12,1: Nouvelle Édition du Fragment Adler (ENA 2536-2)," *RevQ* 25 (2012): 575–604.

might have misread the parent text and created in his mind an alternative parent text that did not exist;[8] he might not understand the Hebrew text and as a result render it interpretively or gloss it (e.g., *not* exegetically or theologically); or he might render the text according to some exegetical or theological agenda. So, we are engaged in a two-step process: first, to identify the differences in any given verse and second, to account for those differences.[9] At the conclusion, I will make some summary remarks about how the translator worked in this passage.

The Texts

10:1

שופט עם יוסד עמו
וממשלת מבין סרידה

κριτὴς σοφὸς παιδεύσει τὸν λαὸν αὐτοῦ,
καὶ ἡγεμονία συνετοῦ τεταγμένη ἔσται.

In this verse we see right away the basic approach that the translator took to his parent text as a matter of course, which was to move sequentially through the verse, rendering morpheme for morpheme. This isomorphic approach generally characterizes Sirach, as we will see.[10]

Of course, we always have to reckon with the possibility of a different *Vorlage* from what MS A has, and we find a likely example right off the bat in the equivalence of עם and σοφός. The Hebrew עם is almost certainly a mistake in transmission, perhaps originating due to attraction to the same noun in the second *stichos* or perhaps from the same term in verse

8. These first two situations are exceedingly difficult, if not impossible to distinguish in practice. See Emanuel Tov, *The Text-Critical Use of the Septuagint in Biblical Research*, rev. ed. (Jerusalem: Simor, 1997) 162–71, who calls these pseudo-variants when reconstructing the *Vorlage* of a Greek translation. For a different assessment, see John Screnock, "Translators as Scribes—A Comparison of Scribal Practice and Translation Practice: Exodus 1–14 in the Hebrew Manuscript Tradition and the Old Greek" (Ph.D. diss., University of Toronto, 2015).

9. This is essentially the method of operation in the Society of Biblical Literature Commentary on the Septuagint, which is a follow-up series to the NETS project (http://tinyurl.com/SBL60467k).

10. On isomorphism as a translation approach in the LXX/OG corpus, see Pietersma, "A New Paradigm"; Boyd-Taylor, *Reading between the Lines*; Albert Pietersma and Benjamin G. Wright, "To the Reader of NETS," in *A New English Translation of the Septuagint*, xiii–xx.

2. Although elsewhere in Sirach the translator does not establish a default equivalence between σοφός and חכם as one might perhaps expect, all of the other equivalents in the book for σοφός have to do with being wise or intelligent. Almost certainly the parent text had חכם or perhaps משכיל (intelligent) or ערום (wise, sly, cunning) especially since the Hebrew text creates a contrast with the neglectful ruler in verse 3.[11] The latter of the three might well provide a graphic path from a parent text that could have stood in front of the Greek translator to the text of MS A.

The graphic similarity between *daleth* and *resh* accounts for the translation of παιδεύσει. The Hebrew uses the verb *yod-samech-daleth*, to establish or found, rather than *yod-samech-resh*, to correct or discipline, which the translator elsewhere renders with the Greek root παιδεύω (cf. 7:23; 10:1; 40:29).[12]

Finally, the last word in the verse in MS A looks to be corrupt. The translator has likely read סדורה, which might well have been in his *Vorlage* and suits the translation well, although he has taken the participle of the verbless clause in Hebrew and turned it into a periphrastic verb in Greek, an understandable rendering. The scribe of MS A has vocalized the texts as if the reading were סדורה. The only other instance of the root *samech-daleth-resh* is in 50:14, where the Greek is from the verb κοσμέω.

10:2

כשופט עם כן מליציו
וכראש עיר כן יושביו[13]

11. The Syriac has ܚܟܝܡܐ in this verse, which supports the reading of the Greek translation. I thank Jeremy Corley for the suggestion of ערום, which occurs once is the extant Hebrew of Sirach at 6:32.

12. The text in the Accordance electronic database reads יוסר, but in the photograph of MS A, even though the *daleth* in this verse is not typical of others in the manuscript, the letters of this verb are, in my estimation, best read as *yod-waw-samekh-daleth*. Compare the *daleth* in צדק in 9:16 (MS A 3:15). Some scholars who read *daleth* are Rudolph Smend, *Die Weisheit des Jesus Sirach erklärt* (Berlin: Georg Reimer, 1906), 89 and Ze'ev Ben-Ḥayyim, *The Book of Ben Sira: Text, Concordance and an Analysis of the Vocabulary* (Jerusalem: The Academy of the Hebrew Language and the Shrine of the Book, The Historical Dictionary of the Hebrew Language, 1973), 12. Among the scholars reading *resh* is Pancratius C. Beetjes, *The Book of Ben Sira in Hebrew: A Text Edition of All Extant Hebrew Manuscripts and a Synopsis of All Parallel Hebrew Ben Sira Texts*, 2nd ed., VTSup 68 (Leiden: Brill, 2006), 34.

13. The Hebrew text of MS A in this section often has vocalization added. I have

κατὰ τὸν κριτὴν τοῦ λαοῦ αὐτοῦ οὕτως καὶ οἱ λειτουργοὶ αὐτοῦ,
καὶ κατὰ τὸν ἡγούμενον τῆς πόλεως πάντες οἱ κατοικοῦντες αὐτήν.[14]

In MS A, verses 2–5 are in the order 3, 2, 5, 4, which is different from the Greek and which creates a somewhat different picture. The Syriac has the same order as the Greek, and so the Greek likely represents the correct verse order. It is difficult to know which order one ought to prefer—although it seems probable to me that the *Vorlage* of the Greek had a different order from MS A—but since I am concentrating on the Greek, I follow its verse order.

At the beginning of the verse, the translator takes the conjunction in a verbless clause as a preposition, and this reading conditions the translation of the entire verse, including the parallel beginning to the second *stichos*. While the translator makes good sense of the verse, he does not render it into a more elegant Greek that might be possible if he had construed the verse properly.

While the Greek translator generally tends not to add words that are not in the Hebrew, we have two cases here where the Greek is longer.[15] The first possessive pronoun *αὐτοῦ* has no equivalent in Hebrew, but it makes good sense, and it is hard to determine whether it was in the translator's *Vorlage*, especially in light of the possessive pronoun at the end of the verse (see below).

The *καί* after *οὕτως* has been added adverbially for emphasis. Perhaps the verbless clause has also prompted the translator to add the *καί*.

Interestingly, the translator has attributed a good sense to מליציו, which comes from the verb *lamed-yod-tsade* with a base meaning of scorn. In the *hiphil*, however, it can mean to speak on behalf of someone, and it refers to an ambassador in 2 Chr 32:31. Still, *οἱ λειτουργοί* is probably an interpretive rendering of the Hebrew, based on the context, since the

---

given the consonantal text only, since the translator likely had a consonantal text before him.

14. Ziegler's text does not have *αὐτοῦ* in the first clause. He bases the reading on the commentary of Antonius Melissa in contrast with the entire Greek manuscript tradition, since this agrees with the Hebrew. I think that the pronoun probably belongs in the text and I have retained it. For Ziegler's critical text, see Joseph Ziegler, *Sapientia Iesu Filii Sirach*, 2nd ed., SVTG 12.2 (Göttingen: Vandenhoeck & Ruprecht, 1980).

15. Wright, *No Small Difference*, 67–91.

Greek is not a close semantic match of the Hebrew and elsewhere in Sirach the same noun renders the root *shin-resh-taf* (cf. 7:30; 50:14).

The grandson has also understood the connotation of ראש here and rendered it appropriately. He uses a Greek word from the same semantic group as ἡγεμονία in verse 1, which he employed to render a different Hebrew root and which results in some semantic leveling between the two verses.

In the second *stichos*, we can observe two variations between the Greek and MS A. Rather than reflecting a parallel structure between the two *stichoi*, the Greek translation has πάντες, which represents a presumed *Vorlage* of כל rather than כן. Whether the translator had כל in his Hebrew text or not is difficult to determine, but it seems likely that he did.

An interpretive problem attends the last word, יושביו. The Hebrew has a masculine possessive pronoun, which seems to go back to שופט as the antecedent, since עיר is feminine (cf. the Hebrew of v. 3). The Greek translator understandably took the inhabitants to be those living in the city rather than people belonging to the judge, as the Hebrew has it, and thus the accusative case pronoun in Greek has τῆς πόλεως as the antecedent, which results in "and according to the ruler of a city are all those who inhabit it."[16] The masculine pronoun in the Hebrew perhaps could have arisen in the interests of rhyming with the first *stichos*, which ends with the masculine pronoun.[17]

10:3

מלך פרוע ישחית עיר
ועיר נושבת בשכל שריה

βασιλεὺς ἀπαίδευτος ἀπολεῖ τὸν λαὸν αὐτοῦ,
καὶ πόλις οἰκισθήσεται ἐν συνέσει δυναστῶν.

The equivalence of ἀπαίδευτος with פרוע is unique in the LXX/OG corpus. In this verse, the translator produces a translation that sets up a contrast between the judge who educates his people and the uneducated king who destroys them. Rather than the king simply being neglectful, as

16. Another possibility is that in the process of transmission, the noun עיר, city, was taken as a masculine noun and the pronoun actually does refer to the city. I find this less likely than that the pronoun refers to the head/leader of the city, particularly since elsewhere in Sirach the word is taken as feminine. See v. 3.

17. My thanks to Brad Gregory for the suggestion.

in the Hebrew, the translator makes the issue one of training/education—not a surprising interpretation in a sapiential text.[18]

At the end of the first *stichos*, the Hebrew of MS A has עיר while the Greek presumes עם. Although, the translator might be interpreting here, the Greek translator almost certainly had a parent text that differed from MS A, since the Syriac as well has "his people," thus confirming that this most likely was the reading of the Hebrew *Vorlage*. The Greek parallels the two nouns in the same order from verse 2, people-city, which also could support a different parent text, especially since in 10:1–18 the Hebrew text contains a number of differing parallel elements. For the translator, the people whom the king rules belong to him, which accounts for the addition of the possessive pronoun.

As we saw in verse 2, the use of pronouns varies between the Hebrew as represented in MS A and the Greek. In the first *stichos*, the translator has the possessive αὐτοῦ for which there is no Hebrew equivalent and at the end of the verse the Greek lacks a possessive where MS A has one that has "city" as its antecedent.

10:4

ביד אלהים ממשלת תבל
ואיש לעת יעמד עליה

ἐν χειρὶ κυρίου ἡ ἐξουσία τῆς γῆς,
καὶ τὸν χρήσιμον ἐγερεῖ εἰς καιρὸν ἐπ' αὐτῆς.

The lack of the definite article before χειρί (see also v. 5) produces a rather odd Greek phrase, "in a hand," which testifies to the literalistic approach that the translator sometimes takes, since he apparently has not read the morpheme with the vocalization that would indicate the presence of the definite article. The translator also takes the same approach in 48:20 and 49:6. This way of rendering the phrase is characteristic of other LXX/OG texts as well (see Prov 10:10; 21:1).[19]

The use of κύριος to render the divine name in whatever form it comes in the Hebrew is standard practice for the translator. The Hebrew manuscripts at various places have אל, אלהים, or the Tetragrammaton (often

18. Jeremy Corley suggested to me that perhaps פרוע should be translated as "unrestrained," which would trade on one meaning of the term, "wild." This meaning would cohere more with the Greek ἀπαίδευτος.

19. Thanks to Jeremy Corley for pointing this out.

abbreviated with three *yods* in MS B), and the translator uses κύριος for all of them.

The use in Hebrew of ממשלת in relation to God's rule parallels its use in verse 1 for intelligent human rulers. In this case, however, the translator has chosen a different term, employing ἐξουσία, which emphasizes God's omnipotence over the cosmos rather than simply his governance and which might point to a concern for *variatio* on the part of the translator.

Throughout the book, the translator takes an interpretive approach to the Hebrew noun תבל, which connotes the entirety of the world. Here, as also in 16:19, he renders it with γῆ, land, rather than with a more encompassing term that would suit the Hebrew. In Sir 37:3 and 39:2 he interprets the Hebrew using the adjective ξηρός, dry or withered, and in 43:3 he employs χώρα, country. In each case, where the Hebrew connotes the entire compass of the earth or world, the Greek reduces the scope.

The Greek rendering of the second *stichos* results in an interpretive rendering that departs from the meaning of the Hebrew. In MS A, the Hebrew prepositional phrase לעת goes together with the preceding noun to characterize "a man for the time," that is, the right person. The translator apparently does not recognize the connection, and by separating out the prepositional phrase and making it adverbial, he does not simply leave it that God raises up a person, which results in the rendering "a useful person" (χρήσιμος). The Greek thus has "and he will raise up a useful person at the right time over it."

10:5

ביד אלהים ממשלת כל גבר
ולפני מחוקק ישית הודו

ἐν χειρὶ κυρίου εὐοδία ἀνδρός,
καὶ προσώπῳ γραμματέως ἐπιθήσει δόξαν αὐτοῦ.

The lack of the definite article with χειρί matches the same construction in the previous verse.

The Greek εὐοδία does not seem to render the Hebrew ממשלת. The Hebrew has a parallel structure that God governs the world (v. 4) and also rules over all people (v. 5). It is difficult to think that the translator rendered this Hebrew—whether as an actual parent text or a presumed one. The Greek term appears in two other places in Sirach, in 20:9 where no Hebrew is extant and in 38:13 where it more appropriately renders מצלחת,

success or fortune. It appears a good possibility that the translator read this Hebrew term in verse 5.

For all intents and purposes, the Hebrew כל is simply ignored. Thus, where the Hebrew reads “in the hand of God is the governance over every man,” the Greek has “in the hand of the Lord is a man’s success.” Thus, the meaning of the Greek and that of the Hebrew as represented by MS A differ a great deal in the first *stichos*.

The phrase *προσώπῳ γραμματέως* creates a rather awkward line in Greek that significantly interprets the Hebrew. The use of *πρόσωπον* in the dative case for the Hebrew preposition לפני does not constitute a preposition in Greek. Moreover, the Hebrew מחוקק refers to a type of ruler throughout the Hebrew Bible, and the LXX/OG translators recognize that meaning. Throughout the LXX/OG translations the earlier translators use *γραμματεύς* for שטר, a kind of foreman, and the later translators employ it for ספר, scribe. The equivalence in Sirach transforms the point of the Hebrew, which is that God sets his splendor on the ruler. The grandson introduces the scribe into the ruling hierarchy, making God set God’s glory on his face. I wonder here whether the grandson is making an allusion to Moses’s face shining as he descended from the mountain with the Law in Exod 34:29, where it says that the skin on Moses face was “charged with glory” (NETS; *δεδόξασται* LXX). If that is the case, the translator not only inserts the scribe into the ruling hierarchy, he subtly connects the scribe, who teaches the law, with Moses who brought it to the Israelites. On the other hand, one could conceivably read the verse a nonexegetical manner if one were simply to understand מחוקק as a scribe, an equivalence that we see as well in Sir 44:4 (cf. the Masada manuscript). So, this passage highlights beautifully the problem of deciding whether a translator is working at finding a rendering for the text in front of him or whether he has a deliberate exegetical reading of it, that is, he has shaped the translation to express a view not necessarily resident in the source text. In my view, he have here an exegetical approach to the verse.

The equivalent of *δόξα* and הוד is not usual in Sirach; it does occur in two other passages, 42:25 and 43:1—in both cases referring to nature not to humans as here. The more usual equivalent is כבוד, although the translator does use the Greek term for other Hebrew terms and constructions on occasion.

10:6

[ב]כל פשע אל תשלים רע לריע
ואל תהלך בדרך גאוה

ἐπὶ παντὶ ἀδικήματι μὴ μηνιάσῃς τῷ πλησίον,
καὶ μὴ πρᾶσσε μηδὲν ἐν ἔργοις ὕβρεως.

For this verse the Greek gives an interpretive rendering. In the first *stichos*, the Hebrew contains a play on words with "evil" and "neighbor": "Do not pay your neighbor evil for any transgression." The Greek captures the essential thought, although the translator's rendering of תשלים רע with *μηνιάσῃς* shifts the meaning, since the Greek means to hold onto anger or hold a grudge, and it also conditions other translation equivalences such as *ἐπί* for ב. Two explanations seem possible: (1) the translator took these two Hebrew words together and rendered them with a single Greek verb or (2) the translation resulted from a parablepsis due to the graphically similar Hebrew words. Whatever the case, the Greek—"For every wrong, do not be angry with your neighbor"—shifts the focus from visiting evil on one's neighbor to holding onto anger against one's neighbor.

The second *stichos* is interpretive as well. Rather than walking in the way of insolence/arrogance, the Greek moves in a different direction. The translation of תהלך with *πρᾶσσε* is unique in Sirach, since in most cases the equivalent for הלך is *πορεύω* or *περιπατέω*. The thought of the Greek verse moves from an inner state—holding onto anger—to action, presumably generated by that inner disposition. Whether, then, the rendering of the first *stichos* conditioned the second is not certain, but it very well might have. The entire second half of the verse looks to be a gloss on the Hebrew rather than any straightforward translation.

This raises the question of whether the translator had the Hebrew of MS A in front of him. I see no necessary reason to propose a variant *Vorlage*, since at least in the first *stichos* the path from the Hebrew to the Greek is understandable enough. If the first part of the verse determined the gloss of the second, then we have here a translation that plays fast and loose with the parent text, although still within an isomorphic approach to translation, since we see in the second *stichos* that the translator still seems to be concerned to have Greek morphemes in place of Hebrew morphemes.

10:7

שנואה לאדון ואנשים גאוה
ומשניהם מעל עשק

μισητὴ ἔναντι κυρίου καὶ ἀνθρώπων ὑπερηφανία,
καὶ ἐξ ἀμφοτέρων πλημμελὴς ἡ ἀδικία.[20]

The first *stichos* of the Greek follows the Hebrew word-for-word, to the degree that the a:b:b':a' word order is retained, the Hebrew participle is rendered with an adjective in Greek, and the clause is left without an explicit verb, unlike in other verses where the translator makes sure to express some verbal action. The translator does employ a different noun for the Hebrew גאוה from the one he used at the very end of verse 6, thus creating semantic differentiation in the Greek where none exists in the Hebrew. This kind of variation characterizes the translation in general and might indicate a rhetorical concern for *variatio*.[21]

The Hebrew of the second *stichos* might have seemed somewhat obscure to the translator, so he kept close to the Hebrew, creating a somewhat awkward clause that lacks an explicit verb. The Greek *ἐξ ἀμφοτέρων* follows the Hebrew but without the pleonastic pronoun. If one takes the preposition as indicating origin, as it can in Greek, then we have, "And for both, injustice is wrong (or perhaps: a trespass)." This translation is close to the Hebrew, although the final two nouns in Hebrew express a slightly different sentiment from the adjective-noun in Greek. When we look elsewhere in Sirach for these equivalents, we discover that the translator does not have a standard set of equivalences for Hebrew words having to do with sin, error, wrong, evil, etc. So, for example, although in 10:7, עשק comes into Greek as *ἀδικία*, in 21:18 this Greek word renders מעל. Thus, it is difficult to tell the extent to which the translator is trying to draw distinctions among the various terms or whether they constitute rough synonyms for him.

10:8

מלכות מגוי אל גוי תסוב
בגלל חמס גאוה

βασιλεία ἀπὸ ἔθνους εἰς ἔθνος μετάγεται
διὰ ἀδικίας καὶ ὕβρεις καὶ χρήματα.[22]

20. The form *πλημμελὴς* is a conjecture on the part of Rahlfs and Ziegler based on the form *πλημμελησῃ* in S* A V 315. The other Greek manuscripts have different forms of a similar noun or a verb.

21. On variation of nouns and verbs, see Wright, *No Small Difference*, 91–112.

22. This verse is the only one in 10:1–18 that has a GK II addition with two *stichoi* added to the two from GK I.

Except for the very end of the verse, which is actually one sentence, the translator understands the point of the Hebrew and at the same time renders it in an isomorphic fashion. The first part, through the preposition בגלל, proceeds word by word. Although the Greek verb *μετάγεται* is not an exact lexical equivalent for the Hebrew verb, it brings the thought of the Hebrew into Greek adequately.

At the very end of the verse, the translator does not seem to have recognized the construct state of the two Hebrew nouns. Thus, "violence of the arrogant" becomes a list, to which the translator adds an additional element: "injustice and insolence and money." Whether the additional noun in the list was in the *Vorlage* or not is difficult to determine. The translator adds a specific reference to money in 33:20, where the Hebrew has שלך. (He probably does in 37:6, although the Hebrew of both MSS B and D have שללך, indicating a possible misreading on the part of the translator.) My inclination, as it is in most ambiguous cases, is not to attribute the addition to a variant parent text but rather to the translator, which suggests some exegetical interest in wealth on his part.

In this list, the translator has returned to the equivalence of ὕβρις for גאוה that we saw in verse 6 and from which he departed in verse 7.

10:9

מה יגאה עפר ואפר
אשר בחייו יורם גויו

τί ὑπερηφανεύεται γῆ καὶ σποδός;
ὅτι ἐν ζωῇ ἔρριψα τὰ ἐνδόσθια αὐτοῦ.

The first *stichos* is translated in a relatively straightforward manner. Note the equivalence of the verbs in Hebrew and Greek for which the translator now switches back to the same root equivalences as he had for the nouns in verse 7. For the repetition of the root *gimmel-aleph-heh* in verses 6–9, the translator has introduced some *variatio*, presumably to reduce the repetition he found in the Hebrew.

The Hebrew phrase עפר ואפר perhaps alludes to the creation story in Gen 3, but the exact phrase appears in Abraham's negotiations with God over Sodom in Gen 18:27, where it expresses Abraham's unworthiness to speak to God. The same phrase comes again in Job 32:19 and 42:6 with the same sense, human unworthiness to speak before God. In each of these passages, the Greek has a combination of *γῆ* and *σποδός* as we have in Sirach. Although the meaning of the phrase in this verse is not exactly that of Genesis and Job, the idea of human frailty before God is fairly close, and it seems likely that both Ben Sira and his grandson knew this phrase from one of these precursor texts.

Confusion reigns in the second *stichos* in Greek. Almost certainly the problems stem from the translator's inability to recognize the Hebrew verb רמם, to decay or be full of worms. Perhaps he read the verb as coming from the root *resh-waw-mem* in the sense of lifting up to remove or perhaps from the Hebrew root *resh-mem-heh* or the Aramaic verb *resh-mem-yod*, both of which mean to throw.[23] Finding some rationale for the equivalence does not solve the problem of the shift from third to first person in the verb, however. Yet, if the translator interpreted the Hebrew verb in either of the ways that I have speculated, then the first person here might indicate that in the translator's view God should be speaking, and the second *stichos* is thus taken as God's punishment in one's life—a theme that we see throughout Ben Sira—a consequence of dust and ashes being proud or arrogant. This explanation also helps us to understand the rendering of אשר with ὅτι in the sense of when, which makes the second *stichos* in the Greek a consequence of the first. On this account, we do not have deliberate exegesis in this translation but rather a translator struggling to make sense of a verse whose Hebrew did not make sense to him. It is impossible to judge the extent to which the translator might have had in mind previous models of the suffering of unrighteous persons, especially kings, such as we see in the death of Antiochus in 2 Macc 9, although rulers make up the subject of much of Sir 10:1–18.

One last note on this verse. The translator did not render the possessive pronoun in the Hebrew morpheme בחייו.

10:10

שמץ מחלה יצהיב רופא
מלך היום ומחר יפול

μακρὸν ἀρρώστημα σκώπτει ἰατρόν·
καὶ βασιλεὺς σήμερον, καὶ αὔριον τελευτήσει.

Both the Hebrew and the Greek contain problems. If the Hebrew שמץ, in biblical Hebrew meaning a slight whisper and in Mishnaic Hebrew a slight or suspicion, was the parent text of the translation, then the transla-

23. I am grateful to Brad Gregory and Jan Joosten for drawing my attention to this possibility. The verb *resh-mem-heh* occurs in Exod 15:1 with the sense of to throw.

tor did not really understand it. He glosses the term with *μακρόν*. Bradley Gregory has suggested on the basis of the Latin translation of *brevem* that the Greek could be a transmission error for *μικρόν*.[24]

The Hebrew verb יצהיב, to gleam or shine bright yellow, does not really make good sense, although in Mishnaic Hebrew the *hiphil* can heave the sense of to grieve, provoke or make angry.[25] If Ben Sira did employ this verb, perhaps the idea is that when an illness is just a whisper, the physician is joyful, that is, he beams, since a more severe illness would be more of a challenge and a greater threat to the patient, or conversely, even a slight illness grieves a physician, since healing is not a foregone conclusion. Whether the parent text of the Greek had that verb or something else is hard to tell, but a variant *Vorlage* for the Greek, which has *σκώπτει*, mock, seems possible, although the translator might be seen as glossing a difficult text. The translator ends up producing a sensible text in Greek, however—"A long (or perhaps, short) illness mocks a physician"—but it differs markedly from the admittedly opaque sense of the Hebrew of MS A: "A whisper/suspicion of illness, a physician gleams(?)/grieves."

In the second *stichos* the translator makes two separate clauses out of the verse by adding *καί* as a connector, whereas the Hebrew has no obvious join between the two halves of the verse.

For the verb in the second *stichos*, the translator eschews a literal translation with some form of *πίπτω*. Instead, he brings out the sense of the Hebrew quite nicely.

In this verse the translator's attempt to make sense of it results in an overall difference of meaning between the two texts. The gist of the Hebrew is that an illness could be so small that the physician does not worry, but in a short time the king could be dead (or perhaps he does worry precisely because the king might be dead in a short time). The Greek goes somewhat in the opposite direction, as a result of the translator's reading of the Hebrew. A long illness (in the text as we have it) frustrates the physician's attempt to cure it and thus, one day the king is king; the next, he is gone. Rather than an exegetical translation, here the translator appears to be doing his best to tackle a Hebrew text that he found difficult.

---

24. Bradley C. Gregory, "Historical Candidates for the Fallen King in Sirach 10,10," *ZAW* 126 (2014): 589–91, here 589 n. 1.

25. Gregory, "Historical Candidates," 589 n. 1.

10:11

במות אדם ינחל רמה
ותולעה כניום ורמש

ἐν γὰρ τῷ ἀποθανεῖν ἄνθρωπον
κληρονομήσει ἑρπετὰ καὶ θηρία καὶ σκώληκας.

The Hebrew of MS A and the Greek have significant differences in this verse. Initially, the Hebrew has no conjunction to connect verses 10 and 11. The Greek has used *γάρ*, which takes the second position and which is a favorite conjunction of the translator.[26]

The initial phrase in Hebrew could be taken as preposition and noun or as a preposition and infinitive construct that has a temporal sense "when a person dies." Depending on which Hebrew construction we prefer, the noun אדם is either the subject of the finite verb or the subject of the infinitive in the temporal clause. The Greek translator has clearly understood it as the latter and has rendered it literally with preposition and infinitive in Greek with the subject of the infinitive in the accusative case.

The end of the verse poses the most difficult issues. The Hebrew has four elements and the Greek only three, and they are in a different order. In the Hebrew, the first two elements, רמה and תולעה, are roughly synonymous, the closest equivalent in the translation for these terms being *σκώληκας*, worms. The same two words occur in parallel in Isa 14:11 and Job 25:6. The Greek *σκώκηξ*, renders both Hebrew terms in the LXX/OG corpus. It seems possible, even likely, then, that the Hebrew of MS A has been harmonized to the biblical parallels in the process of transmission, resulting in a text longer than the Greek, which originally would have had only one of the two terms, perhaps רמה, which would create an alliteration with רמש, creeping thing, which probably has *ἑρπετά* as its equivalence.[27]

26. The conjunction appears 149 times in Sirach according to a search of Ziegler's text in the Accordance electronic text.

27. On the harmonization of passages in Ben Sira to biblical passages in the process of transmission, see Pancratius C. Beentjes, "The Book of Ben Sira in Hebrew: Preliminary Remarks towards a New Text Edition and Synopsis," in *"Happy the One who Meditates on Wisdom" (Sir. 14,20): Collected Essays on the Book of Ben Sira*, CBET 43 (Leuven: Peeters, 2006), 283–91, esp. 288; Benjamin G. Wright, "Preliminary Thoughts about Preparing the Text of Ben Sira for a Commentary," in *Die Septuaginta: Text—Wirkung—Rezeption*, ed. Wolfgang Kraus and Martin Karrer (Tübingen: Mohr Siebeck, 2014), 89–109, especially 95–100. Brad Gregory has suggested to me that perhaps רמה and תולעה are a hendiadys and that the Greek translator is treating them

That leaves the Hebrew כנים, gnats, and θηρία, which are not at all lexical equivalents. (The Hebrew of MS A, כניום, is an error for כנים. The scribe has vocalized the text according to the word כנים.) In the other two places in Sirach where the Greek has the noun θηρίον, it translates the Hebrew חיה, animal. What the translator might have had in his *Vorlage* is not immediately apparent. At the least, we can say that the Hebrew probably had three terms originally, as does the Greek. What exactly those terms were is more difficult to sort out.

10:12

תחלת גאון אדם מועז
ומעשהו יסור מלבו

ἀρχὴ ὑπερηφανίας ἀνθρώπου ἀφίστασθαι ἀπὸ κυρίου,
καὶ ἀπὸ τοῦ ποιήσαντος αὐτὸν ἀπέστη ἡ καρδία αὐτοῦ.

If the Hebrew of Ben Sira was that of MS A, then the translator did not appear to understand it very well. Granted, the meaning of the Hebrew of the first *stichos* is not immediately transparent. Two issues pertain here. Should אדם be understood as in a construct relationship with גאון? Or does it go with the participle מועז, which itself is not clear? The translator seems to have had some difficulty, and so he glossed the *stichos* taking אדם as in construct as witnessed by the genitive case.[28] In addition, he may well have considered his rendering of the first *stichos* in light of the second, which he translates very straightforwardly, since he uses the same verb in Greek, ἀφίστημι, which is an all-purpose verb for the translator and which he uses for the Hebrew verb סור in 38:10. The other possibility is that he misread (or read) מועז as מועל, from the verb מעל, having already had the noun in verse 7. The fact that he used the infinitive in Greek suggests something of this sort might have occurred. In keeping with the verse as a whole, the translator added "from the Lord," apparen.tly since leaving the verb with no complement would make little sense in Greek.

Note that here ὑπερηφανία translates גאון, a related word to גאוה in verse 7, for which he used the same equivalent. One wonders whether, in

---

that way here. Jastrow in his lexicon gives one example where the two nouns seem to work this way, but this is unusual. It seems to me that a harmonizing to the biblical passages is a more likely explanation of the situation.

28. As does the Syriac; see Rey, "Si 10,12–12,1," 590.

light of the equivalence of גאוה and ὕβρις in verses 6 and 8, the translator might have read גאון in verse 7.

The prepositional phrase מלבו makes the second *stichos* somewhat difficult to interpret. The Greek has "heart" as the subject of the clause, thus reversing the grammatical relationships of the clause in Hebrew. The Syriac also lacks the preposition and thus, makes it likely that the *Vorlage* of the Greek read לבו.

Note the lovely alliteration in Greek with *alpha* that begins with the first word and extends throughout the verse.

10:13

כי מקוה זדון חטא
ומקורה יביע זמה:
על כן מלא לבו <רע ויבא> אלה[י]ם נגעה
ויכהו עד כלה

ὅτι ἀρχὴ ὑπερηφανίας ἁμαρτία,
καὶ ὁ κρατῶν αὐτῆς ἐξομβρήσει βδέλυγμα·
διὰ τοῦτο παρεδόξασεν κύριος τὰς ἐπαγωγὰς
καὶ κατέστρεψεν εἰς τέλος αὐτούς.

Both the Hebrew and the Greek have four separate clauses. The Hebrew has a marginal correction that actually brings the verse to five clauses and that agrees more with the Greek than the main text does. Several other differences occur between the two texts.

The Greek translator took the noun מקוה as parallel with תחלה in verse 12 to mean source/beginning, and he levels the semantic difference between the two terms, rendering both with ἀρχή, thus effacing the image of the cistern in the Hebrew.[29] He also continues the *alpha* alliteration for one more *stichos*.

The translator creates something of a minor theme of arrogance while at the same time leveling the text semantically by using the word ὑπερηφανία for the third time since verse 1, in this instance rendering the Hebrew noun זדון.[30]

The Hebrew text has a nice alliteration with מקוה and מקורה. The Greek translator either did not understand the beginning of the second

29. See also Bradley C. Gregory, "Pride and Sin in Sirach 10:13 (15): A Study in the Interdependence of Text and Tradition," *HTR* 108 (2015): 213–34. I thank the author for making a prepublication version available to me.

30. Gregory makes the same point in "Pride and Sin."

stichos, or he had a different parent text. In the two other cases where Hebrew is extant in Ben Sira, the Greek verb *κρατέω* translates the Hebrew verb תמך (4.13; 38.25). Whatever the case, the Greek says something different from the Hebrew of MS A.

In the third *stichos*, the Greek seems to presume a parent text that did not have the third colon of MS A and had the verb of the marginal correction, something like על כן יבא אלהים נגעה. The Hebrew מלא לבו רע has no equivalence in the Greek and could be a harmonization to Qoh 8:11 and 9:3.[31]

The relatively rare verb *παραδοξάζω* occurs in Exod 8:22(10), 9:4, and 11:7 and refers to Pharaoh. The additional phrase in the Hebrew also occurs on MS A at Sir 16:15 and might be an allusion to Pharaoh hardening his heart, as in Exod 8:15, 32, added in the process of transmission.[32]

In the last clause the translator has glossed the Hebrew verb. Whether he has understood it or not remains unclear, but in any case, the two verbs are not lexical equivalents. He has gotten the sense of עד כלה, but for some unknown reason he has positioned the pronomial object of the verb at the end of the clause.

10:14

כסא גאים הפך אלהים
וישב עניים תחתם

θρόνους ἀρχόντων καθεῖλεν κύριος
καὶ ἐκάθισεν πραεῖς ἀντ' αὐτῶν·

The translator has rendered this verse largely isomorphically. The major discrepancy between the Hebrew and the Greek is the equivalence of גאים and *ἀρχόντων*. In this and the previous stanza, the Hebrew has moved back and forth between focusing on rulers and people in general. It appears that the translator wants to push the entire section in the direction of a discussion of rulers. So, rather than the proud, he inserts rulers. Thus, the change likely reflects an exegetical goal to make the poem more consistently about good and bad rulers.

31. Segal, ספר בן סירא השלם, 63. For the various possibilities of where the marginal correction was intended to be placed, see Rey, "Si 10,12–12,1," 581.

32. My thanks to Jeremy Corley for this suggestion.

10:15
ῥίζας ἐθνῶν ἐξέτιλεν κύριος
καὶ ἐφύτευσεν ταπεινοὺς ἀντ' αὐτῶν·

No Hebrew is extant for this section, but both the Greek and the Syriac have the verse. It probably dropped out as a result of a scribal parablepsis, since the Greek translation of verses 15 and 16 begin with a similar construction.[33] It appears that a scribe's eye likely skipped from the word גוים in verse 15 to the same word in verse 16, thereby resulting in elimination of verse 15 in the Hebrew of MS A.[34]

10:16

עקבת גוים טמטם אלהים
ושרשם עד ארץ קעקע

χώρας ἐθνῶν κατέστρεψεν κύριος
καὶ ἀπώλεσεν αὐτὰς ἕως θεμελίων γῆς·

The parent text of the Greek is not certain for this verse.[35] To begin with, the equivalence of χώρας with עקבת differs lexically. The translator certainly knows the meaning of עקב, since he translates it appropriately in 12:17 and 13:26. Segal has the note that the Greek is a "free" translation, but there could just as well be a different Vorlage. Not an easy decision to make.[36] Jean-Sébastien Rey has suggested that the Hebrew עקבת should be read with the sense of trick or ruse, a meaning it has in 2 Kgs 10:19. While this is a reasonable reading of the Hebrew, it still does not explain the Greek translation. Rey also thinks that on the basis of the Syriac and elsewhere in the Septuagint, the second word in the verse should be read as a defective spelling of גאוים, proud.[37] The Greek translator has obviously read the text in front of him as peoples, nations.

The verb טמטם, stop or fill up, does not have the same meaning as καταστρέφω. In all, if the Greek translator had the Hebrew as in MS A, he

33. See Rey, "Si 10,12–12,1," 591.

34. Another possible explanation suggested to me by Brad Gregory is that the Greek has added this verse. Without it, the section from 9:17–10:18 has twenty bicola, which matches the twenty bicola of the following poem in 10:19–11:6. Also within the poem in 9:17–10:18 there would be a 7/6/7 bicola symmetry.

35. See especially the commentary of Segal, ספר בן סירא השלם, 63.

36. Segal, ספר בן סירא השלם, 63.

37. Rey, "Si 10,12–12,1," 591.

glossed the verse for some reason, rendering "God fills up the traces/footprints of the nations" (or, as Rey would translate MS A, "Dieu rend stupide la ruse des orgueilleux") as "The Lord has ruined the lands of the nations." The various suggestions for a parent text different from MS A do not solve all of the problems in the translation. MS A actually has an indication in the margin and above the verb טמטם that there should be a correction, but no correction is made. Segal suggests טאטא as the possible intent and perhaps the reading of the translator, but that verb also does not really have lexical equivalence with the Greek either.[38] The use of *καταστρέφω*, however, might go back to verse 13, where the translator uses the verb of leaders who are arrogant and who continue to sin.[39]

In the second *stichos*, the translator apparently has taken שרשם as a verb with pronomial object rather than a noun with a possessive pronoun, perhaps with the verb φυτεύω in verse 15 in mind. This reading conditions his understanding and translation of the entire clause. Unfortunately, he does not represent the contrast between planting and uprooting in his translation, and thus, he levels the picturesque Hebrew. Also by taking שרשם as a verb, he must do something with קעקע, the verb in the Hebrew of MS A. Whether in his actual parent text or not, it looks as if he has read the word as קרקע, floor or bottom, and rendered it with θεμέλιον. Thus, the Hebrew "And their root he will tear down unto the earth" becomes in Greek "He will destroy them to the foundations of the earth."

10:17

<<ו>>{{י}}סתם[40] מארץ ויתשם
וישבת מארץ זכרם

38. Segal, ספר בן סירא השלם, 63. I am grateful to Jean-Sébastien Rey for a conversation that helped to clarify some aspects of this verse, especially regarding the verb in the first *stichos*.

39. The Syriac reads, "the footprints/traces of the proud," which Patrick W. Skehan and Alexander A. Di Lella, *The Wisdom of Ben Sira*, AB 39 (Garden City, NY: Doubleday, 1987), 222, translate as Ben Sira's text with no argumentation. See Rey, "Si 10,12–12,1," 591.

40. MS A has an interesting correction here. It looks as if the initial scribe had a *yod*, which a corrector or perhaps the original scribe tried to elongate into a *waw*. Thus, the original reading of the manuscript was יסתם, but it was corrected to וסתם. The Greek translator clearly read the clause as not having a conjunction.

ἐξῆρεν ἐξ αὐτῶν καὶ ἀπώλεσεν αὐτοὺς
καὶ κατέπαυσεν ἀπὸ γῆς τὸ μνημόσυνον αὐτῶν.[41]

The verse has three clauses in both Hebrew and Greek. In verse 17a, the Hebrew prepositional phrase מארץ has no equivalent in Greek, leaving the sentence incomplete, since ἐξαίρω is normally a transitive verb and the Greek has no direct object, although the pronoun in the partitive phrase functions as an object, perhaps reflecting a Hebrew *Vorlage* of מהם.[42]

In the first clause the translator looks to have rendered the Hebrew verb according to the idea rather than with an exact lexical equivalent. To scrape is much more colorful than to remove or carry off.

Again, as we have seen in a couple of places, and in contrast to the beginning of the verse, the Greek is not as colorful as the Hebrew. Here the Hebrew uses "uproot," continuing with the planting and root metaphors, which the Greek again defaults to ἀπώλεσεν as in the previous verse, resulting in a leveling of the semantic differentiation of the Hebrew.

The Greek in the third clause represents the Hebrew quite literally, using the verb καταπαύω for the Hebrew root *shin-bet-tav*.

Although not an issue with the translation, note the clever play in Hebrew on the sound of the verbs in the second and third clauses.

10:18

לא נאוה לאנוש זדון
ועזות אף לילוד אשה

οὐκ ἔκτισται ἀνθρώποις ὑπερηφανία
οὐδὲ ὀργὴ θυμοῦ γεννήμασιν γυναικῶν.

The translator, as we have seen so often in this section, gets the gist of the Hebrew, even if he does not always translate it very literally.

Rather than a verbless clause that assumes the copula, the Greek translator employs a verb and thus destroys the image of the Hebrew. Rather than pride being unseemly for a person, the translator harks back to creation to argue that pride was not created for human beings. If his Hebrew was that of Ms A, then in his use of the verb κτίζω and the generalization to all human beings, we have a good example of a theologizing translation,

41. For ἐξῆρεν ἐξ αὐτῶν, Ziegler reads ἐξῆρεν ἐξ ἀνθρώπων apparently thinking it an abbreviation that was filled out incorrectly in the tradition.

42. This suggestion was made to me by Jeremy Corley.

taking a general sapiential point and turning it into a statement about the nature of creation. This transformation results in a loftier conclusion to this stanza and an effective introduction to the next section about human offspring in the beginning of verse 19.

In the second *stichos*, the translator makes the negative explicit in Greek where it is implicit in the Hebrew, the negative particle being understood from the first clause.

He also glosses the Hebrew "strong anger" to produce the more intense Greek "violent anger." The phrase ὀργὴ θυμοῦ is a septuagintalism and does not occur in classical writers. It is relatively frequent in the LXX/OG translations as a rendering of the collocation חרון or חרי with אף.

As in the first clause and keeping with the idea there, the translator generalizes from "a person born of a woman" in Hebrew to "those born of women" in Greek. As in other places, note the use of the dative case to represent the preposition ל in Hebrew.

Conclusions

Even from such a small sample of eighteen verses, we can see some of the ways that this translator works. As a general description, he proceeds in essentially an isomorphic manner, that is, he moves sequentially through each verse from morpheme to morpheme. Most of the interpretive translations and even the theological/exegetical translations take place within this general framework. In these verses we see very few word-order displacements, for example—only the prepositional phrase in verse 4, perhaps the list of creatures at the end of verse 11 and the noun θεμέλιον in verse 16, which might be the result of a misreading. In some cases, however, the translator does gloss his Hebrew text, which results in a very loose relationship between the Hebrew parent and the Greek target.

As we discovered on numerous occasions above, this observation does not mean that the translator produced a translation that matched the Hebrew. In some cases the Greek has a very different meaning from the Hebrew as we have it in MS A. Yet, the translator largely engages in his interpretive translations from within the framework of an isomorphic approach. In most of these cases, I do not think that the translator was deliberately engaging in some systematic exegesis of his parent text. A good example would be verse 9. The translator moves through this verse sequentially, with a likely allusion to Genesis or Job, but when he comes to the end of the verse, it appears as if he did not understand the verb. In order to derive some meaning, he interpreted the last verb and object as an action of God and made the third-person verb of the parent into a first-person verb in the translation. As I see it, he was battling the text for its meaning, not importing some predetermined theological position into it.

In other cases, the translator almost certainly injected some theological or exegetical ideas into a Hebrew text that did not have them. The two clearest cases here are verses 5 and 18. In verse 5, the translator inserted the scribe into the hierarchy of officials with which the text is concerned, and the setting of "his" (i.e., God's) glory on the scribe's face seems to allude to Moses' shining face as he descended Mt. Sinai. Given the high status attributed to the scribe in other passages in the book, this assessment of the verse gains traction. Verse 18 works more subtly. Again, the translator seems to move through the verse sequentially, but with a change of the verb and the use of plural nouns, the translator takes a common sapiential thought—pride is not seemly for a person—and transforms it into a statement grounded in the created order—arrogance was not created for human beings—a thought he extends through the entire verse.

In some cases, it is more difficult to decide what the translator's intention was. We can look at verse 6 as a good example. The Hebrew verse has two parallel cola that teach one not to "repay evil to a neighbor" and not to "walk in the way of arrogance." The Greek transforms that sentiment into two different ideas, the first emphasizing an interior state and the second focusing on the external action. Although the two texts are different, nothing convinces me here that the translator had a different Vorlage; he has taken certain liberties with the parent text, which results in a different sentiment in the Greek from the Hebrew. The translator uses the same thought about holding a grudge against a neighbor in 28:7, using the same phrase. Unfortunately, no Hebrew is extant for that passage, and so we cannot evaluate what he might have done there. Is this deliberate exegesis of the verse or an attempt to make some meaning out of it in an ad hoc manner?

In other passages, I suspect that a different parent text explains the differences between the Hebrew and the Greek texts. Verse 1 almost certainly has a different parent text, with חכם, משכיל, or ערום, the likely word in the translator's *Vorlage*. The same is true for verse 11 at the end, where the list of creatures in MS A has likely suffered in the course of transmission. Less clear is verse 12 in which the Greek varies so much from the text of MS A that if this Hebrew had been in front of the translator, he almost completely abandoned his normal working methods in order to produce this translation. Perhaps somewhat surprisingly, I did not find many cases in this section where I am convinced that the translator had a different parent text from the Hebrew that is preserved in MS A. In that light, this exercise in close examination of a passage that we might take to be representative of the grandson's approach to translating offers us significant insight into how he worked and what his approach to his Hebrew text was.

Finally, this short examination reinforces for me the conclusion that the Hebrew and the Greek of Ben Sira (as well as the Syriac and Latin) constitute different versions of the book. This kind of close examination should impel caution when on the basis of the Greek we want to speak of what Ben Sira said or to make historical reconstructions of Ben Sira's world. I know that I have been guilty of taking this approach—of assuming that when we read the Greek text, we essentially have what Ben Sira said. To a certain degree working in this manner cannot be helped; for many passages, the Greek is really the best text from which to work, but the Greek translation of 10:1–18 reminds us that discovering what Ben Sira said and reconstructing his thought based on the translation is an enterprise fraught with uncertainty. As I begin to move toward writing a commentary on this complex but incredibly fascinating book, this type of analysis admonishes me that these considerations must remain constantly at the forefront of my work not buried somewhere in the background.

Language and Textual History of Syriac Ben Sira

Jan Joosten

The Riddle of the Syriac Version of Ben Sira

The Syriac book of Ben Sira is enigmatic on several accounts. To begin with, the canonical status of the book is anomalous. The Syriac Version of Ben Sira has come down to us as one of the books of the Syriac Bible, the Peshitta.[1] It figures in early pandects such as the Codex Ambrosianus of the sixth or seventh century and is quoted as Scripture by Christian authors from the fourth century onward.[2] The presence of the book in the canon of the Syriac church may seem natural in light of the practice of the Greek church, where Ben Sira was read as Scripture from early on.[3] Jews and Christians, it appears, adopted different canons from the second century onward, and Ben Sira was one of the books rejected by Jews but retained by Christians. The picture is perturbed, however, when one realizes that Ben Sira was translated into Syriac from a Hebrew text, not from the Septuagint.[4] Other deuterocanonical books received by the early Syriac church—such as Judith, Tobit, and the Wisdom of Solomon—were translated into Syriac from the Greek. It stands to mind that the Syriac

1. On the Peshitta in general, see Michael Weitzman, *The Syriac Version of the Old Testament: An Introduction*, UCOP 56 (Cambridge: Cambridge University Press, 1999).

2. See W. Th. van Peursen, *Language and Interpretation in the Syriac Text of Ben Sira: A Comparative Linguistic and Literary Study*, MPIL 16 (Leiden: Brill, 2007), 3–8.

3. On the question of Ben Sira's presence in the Septuagint canon, see Jan Joosten, "The Origin of the Septuagint Canon," forthcoming in the proceedings of the fifth Wuppertal conference on the Septuagint.

4. In many places, the Syriac text can only be understood on the basis of Hebrew text forms attested in various manuscripts, not on the basis of the multiple form of the Greek. See the discussion in van Peursen, *Language and Interpretation in the Syriac Text of Ben Sira*, 16–23.

church adopted them under the influence of the Greek-speaking church. Ben Sira is different. It must have come to Eastern Christianity through an independent channel. Since only Jews would have known enough Hebrew to translate such a difficult book as Ben Sira into any other language, one submits that that channel was Jewish. This leaves the canonical status of the book in the Syriac church unexplained: for all we know, it does not reflect the Septuagint canon, but it does not correspond to any other attested practice in Judaism either.

The theological profile of Syriac Ben Sira, too, raises difficult questions. Translation from the Hebrew assimilates the Syriac version of Ben Sira to most of the other books of the Old Testament Peshitta.[5] As in the case of Ben Sira, the fact that the main part of the Old Testament Peshitta was translated from Hebrew suggests that it is the work of Jewish scholars and was handed down to the Syriac church from Jewish circles. Jewish origin is further confirmed by the presence of midrashic material in the version.[6] For the core Old Testament Peshitta, it has been assumed that the Jewish community that produced the Syriac translation, or at least part of that community, had accepted the Christian message at some point and took their scriptures with them.[7] But at the same time, the Syriac version of Ben Sira manifests several features setting it apart from the Old Testament Peshitta corpus. Perhaps its most notable characteristic is the incontrovertible presence, within the text of the version, of allusions to the New Testament.[8] These allusions can hardly be attributed to a Jewish translator. Once again, Syriac Ben Sira appears to stand somewhere in the middle: it is both Jewish and Christian, a hybrid creation.

5. As is well known, all the books that are part of the Hebrew canon were translated into Syriac from the Hebrew. Influence from the Septuagint can be demonstrated, but it always remains secondary and marginal. See in much more detail Weitzman, *Syriac Version of the Old Testament*, 68–85.

6. See ibid., 86–148; Yĕšaʿyahū Maʾōrī, *The Peshitta Version of the Pentateuch and Early Jewish Exegesis* [Hebrew], Publication of the Perry Foundation for Biblical Research in the Hebrew University of Jerusalem (Jerusalem: Magnes Press, 1995).

7. Weitzman, *Syriac Version of the Old Testament*, 258–62.

8. See Robert J. Owens, "Christian Features in the Peshitta Text of Ben Sira," in *The Texts and Versions of the Book of Ben Sira: Transmission and Interpretation*, ed. Jan Joosten and Jean-Sébastien Rey, JSJSup 150 (Leiden: Brill, 2011), 177–96. Allusions of this type are not found in the Old Testament Peshitta. For allegedly Christian features in the Old Testament Peshitta, see Weitzman, *Syriac Version of the Old Testament*, 240–44.

A third anomaly is the language of Syriac Ben Sira.[9] While most of the book is written in idiomatic Syriac, it also exhibits a few words that are otherwise unattested in Syriac, but well known from western, Targumic, Aramaic:[10]

Ben Sira	Targumic Aramaic	Standard Syriac
ܐܒܥ "to hasten" (36[33]:8)	אבע	ܣܪܗܒ
ܠܚܕܐ "very" (1:29; 51:24)	לחדא	ܛܒ
ܚܫܝܟܐ "poor" (4:1)	חשיכא	ܡܣܟܢܐ
ܐܬܪܥܝ "to be pleased" (37:28)	אתרעי	ܨܒܐ or ܐܨܛܒܝ

The foreign elements are used only occasionally in Syriac Ben Sira. In other passages, the standard Syriac equivalents are used: ܣܪܗܒ for "to hasten" (Sir 43:5), ܛܒ for "very" (7:17; 25:2; 47:24), ܡܣܟܢܐ for "poor" (4:3, 8; 31:4), and ܨܒܐ (45:4, 16) or ܐܨܛܒܝ (15:16, 51:13) for "to choose, to be pleased with." Again, Syriac Ben Sira presents two faces: the larger part of it is written in Syriac, but some of it is not.

Thesis

The hybrid and in-between character of Syriac Ben Sira could be explained in different ways. The canonical status might be witness to a Jewish community, in Mesopotamia or in Palestine, maintaining a canon with Ben Sira

9. See also my earlier studies: Jan Joosten, "Éléments d'araméen occidental dans la version syriaque de Ben Sira," in *Mishnaic Hebrew and Aramaic*, vol. 2 of *Studies in Hebrew, Aramaic and Jewish Languages Presented to Moshe Bar Asher*, ed. Aharon Maman, Steven E. Fassberg, and Yochanan Breuer, trans. Moshe Bar-Asher (Jerusalem: Bialik Institute, 2007), *42–55; Joosten, "Archaic Elements in the Syriac Version of Ben Sira," in Joosten and Rey, *Texts and Versions of the Book of Ben Sira*, 167–75.

10. The table contains only the most striking cases. More examples can be found in the articles referred to in the preceding note.

but no other deuterocanonical books. A solution for the mixed theological profile has been sought in the notion that the translator was a Jewish Christian.[11] The linguistic evidence might be taken to point to a translator juggling with two Aramaic dialects: a Jewish Christian from Galilee, say, who had settled in Edessa and learnt the local dialect might have produced the type of impure Syriac we find in Ben Sira. These are, however, all ad hoc attempts, supported by no evidence except the problematic facts they seek to explain.

It is preferable, then, to attribute the mixture of elements to the redactional history of the translation. It appears that the version was created in two stages: at first, Ben Sira was translated from Hebrew into Targumic Aramaic, in a Jewish milieu; in a second step, the Aramaic version was systematically "Syriacized" by a Christian reviser who no longer had access to the Hebrew text. This hypothesis would account for the linguistic evidence. The "Targumic" words appear to be elements overlooked by the reviser. It would also go some way to explain the mixed theological profile of the version, with more typically Jewish features reflecting the first stage of the version, and the more typically Christian features the second stage.

Application to Some Test Cases

It is notoriously difficult to demonstrate redactional stages when all one has to go on is the final redacted text. Nevertheless, a comparison of the Syriac version with the Hebrew evidence and with the Septuagint shows that the working hypothesis makes good sense in many passages.

Sir 23:4[12]

Geniza fragment Adler 3053[13]: אל אבי ואדון חיי אל תפילני בעצתי
God my father and lord of my life, do not throw me upon my own counsel

---

11. Moshe Z. Segal, ספר בן סירא השלם [*The Complete Book of Ben Sira*], 2nd ed. (Jerusalem: Bialik, 1958), 59–63; Michael M. Winter, "The Origins of Ben Sira in Syriac," *VT* 27 (1977): 237–53, 494–507. Winter's theory was ably criticized by Robert J. Owens, "The Early Syriac Text of Ben Sira in the Demonstrations of Aphrahat," *JSS* 34 (1989): 39–75.

12. This passage was already included in Joosten, "Archaic Elements in the Syriac Version of Ben Sira." It merits to be revisited because new evidence allows a better understanding of the literary process.

13. Joseph Marcus, "Ben Sira, the Fifth Manuscript and a Prosodic Version of Ben Sira," *JQR* 21 (1930): 238.

LXX 23:1: κύριε πάτερ καὶ δέσποτα ζωῆς μου, μὴ ἐγκαταλίπῃς με ἐν βουλῇ αὐτῶν
O Lord, Father and Master of my life, do not abandon me to their design (i.e., of my mouth and lips)

Syr: ܐܠܗܐ ܐܒܝ ܘܡܪܗܘܢ ܕܚܝܝ ܠܐ ܬܪܡܝܢܝ ܠܛܥܝܘܬܗܘܢ
God my father and lord of my life, do not throw me into their apostasy.

While neither 23:1 nor 23:4 are attested in the extant Hebrew manuscripts, the Hebrew source text has nevertheless been preserved in a secondary witness. A Hebrew poem retrieved from the Cairo Geniza, based on Sir 22:26–23:5, echoes the Hebrew wording underlying the versions.[14] This indirect witness proves beyond reasonable doubt that the Hebrew text read בעצתם at the end of the clause (rendered ἐν βουλῇ αὐτῶν in Greek). A question that arises at this point is how the Syriac phrase "in their apostasy" reflects "in their counsel" in the Hebrew. Moshe Z. Segal, in his commentary, cautiously suggests that the Syriac ܠܛܥܝܘܬܗܘܢ is a corruption of the more original ܠܥܛܝܘܬܗܘܢ, "their counsel." Wido Th. van Peursen argues similarly that the original Syriac text was ܠܥܛܬܗܘܢ, "their counsel" and that this was corrupted into ܠܛܥܝܘܬܗܘܢ. The proposals of these scholars are attractive: they explain the divergence between the Hebrew and the Syriac by a simple metathesis of two letters.

What neither of these authors remarks upon, however, is that the words they reconstruct, ܥܛܝܘܬܐ and ܥܛܬܐ, are unattested in Syriac. The meaning "counsel" is consistently expressed by the word ܡܠܟܐ in this language. If the word ܥܛܬܐ (or ܥܛܝܘܬܐ?), "counsel," was found in an earlier version of this passage, this would imply that the language was not Syriac, but Targumic Aramaic. The word עטה, "counsel," occurs in the Targums to the Writings and in Pseudo-Jonathan.[15] Moreover, the word itself is old, being attested several times in the Ahiqar text found in Elephantine and once in Biblical Aramaic (Dan 2:14).[16] The change into ܛܥܝܘܬܐ is perhaps not an accident but may have come about because a Syriac reviser did not know what to make of a word that did not exist in his language. The change

14. I thank Franz Böhmisch, who kindly pointed this out to me in an email message dated August 13, 2014.

15. See the Targum to Ruth 3:4; 4:22; Esth 1:1; Pseudo-Jonathan to Gen 10:11; 11:1; 29:22.

16. Note also that the spelling with *teth* indicates that this is not a loanword from Hebrew.

is made easily enough, but it completely transformed the meaning of the verse. In the reconstructed Hebrew and in the Greek version, the pronoun in "their counsel" refers to the mouth, lips and tongue of the speaker: "Do not throw me back upon the counsel of my mouth." In Syriac, the apostasy must be that of the enemies mentioned in verse 3. One might go as far as to suggest that the verse was displaced from 23:1 to 23:4 for this reason. From "Do not let me be misled by my own lips" the text now means: "Do not let me perish in the apostasy of my enemies."

The divergence in the Syriac of Sir 23:4(1) should not be regarded as an ad hoc adjustment or a simple scribal mistake. It is a tell-tale indication of a process that affected the entire book. A translation into Targumic Aramaic was partly rewritten in a Syriac milieu where the Hebrew text was no longer accessible.

Sir 7:5

A: ופני מלך אל תתבונן
Do not gaze upon the face of the king (?)

LXX: καὶ παρὰ βασιλεῖ μὴ σοφίζου
Do not act wise in the presence of the king

Syr: ܘܩܕܡ ܡܠܟܐ ܠܐ ܬܗܘܐ ܣܟܠܐ
Do not be a fool in the presence of the king

Although the Syriac could be explained as a very free rendering, it is preferable to seek an interpretive path leading from the Hebrew to the version. Segal suggests that instead of תתבונן, the Hebrew source text of the Syriac had תסתכל with the meaning "to look at."[17] This verb was misunderstood and interpreted as meaning "to be foolish."[18] It is to be noted, however, that the verb סכל is not attested in the Hebrew tradition of Ben Sira.

Our hypothesis would favor a slightly different scenario. The Hebrew verb would seem to have been rendered תסתכל in the first stage of the version. The *ethpaal* of סכל is the normal Targumic equivalent of Hebrew

---

17. Whether or not this was the correct interpretation is immaterial in this regard.
18. Segal, ספר בן סירא השלם, 44.

התבונן,[19] and it is a common equivalent of this Hebrew verb also in Syriac Ben Sira.[20] When the verse was read in a Syriac milieu, however, it became problematic. While in Targumic Aramaic הסתכל can express the meaning "to gaze, to direct the eyes, to look (physically)," in Syriac the *ethpaal* of ܣܟܠ can only mean "to perceive, to understand." Unable to make sense of the phrase: "do not understand before the king," the Syriac reviser decided to interpret the verb after the homonymous root ܣܟܠ as "to be foolish," and slightly rewrote the verse accordingly.

Again, this test case shows how a Syriac text saying something rather different from the Hebrew source text came into being.

1:8

LXX: εἷς ἐστιν σοφός, φοβερὸς σφόδρα
One is wise, greatly to be feared

Syr: ܚܕ ܗܘ ܘܕܚܝܠ ܒܠܚܘܕܘܗܝ
He is one, and to be feared alone

The Hebrew of this verse is unfortunately still lacking. The Greek and the Syriac diverge. Although both make sense in the context, one wonders how the divergence can be explained. If σφόδρα corresponds to מאד in the Hebrew source text, the Syriac could be explained in the framework of our hypothesis: מאד would have been rendered with Targumic לחדא in the first stage, as it is preserved still in 1:29 and 51:24; in the second stage, the meaningless לחדא (literally "for one") would have been interpreted as "alone."[21]

Historical Implications

The two-stage hypothesis also helps us understand the historical problem of the version's origin. As was noted above, the fact that Syriac Ben Sira is based on a Hebrew source text is somewhat surprising in view of the clear

19. See, e.g., Targum Jonathan to 1 Kgs 3:21; Isa 1:3; 14:16.

20. See, e.g., Sir 3:22; 6:37; 14:21; 39:32.

21. Similarly in Sir 39:16, σφόδρα "very" in the Greek version corresponds to ܐܟܚܕܐ "together" in Syriac. Here too both texts make sense, yet the divergence between them may indicate that the Syriac text originally read ܠܚܕܐ.

Christian coloring in some passages. But our hypothesis provides a ready solution. It would seem that the use of a Hebrew source text and the insertion of references to the Syriac New Testament reflect distinct phases in the history of the version.

In the first stage, a Hebrew manuscript representing one of the expanded recensions of Ben Sira would have been translated into Targumic Aramaic. This stage could be dated perhaps to the second or early third century CE, and situated, possibly, in the land of Israel. The west-Aramaic elements contained in the version would all have been part of this stage. Also going back to this first stage would be Targumic expressions and turns of phrase that typify Syriac Ben Sira: ܡܐܡܪܐ ܕܡܪܝܐ "The word of the Lord" (11:12, for Hebrew "the eye of the Lord"); ܫܟܝܢܬܐ "the Shekina" (36:13); ܓܠܐ ܩܕܡܘܗܝ "revealed before him," and several others noted in the literature.[22] Midrashic elements identified by several scholars, to the extent they were not already present in the Hebrew *Vorlage*, would also have been introduced into the version at this stage. How this Jewish-Aramaic version found its way to the Christian community of Edessa is impossible to say. It has often been observed, however, that the earliest Syriac Christian authors such as Aphrahat and Ephrem show knowledge of Jewish traditions that were not present in the Old Testament Peshitta.[23] There must have been contacts and exchanges between the early Christian movement and Jewish scholars in Mesopotamia in the second and third century CE. It does not seem far-fetched to imagine that these exchanges could also have involved the book of Ben Sira.

Whether this scenario can account for the canonical status of the writing in the Syriac church is doubtful. The fact that the book was translated into Targumic Aramaic in a Jewish setting does mark it out as a special case. But how and when exactly the book came to be regarded as Scripture remains a mystery.

The version originally borrowed by the church was unsuitable for a Syriac-speaking community. Many of the words it contained would have sounded strange, and some of them would have been incomprehensible. The Targumic version was therefore, in a second stage, thoroughly reworked. To begin with, the language of the version was adapted to the local dialect, Syriac: we must suppose that the west-Aramaic elements that

22. See van Peursen, *Language and Interpretation in the Syriac Text of Ben Sira*, 72.

23. See, e.g., Sebastian P. Brock, "Jewish Traditions in Syriac Sources," *JSS* 30 (1979): 212–32.

can be identified today are a residue of a much more wide-spread phenomenon. The Syriacization of the version was done without reference to the Hebrew source, nor to the Septuagint as far as we can tell, resulting in many alterations of the original meaning. In addition, the reviser seems at times to have taken the liberty to introduce references to the New Testament into the text, and perhaps even his own pious thoughts. This second stage may have been planned by a single author or group and carried out over a short period of time, or it may have been a longish and more or less spontaneous process involving many different hands. In any case, it must be situated in or around Edessa at a period when the New Testament had already made a mark on the local Christian community. This would situate the second stage not before the beginning of the third century and most probably rather later. The end result is a version that is much removed from the source text used in stage one, and all the more so from the original book of Ben Sira.

Conclusion

If the hypothesis proposed in the present paper is accepted, the Syriac version of Ben Sira would turn out to be potentially more valuable than was formerly thought. Although many passages of the version may be secondary elaborations by the Syriac reviser, cut off from any contact with Hebrew text forms of the book, there is a substratum of readings going back to the second or even the first century CE.

Die Vorlage der syrischen Sirachübersetzung und die gereimte hebräische Paraphrase zu Ben Sira aus der Ben-Ezra-Geniza

Franz Böhmisch

Die syrische Übersetzung des Sirachbuches und ihre Vorlage

Die Komposition des syrischen Sirachbuches bis hin zu der heute vorliegenden Gestalt hat mehrere Schritte durchlaufen. Doch welche dies sind, ist immer noch in Diskussion. Nach den Grundlagenstudien von Rudolf Smend, Conleth Kearns und Moshe Segal[1] hatte Michael Winter den syrischen Sirachtext neu kollationiert, darüber eine höchst hilfreiche Konkordanz erstellt und eine „Vetus Syra"-Theorie für das syrische Sirachbuch (SirSyr) aufgestellt, nach der eine erste angeblich ebionitische syrische Übersetzung später von orthodoxen Christen überarbeitet worden wäre.[2] Michael D. Nelson, Vinzenz Reiterer, Robert Owens, W. Th. van Peursen, Jan Joosten, Calduch-Benages/Ferrer/Liesen und kürz-

1. Vgl. Rudolf Smend, *Die Weisheit des Jesus Sirach erklärt* (Berlin: Reimer, 1906), §12 Der Syrer, cxxxvi–cxlvi; Moshe Z. Segal, ספר בן־סירא השלם [*The Complete Book of Ben Sira*], 3. Aufl. (Jerusalem: Bialik, 1972), 59–62; ders. = Moshe H. Segal, "The Evolution of the Hebrew Text of Ben Sira," *JQR* 25.2 (1934): 91–149; Conleth Kearns, "The Expanded Text of Ecclesiasticus: Its Teaching on the Future Life as a Clue to Its Orgin" (Diss., Rom, 1951), publiziert 2011 als Conleth Kearns, *The Expanded Text of Ecclesiasticus: Its Teaching on the Future Life as a Clue to Its Origin*, DCLS 11 (Berlin: de Gruyter, 2011).

2. Vgl. Michael M. Winter, "Ben Sira in Syriac" (Diss., Fribourg, 1974), 88–108; Michael M. Winter, "Theological Alterations in the Syriac Translation of Ben Sira," *CBQ* 70 (2008): 300–12.

lich Michal Bar-Asher Siegal[3] haben die Übersetzungspraxis des syrischen Übersetzers untersucht und der These einer ersten ebionitischen Version des syrischen Sirachbuches den Boden entzogen.

Ich hatte in meinem Aufsatz „Haec omnia liber vitae" postuliert, dass strukturierende Erweiterungen und eine systematische Redaktion über das ganze syrische Sirachbuch (SirSyr) zum Thema „Buch des Lebens" auf eine hebräische Vorlage zurückgeführt werden müssen. Das Problem war bisher, dass nur selten hebräische Handschriften (hauptsächlich MS A) diese postulierte hebräische Vorlage vereinzelt belegen und man gestützt auf exegetische Autoritäten wie Rudolf Smend aus dem syrischen Text die durchscheinende hebräische Vorlage wahrscheinlich machen musste. Durch neue Funde im Jahr 2014 hat sich diese Lage geändert. Gerhard Karner konnte auf der Eichstätter Sirachtagung im September 2014 berichten, dass er und wie sich später herausstellte unabhängig davon auch Eric Reymond entdeckt haben, dass man in Spiegelschrift neue hebräische Belege zu Sir 1 als Abklatsch auf der gegenüberliegenden Seite in MS A aufweisen kann, die einen zur Vorlage von SirSyr 1,*9–*12 ähnlichen Text mit den redaktionellen Erweiterungen zum „Buch des Lebens" indirekt belegen.[4] In meinem Vortrag zur „Komposition des syrischen Sirachbuches" auf dieser Tagung konnte ich zudem auf den hebräischen Text zu Sir 22–23 im Manuskipt ENA 3053.3 eingehen, den der Piyyutforscher Joseph Marcus zusammen mit MS E schon 1931 veröffentlicht und mit der Vorlage von SirSyr in Verbindung gebracht hatte.[5] Moshe Segal hatte

3. Vgl. Michal Bar-Asher Siegal, "The Treatment of Poverty and Theodicy in the Syriac Translation of Ben Sira," *Aramaic Studies* 7.2 (2009): 131–54 = Michal Bar-Asher Siegal, "בעיית הרוע בתרגום הסורי של ספר בן־סירא בדיקה מחודשת של ההבדלים שבין הנוסח הסורי לנוסח העברי / The Problem of Evil in the Syriac Translation of the Book of Ben Sira: the Differences between the Hebrew and the Syriac Texts Reconsidered," *Shenaton leHeqer haMikra* 19 (2009): 137–51.

4. Eric D. Reymond, "New Hebrew Text of Ben Sira Chapter 1 in Ms A (T-S 12.863)," *RevQ* 27 (2015): 83–98; Gerhard Karner, "Ben Sira Ms A Fol. I Recto and Fol. VI Verso (T-S 12.863) Revisited," *RevQ* 27 (2016):177–203.

5. Joseph Marcus, "A Fifth MS. of Ben Sira," *JQR* 21 (1931): 223–40, als Separatdruck Marcus, *The Newly Discovered Original Hebrew of Ben Sira (Ecclesiasticus xxxii,16–xxxiv,1); The Fifth Manuscript and a Prosodic Version of Ben Sira (Ecclesiasticus xxii,22–xxiii,9)* (Philadelphia: Dropsie College for Hebrew and Cognate Learning, 1931. Vgl. Marcus, גנזי שירה ופיוט[*Liturgical and Secular Poetry of the Foremost Mediaeval Poets, from the Genizah Collection in the Library of the Jewish Theological Seminary of America*] (New York: Anglo-Hebrew Publication, 1933).

diesen Text in seine Sirachfragmente aufgenommen und in seinem Kommentar ausführlich verwendet, doch wurde das von der Sirachforschung zu Sir 22–23 jahrzehntelang nicht zur Kenntnis genommen, ebenso die Publikation weiterer Funde von dem Piyyutforscher Ezra Fleischer 1990 und 1997, die ich zum Zeitpunkt der Tagung selber noch nicht vollständig kannte und in ihrem textkritischen Wert unterschätzt hatte. Durch neue eigene Funde nach der Tagung von Oktober 2014 bis Januar 2015 ist diese „gereimte hebräische Paraphrase zu Ben Sira" mit ENA 3053.3 als erstem Blatt umfangreich angewachsen—und belegt klar eine Verbindung dieses hebräischen Textes zur hebräischen Vorlage des syrischen Sirachbuches. Damit ist für diesen Beitrag ein Dreischritt vorgegeben: (1) Eine kurze Darstellung und Kritik der bisherigen Thesen zum syrischen Sirachbuch, (2) ein Nachweis der großräumigen Redaktion im SirSyr und (3) neue Belege aus den älteren und neuen Texten der gereimten Sirachparaphrase (SirPar) im Vergleich mit SirSyr.

Positionen zur syrischen Übersetzung des Sirachbuches

Friedrich V. Reiterer hat in seinem Vergleich der Masadahandschrift mit den anderen Textformen die syrische Version grundlegend verglichen. Es zeigt sich, dass SirSyr wenige Auslassungen, Einfügungen oder auch Umstellungen im Vergleich zur Mas hat[6] und man die syrische Übersetzung daher neu würdigen muss: „Als semitische und daher dem Hebräischen nahe stehende Übersetzung ist sie eine nicht zu unterschätzende Informationsquelle für die Textüberlieferung".[7]

In der Frage, welche theologisch motivierten Änderungen der syrische Übersetzer eingefügt hat, wurde der Ansatz von Winter einer kritischen Analyse unterworfen und es blieben, wenn man vor allem van Peursen, Owens und Calduch-Benages/Ferrer/Liesen zusammenfasst, in der aktuellen Forschung wohl folgende Punkte in der Beschreibung des syrischen Übersetzers übrig:[8]

6. Vgl. Friedrich V. Reiterer, *"Urtext" und Übersetzungen: Sprachstudie über Sir 44, 16–45, 26 als Beitrag zur Siraforschung*, ATSAT 12 (St. Ottilien: EOS-Verlag, 1980), 59.

7. Friedrich V. Reiterer, "Jesus Sirach / Sirachbuch," *WiBiLex*, http://tinyurl.com/SBL0467a; vgl. Reiterer, "Handschriften—Texteditionen—Übersetzungen," in *Zählsynopse zum Buch Ben Sira*, FoSub 1 (Berlin: de Gruyter, 2003), 1–77.

8. Vgl. W. Th. van Peursen, *Language and Interpretation in the Syriac Text of Ben*

- Einige forcierte Thesen Winters wie der angebliche Vegetarismus des Übersetzers (aus einer Textstelle abgeleitet) und seine Zugehörigkeit zu den Ebioniten, das Vermeiden von Aussagen über die Erschaffung der Weisheit und einer spätere antiarianischen Revision, das Vermeiden von Prophetenzitaten, kann man nicht aufrechterhalten.

Bestand haben nach van Peursen und Owens bisher:

- Der Übersetzer zeige eine indifferente bis feindliche Haltung gegenüber dem Opfer- und Tempeldienst und ersetzt sie durch Gebet.
- Sowohl Wertschätzung von Armut wie auch Belege für verstärkte Sorge gegenüber den Armen spielen im syrischen Sirachbuch eine wichtige Rolle.
- Bezüge zum Gesetz werden reduziert (Owens[9]).
- Eschatologisch werden an vielen Stellen das letzte Gericht und zahlreiche Belege einer Vorstellung vom Leben nach dem Tod eingetragen.
- Weitzmann und mit ihm Calduch-Benages/Ferrer/Liesen erkennen einzelne targumisch anmutende Änderungen, die z.B. anthropomorphe Ausdrücke zu vermeiden versuchen. Da diese Forscher die Änderungen bereits in der Vorlage der syrischen Übersetzung und diejenigen, die durch den Übersetzer erfolgt sind, kaum unterscheiden, ist es jedoch schwer auszumachen, ob diese Änderungen wirklich dem Übersetzer zuzurechnen sind oder ob er sie in seiner hebräischen Vorlage schon vorfand.
- Eine christliche Interpretation hat Weitzmann in Sir 48,10 aufgezeigt: „und er wird kommen bevor der Tag des Herr kommt,

---

Sira: A Comparative Linguistic and Literary Study, MPIL 16 (Leiden: Brill, 2007), 95; Robert Owens, "Christian Features in the Peshitta Text of Ben Sira," in *The Texts and Versions of the Book of Ben Sira: Transmission and Interpretation*, hrsg. Jan Joosten and Jean-Sébastien Rey, JSJSup 150 (Leiden: Brill, 2011), 178; Núria Calduch-Benages, Joan Ferrer, and Jan Liesen, *La sabiduría del escriba: Edición diplomática de la versión siriaca del libro de Ben Sira según el Códice Ambrosiano, con traducción española e inglesa / Wisdom of the Scribe: Diplomatic Edition of the Syriac Version of the Book of Ben Sira according to Codex Ambrosianus, with Translations in Spanish and English*, Biblioteca Midrásica 26 (Estella: Verbo Divino, 2003), 48.

9. *Owens, "Christian Features in the Peshitta Text of Ben Sira," 178.*

um umzukehren die Söhne zu den Vätern und zu predigen den Stämmen Jakobs".[10] Weitere Beispiele hat Owens im genannten Aufsatz ergänzt.

- Segal hat in seinem Kommentar viele Beispiele aufgeführt, dass der syrische Übersetzer mit jüdischen Gepflogenheiten so vertraut gewesen sei, dass er einerseits ein orthodoxer Christ (ein Christ fromm in seinem Glauben) "נוצרי אדוק באמונתו", andererseits aber eindeutig jüdischer Herkunft gewesen sei.[11] Ein schlagendes Beispiel für jüdische Wurzeln des SirSyr nennt auch van Peursen mit Verweis auf Sir 36,15 (=36,13 alte syrische Zählung):

ܪܚܡ ܥܠ ܩܪܝܬܐ ܕܩܘܕܫܟ ܥܠ ܐܘܪܫܠܡ ܐܬܪܐ ܕܫܟܝܢܬܟ.

Erbarme dich über die Stadt deiner Heiligkeit, über Jerusalem, den Platz deiner Schechina.[12]

Dieser Übersetzer war in beiden Traditionen zu Hause (jüdisch inklusive Sprachkompetenz im Hebräischen, christlich inklusive Sprachkompetenz im Syrischen und wohl auch im Griechischen). Diese zu jener Zeit ungewöhnliche kulturübergreifende Sprachkompetenz des syrischen Übersetzers des Sirachbuches, die van Peursen herausgearbeitet hat, ist m.E. mehr zu berücksichtigen.

- Nach Segal habe sich dieser judenchristliche Übersetzer jedoch christlich spiritualisierend von der Opferpraxis und der Hochschätzung eines ewigen Israel verabschiedet, ohne sich ganz lösen zu können.[13]

Diese letzte in der Forschung zum syrischen Sirachbuch mit kleineren Nuancen gängige These, der syrische Übersetzer habe absichtlich die Bemerkung über die Ewigkeit Israels in Sir 37,25 getilgt (so Smend, Segal, Kearns, Owens, van Peursen u.a.), worin sich eine Reserve gegen Israel zeige, möchte ich jedoch angreifen. Der Vers lautet „Des Menschen Leben

10. Calduch-Benages, Ferrer, and Liesen, *La sabiduría del escriba*, 49.
11. Vgl. Segal, ספר בן־סירא השלם, §78, 60.
12. W. Th. van Peursen, "The Peshitta of Ben Sira: Jewish And/or Christian?," *AS* 2.2 (2004): 247.
13. Segal, ספר בן־סירא השלם, 60.

währt zählbare Tage, das Leben Jeschuruns (Alternativtext: des Volkes Israel) unzählbare Tage".

Zur Korrektur des Blickwinkels kann in diesem Fall sogar ein Blick in die noch aktuelle Einheitsübersetzung des Sir von Vinzenz Hamp helfen:

19 Es gibt Weise, die für viele weise sind, /
für sich selber aber sind sie Toren.
20 Es gibt Weise, die trotz ihres Wortes verachtet sind, /
von allen Genüssen sind sie ausgeschlossen. =>

21 [Denn vom Herrn wurde ihm keine Huld zuteil, /
weil ihm alle Weisheit fehlt.] -H^{BCD} +GI +VL -S

22 A1= Es gibt Weise, die für sich selbst weise sind; /
die Frucht ihres Wissens zeigt sich an ihrem Leib.
23 B1= Es gibt Weise, die für ihr Volk weise sind; /
die Frucht ihres Wissens ist von Dauer.
24 A2= Wer weise ist für sich selbst, sättigt sich an Genüssen, /
alle, die ihn sehen, preisen ihn glücklich.
25 [Des Menschen Leben währt zählbare Tage, /
das Leben Jeschuruns[des Volkes Israel]
unzählbare Tage.] +H^{BDm} -H^{C} +GI +VL -S
26 B2= Wer weise ist für das Volk, erlangt Ehre, /
sein Ruhm wird dauernd weiterleben.

Vinzenz Hamp hat in seinem Kommentar zu Sir 37,25 kurz bemerkt: „fehlt Syr; G hinter, M vor 24. Wohl eine alte Glosse"[14] und geht damit auf Norbert Peters[15] zurück.

Hätte SyrSir 37,21 übersetzt, dann könnte man argumentieren, dass er Vers 37,25 absichtlich weggelassen hätte. Dem ist jedoch nicht so. Und neben den textkritischen Argumenten ist leicht erkennbar, dass die beiden Verse den klaren Aufbau des Gedichts über die vier Typen von Weisen stören, weshalb man basierend auf Peters und Hamp feststellen muss, dass es sich in Sir 37,21 und Sir 37,25 um Zusätze in der Vorlage von GI handelt. Diese zwei kommentierenden Zeilen stammen nicht von

14. Vinzenz Hamp, *Sirach*, EB.AT 13 (Würzburg: Echter-Verlag, 1951), 99.

15. Vgl. Norbert Peters, *Das Buch Jesus Sirach oder Ecclesiasticus*, EHAT 25 (Münster: Aschendorff, 1913), 309.

Ben Sira, sondern sind auf dem fünfzigjährigen Weg von Ben Sira zur ersten hebräischen Fassung, die sein Enkel ins Griechische übersetzt hat, als Kommentar in den Text eingebaut worden. Eine wertvolle Erweiterung wohlgemerkt, aber eine Erweiterung, die man im Vergleich von MS B mit MS D und mit der syrischen Übersetzung, evtl. auch (vorsichtig) mit dem Florilegium MS C und exegetischen Argumenten als solche identifizieren kann. Die Textfassung, die dem syrischen Übersetzer vorlag, um einige Jahrhunderte später als dem Enkel in Ägypten, hat diese beiden Verse dagegen nicht enthalten. Auch wer diese Deutung nicht teilt, muss einen anderen Grund für das Fehlen des Verses im Syrischen in Erwägung ziehen, der in der erläuterten Struktur des Textes liegt, die durch den Vers durchbrochen wird und jedem Übersetzer auffällt. Ich meine jedoch, dass dieser Befund zu jenen Passagen gehört, in denen die hebräische Textform, die der syrischen Übersetzung zugrundeliegt, in diesem Abschnitt einen Zustand bewahrt, der aus einer zu postulierenden Primärtextform H0[16] und damit weitgehend von Ben Sira selbst stammt. SirSyr 37,25 ist daher nicht als absichtliche Auslassung des Übersetzers zu deuten. Die israelfreundlichen Passagen, die sich im SirSyr finden und seltsamerweise nicht getilgt worden wären, sprechen zudem gegen diese These.

Ein weiteres Problem erkennt man an der Dublette von Sir 30,17 im MS B. [17] Der Vers ist dort hebräisch doppelt überliefert:

30,17
I Besser der Tod als ein nichtiges Leben und ewige Ruhe als dauernder Schmerz.
II Besser der Tod als frevlerisches Leben und in die Scheol zu gehen als beständiger Schmerz.

16. W. Th. van Peursen, "The Alleged Retroversions from Syriac in the Hebrew Text of Ben Sira Revisited: Linguistic Perspectives," in *Beiträge Des 4. Mainzer Hebraistischen Kolloquiums Am 4. November 2000*, hrsg. Reinhard G. Lehmann, KUSATU 2 (Waltrop: Spenner, 2001), 47, Anm.1, hat dafür einmal das Siglum H* verwendet. Ich möchte wie in der Computertechnik und Mathematik von 0 ausgehend zählen und damit zunächst keine Wertungen abgeben, nur die Textunterschiede in den Handschriften feststellen und in Textformen bündeln. Mit der Einführung von H0 lässt sich für ein neu zu erarbeitendes Stemma der Sirachtextformen eine bessere Basis schaffen, um die Theorie der Abhängigkeiten neu formulieren können: HI ist in dieser Sicht nicht der Ausgangspunkt der Textentwicklung, sondern schon ein erster Zwischenschritt.

17. Vgl. Kearns, "The Expanded Text of Ecclesiasticus," 69–70.

Die erste Version ist in der griechischen Handschrift 493 und im Lateinischen übersetzt: „Tod ist besser als ein bitteres Leben und ewige Ruhe als andauernde Krankheit.“

GI lässt „ewige Ruhe“ weg und schreibt: Tod ist besser als bitteres Leben oder eine andauernde Krankheit.“

Syrisch übersetzt: „Besser zu sterben als schlechtes Leben und in die Scheol abzusteigen als andauernder Schmerz“.

Die meisten Exegeten sehen in der Vorlage von GI den originalen Text. An dieser Dublette in MS B ist zum Einen interessant, dass sie die hebräische Vorlage des abweichenden SirSyr enthält, und dass diese Vorlage in mischnischem Hebräisch verfasst ist.[18] Am hebräischen Sirachtext muss also auch in einer Zeit, in der mischnisches Hebräisch verwendet wurde, weitergearbeitet worden sein. Zum Anderen das ebenso häufig zu beobachtende Phänomen, dass SirSyr sehr genau aus seiner Vorlage übersetzt, die ihm allerdings in signifikant anderer Gestalt vorliegt. Hatte man bisher keine hebräische Vorlage gefunden, so erschien die Übersetzung des SirSyr als sehr frei. Segal hat gezeigt, dass die hebräische Version, die dem syrischen Sirachbuch vorlag, von volkstümlichen Adaptierungen aus dem rabbinischen Gebrauch des Buches geprägt gewesen ist: „Accordingly we reach the conclusion that Syr. is based upon a Hebrew text which embodied popular paraphrases of certain verses originally current orally in Jewish circles of the talmudic period“[19]. Diese hebräische Textform des Sirachbuches kann also nicht in einer Höhle am Toten Meer geparkt und erst um 800 wiedergefunden worden sein (was auf andere Versionen durchaus zutreffen mag). Verschiedene Fassungen des hebräischen Sirachbuches waren im Judentum in zwar eingeschränkt breitem aber andauerndem Gebrauch.[20]

Die hebräische Vorlage des syrischen Sirachbuches wies jedoch nicht nur in einzelnen Versen solche verifizierbaren spätere Überarbeitungen auf, sondern wurde vorher schon vor allem in strukturell wichtigen Text-

18. Vgl. Segal, ספר בן־סירא השלם, p. קפז. Viele weitere Beispiele zusammengestellt in den §§77–80 unter der Überschrift „Die hebräische Fassung der syrischen Übersetzung“, ibid., 59–61 und §§81–82, „Das Verhältnis Syr zu G und H“, ibid., 61–63.

19. Segal, “Evolution of the Hebrew Text of Ben Sira,” 123.

20. Vgl. Moshe Z. Segal, “ספר בן-סירא בקומראן/ The Book of Ben-Sira in Qumran,” *Tarbiz* 33 (1963–1964): 243–46; Jenny R. Labendz, “The Book of Ben Sira in Rabbinic Literature,” *AJS Review* 30 (2006) 347–92.

abschnitten einer gezielten Redaktion unterworfen, die um das Konzept des „Buch des Lebens" kreist.

Redaktionelle Signale im syrischen Sirachbuch

Der umfangreiche Zusatz in Sir 1 gibt dabei das Thema „Buch des Lebens" für das ganze syrische Sirachbuch vor.

In der Ausgabe des syrischen Sirach mit Übersetzungen von Calduch-Benages/Ferrer/ Liesen und im Aufsatz von Calduch-Benages über diesen Zusatz wurde dieser dem Übersetzer zugesprochen. Mit guten Argumenten wurde aber dieser deutende Zusatz in SirSyr 1,20a–z bereits von Smend bis Kearns und Segal auf eine hebräische Vorlage zurückgeführt, die bisher nicht erhalten war. Damit bekommt der Übersetzer natürlich ein ganz anderes Gesicht, als wenn man postuliert, dass der Übersetzer selbst so stark in den Text eingegriffen hätte.[21]

1,20ab		Ihre Wurzeln sind das ewige Leben	und ihre Zweige ein langes Leben.
cd	1	Wohl dem Menschen, der über sie nachsinnt,	denn sie ist besser für ihn als alle Schätze.
ef	2	Wohl dem Menschen, der sich ihr nähert,	und gemäß ihren Geboten handelt.
gh	3	Zu einer ewigen Krone macht sie ihn,	und zu immerwährender Gerechtigkeit inmitten der Heiligen.
ij	4	Er freut sich über sie und sie freut sich über ihn,	und sie verwirft ihn nicht in alle Ewigkeit.

21. Zum syrischen Text vgl. ausführlicher Franz Böhmisch, "Haec omnia liber vitae: Zur Theologie der erweiterten Textformen des Sirachbuches," *SNTU.A* 22 (1997): 160–80; *Die Textformen des Sirachbuches und ihre Zielgruppen*, *PzB* 6.2 (1997): 87–112. Andere Analysen bieten Thierry Legrand, "Siracide(Syriaque) 1,20 C-Z: Une addition syriaque et ses résonances esséniennes …," in *Etudes sémitiques et samaritaines offertes à Jean Margain*, hrsg. Christian-Bernard Amphoux et al., Histoire du texte biblique 4 (Lausanne: Zèbre; Editions du Zèbre, 1998), 123–34; und Núria Calduch-Benages, "Traducir—Interpretar: La versión siríaca de Sirácida 1," *EstBib* 55 (1997): 313–40. Eine neuerliche Analyse ist erst mit dem vollständig publizierten neuen Textbestand zu MS A in Sir 1 sinnvoll.

kl	5	Die Engel Gottes freuen sich über ihn,	und (er)zählen alle Herrlichkeiten des Herrn.
mn	6	Dies ganze Buch ist voll von Leben,	Wohl dem Menschen, der hört und danach tut!
op	7	Hört auf mich, ihr Gottesfürchtigen,	und merkt auf und achtet auf meine Worte!
qr	8	Wer das Leben erben will,	als ewigen Gewinn und große Freude,
st	9	Alle meine Worte höre und tue,	und du wirst aufgeschrieben werden in den Büchern des Lebens.
uv	10	Liebe die Furcht des Herrn,	und festige in ihr dein Herz, so wirst du nichts fürchten.
wx	11	Nähere dich und säume nicht,	so wirst du Leben finden für deine Seele.
yz	12	Und wenn du dich nähern wirst:	wie ein Held und wie ein Starker.

Einige Begriffe sind den Abschnitten zuvor entnommen, wie Schätze der Weisheit (1,17), Krone (1,11.18), Freude (1,12), wurden jedoch ganz neu komponiert und auf die Weisheit konzentriert. Aus der ersetzten Passage Sir 1,21–27 ist im zweiten zusätzlichen Distichon das Tun der Gebote als Weg zur Weisheit integriert.

Die vier Distichen 6–9 entwickeln eine Lehre von der Rolle des vorliegenden Buches als Weg zum Leben:

> Dies ganze Buch ist voll von Leben;
> wohl dem Menschen, der hört und danach tut.
> ↓
> Alle meine Worte höre und tue,
> und du wirst aufgeschrieben werden in den Büchern des Lebens.

Spricht der ganze Abschnitt wie auch Sir 1 in der griechischen Version von der Weisheit in dritter Person, so wechselt im zweiten Teil des Zusatzes die Weisheit ohne ausdrückliche Einleitung in die erste Person. Dieser auffällige Wechsel zwischen Rede in dritter Person und der Wechsel in die Rede in erster Person ist eine weitere Auffälligkeit der syrischen Version, die in SirSyr 1; 4 und 51. begegnet. Die Weisheit empfiehlt in Ichrede das vorliegende Buch Jesus Sirach den Gottesfürchtigen als Leitfaden, angefüllt mit Leben: wer den Inhalt des Buches hört und tut, wird in die Bücher des Lebens eingetragen.

Der dritte Abschnitt aus drei Distichen spricht von der Liebe zur Gottesfurcht und ruft abschließend nochmals dazu auf, sich zu nähern. Da immer noch die Weisheit spricht und appelliert, ist als Ziel des Nahens die Weisheit einzusetzen. Vom Aufbau des gesamten Zusatzes her[22] zeichnet sich ab, daß jeweils das Ende eines Abschnitts in der himmlischen Sphäre spielt: die Engel in Zeile 5, die Bücher des Lebens in Zeile 9 und nun analog in der letzten Zeile des dritten Abschnitts der Gottesfürchtige, der der Weisheit nahegekommen ist und wie ein Held und Starker sein wird. Kearns zeigt die Leitlinien dieses Abschnitts im ganzen syrischen Sirachbuch auf:

> The just, inscribed in the Book of Life, will enter the World of the Righteous to receive eternal life, to share an everlasting crown and eternal righteousness with the Holy Ones, the angels of God. In their company the just will rejoice for all eternity, telling forth the glory of God. Syr. thus introduces two ideas not found in Gr. II, viz the written record of man's bad deeds, and the just man's fellowship with the angels in the world of the righteous. Apart from that, Syr.'s eschatology is close to Gr. II's, covering (more cursorily) the same ground and sharing the same ideas.[23]

Die von Smend aufgestellte These, dass die umfangreiche Erweiterung in Sir 1 nicht Schöpfung des syrischen Übersetzers war, sondern in dessen hebräischer Vorlage stand, wird durch die neuen Arbeiten von Eric Reymond und Gerhard Karner zum Textbestand von Sir 1 im MS A eindrucksvoll untermauert. MS A ist ein Manuskript, das nicht nur HI bewahrt, sondern auch Texte enthält, die HII und GII gemeinsam haben und zudem Texte, die nur mit SirSyr gemeinsam sind, darunter die großen redaktionellen Eingriffe in Sir 1 und auch einige spätere volkstümliche Umgestaltungen in mischnischem Hebräisch.

22. Mir erscheint diese Gliederung des Zusatzes SirSyr 1,20a–z immer noch zutreffend.

23. Conleth Kearns, "Ecclesiasticus or the Wisdom of Jesus the Son of Sirach," in *A New Catholic Commentary on Holy Scripture*, hrsg. Reginald C. Fuller et al. (London: Nelson, 1969), 549.

SirSyr 4, 11–14.15–19 Ich-Rede der Weisheit // MS A

Die griechische Konzeption, die z.B. Marböck in seinem Kommentar abdruckt, weil er sich bewusst nach der griechischen Tradition orientiert, formuliert den ganzen Abschnitt in der dritten Person. Die hebräische Textform, die in MS A belegt ist, sowie die syrische Übersetzung wechseln (mit kleineren Detailunterschieden) im zweiten Teil in eine Ich-Rede der Weisheit:

Sir 4,11–19[24]

[Griechisch nach Marböck[24]]	Syrisch
Die Weisheit erhebt ihre Söhne und nimmt sich derer an, die sie suchen.	Die Weisheit hat ihre Söhne gelehrt und erleuchtet alle, die sie suchen.
Wer sie liebt, liebt das Leben und die sie eifrig suchen, werden von Freude erfüllt.	Ihre Freunde sind die, die das Leben lieben und die sie suchen, empfangen Glück vom Herrn.
Wer sie ergreift, wird Ruhm erben, und wo er eintritt, segnet der Herr.	Und die sich an sie kleben werden Ruhm von Gott finden und ein Platz gesegnet durch den Herrn ist das Haus ihrer Wohnung.
Die ihr dienen, leisten Dienst am Heiligenbund die sie lieben, liebt der Herr.	Die ihr dienen sind Diener der Heiligkeit und das Haus ihrer Wohnung liebt Gott.
SIE	ICH
Wer auf sie hört, wird Nationen richten, und wer auf sie achtet, wird in Sicherheit das Zelt aufschlagen.	Der mich anhört wird wahr richten und der mir lauscht wird sich niederlassen innen von mir.
Wenn er Vertrauen hat, wird er sie erben, und in ihrem Besitz werden seine Nachkommen sein.	Wenn er in mich Vertrauen hat, wird er mich erben und er wird mich empfangen für alle Generationen der Welt.

24. Johannes Marböck, *Jesus Sirach 1–23*, HThKAT (Freiburg: Herder, 2010), 90.

Denn auf gewundenen Wegen wird sie vorerst mit ihm wandern, Furcht und Zagen wird sie über ihn bringen	Wegen der Umkehr werde ich mit ihm gehen und zuerst werde ich ihn prüfen. Furcht und Zittern werde ich legen auf ihn
und sie wird ihn im Prozess ihrer Zucht schmerzhaft erproben, bis sie zu ihm Vertrauen gewonnen hat, und sie wird ihn prüfen mit ihren Anordnungen.	und ich werde ihn prüfen in meinen Versuchungen bis zur Zeit da er erfüllt sein Herz mit mir.
Und sie wird auf geradem Weg wieder zu ihm zurückkehren und ihn erfreuen und ihm ihre verborgenen Dinge enthüllen.	Ich werde kehrt machen und werde auf ihm fest machen und werde ihm enthüllen alle meine Geheimnisse.
Wenn er aber abirrt, wird sie ihn verlassen und ihn der Gewalt seines Sturzes übergeben.	Wenn er aber kehrt macht von mir werde ich ihn wegschütten und ihn ausliefern in die Hand der Räuber.

Die Parallelen in Sir 4,11–19 zwischen der syrischen Version und dem hebräischen MS A im Personwechsel belegen, dass MS A hier einen hebräischen Text bezeugt, der mit der hebräischen Vorstufe des syrischen Sirachbuches verwandt ist, auch wenn viele Unterschiede im Detail bestehen. Die auffällige systematische Bearbeitung hin zur ersten Person in der Rede der Weisheit geht konform mit den Beobachtungen in SirSyr 1, was mir als weiteres Indiz für die redaktionelle Überarbeitung in der Vorlage der syrischen Version erscheint.

Sir 9,7 und die Dubletten von 9,9

In SirSyr 9,7–9 erkennt man die Übersetzung einer Dublette von Sir 9,9, die bereits in der hebräischen Vorlage gestanden haben muss, weil sie der syrische Übersetzer vor 9,8 und am ursprünglichen Ort nach 9,8 vorfindet und sorgfältig zweimal übersetzt. Man erkennt eine (nach Marböck wohl ursprüngliche[25]) drastische und eine abgeschwächte Version, wobei im Syrischen die drastische Version am falschen Ort vor 9,8 eingetragen ist, so dass naheliegt, dass der spätere Text in einem hebräischen Manuskript, das nur die abgeschwächte Form am ursprünglichen Ort enthielt, am Rand als Korrektur eingetragen wurde und bei der nächsten Abschrift dann vom Rand vor 9,8 in den Text hineingeschrieben wurde. Dem syri-

25. Vgl. ibid., 142.

schen Übersetzer lag dann die Reihenfolge Sir 9,7 → 9,9 (sekundär) → 9,8 → 9,9 (primär) vor. Es ist daher auch anzunehmen, dass der vorherige Vers SirSyr 9,7 getreu aus der Vorlage übersetzt ist. Er lautet im Syrischen: ܘܬܬܠܛ ܒܫܘ̈ܩܝ ܡܕܝܢܬܐ. ܘܬܬܟܬܒ ܒܓܘܪܐ ܕܚܛܗ̈ܐ. „und du wirst verflucht in den Straßen der Stadt und du wirst eingeschrieben in die Spalte der Sünde". ܓܘܪܐ hat im Syrischen zwei Bedeutungen: (1) Ehebruch und (2) Buchspalte (Payne-Smith[26]). Der syrische Übersetzer hat diesen Begriff hier absichtlich zweideutig verwendet und ein Wortspiel beabsichtigt. Es ist jedoch wahrscheinlich, dass in der hebräischen Vorlage von SirSyr 9,7 ein gängiger Ausdruck für das „Buch der Sünde" stand, der mit der zu SirSyr 1 beschriebenen Redaktion in Verbindung steht.

Sir 50,27–30 Programmatischer Buchschluss

Dem Abschnitt SirSyr 1,20 a–z korrespondiert in Form einer Klammer Sir 50,27–30. In Sir 50,27 bieten die hebräischen und griechischen Textzeugen das erste Kolophon mit leicht unterschiedlichen Namensnennungen Ben Siras, in SirSyr wird der Name des Ben Sira an dieser Stelle völlig getilgt. Auch Gr II hat in 50,29c–d dem Buch einen klaren Schluß gegeben. In SirSyr lautet dieser vorgezogene Buchschluss jedoch Sir 50,27–29:

> Alle Sprüche der Weisen und ihre Geheimnisse sind geschrieben in dieses Buch. Wohl dem Mann, der über sie nachsinnt und sie lernt und sie weiß und sie tut. Die Erhabenheit der Gottesfurcht über allem ist sie erhaben. Schau auf sie, mein Sohn, und du wirst sie nicht verlassen.[27]

Sir 50,27 bietet in GI ein Kolophon: Παιδείαν συνέσεως καὶ ἐπιστήμης ἐχάραξεν ἐν τῷ βιβλίῳ τούτῳ Ἰησοῦς υἱὸς Σιραχ Ελεαζαρ ὁ Ιεροσολυμίτης, ὃς ἀνώμβρησεν σοφίαν ἀπὸ καρδίας αὐτοῦ. auch VL: *doctrinam sapientiae et disciplinae* ***scripsi in codice isto***, jeweils gefolgt von der Namensnennung. In Sir 50,27 Syr steht wie in Sir 24,23a ܣܦܪܐ der Plural in Sir 1,20t Syr ist davon abzuheben), während in Sir 1,20m wie in Sir 39,32b; 44,5b und 47,17a ܟܬܒܐ benutzt ist, woraus man eine inkonsistente Übersetzung aus der hebräischen Vorlage vermuten kann. Der hebräische Text in MS

26. „a) *adultery*" und „b) *the column* of a book or account": Jessie Payne Smith, ed., *A Compendious Syriac Dictionary Founded upon the Thesaurus Syriacus of R. Payne Smith* (1903; Abdr., Oxford: Clarendon, 1967), 66.

27. Zu Details vgl. Böhmisch, "Haec omnia liber vitae," 177–78.

B bietet die zweite Hälfte mit der Nennung des Buches nicht. Wegen der Tilgung des Subjekts (Name des Ben Sira) wird in SirSyr das Objekt zum Subjekt und die 1. p. sg. in die 3. pl. gewendet. Eigengut der syrischen Version ist die Anrede an den Schüler als „Buchschluss" vor dem Gebet in Sir 51 als Appendix.

Sir 51,8–12: Personenwechsel zwischen den Versionen

Sir 51,1–4 redet im Syr wie in MS B Ben Sira direkt zu Gott, wechselt dann aber ab Vers 8 in Syr und MS B in eine Erzählung über die Rettung durch Gott.[28] Hier ist also ein Wechsel von der ersten in die dritte Person festzustellen. Im Gegensatz dazu ist in Gr und VL dieser Personwechsel nur in einzelnen und jeweils verschiedenen Versen präsent. Es erscheint mir plausibel, hier die (schwierigere) Struktur von MS B und dem Syrischen als ursprünglicher anzunehmen. In diesem Abschnitt Sir 51,1–12 kann MS B nicht aus dem Syrischen rückübersetzt sein, weil der syrische Übersetzer hier viele Ausdrücke des Hebräischen umschreibt und der umgekehrte Übersetzungsweg nicht plausibel ist. Unterschiede in den Textformen bzgl. des Wechsels zwischen erster und dritter Person sind also in Sir 1; 4 und 51 zu beobachten. Es ist noch zu klären, in welcher Fassung ein systematisches Interesse in der Gestaltung der Personwechsel ausgemacht werden kann. Eine redaktionelle Gesamtstruktur des SirSyr, die sich von den anderen Textformen abhebt, ist deutlich erkennbar.

Eine dritte hebräische Textform HIII

Moshe Segals Theorie von einer dritten hebräischen Textfassung,[29] die der syrischen Übersetzung des Sirachbuches zugrundeliegt, kann die Sicht auf die syrische Übersetzung wesentlich verändern.

Kearns bestätigte den Ansatz von Segal im Wesentlichen:

---

28. Vgl. Maurice Gilbert, "The Vetus Latina of Ecclesiasticus," in *Studies in the Book of Ben Sira: Papers of the Third International Conference on the Deuteronomical Books, Shime'on Centre, Pápa, Hungary, 18–20 May 2006*, hrsg. Géza G. Xeravits and József Zsengellér, JSJSup 127 (Leiden: Brill, 2008), 3.

29. Vgl. Segal, ספר בן־סירא השלם, §77: Die hebräische Fassung der syrischen Übersetzung.

> This careful study of Segal has confirmed the conclusions of previous workers on four [*sic*] important points:
>
> (1) The existence of a distinct Hebrew recension underlying Gr I.
>
> (2) The occurrence in Gr II of interpolations based on an expanded Hebrew.
>
> (3) The occurrence in it also of interpolations of purely Greek origin.
>
> (4) The Jewish origin and pre-Christian date of Gr II. Segal has advanced good grounds, too for holding.
>
> (5) That not all the peculiarities of Syr are due to the translator, but that many of them belong to the Hebrew text which he was rendering into Syriac.
>
> (6) That this Hebrew text was a distinct recension of Heb, and that Syr is thus textually independent of Gr II.[30]

Man beachte den genauen Sprachgebrauch von Kearns: Die hebräischen Textformen hinter SirGI (HI) und SirSyr stellen klar erkennbare Rezensionen dar, während in GII nur Interpolationen aus einem erweiterten hebräischen Text feststellbar sind. Zudem stellt er ebenso die klare Unabhängigkeit der hebräischen Textform hinter SirSyr, die eine eigene Rezension darstellt, von GII und GI fest. Diese hebräische Textform hinter SirSyr sollte man im Gefolge von Segal die dritte hebräische Textform des Sirachbuches (HIII) nennen.

Die gereimte hebräische Sirachparaphrase aus der Ben-Esra-Geniza in Kairo

Bisher ist in der Sirachforschung im englischsprachigen Aufsatz zur Evolution der Textformen von Moshe Segal (dort Seite 116) und in seinem Kommentar zu Sir 22–23 hartnäckig überlesen worden, dass er mit dem Erstherausgeber Joseph Marcus im Piyyut-Manuskript ENA 3053.3 (Elkan Nathan Adler collection, New York), das große Teile von Sir 22–23 hebräisch enthält, eine direkte Vorlage der syrischen Version in diesen zwei Kapiteln aufzeigen kann und bereits in seinem Kommentar eingearbeitet hat.

Schechter hatte 1900 in der JQR in einem Anhang zu einem Sirachmanuskript bereits den Text eines anderen Fragments herausgegeben, das Bezüge zu Sir 12–13 aufwies.[31] Wie sich durch die Forschungen von

30. Kearns, "Expanded Text of Ecclesiasticus," 85–86.

31. Solomon Schechter, "A Further Fragment of Ben Sira: Prefatory Note," *JQR* 12 (1900): 459.

Schirmann und Fleischer mittlerweile erwiesen hat, gehören diese Fragmente zu der mittelalterlichen Weisheitsschrift des Said ben Babshad (Iraq oder Iran), die Ezra Fleischer 1990 zusammen mit „der" mittelalterlichen Weisheitsschrift aus der Geniza (in Deutschland bekannt durch die Arbeiten von Berger, Rüger und Nebe) ediert hat. Als dritte Schrift veröffentlichte Fleischer in diesem Buch im Anhang die bis 1990 bekannten Handschriften dieser mittelalterlichen Dichtung über das Buch des Ben Sira, dessen erstes Blatt von Joseph Marcus 1930 entdeckt und als Anhang zu seiner Publikation des MS E von Ben Sira veröffentlicht worden war. Diese heute „gereimte hebräische Paraphrase zu Ben Sira" genannte Schrift, wurde also mehrfach als Anhang zu anderen Schriften vergraben. Die Auswertung für die Textkritik und die Deutung des hebräischen Ben Sira steht noch weitgehend aus.

Ebenfalls im Anhang zu seiner Veröffentlichung von MS C hatte M. Gaster ein Piyyut mitgeteilt, das nach seiner Auskunft sehr beschädigt war. Da nach dem 2. Weltkrieg das von Gaster entdeckte Fragment von MS C verschollen ist, wird wohl auch das in dessen Anhang ohne Signatur publizierte Piyyut verloren sein.[32] Ob der von Gaster abgedruckte Text mit einer der genannten umfangreichen mittelalterlichen Dichtungen in Verbindung steht oder ein vereinzeltes Piyyut darstellt, ist zu überprüfen. Es wird höchste Zeit, die auf Ben Sira aufbauenden verschiedenen Piyyuttexte, mittelalterlichen Weisheitsdichtungen und „Ben-Sira-Imitationen" (Giuseppe Veltri)[33] aus den Anhängen herauszuholen.

Nach der Sirachtagung in Eichstätt im September 2014 konnte ich über einen Zugang zum Internetportal http://www.genizah.org des Friedberg Genizah Project im Zeitraum Oktober 2014 bis Januar 2015 systematisch in den zu diesem Zeitpunkt 474022 Bildern der gescannten Genizafragmente aus den beteiligten Bibliotheken recherchieren. Mit Hilfe der Daten der physikalischen Analyse, die durch die Software Genazim mit

32. Moses Gaster, "A New Fragment of Ben Sira," *JQR* 12 (1900): 702. Der Verbleib der Gasterfragmente zu Sirach (MS C) seit dem zweiten Weltkrieg und der Auslagerung in Kellern in London ist nach Gary A. Rendsburg und Jacob Binstein unklar http://tinyurl.com/SBL060467c. Die Sirachforschung arbeitet mit dem Facsimile der Veröffentlichung von Gaster in *JQR*.

33. Giuseppe Veltri, "Mittelalterliche Nachahmung weisheitlicher Texte," in *Gegenwart der Tradition: Studien zur jüdischen Literatur und Kulturgeschichte*, hrsg. Giuseppe Veltri, JSJSup 69 (Leiden: Brill, 2002), 257. Vgl. Giuseppe Veltri, *Libraries, Translations, and 'Canonic' Texts: The Septuagint, Aquila, and Ben Sira in the Jewish and Christian Traditions*, JSJSup 109 (Leiden: Brill, 2006), 190–222.

den Großrechnern der Universität von Tel Aviv über die vorliegenden Bilder durchgeführt worden war[34], lassen sich ausgehend von Schrifthöhe, Zeilenhöhe, Zeilenzahl, Seitenmaß und Schriftdichte der bekannten Fragmente weitere neue finden. Ebenso steuerte das in der Friedberg Genizah Project Webpage eingebaute „Joins Suggestion Tool“ zu den einzelnen Fragmenten noch je 100 physikalisch vergleichbare Fragmente bei, in denen sich dann zwei weitere zugehörige Fragmente, sogenannte „joins“ fanden, sowie Piyyutim und Bibelhandschriften von derselben Schreiberhand.[35] Hierbei hat sich bewährt, von grafisch stark verdunkelten und beschädigten Fragmenten auszugehen, um weitere stark beschädigte Fragmente im FGP-Portal zu finden. Eine ergänzende Recherche an Mikrofilmen der Firkowitch-Sammlung und der Antonin-Sammlung von St. Petersburg sowie einiger bisher nur in Mikrofilm reproduzierter Fragmente der Rylands-Bibliothek in Manchester, die bisher nicht in FGP integriert sind, in der Nationalbibliothek von Israel in Jerusalem vom 14.–18. Februar 2016 hat bisher keine weiteren Funde zur SirPar gebracht.

Die Schreibung einzelner Buchstaben in der Sirachparaphrase (א wie ein lateinisches N, מ genau spiegelverkehrt, ב eher wie ein in der Mitte etwas spitzeres כ oft nur durch Rafe davon unterscheidbar, ל wie arabisches Lam, ziemlich konsequent Rafe über den Begadkefat, einige auffällige vom Arabischen geprägte Ligaturen) sowie der spezifisch „ansteigende“ Schriftduktus ohne Linierung und vor allem die konsequente Setzung des Sof Pasuq am Ende des Doppelzeilers waren eine besondere Hilfe bei der Identifikation dieser Handschrift gegenüber den Piyyutim aus dem gleichen Schreiberumfeld. Die durchgehende Vokalisierung mit der Schreibung eines Segol statt Patach ist ebenfalls eine auffällige Eigenheit dieser Handschrift. Die Handschrift bestand aus lauter gefalteten hintereinandergelegten bifolium-Blättern und hatte jeweils auf der vierten Seite das Anfangswort des nächsten Blattes nach mittelalterlicher Praxis am äußeren (linken) unteren Rand. Die Zahl der Zeilen je Seite in der Handschrift

34. Vgl. die in http://tinyurl.com/SBL060467d leicht zugänglichen Publikationen zur computertechnischen Umsetzung und den Algorithmen hinter Genazim und dem Webportal des FGP. Da das Fragment HUC 1301 z.B. nicht durch Genazim physikalisch analysiert ist („no data“) kann es auch nicht als Join aufscheinen.

35. Zu den Fragmenten vom selben Schreiber gehört eine zweisprachige Tafsirhandschrift zum Sprüchebuch in Moss. III,238.2, T-S NS 185.9, T-S NS 285.56 (drei Blätter), und ENA 2919.5 mit jeweils der hebräischen und dann der übersetzten judäo-arabischen Zeile und mehrere Piyyutdichtungen.

schwankt zwischen 13 und 16.[36] Insgesamt ist (Stand Februar 2016) der Bestand dieser gereimten mittelalterlichen Sirachparaphrase auf 26 Seiten auf 2 bifolium- und 9 folio-Blättern angewachsen. Darunter ist auch das von M. Zulay entdeckte Mikrofilmreplikat „Frankfurt 177" aus dem Schocken-Institut in Jerusalem, dessen Original als eines der 4314 Genizafragmente[37] der Sammlung Freimann in Frankfurt im zweiten Weltkrieg verbrannt ist, und das als Negativbild in der Datenbank mit den genannten Methoden unmöglich zu entdecken gewesen wäre, jedoch bereits in der Edition von Ezra Fleischer enthalten ist. Der von Ezra Fleischer edierte Textbestand der gereimten Sirachparaphrase ist (unvokalisiert) schon länger Bestandteil der Datenbank des Instituts für hebräische Sprache in Jerusalem und über die Webseite מאגרים Maagerim (http://maagarim.hebrew-academy.org.il) zu finden (http://tinyurl.com/SBL060467e), mit exakter Nennung der Fragmentbezeichnung der aufbewahrenden Bibliothek und der Fragmentnummer von Fleischer. In dieser Datenbank ist für SirPar (ID: 960002) als Datierung „vor dem Jahr 1050?" hinterlegt. Ezra Fleischer datiert SirPar auf das 13 Jahrhundert:

> The work, authored by an anonymous poet who apparently flourished in Babylon at the beginning of the 13th century, presents a rather simplified version of the ancient book. Though its being based on the Hebrew original of Ben Sira is beyond doubt, it also contains a rather great deal of additional material of unknown origin. The medieval versifier seems to have based himself on an extended, possibly popular, version of Ben Sira.[38]

Da die Fragmentnummerierung von Fleischer wie in folgender Liste ersichtlich nicht mehr tragfähig ist, eine neue jedoch noch nicht sinnvoll, verwende ich die Fragmentnummer der Bibliotheken, wenn nötig mit Angabe der Seitenzahl recto/verso nach der Konvention des FGP, z.B. ENA 3053.3 1r.

---

36. Fleischer, משלי סעיד בן באבשאד, 276.

37. Vgl. Rachel Heuberger, *Aron Freimann und die Wissenschaft des Judentums*, Conditio Judaica 51 (Tübingen Niemayer, 2004), 74–75.

38. Ezra Fleischer, "Additional Fragments of the 'Rhymed Ben Sira'" [Englisch Zusammenfassung], in *Tehillah Le-Moshe: Biblical and Judaic Studies in Honor of Moshe Greenberg*, hrsg. Mordechai Cogan, Barry L. Eichler, and Jeffrey H. Tigay (Winona Lake, IN: Eisenbrauns, 1997), 324.

Handschriftenbestand der gereimten Paraphrase zu Ben Sira
(פרפרזה מחורזת לבן סירא)

Fragment	Umfang	Bezug	Fund	Fleischer	Average Line Height Text / Average Line Height Total / Average Text Density		
ENA 3053.3	folio	Sir 22–23	Joseph Marcus	א1	4.572 5.180	9.991 9.692	28.169 —
Es fehlen mehrere bifolium-Blätter. Das nächste würde mit מוסר פה Sir 23,7 am Anfang beginnen und evtl. Sir 24 enthalten. Da diese markanten Texte in der Genizaforschung bei der ersten Durchsicht auffallen würden, wird es wohl verloren sein.							
T-S NS 193.99	folio	Sir 34–35	FB		4.084 —	7.914	23.012
T-S AS 137.436	folio	Sir 35–36	FB		3.895 4.741	9.144 9.483	23.817 21.273
T-S NS 108.43	bifolium	Sir 34–39	Schirmann	ב2	4.710 4.878	9.083 8.579	24.510 24.510
T-S NS 93.80	folio	Sir 39–40	Fleischer	ג3	4.778 4.904	9.808 10.059	22.825 23.994
T-S NS 93.79	folio	Sir 40–42	Fleischer	ד4	5.155 4.150	10.059 8.425	21.512 21.043

Das nächste bifolium beginnt mit חונן am Anfang. Ob hier noch ein bifolium fehlt ist wegen der Beschädigungen von T-S AS 124.103 noch nicht klar.							
T-S AS 124.103	folio		FB		5.336 5.123	11.739 10.459	20.765 24.603
T-S AS 124.104	folio	Sir 44–45	FB		4.696 5.336	10.672 11.739	19.459 20.765
T-S AS 133.74	folio	Sir 48	FB		4.595 4.262	10.083 10.910	24.822 22.817
Es fehlen wohl zwei folio-Blätter.							
Frankfurt 177	folio		Zulay	ה5	—		
HUC 1301	bifolium	Sir 50–51	Fleischer 1997	ו6	—		

SirSyr 22–23 und die Sirachparaphrase

M. Segal beschrieb in seinem Aufsatz über die Evolution der Sirachtextformen[39] und in seinem Kommentar zu Sir 22,22–23,9 das Fragment ENA 3053.3 (Elkan Nathan Adler Collection, JTS New York) aus der SirPar und die deutlichen Bezüge zur syrischen Übersetzung des Sirach und entwarf auf der Suche nach dem vollständigen Ben Sira (בן סירא השלם) seine hebräische Rekonstruktion aus SirPar, GI und Syr.[40] Im Vergleich zwischen dem englischen Aufsatz und dem später erschienenen Kommentar in Ivrit ist eine stärkere Rezeption und Akzeptanz des Textes der SirPar // SirSyr zu Sir 22,26 festzustellen. Die strukturellen Unterschiede der beiden Übersetzungen ins Griechische und Syrische, die Vinzenz Reiterer unabhängig davon deutlich aufgezeigt hat, lassen eine harmonische Integration in eine Textform nicht zu.[41] Reiterer hat aus dem Vergleich der griechischen und syrischen Version von Sir 22–23 bereits geschlossen: „Da man wohl nicht davon ausgehen kann, dass die Übersetzer im Laufe der Übertragung neue poetische Strukturen gebildet haben, zeigt sich, dass Γ und Syr markant voneinander abweichende Vorlagen besessen haben".[42] Der unterschiedliche Gestaltungswille in den Vorlagen von Sir 22–23 in SirGI und SirSyr ist deutlich erkennbar.

Der Erstherausgeber des ersten Blattes zur SirPar Joseph Marcus hatte in rabbinischer Kürze das Fragment ENA 3053.3 (unter Nennung nur des beinhaltenden Volume ENA 3053) und die Peschitta dazu abgedruckt sowie einen hebräischen Rückübersetzungsversuch der griechischen Handschrift 248, weil diese griechische Handschrift hier einige Parallelen zu SirPar und SirSyr aufweist. Die VL hat noch mehr Parallelen zu SirPar // SirSyr in Sir 22–23. Segal nennt diese Handschrift aus dem Mittelalter wie die anderen nur „fragment" bzw. קטע. Er schreibt selbst in seinem Kommentar: [43]

---

39. Segal, "Evolution of the Hebrew Text of Ben Sira," 116.

40. Ibid.; Segal, ספר בן־סירא השלם, p. קלה.

41. Friedrich V. Reiterer, "Gott, Vater und Herr meines Lebens: Eine poetisch-stilistische Analyse von Sir 22,27–23,6 als Verständnisgrundlage des Gebetes," in *Prayer from Tobit to Qumran: Inaugural Conference to the ISDCL at Salzburg, Austria, 5–9 July 2003*, hrsg. Renate Egger-Wenzel and Jeremy Corley, DCLY 2004 (Berlin: de Gruyter, 2004), 137–70.

42. Ibid. 165.

43. Segal, ספר בן־סירא השלם, §55: „Es sind uns auch zwei Fragmente von Dichtern aus dem Mittelalter erhalten geblieben, die Weisheitssprüche in Reimen enthal-

> נשתמרו לנו גם שני קטעים של ממשלנים בימי־הבינים, המכילים פתגמי חכמה בחרוזים והמיוסדים על פתגמי ב״ס, והמוסרים לפעמים הרבה מלשונו של ב״ס, כפי שנשתמרה בשתמרה בשרידים שלנו. הם מקבילים לב״ס יב ב־ד יג, כב כה-כג יא; ע׳ בפירושנו למקומות אלו. אין כל ספק שהספר היה הידיהם של משלנים אלמונים אלו, אבל אין אנו יודעים מתי ואיפה נכתבו הקטעים הללו, ומי היו מחבריהם (או מחברם).

Segal sieht also die beiden Handschriften zu (1) Sir 12–13 und zu (2) Sir 22, die wir heute einerseits (1) als Teil der Weisheitsschrift des Said ben Babshad und (2) als gereimte Sirachparaphrase (SirPar) kennen, noch nicht klar getrennt, bemerkt aber, dass es mehrere Verfasser sein könnten. Es ist zu erkennen, dass Said ben Babshad in der Rezeption von Sir 12–13 viel freier umgeht.

Jeremy Corley hat vier Verse aus SirPar mit Übersetzung abgedruckt, aber weil es für die von ihm untersuchte Problematik kaum etwas hergab, diese Spur nicht weiterverfolgt.[44] Auch die anderen Ausleger, die zu Sir 22–23 Beiträge veröffentlicht haben (z.B. Beentjes, Gilbert, Reiterer, Marböck)[45] haben die Textfragmente der SirPar nicht verwendet und auch Segals Analyse mit Hilfe der in dieser Handschrift erhaltenen Zeilen in dessen Kommentar nicht aufgenommen. Calduch-Benages nennt in ihrer jüngsten Veröffentlichung 2015 das Marcus-Fragment aus

---

ten, die auf Sprüchen von Ben Sira basieren und manchmal viel von der ursprünglichen Sprache von Ben Sira überliefern, wie sie in unseren Überresten erhalten sind. Sie entsprechen Sir 12,2–4; 13; 22,25–23,11 (siehe in unserer Auslegung zu den Stellen). Es besteht kein Zweifel, dass das Buch im Besitz dieser anonymen Dichter war, aber wir wissen nicht, wann und wo diese Fragmente geschrieben wurden und wer ihre Verfasser waren (oder ihr Verfasser)". [Übersetzung Franz Böhmisch]

44. Jeremy Corley, *Ben Sira's Teaching on Friendship*, BJS 316 (Providence: Brown Judaic Studies, 2002), 192.

45. Vgl. Pancratius C. Beentjes, "Sirach 22:27–23:6 in zijn context," *Bijdragen* 39.2 (1978): 144–51; Johannes Marböck, "Gefährdung und Bewährung: Kontexte zur Freundschaftsperikope Sir 22,19–26," *Freundschaft bei Ben Sira: Beiträge des Symposions zu Ben Sira, Salzburg 1995*, ed. Friedrich V. Reiterer, BZAW 244 (Berlin: de Gruyter, 1996), 87–106; Friedrich V. Reiterer, "Gott, Vater und Herr meines Lebens: Eine poetisch-stilistische Analyse von Sir 22,27–23,6 als Verständnisgrundlage des Gebetes," in *Prayer from Tobit to Qumran: Inaugural conference of the ISDCL at Salzburg, Austria, 5–9 July 2003*, ed. Renate Egger-Wenzel and Jeremy Corley, DCLY 2004 (Berlin: de Gruyter, 2004), 137–70; Maurice Gilbert, "The Vetus Latina of Ecclesiasticus," in Xeravits and Zsengellér, *Studies in the Book of Ben Sira*, 1–10.

der SirPar, verwendet es jedoch nicht.[46] Der Piyyutforscher Ezra Fleischer hat 1990 alle früheren Funde zur hebräischen Sirachparaphrase von Joseph Marcus, M. Zulay (publiziert in der Zeitschrift Haaretz, die seinem Auftraggeber Schocken gehörte),[47] Schirmann (in dessen Piyyut-Anthologie *Schirim chadaschim*)[48] und seine eigenen Funde zusammengestellt, mit dem Sirachkommentar von Segal verglichen und in seinem Buch über die Weisheitsschrift des Said ben Babshad in Ivrit als Anhang ediert.[49] In einem Aufsatz in der FS Greenberg 1997 konnte Fleischer ein weiteres Blatt der SirPar mit Bezügen zu Sir 50–51 veröffentlichen.[50] M. Kister hatte in einigen Aufsätzen in Ivrit bereits die SirPar verwendet und so konnte Fleischer auf Segals Kommentar und auf Kisters Beiträge und dessen Feststellung zur SirPar zurückgreifen, dass sie dem syrischen

---

46. Calduch-Benages, Núria, "Emotions in the Prayer of Sir 22:27–23:6," *Ancient Jewish Prayers and Emotions: Emotions Associated with Prayer in the Jewish and Related Literature of the Second Temple Period and Immediately Afterwards*, ed. Stefan C. Reif and Renate Egger-Wenzel, DCLS 26 (Belin: de Gruyter 2015), 147 n. 13. Sie belegt in diesem Aufsatz die Forschung zu diesem Gebet bis 2015.

47. Vgl. im Sammelwerk der Beiträge von M. Zulay zu Piyyutim in Haaretz 1936–1954 von Shulamit Elizur: Menahem Zulay, מפי פייטנים ושופכי שיח [*From the Lips of Poets and Precentors*] (Jerusalem: Ben-Zvi; Hebrew University of Jerusalem, 2004–2005]), קפה-קפח und die Belege bei Ezra Fleischer, משלי סעיד בן באבשאד [*The Proverbs of Sa'id Ben Babshad*] (Jerusalem: Ben-Zvi; Hebrew University of Jerusalem, 1990), 43 Anm. 102–7.

48. Ḥayyim J. Schirmann, שירים חדשים מן הגניזה [*New Hebrew Poems from the Genizah*] (Jerusalem: The Israel Academy of Sciences and Humanities, 1965), 436–39 mit dem Erstabdruck des Fragments T-S NS 108.43.

49. Fleischer, משלי סעיד בן באבשאד. Vgl. zu Fleischers Arbeiten an der Sirachparaphrase. Yehoshua Granat, "בשלל צבעים, באלפי צלילים מעודנים, באותנטיות עמוקה וחדה: על פועלו של עזרא פליישר בחקר שירת החול העברית בימי הביניים / Diverse Colours, Thousands of Delicate Echoes, An Authenticity Deep and Sharp": On Ezra Fleischer's Studies of Medieval Secular Poetry," *Jewish Studies* / מדעי היהדות 45 (2009): 149, Anm.17 und zu Said Ben Babshad vgl. Yehoshua Granat, "שיר תהילה על החכמה בפאתי מסורה וקבלה: חטיבה חדשה מפתיחת משלי סעיד בן בבשאד וגל-גולי מסירתה / An Ode to Wisdom within Realms of Massorah and Kabbalah: A Newly Identified Section of the Proverbs of Sa'id ben Babshad and Its Unique Reception," in אסופת מאמרים לזכר מנחם זולאי / *Essays in Memory of Menahem Zulay*, hrsg. Shulamit Elizur et al., Jerusalem Studies in Hebrew Literature 21 (Jerusalem: Mandel Institute of Jewish Studies, [2007]), 183–220.

50. Fleischer, "Additional Fragments of the 'Rhymed Ben Sira,'" in Cogan, Eichler, und Tigay, *Tehillah Le-Moshe*, 205*–18*.

Sirach sehr nahe steht: „דרכו של קטע זה שהוא קרוב מאוד לסורי“.[51] In der Sirachforschung außerhalb Israels muss die Arbeit an dieser Handschrift der Sirachparaphrase weitgehend erst beginnen. Die Forschung an den Sirachbearbeitungen und ihrem Umfeld in den Piyyut könnte jedoch generell eine Bereicherung darstellen, um die Traditionsstöme der hebräischen Sirachhandschriften aus der Ben-Ezra-Geniza von Kairo besser zu verstehen.

Der Dichter dieser mittelalterlichen gereimten Sirachparaphrase hat verschiedene Methoden verwendet, um aus dem Sirachtext einen gereimten Text zu machen:

So hat er ein Distichon aus Ben Sira genommen, das z.B. nach dem Parallelismus a : b aufgebaut war und am Ende von b ein Adjektiv ersetzt, um zu seinem Reim mit a zu kommen, oder ein Verbum hinzugefügt oder die erste Person in die zweite gewendet, oder a und b vertauscht, um auf das Ende von b durch Änderung von a reimen zu können etc.

Dabei ist aber sein Bemühen zu erkennen, möglichst viel und das für ihn Wichtigste vom originalen Text einzubauen und darüber sein kunstvolles über viele Kapitel des Sirachbuches laufendes Gedicht zu gestalten, wobei die Freiheit von der Vorlage in den hinteren Kapiteln zunimmt. Im Vergleich dieses hebräischen Fragments mit dem Textbestand in Gr II, der gerade in Kapitel 23 überraschend gut erhalten ist, VL und vor allem Syr, wie es bereits der Erstherausgeber Marcus ganz klar erkannt hat, ist der frühe Textbestand eines Großteils dieses Abschnitts in dieser alternativen hebräischen Textform, die der syrischen Übersetzung zugrundeliegt, klar

51. Menahem Kister, "בשולי ספר בן-סירא / Notes on the Book of Ben Sira," *Leshonenu* 47.2 (1982–1983): 127; vgl. Kister, "נוספות למאמר בשולי ספר בן-סירא / Additions to the Article 'Notes on the Book of Ben Sira,'" *Leshonenu* 53 (1988–1989): 36–53; Kister, "לפירושו של ספר בן-סירא / A Contribution to the Interpretation of Ben Sira," *Tarbiz* 59 (1990): 308–78; gekürzt in Kister, "Some Notes on Biblical Expressions and Allusions and the Lexicography of Ben Sira," in *Sirach, Scrolls, and Sages: Proceedings of a Second International Symposium on the Hebrew of the Dead Sea Scrolls, Ben Sira, and the Mishnah, Held at Leiden University, 15–17 December 1997*, hrsg. Takamitsu Muraoka and John F. Elwolde, STDJ 33 (Leiden: Brill, 1999), 160–87 und zu SirPar und dem Begriff יצר bei Ben Sira in Sir 22 Kister, "יצר לב האדם, הגוף והטיהור מן הרע: מטבעות תפילה ותפיסות עולם בספרות בית שני ובקומראן וזיקתם לספרות חז״ל ולתפילות מאוחרות / 'The Imagination of Man's Heart': Body and Purification from Evil: Prayer Formulas and Concepts in Second Temple Literature and Their Relationship to Later Rabbinic Literature," *Meghillot* 8 (2010): 243–84. (Ich bedanke mich bei Prof. M. Kister für diesen Literaturhinweis) .

zu entdecken. Es scheint nun so, dass die hebräischen Vorlagen der Peschitta und der VL zu Sir 22, 27–23,6 sich nahestehen und nach der Darstellung von Gilbert[52] gegenüber Gr I die ursprünglichere Textform darstellen könnten. Die Diskussion, welche der Textformen in diesen Kapiteln Sir 22–23 auf das ursprüngliche hebräische Sirachbuch und Ben Sira zurückgeht, ob es wie meist selbstverständlich angenommen die in GI sichtbare Gestalt ist oder die alternative Textform im Syrischen, oder doch beide wie in einem synoptischen Problem auf eine andere primäre Textform zurückgehen, wird nach einer Durcharbeitung der SirPar evtl. zu klären sein.

Van Peursen hat im Vergleich der verschiedenen Textbezeugungen (Handschriftenfragmente, Florilegien, gereimte Neudichtungen) zum Sirachbuch festgestellt: „The transmission of the Hebrew text was very fluid and receptive to all kinds of changes and additions".[53] Nach van Peursen muss daher auch diese gereimte Weisheitsdichtung unter die Quellen für Sirach eingegliedert werden, auch wenn es sich um keinen Sirachtext und auch nicht um ein Florilegium handelt, sondern eben um eine eigene umfangreiche Weisheitsschrift über den Sirachtext mit Elementen von Piyyut:

> The existence of witnesses that are loosely related to Sirach, such as the Geniza Ms C, which can be called a *florilegium*, the so-called prosodic version of Ben Sira in MS Adler 3053, and a Geniza Fragment published by S. Schechter. The fact that Ms C is treated as a witness to the book of Sirach and is included in the text editions, while the others are not, should not blind us to the variety of ways in which this book or parts of it were transmitted.[54]

Die gereimte Gedichtform erfordert, wo kein anderer hebräischer Textzeuge vorliegt wie in Sir 22–23, eine detaillierte Kollation mit den Übersetzungen, aus denen dann die Veränderungen durch den Dichter und dessen Vorlage rekonstruiert werden können. Eine solche Beschreibung der Handschrift der SirPar und der Einordnung in die Traditionsströme, in die sie hineingehört, kann hier nicht geleistet werden.[55]

---

52. Gilbert, "Vetus Latina of Ecclesiasticus," 5.

53. Van Peursen, *Language and Interpretation in the Syriac Text of Ben Sira*, 115.

54. Ibid., 116.

55. Ich erarbeite in den nächsten Monaten eine Edition der SirPar, in der eine ausführliche Beschreibung der Handschrift enthalten sein soll.

Die Analyse von Segal zu Sir 23,9–11 und damit indirekt die SirPar spielt bereits in der neutestamentlichen Diskussion über das Schwurverbot Jesu eine gewichtige Rolle.[56]

Sir 22,22–23,7 in der SirPar

Diesen Text biete ich hier (ohne die in der Handschrift und der Edition von Fleischer enthaltenen Vokale). Ich ergänze die Einrückung am Anfang der Strofe zu Sir 23,1, die Marcus und Fleischer nicht berücksichtigt haben. Diese Einrückungen strukturieren klar erkennbar die Strofen in der gesamten SirPar. In der deutschen Übersetzung versuche ich die Reimung und einige poetische Beobachtungen soweit mir möglich nachvollziehbar zu machen.

הוצאת סוד חרפה גדולה	Das Rausbringen eines Geheimnisses ist eine große Schande
ומכת סתר תביא קללה	und ein verborgener Schlag führt Fluch heran.
לפני אש תימרות עשן	Vor dem Feuer sind Säulen von Rauch
ולפני שפך דם צרה תעשן	und vor dem Vergießen von Blut Bedrängnis raucht.
מסתיר סודו לא יבוש	Wer sein Geheimnis verbirgt wird der Scham entrinnen
ומטמין דבה רעתו יכבוש	und wer Nachrede zurückhält wird seinen Freund gewinnen.
אם גלה לך רעך סודו	Wenn dir dein Freund sein Geheimnis enthüllt,
אל תגלהו	enthülle du es nicht,
פן תהי כנבל בהוציאו	damit du nicht wie ein Tor bist, der es rausbringt
ויזהר ממך שומעהו	und er, wenn er es hört, schaltet vor dir auf Vorsicht.
שים על פיך משמר	Setze auf deinen Mund einen Riegel
ועל שפתך חותם נגמר	und auf deine Lippen ein vollendetes Siegel.

56. Vgl. John P. Meier, *Law and Love*, Bd. 4 von *A Marginal Jew: Rethinking the Historical Jesus*, ABRL (New Haven: Yale University Press, 2009), 210–11 (Anm. 11 und 12); Jonathan Klawans, "The Prohibition of Oaths and Contra-Scriptural Halakhot: A Response to John P. Meier," *Journal for the Study of the Historical Jesus* 6 (2008): 33–48.

למען לא תידמה במגלים סודות	damit du nicht verglichen wirst mit Verrätern der Geheimnisse
ולא תתן לנבלות אלך אודות	und du nicht gibst zu Torheiten über dich Anlässe.
תשחית נפשך בגילוי סודך	Du verdirbst deine Seele beim Enthüllen deines Geheimnisses
ורעך אשר האמינך והבא עדך	und deinen Freund, der an dich glaubte und der zu dir kam.
אמור ליוצרך אל	Sag zu deinem Schöpfer: Gott, mein Vater und
אבי ואדון חיי	Herr meines Lebens
אל תפילני בעצתי ומאויי	Lass mich nicht fallen durch meinen Ratschluss und meine Begierde.
רדני על יצרי והצילני ממגורי	Lass mich herrschen über meinen Trieb und reiße
ומחול על חטאי כי אתה בוראי	mich heraus aus meiner Furcht und aus dem Kreisen um meine Sünde, denn du bist mein Schöpfer.
למען לא ירבה פשעי	damit nicht mehr wird mein Vergehen
ולא יוסיף רשעי	und nicht hinzukommt mein Frevel.
אל תשמח עלי אויבי	Nicht soll sich freuen über mich mein Feind
ואל יזנחוני רעי וקרובי	und nicht sollen mich verachten meine Nächsten und Freund.
גבה עינים אל תתנני	Hochmütige Augen gib nicht zu mir
ולב פחז הרחק ממני	und ein leichtfertiges Herz halte fern von mir.
נפש עזה אל תמשל בי	Eine freche Seele soll nicht herrschen in mir
וטהר רעיון לבבי וקרבי	und reinige das Streben meines Herzens und des Inneren in mir.
פחזי יצר אל יחפיזוני	Die Leichtfertigkeiten des Triebes sollen mich nicht verleiten
ומליצי רע אל יליצוני	und mein böses Rätsel soll mich nicht verspotten.
בשפתי אל תפילני	Durch meine Lippen lass mich nicht fallen
ולשוני אל ילכדני	und meine Sprache soll mich nicht fangen.
לשבועה אל תאלפני	Mit dem Schwur mach mich nicht vertraut
ולפני שופטים אל תושיבני	und vor den Richtern setz mich nicht aus.
מוסר(פה) ...	Zucht [des Mundes] …

Der mittelalterliche Dichter hat zu Sir 22–23 eine erste Strofe konstruiert, die zuerst mit der dritten Person arbeitet und von ePP der dritten Person und schließlich ab שים von der zweiten Person und ePP der zweiten Person geprägt wird. Zu Sir 23 hat der Dichter eine weitere Ich-Strofe konstruiert, die konsequent von der ersten Person und ePP der 1. Person durchformt ist. Er hat dazu mit אמור ליוצרך eine Anrede an den Hörer/Beter als Überleitung von der zweiten Person eingefügt und seinen Vorlagentext aus Sir 23 in der Folge konsequent zur 1. Person umgebaut. Trotz dieser neuen Metastruktur ist es dem mittelalterlichen Dichter gelungen, wie man im Vergleich mit den Sir-Übersetzungen sieht, einen Großteil seiner Vorlage zu bewahren (manchmal ohne jegliche Änderung im ersten Stichos, oft nur durch einzelne Vokabelersetzung und Personwechsel in den Suffixen und ePP). An anderen Stellen in der SirPar hat der Dichter Strofen mit mehreren maskulinen Pluralketten am Ende gebaut, die auf -im enden, anderswo mit femininen Pluralketten auf -ot und hat sich dazu passende Sirachtexte an die richtigen Stellen platziert. Das führt dazu, dass der Dichter sich zwar grundsätzlich an die Reihenfolge des Sirachbuches hält, für die einzelnen Strofen sich aber Verse aus dem Sirachbuch neu zusammenstellt. Wenn Joseph Marcus schreibt: „Beginning with Ch. 23 Cod. 248 has several variants and additions which may have been influenced by liturgical use“[57], dann könnte er aus seiner Erfahrung als Piyyutforscher einen Schlüssel geliefert haben, wie es in manchen Textformen des Sirachbuches zu ähnlichen sprachlichen Änderungen gekommen sein kann, wie es in diesem piyyutartigen Sirachgedicht der Fall ist. Gerade darin liegt über die textkritische Bedeutung hinaus die spezifische Qualität der mittelalterlichen Paraphrase als Bibeldichtung und hebräische „Kommentierung“ zum Sirachbuch. Zunächst einige Textproben des Ben Sira Textes in der SirPar verglichen mit den Versionen:

Der Vers לפני אש תימרות עשן ולפני שפך דם צרה תעשן zu Sir 22,24 zeigt das einfachste Umgestaltungmuster, indem zum Vers aus der Vorlage einfach am Ende ein Wort (in diesem Fall ein Verb) hinzugesetzt wird, das sich zu Stichos a reimt. Textkritisch ist das ideal, weil man nur den Vers im Vergleich mit den Übersetzungen herausschälen muss. SirSyr hat exakt den Wortlaut übersetzt ܩܕܡ ܢܘܪܐ ܬܢܢܐ. ܘܩܕܡ ܐܫܕ ܕܡܐ ܨܚܝܐ. Wie Segal schon vermerkt, verweist SirSyr 22,24 und seine Vorlage auf Peshitta Joel 3,3 (dort als 2,30 gezählt).[58]

Sir 22,26 entspricht SirPar mit Vertauschung der Reihenfolge der letzten zwei Halbstichen (bei gleichzeitigem Umbau auf den Reim -hu) SirSyr:

---

57. Marcus. "A Fifth MS. of Ben Sira," 240 Anm. 16 bzw. ders., "The Newly Discovered Original Hebrew of Ben Sira," 28 Anm. 16.

58. Segal, "Evolution of the Hebrew Text of Ben Sira," 116.

ܐܢ ܓܠܐ ܠܟ ܚܒܪܟ ܐܪܙܐ.	אם גלה לך רעך סודו
ܠܐ ܬܦܩܝܘܗܝ.	אל תגלהו
ܕܠܐ ܟܠ ܕܫܡܥܟ ܢܙܕܗܪ ܡܢܟ.	פן תהי כנבל בהוציאו
ܘܐܝܟ ܦܘܪܫܐ ܢܚܫܒܟ ❖	ויזהר ממך שומעהו

SirSyr: Wenn dir dein Freund ein Geheimnis enthüllt, gib es nicht heraus, damit nicht jeder, der dich hört, sich vor dir hütet und dich für einen Schuft hält.

Auch zu Sir 23,5 belegt SirPar die Vorlage von SirSyr[59]:

גבה עינים אל תתנני ולב פחז הרחק ממני
ܥܝܢܐ ܪܡܬܐ ܠܐ ܬܬܠ ܠܝ. ܘܠܒܐ ܦܚܙܐ̇ ܐܪܚܩ ܡܢܝ.

M. Kister hat nachgewiesen, dass גבה עינים hier nicht nach biblischem Sprachgebrauch sondern nach den Grundbedeutungen der einzelnen Vokabeln und dem natürlichen Verständnis der „hochmütigen Augen" verstanden werden muss.[60] Auch zu פחז bietet Sir 22 nach der SirPar ein neues Verständnis.[61]

M. Gilbert hat die Gemeinsamkeiten der VL zum SirSyr in Sir 22,27–23,6 hervorgehoben: "Many translators and commentators consider that, when one wants to reach the original text written by Ben Sira, it is necessary to follow the reading of the Vetus Latina and the Peshitta versions. These authors form the majority of scholars and I agree with them".[62] Wenn man nun die hebräischen Belege in der SirPar noch zusätzlich kennt und sie

59. Gerhard Karner hat mich darauf aufmerksam gemacht, dass zu Sir 23,5 in MS 7a1 statt ܦܚܙܐ̇ fälschlich ܒܚܙܐ̇ steht. In der Ausgabe des syrischen Sirach von Paul Anton von Lagarde, *Libri veteris testamenti apocryphi syriace* (Leibzig: Teubner 1861), 23 steht der korrekte Text.

60. Vgl. ausführlich mit Erläuterungen zur SirPar Menahem Kister, "לפירושו של ספר בן-סירא / A Contribution to the Interpretation of Ben Sira," 328–30; gekürzt in Kister, "Some Notes on Biblical Expressions and Allusions and the Lexicography of Ben Sira," 172.

61. Vgl. Kister, "לפירושו של ספר בן-סירא / A Contribution to the Interpretation of Ben Sira," 328. Diese neuen Belege führen über bisherige Studien zu dieser Wurzel hinaus, vgl. Armin Lange, "Die Wurzel פחז und ihre Konnotationen," *VT* 51 (2001): 497–510.

62. Gilbert, "Vetus Latina of Ecclesiasticus," 5.

mit den entsprechenden Übersetzungen in VL, GII (besonders 248) und SirSyr verknüpft, bleibt, auch wenn das noch in einer längeren Analyse gezeigt werden muss, wohl nur diese Konsequenz: In dieser Passage geht der Weg auch zur Primärtextform H0 über eine rekonstruierte Fassung aus SirPar, VL und SirSyr.

אל אבי ואדון חיי „Gott, mein Vater und Herr meines Lebens" das in SirSyr zweimal wörtlich übersetzt ist, kann entgegen der bisherigen Diskussion, die vom griechischen Text ausging, als für Sir 23,1 und 23,4 gesichert gelten. Der griechische Übersetzer variiert die Anrufe, die „auf den selben Basistext zurückgehen, da im Hebräischen gerade die Gleichheit als gelungene Phraseologie gilt".[63] Ben Sira begründet in diesem Gebet eine neue Gebetssprache, die offensichtlich eine große Breitenwirkung entfaltet hat.[64]

Die westaramäischen Belege in SirSyr 22–23

Die Analyse von SirPar ENA 3053.3 (Fleischer 1,8)[65] kann auch in die Diskussion eingreifen, die Joosten angestoßen hat in der Frage (1) der westaramäischen Belege im SirSyr und (2) der Deutung ihrer Entstehung. Joosten nennt als ein Beispiel eines westaramäischen Wortschatzes Sir 23,4.[66]

ܐܠܗܐ ܐܒܐ ܘܡܪܗܘܢ ܕܚܝܝ. ܠܐ ܬܪܡܝܢܝ ܒܡܟܠܘܬܗܘܢ.

Es war wie öfter bemerkt worden, dass hier eine Verschreibung im Syrischen vorliegt und in ܒܡܟܠܘܬܗܘܢ die Reihenfolge von ܠ und ܟ vertauscht wurde. ܡܠܟܘܬܗܘܢ oder ܡܠܟܬܗܘܢ bedeuten westaramäisch „ihre Ratschlüsse", sind jedoch nach Joosten im Syrischen nicht belegt. Mit dieser innersyrischen Konjektur ergibt sich für den syrischen Text:

63. Friedrich V. Reiterer, "Gott, Vater und Herr meines Lebens: Eine poetisch-stilistische Analyse von Sir 22,27–23,6 als Verständnisgrundlage des Gebetes," *DCLY* 2004: 151.

64. Werner Urbanz, "Die Gebetsschule des Jesus Sirach: Bemerkungen zu Inhalten, Subjekten und Methoden des Gebets im Sirachbuch," *PzB* 18 (2009): 31–48.

65. Man begegnet oft ungenauen Benennungen wie „ENA 3053", doch sind unter diesem Siglum viele verschiedene Fragmente zu finden und nur ENA 3053.3 beinhaltet das Fragment zu dieser Handschrift.

66. Joosten, "Archaic Elements in the Syriac Version of Ben Sira," in Joosten und Rey, *Texts and Versions of the Book of Ben Sira*, 169.

„Gott, mein Vater und Herr meines Lebens, überlasse mich nicht ihren Ratschlüssen.“ Dieser Text entspricht exakt dem aus SirPar durch Abstreifen der Zugabe des mittelalterlichen Dichters zu rekonstruierenden hebräischen Text, wie es Segal in seinem Kommentar getan hat.

Auch der hebräische Text zu Sir 23,9 findet sich in der letzten Zeile des von Marcus identifizierten Blattes in die erste Person gewendet, SirPar ENA 3053.3 (Fleischer 1,17): לשבועי אל תאלפני, belegt die Wurzel אלף. Die ungewöhnliche Übersetzung von hebr. אלף durch die etymologisch gleiche aber im Syrischen normalerweise eine andere Bedeutung anzeigende Wurzel ܐܠܦ/ܐܠܦ kann sich ebenfalls durch den Versuch einer möglichst kongruenten Übersetzung aus dem Hebräischen erklären.

Joosten hat mehrere solcher westaramäischen Belege im SirSyr aufgezeigt. Löst aber die Hypothese einer westaramäischen Vorstufe des syrischen Sirachbuches, die für eine ostaramäisch sprechende Leserschaft syrisch überarbeitet wurde, wirklich das Problem? Das würde bedeuten, dass (1) sehr konsequent eine westaramäische Vorstufe ins Syrische transformiert worden wäre (2) dann aber doch einige wenige Belege dieser ansonsten sehr konsequenten Überarbeitung entgangen wären und stehengeblieben sind, (3) ohne dass sich in Handschriften von diesem Übergang noch Spuren fänden (einzelne Wörter, die mal westaramäisch, ein andermal syrisch in den syrischen Handschriften zu finden sind).

Der syrische Übersetzer scheint sich in Sir 23 generell um eine möglichst große Wortkongruenz zwischen seinem hebräischen Ausgangstext und der Zielsprache bemüht zu haben. Skehan hat in den Notes zu seiner Übersetzung von Sir 23,4 aramäische Belege genannt und meint, dass der syrische Übersetzer dieses „equivalent“ verwendet, es jedoch im sonstigen Syrisch nicht überlebt habe: „The noun does not survive in Syriac literature …“.[67] Das könnte selbst hier zutreffen, wenn der syrische Übersetzer für עצה, das man in SirPar findet, mit einem phonetisch verwandten Wort ܚܠܝܨܬܐ ins Syrische übersetzt, das man dann später wie Skehan meint nicht mehr verstanden und textkritisch verunstaltet hat. Wäre nicht denkbar bei einem judenchristlichen Übersetzer, dessen ungewöhnliche Sprachkompetenz so weit reicht, einen poetischen hebräischen Text (evtl. sogar mit gelegentlichen Seitenblicken auf griechische Texte) und unter Berücksichtigung der schon vorliegenden Bücher der syrischen Peshitta

67. Patrick W. Skehan and Alexander A. Di Lella, *The Wisdom of Ben Sira*, AB 39 (New York: Doubleday, 1987), 321.

in das Syrische übersetzen zu können, dass er einige sonst nur westaramäisch bezeugte jüdische Sprachtraditionen kennt und vereinzelte Begriffe in seiner Übersetzung verwendet, die man bis jetzt im syrischen Sprachschatz noch nicht nachweisen konnte? Kann ein Judenchrist, der zu einer solchen Übersetzung fähig ist, nicht von seiner Sozialisierung her auch talmudisches Aramäisch kennen und in seinem syrischen Wortschatz verwenden? Ich vermute, dass diese Sichtweise zur Deutung des von Joosten nachgewiesenen Phänomens westaramäischer Komponenten im syrischen Sirachtext auch hinreichen könnte und die weit größeren Schwierigkeiten einer Vetus-Syra-Hypothese oder einer westaramäischen Sirachtargumthese vermeidet.

Sirachparaphrase T-S NS 108.43 zu Sir 34 (Fleischer 2,13.15–16)[68]

כי מגיש מנחה מחיל דלים	Denn ein Darbringender eine Mincha vom Gut der Armen
כזוביח בניו לשדים ועולים	ist wie ein Opfernder seinen Sohn *den Dämonen und Frevlern.*
…	…
מתרחץ משרץ ושב ונגע בגויתו	Der sich reinigt *vom Ungeziefer* und wieder berührt seinen *Leichnam,*
מה הועילו רחיצתו ושטיפותו	was hat er von seiner Waschung *und seiner Reinigung?*
בן איש צם על חטאתו	So ein Mann, der fastet wegen seiner Sünde ….

Auch hier entspricht bei Vertauschung der beiden Stichen SirPar dem syrischen Text von Sir 34, 24. Die Vertauschung von a und b bewirkt, dass der Dichter auf die Pluralendung von b aufbauen kann und durch Änderung am Ende von a einen Reim herbeiführt. Die Wendung מגיש מנחה, findet sich bereits in Mal 2,12. Es besteht kein Grund, dass der Dichter diese Wendung geändert hätte. Die singuläre Wendung מתרחץ משרץ „der sich Reinigende vom Gewürm" belegt die Wurzel רחץ, die im SirSyr vorausgesetzt ist. Der Ausdruck ersetzt, wie Fleischer zur Stelle erläutert, das zu postulierende (bei Ben Sira wohl defektiv geschriebene) רחץ ממת „ein Waschender vom Tod" aufgrund einer Tradition im Babylonischen Talmud Taanit 16a:65:

68. Fleischer, משלי סעיד בן באבשאד, 269–71.

אדם שיש בידו עבירה ומתודה ואינו חוזר בה למה הוא דומה לאדם שתופס שרץ בידו שאפי׳ טובל בכל מימות שבעולם לא עלתה לו טבילה

Aus phonetischen Gründen setzt der Dichter zudem das hitpael, um sowohl Assonanz wie einen Binnenreim zu erzeugen: mitrachez mischerez.

Träume in SirPar T-S NS 108.43 zu Sir 34,7 (Fleischer 2,2)

רבים תעו דרך בחלומות ויכשלו בהליכתם עד מות	Viele verloren den Weg durch Träume und scheiterten auf ihrem Lebenswandel *zum Tod.*
ܣܓܝܐܐ ܓܝܪ ܒܚ̈ܠܡܐ ܛܥܘ ܐܘܪܚܐ ܘܐܬܬܩܠܘ ܒܫܒܝ̈ܠܝܗܘܢ.	Viele nämlich verloren durch Träume den Weg und sind auf ihren Pfaden gestrauchelt.

ܒܚ̈ܠܡܐ ist in 7a1 mit Seyame als Plural markiert. Die hebräische Rekonstruktion aus dem Syrischen im Kommentar zur SirPar von Fleischer, in der er בחלום im Singular setzt, ist zu בחלומות zu korrigieren.[69] Hier ist wieder auffällig, wie kongruent SirSyr aus der Vorlage übersetzt. Mit diesem Text aus SyrPar kann man nun die Analyse der Traumkritik des Sirachbuches präzisieren.[70]

Sirachparaphrase T-S NS 193.99 zu Sir 35,12

T-S NS 193.99 1r verwendet den Satz, der in MS B zu Sir 35,12ab an den Rand notiert und in SirSyr 35,12c–d übersetzt ist: מלוה ײי נותן לאביון ומי בעל גמולות כי אם הוא (vgl. Spr 19,17). Der Text stand also in der Vorlage der SirPar im Text. Der Dichter ergänzt mit einem Halbsatz aus Sir 35,13a der in SirSyr nicht übersetzt ist: כי אלוה תשלומות הוא. Sir35,13b verwendet der Dichter dann an einer anderen Stelle. Der aus MS B 35,12ab und MS Bm 35,12cd zusammengesetzte Text als Vorlage für SirSyr 35,12 wird

---

69. Ibid., 269.

70. Vgl. Franz Böhmisch, "Spiegelungen der Seele und Gesichter: Traumkritik im Sirachbuch," in *Geistes-Gegenwart: Vom Lesen, Denken und Sagen des Glaubens: Festschrift für Peter Hofer, Franz Hubmann und Hanjo Sauer*, ed. Franz Gruber, Linzer philosophisch-theologische Beiträge 17 (Frankfurt am Main: Lang, 2009), 19–30. Ich kannte damals die Sirachparaphrase noch nicht.

in SirPar bestätigt. Der Dichter hat hier sowohl Binnenreim als auch Endreim erzeugt durch Umstellung weniger Wörter.

מלוה ייי נותן לאביון	Es leiht an JHWH, der dem Armen gibt,
כי הוא בעל [גמולות]	denn er ist der Herr der Vergeltung,
ש|בֵ חביון	[*er bewohnt die Hülle*]
כי גם הוא אלוה תשלומות	denn auch ist er der Gott der Wiedergutmachung.
SirSyr 35,10	
ܗܒ ܠܐܠܗܐ ܐܝܟ ܗܝ ܕܝܗܒ ܠܟ	Gib an Gott gemäß dem, was er dir gibt
ܒܥܝܢܐ ܛܒܬܐ ܘܒܐܝܕܐ ܦܬܝܚܬܐ.	mit gutem Auge und großzügiger Hand.
ܡܢ ܕܝܗܒ ܓܝܪ ܠܡܣܟܢܐ ܠܐܠܗܐ ܗܘ ܡܘܙܦ.	Wer nämlich dem Armen gibt, der leiht an Gott.
ܡܢܘ ܓܝܪ ܦܪܘܥܐ ܐܠܐ ܐܢ ܗܘ.	Wer ist nämlich der Vergelter, wenn nicht er?

In ש|בֵ חביון ist ein Riss im Blatt, der die Lesung auf der Fotografie erschwert, wobei diese aber wohl durch Augenschein noch exakter bestimmbar ist und sich zu „noten leäbjon" reimt. Das Wort חביון, das hier verwendet ist, bedeutet „Hülle", wird aber in SirPar T-S NS 108.43 (Fleischer 2,24) wie beim etwa aus derselben Zeit stammenden Shalomo ibn Gabirol, *Krone des Königreichs* (כתר מלכות)[71], als verhüllte himmlische Wohnung verwendet.

Die Vorlage des SirSyr hatte also wie SirPar diesen Vers an exakt derselben Stelle, während MS B ihn am Rand ergänzt. Aphrahat kennt diese Fassung aus seinem syrischen Sirachtext.[72] Dieses Fragment bezeugt auch zu anderen Versen in Sir 34–36 die meisten Lesarten, die im MS B am Rand stehen. Es ist daher anzunehmen, dass sich ein Großteil der Marginaltradition in MS B aus einer Handschrift herleitet, die mit der Vorlage von SirSyr und SirPar verwandt ist. Eine Hoffnung wäre, dass sich nach einer umfangreichen Kollation der SirPar // SirSyr mit MS. B eine klarere Scheidung der Traditionen in MS B und MS Bm und den anderen Manuskripten auf verschiedene Vorlagen vornehmen lässt.

71. Vgl. den Text in http://tinyurl.com/SBL060467f.

72. Vgl. Robert J. Owens, "The Early Syriac Text of Ben Sira in the Demonstrations of Aphrahat," *JSS* 34 (1989): 39–75.

Das Gebet Sir 36,1–11 in der SirPar T-S AS 137.436 1v

Die Seite 1v des Fragments T-S AS 137.436 enthält mit bemerkenswert wenigen Eingriffen das Gebet um die Rettung Israels. Es wird mit dem Aufruf אמרו eingeleitet, der es dem Dichter erlaubt, von nun an in der 1. P. pl. zu auffälligerweise „אלהי כל“ (sic!) zu beten. Die in Sir 36 virulente Problematik der Unterschiede der Versionen bzgl. 3. P. pl. und 1. P. pl. kann man zumindest auf den ersten Blick mit der SirPar nicht lösen, weil sich der Dichter ausweislich des Textes zu Sir 22–23 die Suffixe für eine einheitliche Gebetsstruktur zurechtbiegen könnte. Der Unterschied liegt jedoch darin, dass die Person für den Reim keine Rolle spielt (hier ist das ePP der 2.m.sg für Gott am Ende der Halbzeilen dominierend). Die Formulierung והשבת ראש אויב Sir 36,10 zu Beginn von Z. 10 des Fragments, die auch in Bm angezeigt wird, ist in SirSyr vorausgesetzt, wobei ראש mit ܬܓܐ „Krone“ übersetzt ist. Sir 36,11 fehlt auch in der SirPar.

Interessanterweise sind auf diesem Fragment (wie auf mehreren anderen der SirPar und verwandter Fragmente) in Spiegelschrift aufgrund Feuchteschäden mehrere deutlich lesbare Abdrucke des darüber liegenden Fragments zu sehen und manchmal zeilenweise lesbar.[73] Damit kann man zumindest überprüfen, ob ein bestimmtes Fragment in der Geniza mit diesem Fragment zusammengelegen war und evtl. kann auch textkritisch etwas dabei herauskommen.

73. Bei einzelnen Stichproben zu Spiegelschriften in MS A und SirPar in den hochqualitativen Fotografien des Friedberg Genizah Project stellte ich fest, dass Computerprogramme eine stärkere Rotfärbung dieser Abklatschfarbe der Spiegelschrift von der gegenüberliegenden Manuskriptseite, die für das menschliche Auge kaum sichtbar ist, feststellen können. Die physikalische Ursache ist mir noch nicht klar, ist jedoch auch an Bildpunkten, in denen die Abklatschfarbe und die ursprüngliche Textzeile dieser Seite überlappen, bemerkbar. Man könnte computertechnisch versuchen, wenn diese Beobachtung generalisierbar wäre, die originale Schreibschicht ab einem angemessenen Schwellwert über der umgebenden Papierfarbe von der durch Wasserschaden spiegelverkehrt abgebildeten Abklatschfarbe mit stärkerer Rottönung zu scheiden und beide getrennt abzuheben. Da dies viel Handarbeit pro Fragment erfordert, der Nutzen aber bei Tausenden von Genizafragmenten mit Feuchteschäden erst zu erwarten ist, wäre das eine typische Aufgabe für ein Computerprogramm in einem solchen Großprojekt.

Sir 39,26–30 in der SirPar T-S NS 93.80 (vgl. Fleischer 3,2–7)

ראש לחיי אדם מי[ם] ויצהר ובגד ודבש
כל אלה לטובים ייטיבו ורעים לזרה יהפכו
יש רוחות לנקם יוצרו ולאסון וצרות נכרו
אש ודבר וצרות ורעות למשפט רשעים הם נוגעות
חית שן פתן ועקרב , ולנקמות כל זין וקרב
כל אלה לצורכם נועדו והמה לעתם יפקדו

Die SirPar hilft hier einige Lücken in MS B und Mas aufzufüllen. לזרה geht in SirPar zu Sir 39,27 gegen B mit Mas.[74] נקם ist im SirSyr als Vorlage vorausgesetzt und ersetzt dort משפט.[75]

Der indirekte Beleg des zusätzlichen Psalms in Sir 51 in der SirPar

Fleischer wies 1997 den Einschub einer Litanei in SirPar (HUC 1301 2r) mit אודה zu Beginn jeder Zeile und Zitaten aus Ps 136 und wenigen Anspielungen auf Sir 51 genau an der Stelle nach, in der sich in MS B ein zusätzlicher bisher unbekannter Psalm findet, der in G, Syr und VL nicht vorhanden ist.[76] Damit hat man einen Beleg, dass dem Dichter in seiner Ben Sira-Handschrift dieser Psalm vorlag. Warum der syrische Übersetzer diesen Psalm entweder nicht vorfand oder (nun fast wahrscheinlicher) nicht übersetzt hat, ist eine zu klärende Frage. Dieser zweite indirekte Beleg des Psalms nach MS B in jener volkstümlichen Fassung, die der SirPar vorlag, lässt tatsächlich neu darüber nachdenken, ob der Psalm bereits in der Originalversion von Ben Sira gestanden haben könnte (Otto Mulder[77]), was mir ob des Fehlens in jeglichem anderen Textzeugen aber immer noch schwer einleuchten mag, oder ob er einer der späteren Erweiterungen zugehört. Es ist m.E. als Vermutung der Schluss zulässig, dass

74. Fleischer, משלי סעיד בן באבשאד, 275.

75. Ibid.

76. Vgl. Fleischer, "קטעים חדשים מן הפרפרזה המחורזת של ספר בן סירא / Additional Fragments of the 'Rhymed Ben Sira,'" 215*; 324 (Englisch Zusammenfassung).

77. Vgl. Mulder, "Three Psalms or Two Prayers in Sirach 51?," in Egger-Wenzel and Corley, *Prayer from Tobit to Qumran*, 171–201. Vgl. Franz Böhmisch, "Ein Liebeslied eines jüdischen Weisheitslehrers auf seine Jugendliebe (Sir 51,13–30)," *Visionen des Anfangs*, hrsg. Andreas Leinhäupl-Wilke, Stefan Lücking, und Jesaja M. Wiegard, Biblisches Forum Jahrbuch 2 (Munich: Biblisches Forum, 2004), 49–70.

der Psalm in Sir 51 in MS B aus der postulierten Textform HIII stammt und wegen der Länge und vielleicht auch den Beschädigungen in der Vorlage des MS B nicht am Rand eingetragen, sondern direkt in den Haupttext eingearbeitet wurde.

Resumee

Die Vorlage des syrischen Sirachbuches ist eine eigene hebräische Rezension, die einer redaktionellen Überarbeitung unterworfen wurde. Sie ist auch in der SirPar-Handschrift als Vorlage auszumachen. Man sollte diese Textform mit Moshe Segal in der Theoriebildung einfach die dritte hebräische Textform nennen (Sir HIII). Segal hat in seinem Kommentar (20 Jahre nach dem englischsprachigen Aufsatz über die Evolution der Sirachtexte in JQR) nicht mehr über SirSyr nur als Teilgruppe der zweiten Textform des Sirachbuches gesprochen, sondern klar von einer dritten hebräischen Rezension. Diese These erscheint mir nach Durchsicht der Parallelen von SirSyr zu MS A in Sir 4 (sowie demnächst auch Sir1) sowie zu den Parallelen von SirSyr und SirPar bestätigt.

Sir Syr 1,20a–z mit der Klammer zu Sir 39 und dem vorgezogenen Buchschluss in Sir Syr 50 und der Überarbeitung zum Thema „Buch voller Leben => Nachsinnen und Tun => Eintrag in das Buch des Lebens" belegen eine bewusste Redaktion dieser „dritten" Rezension, die ich mit Segal deshalb so nenne, weil die Wissenschaftsgeschichte bisher mit HI und HII etablierte Größen diskutiert hat und man diese „dritte" Textform im Textbestand ganz klar von den beiden in GI (Majuskelhandschriften) und GII (248 und verwandte Minuskeln) sichtbaren Textformen unterscheiden kann.

In mischnischem Hebräisch wurde diese Version in jüdischer Tradition volkstümlich weiterentwickelt, bevor sie in SirSyr übersetzt wurde. Zumindest drei diskutierte Belege der von Jan Joosten festgestellten westaramäischen Elemente in der syrischen Übersetzung könnten sich dem Versuch kongruenten Übersetzens aus der hebräischen Vorlage verdanken.

Die hier mit Hilfe der SirPar im Gefolge von Joseph Marcus, Moshe Segal und Ezra Fleischer aufgewiesene alternative hebräische Vorlage der syrischen Sirachübersetzung (=HIII) kann nun ein Ausgangspunkt sein, die Übersetzungspraxis des syrischen Übersetzers annähernd im Vergleich mit seinem Ausgangspunkt genauer zu bestimmen und die Tendenzen von Vorlage (HIII) und Übersetzer jeweils genauer zu beschreiben. Ich möchte in den nächsten Monaten (1) an einer Edition der bisher entdeckten Fragmente der Sirachparaphrase arbeiten und (2) im Vergleich der hebräischen Texte der SirPar mit SirSyr, VL und den griechischen Handschriften das Verständnis der Textformen des Sirachbuches und der Traditionsströme, in denen sie sich bewegten, vorantreiben.

Einige hermeneutische Beobachtungen zur syrischen Version des Sirach

Burkard M. Zapff

Dass eine Übersetzung, gleich in welche Zielsprache, immer auch ein Stück Interpretation ist, ist beinahe schon eine Binsenweisheit, jedoch eine nach wie vor aktuelle Erfahrung, die auch einen modernen Übersetzer verunsichern kann. Nun unterscheiden sich moderne Übersetzungen gewöhnlich von antiken Übersetzungen darin, dass sie sich meistens der damit verbundenen hermeneutischen Probleme mehr bewusst sind als man dies gewöhnlich antiken Übersetzern unterstellt. Dass jedoch das Problem als solches bereits dem ersten Übersetzer des Sirachbuches bekannt war, wird uns eindringlich im Prolog des griechischen Übersetzers vor Augen geführt,[1] wo der Autor bekanntlich in Form einer Art *captatio benevolentiae*[2] seine Leser darum bittet, Nachsicht in den Fällen walten zu lassen, bei denen er in seiner Übersetzungstätigkeit versagt zu haben scheint, obgleich er sich gemäß der Übersetzungskunst um bestimmte Redewendungen für seine Leser emsig bemüht habe. Dabei ist er sich durchaus bewusst, dass ein Abstand besteht zwischen der Ausgangssprache—dem Hebräischen—und seiner Zielsprache—dem Griechischen.[3] Nun gibt es ein solches Vorwort in der syrischen Version des Sirach nicht. Dennoch zeigt sich auch hier, dass Übersetzung immer auch Interpretation beinhaltet. In welcher Form und in welchem

1. Zum Prolog des Sirachbuches vgl. Benjamin G. Wright, "Why a Prologue? Ben Sira's Grandson and His Greek Translation," in *Emanuel: Studies in Hebrew Bible, Septuagint, and Dead Sea Scrolls in Honor of Emanuel Tov*, hrsg. Shalom M. Paul et al., VTSup 94 (Leiden:Brill, 2003), 633–44.

2. Johann Marböck, *Jesus Sirach 1–23*, HThKAT (Freiburg: Herder, 2010), 41.

3. Es geht hier, wie Marböck mit Recht betont, „um die grundsätzliche Grenze und Eigenständigkeit einer Übersetzung" (ibid.).

Ausmaß dies der Fall ist, soll in diesem Beitrag anhand einiger Beispiele belichtet werden.

Die erstmalig von H. P. Rüger 1970 vertretene These,[4] wonach die syrische Übersetzung auf einer hebräischen Vorlage fußt, ist heute ein gewisser *consensus communis*. Dabei scheint sich der Übersetzer jedoch auch G, vermutlich sogar des erweiterten Textes G II bedient zu haben. Als Entstehungszeit gilt heute das 3.–4. Jh. n.Chr. Dennoch weicht der syrische Text gelegentlich in erheblichem Maße sowohl von den uns heute vorliegenden hebräischen Textfragmenten aus der Geniza in Kairo bzw. aus Qumran und Masada wie von den griechischen Textüberlieferungen ab. Diese Abweichungen sind teilweise so gravierend, dass Smend die syrische Übersetzung des Sirach einmal als „das schlechteste Übersetzungsstück der syrischen Bibel" bezeichnet hat.[5]

So stellt sich natürlich die Frage nach dem Grund dieser Abweichungen. In seinem ausführlichen und wegweisenden Werk „Language and Interpretation in the Syriac Text of Ben Sira", hat W. Th. van Peursen 2007 verschiedene Klassifizierungen dieser Abweichungen dokumentiert.[6] Sie reichen von Missverständnissen des Übersetzers hinsichtlich des ihm—vermutlich—vorliegenden hebräischen Textes, über poetische Eigenarten bis hin zu theologischen Anliegen, die der Syrer in seiner Übersetzung berücksichtigt wissen wollte. Aufgrund der Freiheit, die sich der Übersetzer nahm, wird in der neueren Forschung außerdem die Schlussfolgerung gezogen, dass für ihn das Sirachbuch noch keine ausgesprochen kanonische Wertigkeit, sondern lediglich autoritativen Charakter besessen habe. Wie auch immer: Diese Abweichungen, sofern sie intentional sind, lassen möglicherweise Rückschlüsse zu, in welchem sozio-kulturellen und religiösen Umfeld sich der Übersetzer bewegte. Außerdem mahnen sie dazu, nicht unbesehen den syrischen Text da, wo etwa der hebräische Text ausfällt, als Zeugen eines G vorausliegenden hebräischen Textes heranzuziehen. Was nun den religiösen Hintergrund der syrischen Übersetzung

---

4. Hans P. Rüger, *Text und Textform im hebräischen Sirach: Untersuchungen zur Textgeschichte und Textkritik der hebräischen Sirachfragmente aus der Kairoer Geniza*, BZAW 112 (Berlin: de Gruyter, 1970).

5. Rudolf Smend, *Die Weisheit des Jesus Sirach erklärt* (Berlin: Reimer, 1906), cxxxvii: „Die Uebersetzung des Sirach ist wohl das schlechteste Uebersetzungswerk der syrischen Bibel".

6. W. Th. van Peursen, *Language and Interpretation in the Syriac Text of Ben Sira: A Compartive Linguistic and Literary Study*, MPIL 16 (Leiden: Brill, 2007).

anbetrifft, gibt es bisher keinen wirklichen Konsens. Die Thesen reichen von der von M. M. Winter vertretenen Sicht,[7] wonach es sich hier um die Übersetzung eines ebionitischen Christen handle, die später eine orthodoxe Revision erhalten habe, bis hin zu der These M. P. Weitzmans,[8] wonach die syrische Übersetzung ein nichtrabbinisches und antikultisches Judentum widerspiegle, welches später ins Christentum eingemündet sei.

Aufbauend auf den vielfältigen Anmerkungen van Peursens und eigenen Beobachtungen im Zuge meiner Übersetzungsarbeit am syrischen Sirach möchte ich im Folgenden einige Besonderheiten der syrischen Übersetzung darstellen, die aufgrund ihrer Eigenart gewisse Rückschlüsse auf Intentionen des Übersetzers zulassen, ohne jedoch die Frage nach einer jüdischen oder christlichen Autorenschaft letztendlich klären zu können. Ich werde bei meinem Vorgehen zwar auch einige formale Eigentümlichkeiten erwähnen, mich jedoch im Unterschied zu van Peursen schwerpunktmäßig auf inhaltliche Aspekte verlegen, wobei ich selbstredend aufgrund des umfänglichen Materials keine Vollständigkeit anzielen will und kann.

Für die Textauswahl beschränke ich mich, um möglichst große Sicherheit hinsichtlich der Eigenständigkeit des Syrers bezüglich seiner Textvorlage zu gewinnen, vorwiegend auf folgende Texte:

1. Texte, in denen der Syrer sowohl von den uns vorliegenden hebräischen Textfragmenten als auch von der griechischen Version bzw. Versionen abweicht. Zwar ist grundsätzlich denkbar, dass der Syrer hier auf eine verlorengegangene, abweichende Textvorlage Bezug nimmt, jedoch erhöht sich damit die Wahrscheinlichkeit, dass er tatsächlich einer eigenen Interpretationslinie folgt, zumal dann, wenn sie an anderen Textstellen ähnlich wahrgenommen wird. In den Fällen, wo nur die syrische und griechische Version vorliegt, suche ich die postulierte Tendenz durch weitere Textbeispiele abzusichern.

7. Michael M. Winter, "Ben Sira in Syriac: An Ebionite Translation?," in *Studia Patristica XVI: Papers Presented to the Seventh International Conference on Patristic Studies Held in Oxford 1975*, hrsg. Elizabeth A. Livingstone (Berlin: Akademie-Verlag, 1975), 121–23.

8. Michael P. Weitzman, "From Judaism to Christianity: The Syriac Version of the Hebrew Bible," in *The Jews among Pagans and Christians in the Roman Empire*, hrsg. Judith Lieu, John North, und Tessa Rajak (London: Routledge 1992), 153–61.

2. Texte, in denen der Syrer zwar den hebräischen Fragmenten oder dem griechischen Text folgt, jedoch einzelne theologisch aufgeladene Begriffe nicht mit dem entsprechenden, zu erwartenden syrischen Äquivalent wiedergibt, sondern durch andere, allgemeinere Lexemata ersetzt.
3. Textpassagen der hebräischen Textfragmente und des griechischen Textes, die der Syrer unübersetzt lässt. Hier ergibt sich zwar die Möglichkeit, dass diese Texte nicht in der Vorlage des Syrers vorhanden waren. Sollte sich mit diesen Texten jedoch ein gewisses inhaltliches Profil verbinden, das der Syrer auch an anderer Stelle meidet oder zu unterdrücken sucht, kann diese Auslassung als Hinweis auf eine damit verbundene theologische Intention gedeutet werden.

Es ist wohl kaum nötig anzumerken, dass diese Untersuchung auf Vorarbeiten hinsichtlich der Erstellung einer diplomatischen Synopse der vorhandenen hebräischen, griechischen, syrischen und lateinischen Texte fußt. Es soll damit zugleich das Desiderat einer solchen Synopse unterstrichen werden.

Ich beginne mit einigen Beobachtungen zur poetischen Struktur einzelner Verse im syrischen Sirach und deren Bezugnahme auf den jeweiligen Kontext.

1. Poetisch bedingte Modifikationen

In Sir 9,17 finden sich folgende Versionen:

MS A liest:

בחכמי ידים יחשך יושר ומוש[ל] עמי חכם

Bei denen, die mit den Händen geschickt sind, bleibt Redlichkeit aus,[9]
aber wer mein Volk beherrscht, sei weise.

Die Fassung von G lautet:

---

9. Der schwer zu verstehende Text hat zu verschiedenen textlichen Verbesserungsvorschlägen geführt. Georg Sauer, *Jesus Sirach/Ben Sira*, ATD Apokryphen 1 (Göttingen: Vandenhoek & Ruprecht, 2000), 102 Anm. 136, will anstelle von יחשך יחשב „gerechnet werden" lesen und anstelle von יושר יוצר „Künstler", also: „Unter die, die mit den Händen geschickt sind, wird gerechnet der Künstler".

ἐν χειρὶ τεχνιτῶν ἔργον ἐπαινεσθήσεται καὶ ὁ ἡγούμενος λαοῦ σοφὸς ἐν λόγῳ αὐτου

Durch die Hand von Künstlern wird ein Werk gelobt, und der Herrscher des Volkes ist weise in seiner Rede.

S schließlich gibt den Vers folgendermaßen wieder:

ܒܚܟܡܬܗ ܕܕܝܢܐ ܬܬܩܝܡ ܡܕܝܢܬܐ. ܘܕܫܠܝܛ ܒܥܡܡܐ ܢܗܘܐ ܚܟܝܡ ܘܣܟܘܠܬܢ.

Durch die Weisheit des Richters möge die Stadt bestehen, und wer über die Völker herrscht, sei weise und klug.

Wie ist der Unterschied zu erklären? MS A bietet eine Antithese: dem geschickten, aber unredlichen Handwerker steht der weise Herrscher gegenüber. An ihn stellen sich höhere, auch ethische Ansprüche—eine Sicht, die sich auch in der Hochschätzung des Schriftgelehrten gegenüber den handwerklich Tätigen in Sir 38/39 widerspiegelt.[10] In G findet sich ein Vergleich. Dem Handwerker entspricht der weise Herrscher, insofern seine Rede mit dem zu lobenden Werk des Künstlers in Beziehung gesetzt wird. S hingegen bedenkt ausgehend von V17b nur noch die Kunst des Herrschens: Zunächst hinsichtlich des begrenzten Raumes der Stadt und dann hinsichtlich der Völkerwelt. Es wird hier also eine Fokussierung auf das Thema „Herrschen" vorgenommen, während der Handwerker und sein Werk komplett ausgeblendet werden. Dabei scheint S die hebräische Pluralform ידים „Hände" mit ܕܝܢܐ „Richter" in Verbindung gebracht zu haben, so dass trotz der gravierenden inhaltlichen Abweichung im ersten Teil des Verses ein wenigstens schwacher Bezug zur hebräischen Vorlage gewahrt bleibt. Durch die Verwendung des Begriffs „Stadt" stellt S zugleich eine Beziehung zum folgenden Vers 18 her. Dort ist von einem geschwätzigen Mann die Rede, der in der *Stadt* gefürchtet wird. Der syrische Text verwendet dort—offensichtlich mit der Intention einer Variation—anstelle des Wortes ܡܕܝܢܬܐ das Wort ܩܪܝܬܐ. Das heißt, nicht nur innerhalb des Verses geschieht eine Vereinheitlichung, sondern auch über den Vers hinaus wird mittels eines Stichwortes ein Bezug zum Kontext hergestellt. Die Intention dieser Wiedergabe ist also hier vor allem in einem engeren inhaltlichen Bezug innerhalb des Verses, aber auch darü-

10. Vgl. Burkard M. Zapff, *Jesus Sirach 25–51* (Würzburg: Echter, 2010), 260–67.

ber hinaus zu suchen. Hier für den Syrer eine vom hebräischen und griechischen Text abweichende Vorlage anzunehmen, wäre demnach verfehlt.

Ein zweites Beispiel, das die Intention des Syrers veranschaulichen kann, eine stärkere Parallelisierung und Strukturierung innerhalb des Verses zu bewirken, findet sich in Sir 10,19, wo dieses Ziel durch Ergänzungen erreicht wird.

Dort liest das hebräische Fragment MS A[11]:

זרע נכבד מה זרע לאנוש זרע נקלה עובר מצוה

> Nachkommenschaft wird als Ehre betrachtet.—Welche Nachkommenschaft hat der Mensch?—Eine verachtenswerte Nachkommenschaft, die das Gebot übertritt.

Die Auffassung, die Sirach vertritt, setzt sich offenbar mit der These auseinander, dass Nachkommenschaft, vor allem zahlreiche Nachkommenschaft, als Ehre zu betrachten sei. Demgegenüber zählt für Sirach nur eine solche Nachkommenschaft, die das Gesetz beachtet: alles andere ist verachtenswert.

G greift diese These auf, expliziert sie aber in einer ausführlicheren Gegenüberstellung:

σπέρμα ἔντιμον ποῖον σπέρμα ἀνθρώπου
σπέρμα ἔντιμον ποῖον οἱ φοβούμενοι τὸν κύριον
σπέρμα ἄτιμον ποῖον σπέρμα ἀνθρώπου
σπέρμα ἄτιμον ποῖον οἱ παραβαίνοντες ἐντολάς

Eine ehrenhafte Nachkommenschaft—welche (ist es)? Die Nachkommenschaft des Menschen.
Eine ehrenhafte Nachkommenschaft—welche (ist es)? Die den Herrn fürchten.
Eine ehrlose Nachkommenschaft—welche (ist es)? Die Nachkommenschaft des Menschen.
Eine ehrlose Nachkommenschaft—welche (ist es)? Die die Gebote übertreten.

Das heißt: In G wird eine Gegenüberstellung vorgenommen, wonach sich Ehre oder Unehre der Nachkommenschaft des Menschen an der

11. Vgl. MS B, das allerdings im ersten Teil זרע נקלה מה זרע לאנוש liest.

Furcht Gottes bzw. der damit offenbar in Beziehung stehenden Beachtung oder Missachtung der Gebote entscheidet. Entsprechend der parallelen Struktur stehen dabei „die die Gebote übertreten" in Antithese zu denen, „die Gott fürchten"; Einhaltung bzw. Übertretung der Gebote steht damit in enger Verbindung zur beachteten oder missachteten Gottesfurcht.

S genügt offenbar diese in G vorgenommene Parallelisierung bzw. antithetische Struktur nicht, obwohl sie anscheinend daran anknüpft. Sie gibt den Vers folgendermaßen wieder:

ܙܪ̈ܥܐ ܡܝܩܪ̈ܐ ܗܢܐ ܕܙܪܝܥ ܠܒܪܢܫܐ.
ܙܪ̈ܥܐ ܡܝܩܪ̈ܐ ܡܢ ܕܕܚܠ ܠܐܠܗܐ.
ܙܪ̈ܥܐ ܡܝܩܪ̈ܐ ܡܢ ܕܢܛܪ ܦܘܩܕ̈ܢܐ.
ܙܪ̈ܥܐ ܨܥܝܪ̈ܐ ܗܢܐ ܕܙܪܝܥ ܠܒܪܢܫܐ.
ܙܪ̈ܥܐ ܨܥܝܪ̈ܐ ܡܢ ܕܠܐ ܢܛܪ ܦܘܩܕ̈ܢܐ.

Eine geehrte Nachkommenschaft? Das, was vom Menschen gesät ist.
Eine geehrte Nachkommenschaft? Die, die Gott fürchtet.
Eine geehrte Nachkommenschaft? Die, die Weisungen hält.
Eine verachtete Nachkommenschaft? Das, was vom Menschen gesät ist
Eine verachtete Nachkommenschaft? Die, die die Weisungen nicht hält.

Das heißt, es wird hier eine klare Kontrastierung hergestellt, wonach das Einhalten der Weisungen entscheidend ist, ob die Nachkommenschaft eines Menschen geehrt oder verachtet ist. Dabei fügt S eine weitere, der jeweils parallelen Formulierung „Die Nachkommenschaft des Menschen" inhaltlich entsprechende Formulierung ein: „die, die die Weisung hält" bzw. „nicht hält". Da im ersten Teil das Einhalten der Weisungen Explikation der zuvor genannten Gottesfurcht ist, schien es im zweiten Teil S offensichtlich nicht mehr nötig, nun auch noch von der Nachkommenschaft zu sprechen, die Gott *nicht* fürchtet. Auffällig ist auf jeden Fall, dass offensichtlich auch hier die gefälligere poetische Strukturierung leitend war. Das heißt, der syrische Text beruht hier ebenfalls nicht auf einer anderen Textgrundlage, sondern ist der poetischen Form geschuldet. So bezeichnet denn auch van Peursen mit Recht als häufigstes poetisches Merkmal des Syrers die Parallelisierung und die Wiederholung von Worten und Phrasen. Dies, so van Peursen weiter, sei ein Charakteristikum der aramäisch-syrischen poetischen Tradition.[12]

12. Van Peursen, *Language*, 63.

Zu diesem, in der syrischen Übersetzung häufig anzutreffenden Bemühen, den Texten eine stringentere und gefälligere poetische Struktur zu geben, gehören auch inhaltliche Verbesserungen. Zu ihnen zählt z.B. Sir 13,23.

Dort liest MS A:

עשיר דובר הכל נסכתו ואת שכלו עד עב יגיעו:
דל דובר מי זה יאמרו ואם נתקל גם הם יהדפוהו

Ein Reicher redet—alle schweigen, und seine Klugheit lassen sie bis an die Wolken reichen.
Ein Armer spricht—„Wer ist das?“ sagen sie, und wenn er strauchelt, dann geben sie ihm auch noch einen Stoß.

G hat hier folgende Version:

πλούσιος ἐλάλησεν καὶ πάντες ἐσίγησαν καὶ τὸν λόγον αὐτοῦ ἀνύψωσαν ἕως τῶν νεφελῶν
πτωχὸς ἐλάλησεν καὶ εἶπαν τίς οὗτος κἂν προσκόψῃ προσανατρέψουσιν αὐτόν

Der Reiche spricht, und alle schweigen, und seine Rede erhöhen sie bis zu den Wolken.
Der Arme spricht und sie sagen: „Wer ist dieser?“ Und wenn er sich stößt, dann stürzen sie ihn nieder.
Der Syrer hingegen übersetzt:

ܥܬܝܪܐ ܡܡܠܠ ܘܟܠܗܘܢ ܨܝܬܝܢ. ܘܦܐܒܘ̈ܗܝ، ܥܕܡܐ ܠܥܢܢܐ ܡܣܩܝܢ ܠܗ.
ܡܣܟܢܐ ܡܡܠܠ ܘܐܡܪܝܢ ܡܢܐ ܐܡܪ. ܘܐܢ ܬܬܩܠ ܢܣܚܦܘܢܗ.

Der Reiche redet und sie alle lauschen, und seine Befürworter erheben ihn bis zu den Wolken.
Der Arme redet und sie sagen: „Was redet er?“ Und wenn er stolpert, werden sie ihn niederwerfen.

H und G argumentieren also folgendermaßen: Die Person ist ein Reicher, also wird der Inhalt seiner Rede beachtet und gelobt. Ist die Person ein Armer, bleibt der Inhalt seiner Rede außen vor.

Demgegenüber nimmt der Syrer eine stärkere Parallelisierung vor, insofern in beiden Versteilen sowohl Inhalt wie Person des Redenden in den Blick genommen werden: Die Rede des Reichen wird aufmerksam wahrgenommen, die des Armen verworfen. Der Reiche wird zu den Wolken erhoben, der Arme niedergeworfen. Um diese Parallelisierung zu erreichen, muss der Syrer denn auch die Frage „Wer ist das?“ in MS A bzw. „Wer redet?“ in G logischerweise auf den *Inhalt* seiner Rede beziehen: „*Was* redet er?“.

2. Inhaltliche Änderungen auf der Ebene der Semantik

Neben solchen, vor allem von einer stärkeren formalen und inhaltlichen Parallelisierung der einzelnen Sentenzen geleiteten Modifikationen finden sich auch Änderungen, die offenbar bewusst von der mit einzelnen Lexemen verbundenen Semantik der hebräischen Vorlage abweichen.

Dies geschieht z.B. mit dem Ziel einer Abschwächung bzw. Vermeidung bestimmter, theologisch gefüllter Termini. Ein Beispiel findet sich in Sir 3,11. Dort bietet MS A folgenden Text:

כבוד איש כבוד אביו ומרבה חטא מקלל אמו

Die Ehre eines Mannes ist die Ehre seines Vaters, und Sünde vermehrt, wer seiner Mutter flucht.

G weicht im zweiten Versteil inhaltlich deutlich von der hebräischen Version ab, wenn es dort heißt:

ἡ γὰρ δόξα ἀνθρώπου ἐκ τιμῆς πατρὸς αὐτοῦ καὶ ὄνειδος τέκνοις μήτηρ ἐν ἀδοξίᾳ

Denn die Ehre des Menschen (kommt) aus dem Ansehen seines Vaters, und Schmach für die Kinder (ist) eine Mutter in Unehre.

Dabei hat bereits G offensichtlich ein Problem mit der Formulierung „seiner Mutter fluchen“ und macht daraus „eine Mutter in Unehre“. S hingegen orientiert sich offensichtlich an der hebräischen Fassung, allerdings mit einem markanten Unterschied. Es heißt dort:

ܐܝܩܪܗ (ܓܝܪ)[13] ܕܓܒܪܐ ܐܝܩܪܗ ܗܘ ܕܐܒܘܗܝ، ܘܣܓܝܐܐ ܪ̈ܘܪܒܐ ܡܢ ܕܡܨܥܪ
ܠܐܡܗ

13. Nur in 7h3, vgl. de Lagarde.

(Denn) die Ehre eines Mannes ist die Ehre seines Vaters, und große Schulden lädt auf sich, wer seine Mutter *schmäht*.

Aus hebräisch קלל, das entsprechend ThWAT die Bedeutung „herabsetzen", „entehren", „verwünschen", „verfluchen" und „lästern" hat,[14] wobei wohl die Vorstellung mitschwingt, dem Gegenüber eine lebensmindernde Wirklichkeit zu erzeugen, wird beim Syrer ein ܡܨܚܐ, was so viel wie „schmähen", „entehren" bedeutet.[15] Dass sich der Syrer durchaus der Semantik von קלל bewusst ist, zeigt sich in Sir 4,5b, wo er das hebräische קלל mit der Wurzel ܠܛܐ wiedergibt, welches nun eindeutig mit „verfluchen",[16] wörtl. eigentlich mit „verabscheuen" zu übersetzen ist. Diese Abschwächung bestätigt sich auch von Sir 3,16 her, wo zwar der Täter vor seinem Schöpfer verflucht ist—syr. ܡܠܝܛ ܡܢ ܒܪܘܝܗ—jedoch sein Vergehen, nämlich entsprechend MS A seine Mutter zu verfluchen,[17] hebr. מקלל אמו, wiederum lediglich mit „der seine Mutter schmäht", syr. ܘܡܨܚܐ ܠܐܡܗ, wiedergegeben wird. Offensichtlich schien diese—zugegebenermaßen krasse—Vorstellung, seine Mutter zu verfluchen, dem syrischen Übersetzer undenkbar.

Eine Abschwächung der hebräischen Vorlage, bei der im Hintergrund wohl bereits theologische Überlegungen stehen, findet sich in der syrischen Übersetzung bezüglich der Wiedergabe dessen, was die hebräische Vorlage als „Sühnegeschehen" oder „Sühnehandlung" bezeichnet. Es gibt nun in den hebräischen Sirachfragmenten drei Texte, in denen von einem sühnenden Handeln gesprochen wird: Sir 3,30; 45,16b und 23. Jedes Mal wird dabei der klassische hebr. Terminus technicus כפר verwendet.[18] Der griechische Text gibt diese Wurzel regelmäßig mit einer Verbform von ἐξιλάσκομαι wieder.[19] Da diese Wurzel auch in dem nur

---

14. J. Scharbert, "קלל," *ThWAT* 7:43–44.

15. Wenn van Peursen, *Language*, 21, meint syr. ܡܨܚܐ sei eine angemessene Übersetzung von hebr. קלל und deshalb sei keine Emendation im hebräischen Text nötig—etwa zu מקלה—, dann rechnet er m.E. zu sehr damit, dass S in ihrer Übersetzung immer möglichst der hebräischen Semantik zu entsprechen sucht.

16. Jessie Payne Smith, Hrsg., *A Compendious Syriac Dictionary Founded upon the Thesaurus Syriacus of R. Payne Smith* (Abdr., Oxford: Clarendon, 1985), 237: „to curse".

17. MS C spricht hier von der Verstoßung der Mutter: יסחוב.

18. Ausführlich zum Begriff vgl. B. Lang, "כפר," *ThWAT* 4:303–10.

19. Franz Passow, *Handwörterbuch der griechischen Sprache*, Bd. 2.1 (Leipzig: Vogel, 1847), gibt dafür die Bedeutung: „einen sich geneigt machen, aussöhnen, versöhnen, begütigen" an.

griechisch vorliegenden Sir 3,3 verwendet wird, wo wiederum von einem sühnenden Geschehen die Rede ist, ist anzunehmen, dass auch dort in der ursprünglichen hebräischen Textfassung ein כפר stand.[20] Anders ist dies beim Syrer. So wird das in den hebräischen und griechischen Textversionen als sühnendes Handeln bezeichnete Eintreten des Pinchas für sein Volk in Sir 45,23 durch den Syrer lediglich als „Gebet für Israel" in Anlehnung an Ps 106,30 wiedergegeben, wie bereits van Peursen erkannt hat.[21] Ähnlich wird auch das Sühnegeschehen, von dem der hebräische Text in Sir 3,30b spricht, wo es das Almosen ist, welches Sühne bewirkt, beim Syrer durch die Wurzel ܫܒܩ wiedergegeben. Letztere ist mit „loslassen, erlassen, vergeben"[22] zu übersetzen. Diese Wurzel verwendet auch Sir 3,3, wo die Ehre des Vaters zum Erlass der Verschuldungen führt. Lediglich im Fall des kultischen Handelns des Hohepriesters Aaron in Sir 45,16b übersetzt der Syrer auffälligerweise die hebräische Wurzel כפר mit dem syrischen Pendant ܚܣܐ, das zusammen mit der Präposition ܥܠ die Bedeutung „Sühne leisten"[23] annimmt und damit analog zu כפר ein sühnendes Geschehen bezeichnet. Dabei wird in der syrischen Version des Sirach diese Wurzel nur an *dieser einen* Stelle verwendet. Offensichtlich will damit der Syrer sühnendes Geschehen ausschließlich auf den kultischen Bereich und hier nochmals auf das als vergangenes Geschehen verstandene Handeln des Hohepriesters Aaron eingegrenzt wissen,[24] entgegen der hebräischen—und griechischen—Fassung, die durch einen breiteren Anwendungsbereich der Wurzel כפר eine Weitung vornimmt, vielleicht im Sinne eines uneigentlichen Sühnegeschehens.

---

20. Vgl. dazu die Rekonstruktion von Segal: מכבד אב יכפר חטאת.

21. Van Peursen, *Language*, 105.

22. Payne Smith (*A Compendious Syriac Dictionary*, 557) gibt unter anderem folgende Bedeutungen an: „to leave, go away, leave over, leave behind, send away, let go, remit, forgive, forsake, abandon".

23. Ibid., 150.

24. Man kann darüber spekulieren, warum dies so ist. Eine mögliche Erklärung wäre hier vielleicht in christlichen Einflüssen zu suchen, die—abgesehen von den als vergangen angesehenen Sühnehandlungen des Aaron—diese Begrifflichkeit ausschließlich mit dem Heilsopfer Jesu Christi in Verbindung bringen wollten, so dass es jenseits davon keine ausgesprochene Sühnehandlung des Menschen mehr gibt.

3. Tendenzen zur Vereinheitlichung

Auch Ergänzungen mit dem Ziel einer *Vereinheitlichung* lassen sich in der syrischen Übersetzung mehrfach feststellen. Dies zeigt sich nicht zuletzt im „Lob der Väter" und zwar mittels des Begriffs „Schwur" bzw. „schwören"[25], syr. ܝܡܐ[26]. In der hebräischen Fassung von Sir 44,18 (MS B), wo es um Noach geht, findet sich zunächst folgende Formulierung: באות עולם נכרת עמו „in einem ewigen Zeichen wurde mit ihm geschnitten". Die griechische Übersetzung spricht dagegen ausdrücklich von „Bundesschlüssen": διαθῆκαι αἰῶνος ἐτέθησαν πρὸς αὐτόν „Ewige Bundesschlüsse wurden mit ihm geschlossen".

In der syrischen Fassung ist auffälligerweise von „Eiden" die Rede, die ihm Gott „schwor", ܡܘܡܬܐ ܝܡܐ ܠܗ ܒܫܪܪܐ „*Eide schwor* er ihm in Wahrheit".

Ähnlich ist dies in Sir 44,21 im Hinblick auf Abraham. Dort spricht der hebräische Text von einem Eid, in dem Gott ihm etwas zugesichert habe: על כן בש[בו]עה הקים לו „Deswegen richtete er ihm auf in einem Eid", vgl. G: διὰ τοῦτο ἐν ὅρκῳ ἔστησεν αὐτῷ „Deswegen hat er ihm in einem Eid zugesichert." Der Syrer übersetzt wiederum „deshalb schwor ihm Gott in Eiden", ܡܛܠ ܗܢܐ ܒܡܘܡܬܐ ܝܡܐ ܠܗ ܐܠܗܐ.

In Sir 44,22, wo es um Isaak geht, ist zwar nicht von Eiden die Rede, doch findet sich hier das Verb „schwören". So gibt der Syrer den Text mit „und auch dem Isaak schwor er" ܘܐܦ ܠܐܝܣܚܩ ܝܡܐ wieder, während MS B וגם ליצחק הקים בן „und auch dem Isaak richtete er einen Sohn auf" liest. G hat hier: καὶ ἐν τῷ Ισαακ ἔστησεν οὕτως „und auch dem Issak sicherte er so zu".[27]

Schließlich findet sich dieses Thema nochmals in Sir 45,24, wo es um den Pinchasbund geht, den Gott dem Pinchas und seinen Nachkommen aufgrund erwiesener Treue stiftet. Die hebräische Fassung liest hier: לכן גם לו הקים חק ברית שלום „deshalb richtete er auch ihm eine Satzung, einen Bund des Friedens auf", was G in ähnlicher Weise aufnimmt: διὰ τοῦτο ἐστάθη αὐτῷ διαθήκη εἰρήνης „Deshalb wurde ihm ein Bund des Friedens zugesichert".

---

25. So bereits van Peursen, *Language*, 66.

26. Payne Smith (*A Compendious Syriac Dictionary*, 193) gibt folgende Bedeutungen an: „swear, take an oath, swear fealthy".

27. G setzt hier offensichtlich die Variante von MS Bm voraus, die anstelle von בן ein כן liest.

Demgegenüber spricht auch hier der Syrer wiederum davon, dass Gott dem Pinchas „in Eiden schwor“, ܒܡܘܡܬܐ ܝܡܐ ܠܗ ܐܠܗܐ. Es wird also in der syrischen Version mittels derselben Phrase eine Linie gelegt, die von Noach über Abraham und Isaak bis Pinchas reicht. Verbindender theologischer Gedanke scheint dabei zum einen das sich treu bleibende identische Handeln Gottes und zum anderen die Gültigkeit dieses Schwures über den jeweiligen Adressaten hinaus für die nachfolgenden Generationen zu sein.

4. Ergänzungen anhand des alttestamentlichen Bezugstextes

Eine weitere, mehr inhaltliche Eigenart des Syrers ist die *Ergänzung von Bezügen auf das Alte Testament*, die er bereits in seiner Vorlage findet. Zwei markante Beispiele dafür finden sich in Sir 44,17—der Würdigung Noachs—und der eben erwähnten Pinchasepisode. So ergänzt der Syrer nach der Beschreibung des gerechten Noach unter Aufnahme des Stichwortes „schwören“ folgende Formulierung, die sich weder in der hebräischen noch in der griechischen Vorlage findet: „Und es schwor ihm Gott, dass nicht wieder eine Flut sein werde“ ܘܝܡܐ ܠܗ ܐܠܗܐ ܕܠܐ ܢܗܘܐ ܬܘܒ ܛܘܦܢܐ. Diese Ergänzung greift zwar das Stichwort „Flut“ aus den Vorlagen auf, setzt aber in ihrer Formulierung gleichzeitig die Kenntnis von Gen 9,11 voraus: ולא־יהיה עוד מבול.

In der Darstellung der Pinchaserzählung in Sir 45,23 nimmt der Syrer insofern gegenüber seiner Vorlage eine Ergänzung vor, als sich seine Wiedergabe enger an der alttestamentlichen Erzählung in Num 25,6–13 orientiert. Die hebräische Textversion von MS B lautet hier folgendermaßen:

וגם פינחס [ב]ן אלעזר בגבורה נח[ל שלישי בהוד] בקנאו לאלוהי כל
ויעמד בפרץ עמו:

> Und auch Pinchas, der Sohn des Eleazars. Wegen seiner Tapferkeit erbt er das Dreifache an Ehre, wegen seines Eifers für den Gott des Alls und er stand in der Bresche seines Volkes.

Wie man leicht erkennen kann, wird hier Pinchas entgegen des ursprünglichen Sinns des hebräischen Textes im Buch Numeri zum Vorkämpfer des Monotheismus stilisiert, indem er für den „Gott des Alls“ eifert. Bereits die griechische Version weicht davon deutlich ab. Sie liest:

καὶ Φινεες υἱὸς Ελεαζαρ τρίτος εἰς δόξαν ἐν τῷ ζηλῶσαι αὐτὸν ἐν φόβῳ κυρίου καὶ στῆναι αὐτὸν ἐν τροπῇ λαοῦ ἐν ἀγαθότητι προθυμίας ψυχῆς αὐτοῦ.

Und Phinees, der Sohn des Eleazars, war der Dritte an Ehre, indem er ihm nacheiferte in der Furcht des Herrn und er fest stand im Wandel des Volkes, in der Güte des Eifers seiner Seele.

Hier wird Pinchas zum Vorbild und zum Nacheiferer seiner Vorgänger in der Furcht des Herrn, dem er auch in der Wankelmütigkeit des Volkes die Treue hielt. Der Syrer hingegen nähert sich, wie bereits gesagt, wieder der alttestamentlichen Vorlage an. Er nennt nun ausdrücklich den dort ausgeführten eigentlichen Grund des Eifers des Pinchas, wenn er folgendermaßen formuliert:

ܘܐܦ ܦܢܚܣ ܒܪ ܐܠܥܙܪ ܒܓܢܒܪܘܬܗ ܢܣܒ ܬܠܬܐ ܐܝܩܪܝܢ.
ܒܛܢܢܐ ܕܛܢ ܒܡܕܝܢܝܬܐ ܘܒܒܪ ܐܝܣܪܐܝܠ. ܘܩܡ ܒܬܘܪܥܬܐ ܒܥܡܐ

Und auch Pinchas, der Sohn des Eleazars, wegen seiner Tapferkeit nimmt er sich das Dreifache an Ehren. Wegen des Eifers, den er eiferte *wegen der Midianiterin und des Sohnes Israels,* und der in der Bresche des Volkes stand....

Tatsächlich ist ausweislich der biblischen Erzählung die verbotene Vermischung Israels mit fremden Völkern in Gestalt jenes Sohnes Israels, der sich mit einer Midianiterin einlässt, Grund für den Eifer des Pinchas, der beide auf ihrem Lager durchbohrt. Mit dieser kurzen Einfügung verlässt der Syrer die Interpretation der Textstelle im hebräischen wie im griechischen Text und kehrt wieder zum Sinn des ursprünglichen alttestamentlichen Textes zurück. Der Übersetzer hat also nicht nur einen Blick auf seine jeweilige(n) Vorlage(n) des Sirachtextes, sondern gleichzeitig auf die alttestamentlichen Bezugstexte.

Da und dort sind zwar bereits im Zusammenhang mit den Charakteristika des syrischen Textes theologische Intentionen angeklungen, die die syrische Version verfolgt, dies geschah jedoch bisher eher am Rande. Im Folgenden sollen daher theologische Leitlinien im Vordergrund stehen, die die Darstellung des syrischen Sirach prägen.

5. Opferkritische Tendenzen

Erwähnt wurde bereits die vom Syrer gegenüber seiner hebräischen bzw. griechischen Vorlage sehr eingeschränkte Verwendung von ausdrücklicher Sühneterminologie, die im Grunde nur noch im kultischen Handeln des Aaron Anwendung findet. Ähnliches gilt überhaupt für die Bedeutung, die Kult und Opfer beim Syrer spielen.[28] Dies ist nicht nur positiv zu beobachten, etwa anhand der Veränderungen, die der Syrer an einschlägigen Stellen vornimmt, sondern in diesem besonderen Fall auch anhand von Texten und Versen, die er aus seiner Vorlage unübersetzt lässt. Hier wiederum einige Beispiele:

Beeindruckend ist Sir 35, wo sich die Verse 1–12 intensiv mit Opfer und seiner Bedeutung beschäftigen. Die Darstellung leidet allerdings darunter, dass hier lediglich die syrische und griechische Version erhalten ist, demnach eine Absicherung, wie originär der syrische Text hier formuliert, seitens der hebräischen Version nicht möglich ist. Da sich diese opferkritische Tendenz jedoch auch an anderen Stellen im Sirach zeigt, wo ein Vergleich mit der hebräischen Fassung möglich ist, scheint es sich hier tatsächlich um eine Eigenart des Syrers zu handeln. Der Unterschied fällt bereits in V 1 auf. So formuliert hier die griechische Version: *ὁ συντηρῶν νόμον πλεονάζει προσφοράς* „Wer das Gesetz streng beobachtet, vermehrt die Opfergaben". Den Satz kann man dabei grundsätzlich in zweifacher Hinsicht verstehen. Nämlich einmal in dem Sinn, dass Gesetzeseinhaltung der Darbringung von Opfergaben entspricht, also Opfergaben ersetzen kann, oder aber, dass die Einhaltung des Gesetzes eine vermehrte Darbringung von Opfergaben impliziert. Dabei scheint diese alternative Möglichkeit, den Vers verstehen zu können, bewusst angezielt zu sein, werden doch im Folgenden sowohl mildtätiges Tun, wie Opferdienst als Erfüllung des Gesetzes gewürdigt. Demgegenüber formuliert der Syrer eindeutig: ܐܢ ܥܒܕܬ ܡܕܡ ܕܟܬܝܒ ܒܢܡܘܣܐ ܐܣܓܝܬ ܦܘܠܚܢܐ. ܘܕܢܛܪ ܦܘܩܕܢܐ ܛܘܒܘܗܝ ܠܪܘܚܗ „Wenn du etwas tust, was im Gesetz geschrieben ist, vervielfältigst du die Anbetung und wer das Gebot hält: Selig ist sein Geist!" Aus den „Opfergaben" in der griechischen Version wird nun lediglich eine „Anbetung" bzw. ein „religiöser Dienst"[29]—so die wörtliche Bedeutung des hier verwendeten ܦܘܠܚܢܐ.[30] Zum einen wird nun ausdrücklich von einem „Tun" dessen, was im Gesetz steht, gesprochen, zum anderen die „Opfergabe" zu einer Anbetung bzw. einem religiösen Dienst abgeschwächt. Dass es dabei um

28. Ausführlich bereits van Peursen, *Language*, 79–83.

29. Van Peursen, *Language*, 79.

30. Payne Smith (*A Compendious Syriac Dictionary*, 437), gibt als Sonderbedeutung „religious service, worship" an.

Gesetzesobservanz geht, macht der Nachsatz deutlich, der mit einer Seligpreisung verknüpft wird, die an die Segnungen in Dtn 28,1ff. erinnert.

Noch interessanter ist der Folgevers. Dort lautet die griechische Version: θυσιάζων σωτηρίου ὁ προσέχων ἐντολαῖς: „wer ein Dankopfer darbringt, der hält die Gebote". Sir 35,1 wird demnach offenbar in der Weise verstanden, dass Opfern eine Form der Gebotserfüllung ist. Der Syrer hingegen liest:

ܐܓܪܐ ܣܘܓܐܐ ܟܢܫ ܗܘ ܕܡܩܪܒ ܩܘܪܒܢܐ. ܘܥܒܕ ܙܕܩܬܐ ܢܛܪ ܢܡܘܣܐ

Gute Belohnungen häuft derjenige auf, der eine Opfergabe darbringt, und wer ein Almosen macht, hält das Gesetz.

Lässt die Formulierung des Vordersatzes ܕܡܩܪܒ ܩܘܪܒܢܐ zunächst an ein kultisches Geschehen denken, so macht der Nachsatz deutlich, dass es sich bei der vermeintlichen Opfergabe um ein Almosen handelt, somit dieses in den Rang eines quasi kultischen Opfers einrückt. Dass es sich bei beiden nicht um verschiedene Dinge handelt, sie vielmehr in einer inhaltlichen Korrespondenz stehen, wird auch anhand der beiden anderen Formulierungen „Belohnungen aufhäufen" und „Einhaltung des Gesetzes" deutlich. Offensichtlich stehen nämlich auch diese beiden in einem Sinnzusammenhang, insofern wiederum die Segnungen in Dtn 28 vorausgesetzt werden, die dort der Einhaltung des Gesetzes in Aussicht gestellt werden. Ganz auffällig ist diese Tendenz in V 8. Dort formuliert der griechische Text:

προσφορὰ δικαίου λιπαίνει θυσιαστήριον καὶ ἡ εὐωδία αὐτῆς ἔναντι ὑψίστου;

Eine Opfergabe des Gerechten ölt den Altar, und ihr Wohlgeruch bis zum Höchsten.

Zwar wird auch hier die Wirksamkeit und Annahme des Opfers mit der ethischen Integrität des Opfernden in Verbindung gebracht, jedoch ist gleichzeitig—wie die Formulierung „ölt" nahelegt—an eine kultische Handlung gedacht. Ganz anders ist dies in der syrischen Version. Diese formuliert (V 6):

ܩܘܪܒܢܝܗܘܢ ܕܙܕܝ̈ܩܐ ܨܠܘܬܐ ܕܦܘܡܗܘܢ. ܘܡܥܒܕܝܗܘܢ ܫܦܝܪܐ ܩܕܡܝ.

> Die Opfergaben der Gerechten sind das Gebet ihres Mundes, und ihre Taten dringen in den Himmel vor.

Die Opfergaben als kultische Handlung werden nun mit dem Gebet des Gerechten verbunden. Wiederum wird—wie in V 1—aus dem Opfer lediglich ein Gebet. Wie der Opfergabe des Gerechten in G der Wohlgeruch korrespondiert, der bis zum Höchsten gelangt, so dem Gebet der Gerechten ihre guten Taten, die in den Himmel vordringen. Schon fast neutestamentlich mutet die syrische Wiedergabe von V 10 an. Dort formuliert die hebräische Version (MS B): תן לו כמתנתו לך בטוב עין ובהשגת יד „Gib ihm gemäß seiner Gabe an dich, mit einem guten Auge gemäß dem Ertrag der Hand" (vgl. G: δὸς ὑψίστῳ κατὰ τὴν δόσιν αὐτοῦ καὶ ἐν ἀγαθῷ ὀφθαλμῷ καθ' εὕρεμα χειρός „Gib dem Höchsten gemäß seiner Gabe und mit einem freundlichen Auge gemäß dem Ertrag der Hand").

Wiederum ist hier offensichtlich an ein Opfer gedacht, das nicht spärlich ausfallen soll. Zunächst scheint der Syrer diese Aufforderung ohne große Veränderung aufzunehmen, wenn er im ersten Teil von V 10 folgendermaßen formuliert:

ܗܒ ܠܐܠܗܐ ܐܝܟ ܡܐ ܕܝܗܒ ܠܟ. ܒܥܝܢܐ ܛܒܬܐ ܘܒܐܝܕܐ ܪܒܬܐ.

> Gib Gott wie er dir gab, mit wohlwollendem Auge und mit großer Hand.

Wie diese Gabe jedoch zu verstehen ist, wird im Folgesatz deutlich, wo der Syrer offensichtlich ohne Anhalt an einer Vorlage formuliert:

ܡܢ ܕܝܗܒ ܓܝܪ ܠܡܣܟܢܐ ܠܐܠܗܐ ܗܘ ܡܘܙܦ. ܡܢܘ ܓܝܪ ܦܪܘܥܐ ܐܠܐ ܐܢ ܗܘ.

> Denn wer dem Armen gibt, ist einer, der Gott leiht, denn wer ist einer, der zurückzahlt, wenn nicht er?

Dem Armen zu geben, ist also dasselbe, wie Gott selbst zu geben bzw. zu leihen. Im Armen wird Gott zum Empfänger der Gabe. Auch hier wiederum wird das kultische Opfer durch soziales Handeln ersetzt.

In der Forschung hat man nun aufgrund solcher Formulierungen einen möglicherweise christlichen Hintergrund der syrischen Übersetzung zu erheben gesucht, zumal die Ausführungen, wie bereits gesagt, doch sehr neutestamentlich klingen. Demgegenüber verweist van Peursen auf ein durchaus von der Tendenz her vergleichbares Zitat aus Qumran, 1QS IX,4–5, wo es heißt (deutsche Übersetzung von mir):

> Das Opfern der Lippen in Einklang mit der Anordnung wird wie angenehmer Geruch der Gerechtigkeit sein und die Vollkommenheit des Verhaltens wird wie ein freiwilliges Opfer angenommen.[31]

Damit aber wäre auch ein jüdisches Umfeld als geistiger Hintergrund der syrischen Übersetzung denkbar. Schließlich noch ein letztes Beispiel für die distanzierte Sicht des Syrers hinsichtlich kultischen Opferwesens, das diese theologische Tendenz der syrischen Übersetzung, diesmal vor dem Hintergrund der hier vorliegenden hebräischen Fassung bestätigt.

In Sir 38 beschäftigt sich Sirach mit der umstrittenen, weil aus dem hellenistischen Kulturkreis stammenden Institution des Arztes.[32] Im Falle einer Krankheit gibt er dort folgenden Rat. Zunächst die hebräische Version in V 10–11:

> [נו]ס מעול ומהכר פנים ומכל פשעים טהר לב:
> ה[גש ניח]וח [ו]אזכרה ודשן ערוך בכנפי הוניך

> Lass ab vom Bösen und von Parteilichkeit und von allen Sünden reinige dein Herz. Bring den beruhigenden Duft eines Gedenkopfers dar und eine fette[33] Gabe (wörtl.: Aufschichtung) auf den Flügeln deines Vermögens.

Die griechische Fassung formuliert ähnlich:

> ἀπόστησον πλημμέλειαν καὶ εὔθυνον χεῖρας καὶ ἀπὸ πάσης ἁμαρτίας καθάρισον καρδίαν. δὸς εὐωδίαν καὶ μνημόσυνον σεμιδάλεως καὶ λίπανον προσφορὰν ὡς μὴ ὑπάρχων

---

31. Van Peursen, *Language*, 82: „The offering of the lips in compliance with the degree will be like the pleasant aroma of justice and the perfectness of behaviour will be acceptable like a freewill offering", zit. nach E. Chazon, "Psalms, Hymns, and Prayer," in *Encyclopaedia of the Dead Sea Scrolls*, hrsg. Lawrence Schiffman und James VanderKam (Oxford: Oxford University Presss, 2000), 2:714, engl. Übersetzung von Florentino García Martínez and Eibert Tigchelaar, Hrsg., *Dead Sea Scrolls Study Edition* (Leiden: Brill, 2000), 1:91.

32. Ausführlich vgl. Burkard Zapff, "Sir 38,1–15 als Beispiel der Verknüpfung von Tradition und Innovation bei Jesus Sirach," *Biblica* 92 (2011): 347–67.

33. Alternativ kann hier ein Imp. piel gelesen werden: „mach fett".

Halte fern Vergehen und lenke gerade die Hände, und von aller Sünde reinige das Herz. Gib süßen Duft und ein Gedächtnisopfer aus feinstem Weizenmehl, und mach die Opfergabe fett, als seiest du nicht da.

Beide Male also verbindet sich Abkehr vom Bösen mit einer kultischen Handlung, entsprechend der bereits beobachteten Verbindung zwischen ethischem Verhalten und erfolgreicher Opferpraxis. Interessant ist nun die Version des Syrers. In V 10 unterscheidet er sich nur zunächst unwesentlich in der Aufforderung:

ܐܥܒܪ ܒܝܫܬܐ ܘܢܟܠܐ ܘܡܢ ܟܠ ܚܛܗܐ ܕܟܐ ܠܒܟ

Bekehre dich vom Bösen"—wörtlich eigentlich: „Lass das Böse vorbeigehen"—und von Falschheit und von allen Sünden reinige dein Herz.

V 11 hingegen, wo man nun eigentlich entsprechend H und G eine Aufforderung zur kultischen Opferpraxis erwartet, lässt S schlicht unübersetzt.[34] Damit bestätigt sich diesmal—sozusagen ex negativo—auch hier die opferdistanzierte Haltung des Syrers.

Dieser Tendenz des Syrers entspricht auch seine eher distanzierte Sicht des Priestertums. Dies zeigt sich z.B. daran, dass er in Sir 45,8–14, wo die hebräische und griechische Version ausführlich die Ausstattung des als Hoherpriester eingesetzten Aaron beschreibt, lediglich V 8 übersetzt, die restlichen Verse aber schlicht übergeht.

6. Eschatologische Tendenzen

Als letzter Punkt sei schließlich noch auf *eschatologische Tendenzen* hingewiesen, die die syrische Übersetzung da und dort im Unterschied zur hebräischen bzw. griechischen Version prägt. Unter „Eschatologie" werden hier zum einen die Vorstellungen von endzeitlichen Ereignissen, etwa in Gestalt eines Endgerichtes, zum anderen die Vorstellung einer postmortalen Existenz des einzelnen Menschen verstanden. Dies ist nicht zuletzt deshalb erwähnenswert, weil Sirach nach weitverbreiteter Ansicht[35] ursprünglich solche Vorstellungen nicht vertritt. Man verglei-

34. Van Peursen, *Language*, 80.

35. Lutz Schrader, *Leiden und Gerechtigkeit: Studien zu Theologie und Textgeschichte des Sirachbuches*, BET 27 (Frankfurt am Main: Lang, 1994).

che dazu beispielsweise die hebräische Version von Sir 41,4, wo entsprechend der Marginalie in MS B davon die Rede ist, dass es in der Scheol keine Widerreden (אין תוכחות), wohl im Sinne von Klagen aufgrund der vorher genannten unterschiedlichen Lebensdauer von tausend, hundert oder zehn Jahren, gibt. Sirach vertritt hier also offensichtlich die traditionelle alttestamentliche Vorstellung einer allenfalls schattenhaften, depotenzierten Existenz in der Unterwelt, wenn nicht überhaupt eines Todesschlafes ohne Bewusstsein (vgl. Sir 38,21.23). Auch prophetische Zitate, die sich in ihrem ursprünglichen Kontext ausdrücklich auf endzeitliche Ereignisse beziehen, werden bei Sirach häufig nicht auf die Zukunft, sondern auf Situationen der Gegenwart bezogen. Sehr anschaulich ist dies etwa in der Beschreibung der vom Hohenpriester Simeon vollzogenen Liturgie in Sir 50,17. Dort wird das Niederfallen allen Fleisches vor dem Höchsten, dem Heiligen Israels am Ende der Liturgie mit den Worten der Verheißung in Jes 66,23 formuliert, deren Einlösung jedoch bei Jesaja erst für das Ende der Zeit nach der Erschaffung eines neuen Himmels und einer neuen Erde erwartet wird.[36]

Gegenüber diesem Ausfall einer Eschatologie zumindest in den hebräischen Versionen des Sirach gibt es nun in der syrischen Version Texte, die von einem Endgericht, ja offenbar auch von einem ewigen Leben sprechen. Der endzeitliche Gerichtsgedanke spielt etwa in Sir 17,23–24 eine Rolle. Hier ist allerdings leider nur die griechische und syrische Version erhalten. Die griechische Version lautet:

> μετὰ ταῦτα ἐξαναστήσεται καὶ ἀνταποδώσει αὐτοῖς καὶ τὸ ἀνταπόδομα αὐτῶν εἰς κεφαλὴν αὐτῶν ἀποδώσει, πλὴν μετανοοῦσιν ἔδωκεν ἐπάνοδον καὶ παρεκάλεσεν ἐκλείποντας ὑπομονήν.
>
> Danach wird er sich erheben und ihnen vergelten, und ihre Vergeltung lässt er über ihr Haupt kommen, nur denen, die umkehren, gewährt er Heimkehr, und redet denen gut zu, die (ihre) Geduld verlieren.

Der Syrer hingegen liest:

> ܒܬܪ ܗܠܝܢ ܢܬܓܠܐ ܘܢܦܪܘܥ ܐܢܘܢ. ܘܦܘܪܥܢܗܘܢ ܒܪܫܗܘܢ ܢܬܠ.
> ܒܪܡ ܠܬܝܒܐ ܝܗܒ ܬܝܒܘܬܐ ܘܝܗܒ ܠܟܠ ܕܠܐܝܢܐ ܣܒܪܐ.

36. Zapff, *Sirach*, 382.

> Danach wird er sich offenbaren und ihnen vergelten, und ihre Verschuldungen auf ihr Haupt legen. Aber den Bußfertigen gewährt er Umkehr und vernichtet alle, die den Gerechten schaden.

Die Rede von der *Offenbarung* Gottes könnte dabei auf eine endzeitliche Offenbarung hindeuten.[37] Somit ist es folgerichtig, wenn im darauf folgenden Vers eine Unterscheidung zwischen Bußfertigen, somit den Guten, und denen, die sich gegen die Gerechten stellen, eingeführt wird. Dennoch sind die Hinweise darauf, dass es sich hier wirklich um ein Endgericht handelt, doch recht verhalten. Klarer ist dies hingegen in Sir 23,20. Zwar ist auch hier nur die griechische und syrische Version erhalten, doch sind die Unterschiede umso markanter. Eingebettet sind beide Verse zunächst in eine Aussage über die Allwissenheit Gottes, der, wie es in der griechischen Fassung heißt, die Wege der Menschen überblickt und bis in die verborgenen Bereiche hinein beobachtet. S liest dementsprechend: „Und er erkennt in der Dunkelheit, von welcher Gestalt ihre Werke sind".

G liest nun weiter:

> πρὶν ἢ κτισθῆναι τὰ πάντα ἔγνωσται αὐτῷ οὕτως καὶ μετὰ τὸ συντελεσθῆναι.
>
> Bevor es geschaffen war, war ihm alles bekannt, und so (wird es) auch (sein), nachdem es zu Ende gebracht ist.

Zwar scheint hier bereits ein Ende der Welt im Blick zu sein, ohne dass dieses jedoch in besonderer Weise qualifiziert wird: es geht hier nur um den zeitlichen Rahmen, in dem sich die Allwissenheit Gottes bewegt. Demgegenüber formuliert der Syrer:

> ܡܛܠ ܕܥܕ ܠܐ ܗܘܐ ܟܠ ܡܕܡ ܓܠܐ ܗܘ ܩܕܡܘܗܝ. ܘܐܦ ܡܢ ܒܬܪ ܚܪܬܗ
> ܕܥܠܡܐ ܗܘ ܕܐܢ ܠܗ.
>
> Denn als noch nichts war, war alles vor ihm offenbar. Und auch nach dem Ende der Welt richtet er sie (Möglich ist dabei auch ein Bezug des Objektsuffixes auf die zuvor genannte Gestalt ihrer Werke).

---

37. Van Peursen, *Language*, 35.

Erkenntnis Gottes, die über die Weltzeit hinausreicht, wird also nicht lediglich als eine Wahrnehmung Gottes verstanden, sondern mit seinem aktiven richtenden Handeln im Sinne eines Endgerichtes in Verbindung gebracht.

Schließlich scheint auch der Gedanke eines postmortalen Lebens der syrischen Sirachversion nicht fremd zu sein. Deutlich wird dies z.B. in Sir 3,1. Auch hier ist nur die griechische und syrische Version des Textes erhalten. So liest hier G:

> ἐμοῦ τοῦ πατρὸς ἀκούσατε τέκνα καὶ οὕτως ποιήσατε ἵνα σωθῆτε
>
> Meinen Vater hört, ihr Kinder, und so solltet ihr handeln, damit ihr gerettet werdet.

Hingegen formuliert der Syrer:

> ܒܢܝܐ ܕܝܢ ܠܐܒܗ̈ܬܐ ܫܡܥܘ ܘܥܒܕܘ. ܡܛܠ ܕܬܚܘܢ ܚܝ̈ܐ ܕܠܥܠܡ ܥܠܡܝܢ.
>
> Ihr Söhne aber, hört auf die Väter und handelt, damit ihr das Leben für immer und ewig leben werdet.

Ähnlich ist dies auch in Sir 1,12. In der griechischen Version werden die der „Furcht des Herrn" entsprießenden Früchte folgendermaßen beschrieben:

> φόβος κυρίου τέρψει καρδίαν καὶ δώσει εὐφροσύνην καὶ χαρὰν καὶ μακροημέρευσιν.
>
> Die Furcht des Herrn wird das Herz erquicken, und sie wird Frohsinn und Freude und eine Vielzahl an Tagen geben.

Der Syrer hingegen hat hier:

> ܕܚܠܬܗ ܕܡܪܝܐ ܡܚܕܝܐ ܠܒܐ. ܚܕܘܬܐ ܘܕܝܨܐ ܘܚܝ̈ܐ ܕܠܥܠܡ
>
> Die Furcht des Herrn erfreut das Herz: Freude und Jubel und ein Leben für immer.

Die Vielzahl der Tage (so G) wird hier offensichtlich auf ein ewiges Leben hin ausgedehnt. In diese Tendenz fügt sich auch die schon früher formulierte Beobachtung von Winter und Schrader ein, dass der eingangs zitierte Vers Sir 41,4b hinsichtlich eines Nichtvorhandenseins von Klagen in der Unterwelt von S unübersetzt gelassen wird.[38] Die Vorstellung einer Unterwelt, in der es nicht einmal mehr Klagen gibt, passt natürlich nicht in die Konzeption einer postmortalen Existenz.

Diese Beobachtungen sollen genügen. Sie zeigen m.E. überzeugend, dass die syrische Version in vielen Fällen keine ältere, von der hebräischen und griechischen Fassung abweichende Vorlage benutzt, sondern vielfach eine Interpretation aufgrund bestimmter formaler Prinzipien und theologischer Tendenzen darstellt. Sie ist damit durchaus in gewisser Hinsicht mit der Interpretation der hebräischen Bibel durch die Targumim vergleichbar. Dies macht sie für die Erschließung eines möglichen ursprünglicheren hebräischen Textes des Sirach zwar nicht einfach wertlos, mahnt jedoch in dieser Hinsicht zur Zurückhaltung. Eher ist die syrische Übersetzung als ein Beleg für die durchaus lebendige Rezeptions- und Interpretationsgeschichte des Sirachtextes zu werten.

38. Schrader, *Leiden*, 247.

Der lateinische Text des Ecclesiasticus: Von Philipp Thielmann bis zu Walter Thiele*

Pierre-Maurice Bogaert, OSB

In diesem Überblick sollen die großen Etappen dargestellt und erläutert werden, in denen das Buch Jesus Sirach in seiner Überlieferung erforscht wurde. Dabei werden die verschiedenen Sprachen berücksichtigt, mit einem Schwerpunkt auf der lateinischen Übersetzung.

Zu beginnen ist mit dem für die Sirach-Forschung einschneidenden Fund der Handschriften in der Kairoer Geniza am Ende des 19. Jahrhunderts und etwa zeitgleich der Entdeckung einer lateinischen Textversion, die sich von der der Vulgata unterscheidet.

Eine Tabelle gibt uns einen ersten Überblick:

Datum	**Lateinisch**	**Griechisch**	**Hebräisch**	**Syrisch**
1876				A. M. Ceriani
1893–1898	Ph. Thielmann			
1895	C. Douais (Hs. VL 171)			
1896ff.			Kairoer Geniza	
1899	H. Herkenne			
		(Th. Nöldeke)		
1906		Hatch & Redpath Suppl.	R. Smend Hatch & Redpath Suppl.	

* Diesen Beitrag hat Bonifatia Gesche während der Eichstätter Tagung referiert und zur Publikation ins Deutsche übertragen.

1907		R. Smend	R. Smend	
1921	A. Wilmart (Hs. VL 171)			
1928–1931	D. De Bruyne			
1935			M. H. Segal	
1956ff.			2Q, 4Q	
1964	BSR (J. Gribomont)			
1965		J. Ziegler	Masada	
1973			D. Barthélemy	
1974		O. Wahl		
1976–1977				M. M. Winter
1987–2005	W. Thiele, VLB			
1999		Chr. Wagner		
2005		J.-M. Auwers		
2014	A. Forte, VLB			

1. Die Jahre 1895 bis 1906

Als erster ist der hervorragende Philologe und Grammatiker Philipp Thielmann zu nennen, der bei seiner systematischen Suche nach afrikanischen Elementen im Vokabular des lateinischen Sirach feststellte, dass diese bis zum Kapitel 43 häufig sind, aber ab dem Kapitel 44, in dem das „Lob der Väter“ (*laus patrum*) beginnt, fast völlig fehlen, jedoch im 51. Kapitel wieder häufiger werden.[2] Für diese Beobachtung bietet er zwei Erklärungen: (1) Sir 1–43 und Sir 51 wurden von einem afrikanischen Übersetzer übersetzt und Sir 44–50, also das „Lob der Väter“, von einem europäischen. (2) Der Prolog wurde ebenfalls von einem Europäer übersetzt, jedoch vermutlich von einem anderen als dem, der die anderen Kapitel übersetzt hat.

2. Philipp Thielmann, “Die europäischen Bestandteile des lateinischen Sirach,” *Archiv für lateinische Lexicographie und Grammatik* 9.2 (1894): 247–84.

Etwa zur selben Zeit veröffentlichte Célestin Douais eine Seite einer Handschrift, die einen Text des lateinischen Sirach enthält, der nicht mit dem Vulgata-Text übereinstimmt, und teilte diese Entdeckung Thielmann mit der Bitte um Stellungnahme mit. Douais kommt zu dem Schluss, dass dieses Blatt aus Toulouse einen eigenständigen Text überliefert, von dem keine der gut bezeugten Versionen und Editionen abhängt, also um einen anderen Texttyp, nicht nur um die Revision einer bestehenden Textform.[3]

Ebenfalls in dieser Zeit *studierte* Heinrich Herkenne[4] den Text des Sirach-Buches; seine Forschung hat Donatien De Bruyne gewürdigt und rezipiert.[5]

Für den *griechischen* Sirach ist es Theodor Nöldeke, der als erster die Existenz einer zweiten Textform erkennt. Er geht dabei von der Dublette *ἐν νόσοις* (*νόσῳ* Chrysostomus) *καὶ πενίᾳ* (*παιδείαις* 253; ‚*παιδείᾳ*' SyrH) *ἐπ'* (*ἐν* 404') *αὐτῷ πεποιθὼς γίνου* O-S2 *b* 404', Chrysostomus (PG 48,936; 49,184) in Vers 2,4b aus, die sich in einigen Handschriften findet, dort aber fälschlich hinter Vers 2,5 eingeordnet ist, jedoch an der richtigen Stelle in einem Zitat des Johannes Chrysostomus.[6]

Für den hebräischen Sirach spielt die Veröffentlichung der Funde aus der Kairoer Geniza die entscheidende Rolle. Diese Handschriften geben der Sirachforschung eine völlig neue Richtung.[7]

Den Abschluss dieser ersten Phase der Forschungsgeschichte bilden die Arbeiten von Rudolf Smend,[8] und zwar sein Kommentar und sein griechisch-hebräisches Glossar aus dem Jahr 1906 sowie das *Supplement*

3. Célestin Douais, *Une ancienne version latine de l'Ecclésiastique; Fragment publié pour la première fois, accompagné du fac-similé du manuscrit visigoth* (Paris: Picard, 1895), 33.

4. Heinrich Herkenne, *De Veteris Latinae Ecclestiastici capitibus I–XLIII …* (Leipzig: Hinrichs, 1899), viii–268.

5. Donatien De Bruyne, "Étude sur le texte latin de l'Ecclésiastique," *RBén* 40 (1928): 5–48, siehe 9.

6. Nach dem Kommentar von Rudolf Smend, *Die Weisheit des Jesus Sirach hebräisch und deutsch, mit einem hebräischen Glossar* (Berlin: Reimer, 1906), S. xci und 18–19 (Siehe auch T. Nöldeke, "The Original Hebrew of a Portion of Ecclesiasticus," *The Expositor*, 5/29 [1897]: 347–64, v.a. 361–62).

7. Es ist unmöglich, die Vielzahl der Publikationen aufzuführen, die seit 1896 erschienen sind. Auch heute kann man immer noch auf die Entdeckung des einen oder anderen Blattes aus der Kairoer hoffen. Siehe M. Gilbert, "Siracide," *DBS* 12:1389–1439.

8. Smend, *Die Weisheit des Jesus Sirach.*

zur Konkordanz von Hatch und Redpath.[9] Angespornt durch diese Handwerkszeuge, die wir Henry A. Redpath und Rudolf Smend verdanken, wird ein neues Zeitalter der Sirachforschung eingeläutet.

Ebenfalls im Jahr 1906 stellte Rudolf Smend eine erste Zusammenfassung der Forschungsergebnisse vor und publizierte den ersten Kommentar, in dem er die neuen Funde *einverleiben* und in den er neben dem hebräischen Text auch die griechische, syrische und lateinische Überlieferung einbezieht.[10] Beim Vergleich der griechischen Version mit der lateinischen Übersetzung fand er die Vermutung Nöldekes bestätigt, dass es eine zweite griechische Textversion gebe, und stellte eine Liste derjenigen Textstellen dieser Version zusammen, die man wiedergewinnen kann, wenn man den griechischen mit dem lateinischen Text vergleicht. In einer gelehrten und scharfsinnigen Studie des lateinischen Textes untersuchte er die Dubletten und die Übereinstimmungen mit dem hebräischen und dem syrischen Text. Zahlreiche Fehler deuten nach seiner Einschätzung auf eine andere griechische Vorlage des lateinischen Übersetzers oder aber auf einen anderen Übersetzer hin, der während des zweiten Jahrhunderts tätig war.[11]

Des Weiteren müssen wir wegen der sich daraus ergebenden Schwierigkeiten auf die Vertauschung von zwei längeren Textpassagen in Sirach eingehen. Zwei Abschnitte ungefähr gleicher Länge, jeweils etwa 160 Verse im Umfang, sind in allen direkten griechischen Textzeugen, auch in der Hs. 248, vertauscht, jedoch im Syrischen, in den hebräischen Zeugen aus der Geniza und aus Qumran, ebenso wie in der lateinischen Überlieferung (Zählung entsprechend der Vulgata: 30,25–33,16a und 33,16b–36,10a) an der richtigen Stelle überliefert. Wie es zu diesem Fehler kam, ist nach wie vor schwierig zu erklären. Naheliegend ist die Annahme, dass Blattlagen in einem Kodex vertauscht wurden, was voraussetzt, dass der Fehler nicht anhand einer Rolle, sondern in einem Kodex entstanden ist. Sowohl Rahlfs als auch Ziegler folgen in ihrer Edition des griechischen Textes der lateinischen Anordnung, gehen aber unterschiedliche Wege bei der Nummerierung der Kapitel und Verse. Da der lateinische Text oftmals länger ist als der griechische, weicht die Verszählung, die auf die lateinische Version des Robert Estienne (†1559) zurückgeht, häufig von der griechischen ab.

---

9. Edwin Hatch, Henry A. Redpath, *A Concordance to the Septuagint. Supplement* (Oxford: Clarendon, 1906), 163–216.

10. Smend, *Die Weisheit des Jesus Sirach*, xci–cxviii (Ueber eine zweite griechische Übersetzung) und cxviii–cxxix (Die Vetus Latina).

11. Ibid., cxxvii.

Es wäre sinnvoll gewesen, die ursprüngliche Zählung beizubehalten, doch dafür ist es nun zu spät. Jetzt ist der Benutzer mit drei unterschiedlichen Verszählungen in dem Buch konfrontiert, nämlich mit der lateinischen, der griechischen mit ihrer Versumstellung und der griechischen, in der die Versumstellung korrigiert wurde. Ohne die Zuhilfenahme von Konkordanzen ist es kaum noch möglich, den Überblick zu bewahren.[12]

2. Donatien De Bruyne

Bevor wir uns den bedeutenden Forschungen De Bruynes zuwenden, ist noch der Benediktiner André Wilmart zu erwähnen, der seinerseits Entdeckungen zur Textgeschichte beitragen konnte. So konnte er zwei weitere Blätter der Toulouser Handschrift, die, wie schon erwähnt, Douais entdeckt hat, identifizieren und legte im Jahr 1921 eine Edition dieser Texte vor. Dabei erkannte er, dass es sich um eine Textform handelt, die Augustinus in seiner Schrift „De gratia et libero arbitrio“ (Über die Gnade und den freien Willen) zitiert hat—und zwar nur dort.[13]

Zwischen 1928 und 1931 sind dann die wichtigen Arbeiten D. De Bruynes erschienen, von denen die kürzeste, eine Publikation aus dem Jahr 1929,[14] die bedeutendste ist. In weiteren Veröffentlichungen belegte er seine Erkenntnisse detailliert mit Beispielen und stellte seine Folgerungen aus den Beobachtungen der Fachwelt zur Diskussion.[15] Er zeigte, dass die Umstellung der großen Textabschnitte (Kap. 33–36) auf eine Vertauschung der Lagen in einem griechischen Manuskript zurückgeführt werden muss. Außerdem bestätigte er die Existenz von zwei unterschiedlichen griechischen Übersetzungen oder Textformen: Gr I in den großen Unzial-Handschriften und den davon abhängigen Texten, und Gr II als die Vorlage der lateinischen Übersetzung. Auch folgte er Thielmann in der Annahme, dass insgesamt drei Personen die lateinische Übersetzung

12. Friedrich V. Reiterer, *Zählsynopse zum Buch Ben Sira*, FSBP 1 (Berlin: de Gruyter, 2003).

13. André Wilmart, "Nouveaux feuillets toulousains de l'Ecclésiastique," *RBén* 33 (1921): 110–23, v.a. 116.

14. Donatien De Bruyne, "Le prologue, le titre et la finale de l'Ecclésiastique," *ZAW* 47 (1929): 257–63.

15. Donatien De Bruyne, "Étude sur le texte latin de l'ecclésiastique," *RBén* 40 (1928): 5–48; und De Bruyne, "Saint Augustin reviseur de la Bible," *Miscellanea Agostiniana* 2 (1931): 521–606, siehe v.a. 578–82.

zu verantworten haben, nämlich ein afrikanischer Übersetzer für Kap. 1–43 und Kap. 51, ein europäischer für Kap. 44–50 und ein weiterer europäischer für den Prolog. Die Auswertung von griechischen (v.a. Klemens von Alexandrien) und lateinischen patristischen Quellen zeigt die große Bedeutung des lateinischen Textes, der nach Ausscheiden der Dubletten, die nach De Bruynes Ansicht auf eine Revision nach Gr I zurückgehen, als Zeuge für Gr II zu gelten hat. Hierin ist diese Überlieferung auch der Minuskel 248 überlegen. Die Hs. 248 dürfte eine eigene Textversion vertreten, für die De Bruyne die Bezeichnung Gr III erwägt.[16] Dieser Text ist von besonderer Bedeutung aufgrund seiner Ähnlichkeit mit der lateinischen Übersetzung, die die Vermutung zulässt, es könne sich um eine direkte Vorlage handeln.

De Bruyne kommt zu der Erkenntnis, dass Gr II wohl weder das Lob der Väter noch den Prolog enthielt, da er keine Belege für diese Textpassagen in der lateinischen Übersetzung nachweisen kann.

Dass Cyprian und einige andere Väter das Buch nicht dem Siraciden, sondern Salomo zuschrieben (vgl. z.B. die Zuweisung: *ad Salomonem in ecclesiastico*), sieht er im Zusammenhang mit der Beobachtung, dass in einem Traditionsstrang der Prolog fehlt, dafür aber das Gebet des Salomo (= 3 Rg 8,22–31 nach De Bruyne)[17] als 52. Kapitel angefügt ist. Obwohl keine dieser Thesen beweisbar ist, bieten sie immerhin einen möglichen Schlüssel für die Interpretation der zahlreichen lateinischen Varianten.

Die gegensätzlichen Ansichten Smends und De Bruynes fasst Alexander A. Di Lella folgendermaßen zusammen: Nach Smend ist Gr I die Vorlage für die lateinische Übersetzung, in die jedoch zahlreiche Elemente aus Gr II eingeflossen sind. Dagegen geht De Bruyne davon aus, dass der lateinische Text grundsätzlich auf Gr II zurückgeht.[18]

De Bruyne führt seine Forschung dahingehend fort, dass er die Sirach-Zitate bei Augustinus auswertet, wobei er die Erkenntnis Wilmarts bestätigt findet, dass Augustinus in „*De gratia et libero arbitrio*" den Text

16. De Bruyne, "Étude sur le texte latin de l'ecclésiastique," 45.

17. Vermutlich ist das Gebet Salomos jedoch eher mit 2 Par 6,13–22 in Verbindung zu bringen; siehe dazu Robert Weber, *Les anciennes versions latines du deuxième livre des Paralipomènes* (Rome: Abbaye Saint-Jérôme, 1945), xi–xiii.

18. Alexander Di Lella and Patrick W. Shehan, *The Wisdom of Ben Sira: A New Translation* (New York: Doubleday, 1987). In seinen Ausführungen schenkt Di Lella der lateinischen Version nicht die ihr gebührende Beachtung. So geht er z.B. nicht auf das Gebet Salomos ein (57).

zitiert, von dem Douais und Wilmart Fragmente gefunden haben. Dieser Text entspricht dem Typ J in Thieles Beuroner Edition. In anderen Schriften legt Augustinus hingegen einen anderen, ebenfalls korrigierten Text zugrunde, den Thiele als Typ I einordnet. De Bruyne nimmt aber an, dass es sich bei keinem der beiden Texte um eine eigene Textfassung handelt, sondern um eine Revision durch Augustinus selbst.

3. Ein hebräischer Text in Bewegung: M. H. Segal

Seit 1935 verfolgt M. H. Segal die Spur, dass der hebräische Text keinesfalls ein monolithischer Block ist, sondern dass er Veränderungen erfahren und eine eigene Textgeschichte durchlaufen hat. Er geht dabei davon aus, dass laut Prolog der Text des Enkels nicht identisch mit der hebräischen Vorlage des Großvaters ist.[19] Tatsächlich liefern die Textfunde der folgenden Jahre zahlreiche Belege für diese Beobachtungen und demonstrieren die Komplexität der Textgeschichte des hebräischen Sirach.[20] Da es in diesem Überblick über die Forschungsgeschichte nicht in erster Linie um den hebräischen, sondern den lateinischen Sirach-Text geht, sei nur noch darauf hingewiesen, wie sehr die Publikation der neuen Fragmente aus Qumran und Masada die Forschung beflügelt hat. Ganz offensichtlich beginnt die Komplexität der Textgeschichte schon beim hebräischen Text und wird mit der Übertragung in die anderen Sprachen immer größer.

4. Die kritische Edition der römischen Vulgata (1964)

Mit der Herausgabe der kritischen Edition der Vulgata[21] durch die Mönche der Abtei San Girolamo in Rom konnte mehr Klarheit in die Überlieferung

19. Moses Hirsch Segal, "The Evolution of the Hebrew Text of Ecclesiasticus," *JQR* NF 25 (1934–1935): 91–149. Siehe auch Joseph Ziegler, *Sylloge: Gesammelte Aufsätze zur Septuaginta*, MSU 10 (Göttingen, Vandenhoeck & Ruprecht, 1971), 519.

20. Siehe die Einleitung und den Kommentar von Moshe Z. Segal, ספר בן סירא השלם [*The Complete Book of Ben Sira*], 2. Aufl. (Jerusalem: Fondation Bialiq, 1958).

21. *Biblia sacra: Iuxta Latinam Vulgatam versionem ad codicum fidem; Cura et studio monachorum Abbatiae Pontificiae Sancti Hieronymi in urbe O.S.B. edita*, 18 Bde. (Rome: Typis Polyglottis Vaticanis, 1926–1995) (= BSR) (hier Sapientia Salomonis/ Liber Hiesu Filii Sirach). Verantwortlich für diesen Band war Jean Gribomont. Siehe auch Jean Gribomont, "L'édition vaticane de la Vulgate et la Sagesse de Salomon dans sa recension italienne," *Rivista di storia e letteratura religiosa* 4 (1968): 472–96, wo er u.a. Fakten diskutiert, die für Sirach von Bedeutung sind.

des lateinischen Sirach gebracht werden. Der Textbestand wird dadurch gesichert, dass für die Ausgabe zahlreiche Bibelhandschriften kollationiert und dass anhand des Beuroner Zettelkastens eine gut begründete Auswahl an Kirchenväterzitaten zugrunde gelegt wurde. Für die Arbeit stand den Herausgebern unter der Leitung von Dom Jean Gribomont eine vorläufige Fassung der kritischen Göttinger Septuaginta-Ausgabe zur Verfügung, die J. Ziegler ein Jahr nach dem Erscheinen der Vulgata-Edition veröffentlichen konnte (1965). Die Herausgeber folgen in ihrer Einleitung weitgehend ihren Vorreitern Thielmann und De Bruyne. Auch sie gehen von drei Übersetzern aus und nehmen an, dass der Prolog und das Väterlob später hinzugefügt wurden, obwohl beide in allen Handschriften vertreten sind. Sie stellen fest, dass sich die Handschriftengruppen im Abschnitt des „Lobs der Väter" anders zusammensetzen als im Rest des Buches und dass das Florilegium *x* (St. Gallen, Stiftsbibliothek 11) den Text nicht überliefert.[22] Es ist anzumerken, dass die übliche Zuordnung zu Salomo nur dann möglich wäre, wenn der Prolog nicht vorhanden ist, weil der sich auf Sirach, nicht auf Salomo bezieht. Das Gebet des Salomo, das sich als 52. Kapitel in fast allen Textzeugen findet—nur in Angleichung an den griechischen Text ist es bisweilen ausgelassen—, geht auf eine nicht recht einzuordnende griechische Vorlage zurück, die 2 Par 6,13–22 näher steht als dem ähnlichen Text in 3 Rg 8,22–31.[23]

Die Komplexität der lateinischen Handschriftenüberlieferung von Sirach kommt keinem anderen biblischen Buch nahe, auch nicht dem Buch der Weisheit, dessen Handschriftenüberlieferung am ehesten vergleichbar ist. Daher unterscheidet sich die römische Edition sowohl in der Orthographie als auch in diversen textkritischen Entscheidungen von der Sixto-Clementina. Die römische Vulgata mit ihrer detaillierten Untersuchung der Handschriftengruppen und der Vielfalt der Informationen bietet eine gute Basis für die Edition der Vetus Latina.

5. Die kritische Ausgabe der Septuaginta (Joseph Ziegler, 1965)

In der Vorbereitung seiner kritischen Ausgabe für das Göttinger Septuaginta-Unternehmen hat Joseph Ziegler seit 1958 die Ergebnisse seiner

---

22. BSR 12:xi–xii und xiv.

23. BSR 12:Dies muss zu gegebener Zeit anhand der noch nicht erschienenen kritischen Edition der Chronikbücher erneut untersucht werden.

Forschung veröffentlicht.[24] Zunächst war es seine nicht ganz einfache Aufgabe, den Text der wichtigen Kodizes zu edieren, die alle die Version Gr I überliefern; andererseits durfte er die Zitate des Clemens von Alexandrien und die lateinische Tradition nicht aus dem Blick verlieren, die alle die Version Gr II repräsentieren, und dann musste er mit der Minuskel 248 einen weiteren Textzeugen, der mit seinen Zusätzen oft mit der lateinischen Überlieferung übereinstimmt, in seine Erwägungen einbeziehen. Auch musste er berücksichtigen, dass der lateinische Text die Umstellung der Kapitel 30–36 nicht mit vollzogen hat und zudem insgesamt einen guten Text überliefert. Ziegler selbst schreibt: „So ist es auch nicht richtig, von nur einer zweiten griech. Übersetzung zu sprechen, sondern es ist anzunehmen, dass mehrere griech. Übersetzungen im Umlauf waren, von denen uns namentlich im ersten Teil des Buches ziemlich umfangreiche Überreste in der *O-L*-Rezension und vor allem in La(tein) überliefert werden".[25] Bei dieser Aussage müssen wir ausdrücklich zur Kenntnis nehmen, dass Ziegler den ersten Teil des Buches in der Überlieferung der Rezensionen anders einordnet als den zweiten.

6. Konkordanzen (1973–1977)

In den 1970er Jahren wurden die Hilfsmittel zum Studium des Textes dem Stand der Forschung angepasst und die neuen Funde einbezogen.

6.1. Hebräisch

Nachdem Smend seinen Index zu Sirach veröffentlicht hatte, wuchs die Textmenge durch neue Funde aus der Kairoer Geniza, aus Qumran und Masada erheblich an, was eine Neubearbeitung notwendig machte. Dieser Aufgabe haben sich Dominique Barthémely und Otto Rickenbacher gewidmet, die 1973 eine Konkordanz des hebräischen Vokabulars veröffentlichten.[26] Sie gehen vom hebräischen Vokabular aus und ordnen ihm die entsprechenden syrischen und griechischen Wörter zu. Dem Werk ist

24. Die Aufsätze sind in dem Sammelband Ziegler, *Sylloge*. Auf dieses Buch werden wir ggf. verweisen.

25. Joseph Ziegler, *Sapientia Jesu filii Sirach*, SVGT 12.2 (Göttingen: Vandenhoeck & Ruprecht, 2016), 74.

26. Dominique Barthélemy und Otto Rickenbacher, *Konkordanz zum hebräischen Sirach mit syrisch-hebräischem Index* (Göttingen: Vandenhoeck & Ruprecht, 1973).

ein syrisch-griechischer Index beigegeben. Der Zielsetzung dieser Konkordanz entsprechend, beschränkt sich die Textgrundlage auf die im Hebräischen überlieferten Teile des Sirachbuches. Zudem ist die lateinische Version von Jesus Sirach nicht berücksichtigt.

6.2. Syrisch

Michael M. Winter hat eine Konkordanz[27] nach den beiden ältesten syrischen Handschriften, dem Ambrosianus (Edition durch Ceriani 1876), und dem Londoner Text (London, British Library, Add. 12142), den Paul A. de Lagarde veröffentlicht hat (1861), zusammengestellt und 1976 veröffentlicht. Dabei konnte er auf Vorarbeiten von William D. McHardy zurückgreifen. Dieses wichtige Hilfsmittel enthält nun im Unterschied zu den bisherigen Werken den gesamten Sirachtext. Deutlich wird, dass der syrische Text aus dem Hebräischen übersetzt ist, aber auch Einflüsse aus dem Griechischen nachzuweisen sind. Und auch Übereinstimmungen mit dem lateinischen Text, die nicht über die Zwischenstufe des Griechischen vermittelt sind, finden sich nicht ganz selten. Ähnliches lässt sich für die Beziehung des hebräischen zum lateinischen Text beobachten.

6.3. Latein

Alle früheren lateinischen Konkordanzen basieren auf der Sixto-Clementina (1592), die jedoch durch die kritische römische Edition (1964) ersetzt ist, da sie sich gerade im Buch Jesus Sirach deutlich von dem kritischen Text unterscheidet. Bonifatius Fischer, einer der Herausgeber der Stuttgarter Handausgabe der Vulgata, die 1969 erschien,[28] führte seine Editionsarbeit dahingehend weiter, dass er eine lateinische Wortkonkordanz kompilierte, die 1977 in fünf Bänden erschien.[29] Sie gründet auf dem kritischen Text der Stuttgarter Vulgata, bezieht die Clementina jedoch ein. Möglich

27. Michael M. Winter, *A Concordance to the Peshitta Version of Ben Sira*, MPIL 2 (Leiden: Brill, 1976).

28. *Biblia Sacra iuxta vulgatam versionem: Recensuit et brevi apparatu instruxit Robertus R. Weber* (Stuttgart: Deutsche Bibelgesellschaft, 1969, jetzt in der fünften Auflage von 2007).

29. Bonifatius Fischer, *Novae Concordantiae Bibliorum Sacrorum iuxta Vulgatam Versionem critice editam*, 5 Bde. (Stuttgart: Frommann-Holzboog, 1977).

wurde dieses Werk durch die ersten Computerprogramme, die zu jener Zeit unmittelbar für diesen Zweck geschrieben wurden.

7. Ein neuer Zeuge für Gr II, der den lateinischen Text stützt: Die Sacra Parallela (Otto Wahl, 1974)

Als wohl wichtigster Zeuge für die Textform Gr II kann zweifellos Clemens von Alexandrien gelten. Doch ist die Überlieferung aus seiner Hand keinesfalls die einzige Quelle, wie Otto Wahl zeigen konnte. Jahre lang erforschte er die Handschriftenüberlieferung und den Text der sogenannten Sacra Parallela, eines Florilegiums, das im Allgemeinen Johannes von Damaskus zugeschrieben wird. Die Zitate aus Jesus Sirach, die sich in dieser Schrift finden, publizierte er 1974 in einer Monographie, wobei er herausstellte, dass einige Sirachzitate außer in diesem Werk nur noch in der lateinischen Fassung überliefert sind.[30] Folgerungen daraus hat er jedoch nicht gezogen. Die Annahme, dass dem Autor der Sacra Parallela ein Text der Version Gr II als Vorlage diente, ist naheliegend, aber in Ermangelung weiterreichender Studien sind darüber hinausgehende Schlüsse kaum zu ziehen.

8. Walter Thiele (1987–2005)

Einen großen Fortschritt in der Sirachforschung stellt die Edition der Vetus Latina in der Beuroner Reihe dar. Nach Abschluss der Edition des Buches der Weisheit konnte Walter Thiele in den Jahren 1987 bis 2005 in rascher Folge die ersten 24 Kapitel des lateinischen Sirach veröffentlichen.[31] Äußerst sorgfältig und umfassend hat er Aspekte der Textgeschichte untersucht und seine Ergebnisse komprimiert in der Einleitung zu der Edition und im kritischen Apparat der Fachwelt zur Diskussion gestellt. Wenn auch die Richtigkeit einiger seiner Schlüsse bezweifelt

30. Otto Wahl, *Der Sirach-Text der Sacra Parallela* (Würzburg: Echter, 1974), 29. Eine Zusammenstellung dieser Textstellen bietet er nicht. Diese hat dann Jean-Marie Auwers, *Concordance du Siracide (Grec II et Sacra Parallela)* (Paris: Gabalda, 2005), 11–12 vorgelegt. Diese Konkordanz ist ein unentbehrliches Hilfsmittel, weil der Langtext von Jesus Sirach sonst nur beiläufig, nicht aber als eigene Textfassung behandelt wurde.

31. Vgl. dazu BBL 6.673, 7.1.99; 7.3.269; 6.4.352; 7.5.428; 7.8.752.

werden kann, so stellt er doch gut begründete Beobachtungen zusammen, auf denen weitere Forschung aufbauen kann.

Im Folgenden wollen wir kurz anreißen, in welchen Fragen er zu neuen Erkenntnissen gekommen ist:

Zum Titel stellt er eindeutig fest, dass das Buch in der lateinischen Tradition Salomo zugeschrieben wurde, wobei die Nennung „ecclesiasticus" in den Quellen nicht durchgängig hinzugefügt wird. Diese Bezeichnung ist im Griechischen, soweit bekannt, überhaupt nicht bezeugt. Erst seit der zweiten Hälfte des vierten Jahrhunderts wird das Buch in Abschriften oder Kommentaren von Autoren, die von einer entsprechenden Vorlage abhängen, mit „Iesus filius Sirach" identifiziert.[32] Dennoch nimmt Thiele eine griechische Vorlage für diesen Titel als wahrscheinlichste Herkunft an. Thieles Argumentation baut auf dem Faktum auf, dass das Buch Jesus Sirach zu den fünf Weisheitsbüchern gerechnet wird und damit Salomo zugeschrieben werden muss. Eine Verbindung mit der Hinzufügung des Gebetes Salomos zum Sirachbuch erwägt er hingegen nicht. Außerdem zieht er nicht in Betracht, dass die lateinischen Väter sich bisweilen darüber wundern, dass das Buch dem Siraciden zugeordnet wird. Diese Verwunderung ist schwer erklärlich, wenn ihnen der Prolog vorgelegen hat. Doch auch die Bezeichnung „ecclesiasticus", für die keine griechische Vorlage bekannt ist, ist schwierig zu erklären. Zwar nennt Rufin die nicht-kanonischen Bücher, aber es gibt keinen Hinweis darauf, dass die lateinischen Väter Sirach und das Buch der Weisheit anders einordneten als die übrige Weisheitsliteratur. Thiele zufolge handelt es sich um einen Titel, der von Anfang an, d.h. seit Cyprian, verwendet und wohl aus einer griechischen Vorlage übernommen wurde, von der freilich keine Reste mehr überliefert sind.[33]

Ein weiterer Punkt, den Thiele untersucht, ist die Vertauschung der zwei Blöcke in den Kapiteln 30–36, wozu er sich erstaunlich zurückhaltend äußert. Meist wird angenommen, dass die Umstellung durch die mechanische Vertauschung von zwei Lagen in einem griechischen Kodex entstanden ist, der der Archetyp der gesamten Überlieferung war. Das hieße, dass der lateinische Text eine andere Vorlage hatte, die der Vertauschung entgangen ist. Aus verschiedenen Gründen hält Thiele dies nicht für völlig überzeugend. Er erwägt stattdessen, dass schon die ursprüng-

---

32. Walter Thiele, Hrsg., *Sirach (Eccesiasticus)*, VLB 11.2 (Freiburg im Breisgau: Herder, 1987–2005), 153–59.

33. Ibid., 159 (unten).

liche griechische Übersetzung diese Vertauschung enthalten habe. Das würde bedeuten, dass die griechische Vorlage des lateinischen Textes nach einem hebräischen Text korrigiert worden ist.[34]

Ein textgeschichtlich wichtiges Thema sind die zahlreichen Dubletten des lateinischen Textes. In diesem Punkt nimmt Thiele ausführlich Stellung zu der Hypothese D. De Bruynes, die die Forschung bisher geprägt hat, und bis zu einem gewissen Maß zu den Erkenntnissen, die in der römischen Vulgata-Ausgabe publiziert sind. Nach D. De Bruynes Ansicht gehören die Dubletten nicht zum ursprünglichen lateinischen Text und auch nicht zur Version Gr II. Vielmehr handele es sich um Zusätze, die im Laufe der lateinischen Textgeschichte angesammelt wurden. Der Herausgeber müsse also in jedem Einzelfall entscheiden, welche der Dubletten den ursprünglichen Text repräsentiert. Thiele hingegen nimmt an, dass die meisten Dubletten zum ursprünglichen Textbestand der lateinischen Übersetzung gehören und bereits in der griechischen Vorlage vorhanden waren.

Wo die Beurteilung der Dubletten schwierig ist und wo wir die griechische Vorlage nur unzureichend kennen—dass es solche Fälle gibt, zeigen die Sacra Parallela—ist die Ansicht Thieles für die Herausgabe des Textes wohl die sicherste. Doch bleibt bestehen, dass bei Dubletten sehr sorgfältig die Fakten geprüft und abgewogen werden müssen. Viele Entscheidungen bleiben der Einschätzung des Herausgebers überlassen.

Des Weiteren widerspricht Thiele der seit Thielmann gängigen und durch D. De Bruyne und die Herausgeber der römischen Vulgata-Edition[35] aufgegriffenen Ansicht, der lateinische Text sei von mehreren Übersetzern übertragen worden. Dafür sieht er keine Hinweise im Text. Nichts deute darauf hin, dass die Kapitel 44–50, also das Lob der Väter, und der Prolog später hinzugefügt wurden.[36] Es sei nicht zu beweisen, dass sie nicht ursprünglich zum Text gehört haben. Aber Thiele gibt zu, dass die *Oratio Salomonis* seit Beginn zur lateinischen Textüberlieferung

34. Ibid., 148 (oben).

35. BSR 12:xii: "Non enim ad invicem codicum nostrorum familiae eamdem proferunt habitudinem in his capitibus ac in ceteris, nec florilegium *x* Laudem Patrum cum libro Sirach praebet."

36. Thiele, *Sirach (Eccesiasticus)*, 120–24.

gehörte,[37] geht aber nicht den Schritt wie De Bruyne, das Buch ausdrücklich Salomo zuzuschreiben. [38]

9. Lexikalische Forschung am griechischen Text

Keine der bisher erschienen Konkordanzen bezieht den griechischen Langtext ein, sondern sie beruhen in erster Linie auf dem Text der großen griechischen Unzial-Handschriften, die nur in Ausnahmefällen den einen oder anderen Textzusatz überliefern. Erst Jean-Marie Auwers geht andere Wege und bezieht die Zusätze im griechischen Text in seine Konkondanz, die 2005 erschien, mit ein und stellt so ein äußerst nützliches Arbeitsinstrument zur Verfügung, das es ermöglicht, bei lexikalischen Untersuchungen die griechischen Zusätze noch mehr in den Blick zu nehmen, z.B. bei der Erstellung eines griechisch-lateinischen Wörterbuchs zu Sirach, das ein Desiderat der Sirach-Forschung darstellt.[39]

In diese Richtung geht Christian Wagner in seiner Doktorarbeit, in der er die Hapaxlegomena des Sirachbuches untersucht hat.[40] Neuerdings hat auch Muraoka in seinem Septuagintalexikon und in seinem Griechisch-Hebräisch/Aramäischen Index das Sirach-Vokabular[41] mit dem

---

37. Ibid., 12–125.

38. Ibid., 124–25. Es ist ungenau zu sagen, dass De Bruyne die Hinzufügung des *Gebetes des Salomo* dem lateinischen Übersetzer zuschreibt. Er tendiert ausdrücklich zu der Auffassung, dass es schon in der griechischen Vorlage vorhanden war: "Appartient-il (le texte de l'*Oratio Salomonis*) à la traduction primitive de l'Ecclésiastique ou bien a-t-il été ajouté très tôt? Il est difficile de le dire. Puisque cette attribution à Salomon semble avoir été faite dès l'origine, la prière peut avoir été ajoutée dès l'origine" (Bruyne, "Le prologue," 262). De Bruyne, der das Vorhandensein der *Oratio* mit dieser Zuschreibung in Verbindung bringt, weist darauf hin, dass Clemens von Alexandrien das Buch Salomo zugeschrieben hat.

39. Siehe dazu oben Anm. 30 und auch J.-M. Auwers, "L'apport du texte long du Siracide au lexique du grec biblique," in *Interpreting Translation: Studies on the LXX and Ezekiel in Honour of Johan Lust*, hrsg. F. García Marínez and M. Vervenne, BETL 192 (Leuven: Peeters, 2005), 22–44.

40. Christian Wagner, *Die Septuaginta-Hapaxlegomena im Buch Jesus Sirach: Untersuchungen zu Wortwahl und Wortbildung unter besonderer Berücksichtigung des textkritischen und übersetzungstechnischen Aspekts* (Berlin: de Gruyter, 1999).

41. Takamitsu Muraoka, *A Greek-English Lexicon of the Septuaginta* (Leuven: Peeters, 2009), und Muraoka, *A Greek-Hebrew/Aramaic Two-Way Index to the Septuagint* (Leuven: Peeters, 2010). In letzterem Werk bezieht er das Sirach-Buch in den

zusätzlichen Material, das Auwers publiziert hat, berücksichtigt und damit zwei grundlegende Arbeitsinstrumente vorgelegt.

10. Anthony Forte 2014 (Nachfolge von W. Thiele)

Nach Abschluss des ersten Teiles von Sirach, mit der Fertigstellung von Kapitel 24 hat W. Thiele aus Altersgründen die Edition in jüngere Hände übergeben. Anthony Forte vom Bibelinstitut in Rom bekam den Auftrag, die Edition fortzuführen, und er konnte im Jahr 2014 seinen ersten Faszikel, der Sir 25,1 bis 28,23–24 (28,19–20 LXX) umfasst, publizieren. Seine Vorgehensweise, in der er weitgehend Thiele folgt, und seine eigenen Ergebnisse stellt er in den Arbeitsberichten der Vetus-Latina-Stiftung der letzten Jahre (seit 2007)[42] und in weiteren Publikationen vor.[43] Obwohl er sich in vieler Hinsicht an der Editionsweise Thieles orientiert, geht er methodisch doch etwas eigene Wege, indem er die Informationen im kritischen Apparat auf das Notwendige beschränkt.

11. Statt einer Zusammenfassung

11.1. Leseprobe aus der jüngsten Edition: Sir 27,4 (5 lat.)

An diesem Vers lässt sich die Vorgehensweise und die Genauigkeit der Edition zeigen.

- ἐν σείσματι wird durch *in pertusura* (var. *in pertunsura* Z*) wiedergegeben; nur die gelehrte Edition des 13. Jahrhunderts, Ω^S, liest an dieser Stelle *percussura*. Die Glossare bieten für σείω und σεισμός *concutio, concussio, excussio.*[44] *Percussura*, das von dersel-

Kontext des Septuaginta-Vokabulars als Ganzes mit ein, jedoch ausschließlich für die hebräisch überlieferten Passagen, wie es sich aus der Zielsetzung des Werkes ergibt.

42. 51–58. Bericht der Stiftung; 40–47. Forschungsbericht des Instituts, Beuron, 2007–2014.

43. Anthony J. Forte, "The Old Latin Version of Sirach: Editio Critica and Some Textual Problems," in *The Texts and Versions of the Book of Ben Sira: Transmission and Interpretation*, hrsg. Jean-Sébastien Rey (Leiden: Brill, 2011), 199–214, und Forte, "Veteris Latinae Ecclesiastici: Apologia pro interprete latino," *JSCS* 47 (2014): 69–92.

44. Georg Goetz, *Thesaurus glossarum emendatarum: Pars posterior, Accedit index graecus Guilelmi Heraei*, Bd. 7.1 von *Corpus glossariorum latinorum* (Leipzig: Teubner, 1901), 636.

ben Wurzel *abgeleitet* ist, ist auch sonst belegt, also wohl an dieser Stelle korrekt.[45] Die Lesart wurde von den antiken Editoren der Vulgata fortgeführt. Dabei ist daran zu erinnern, dass in visigothischer Schrift c und t leicht zu verwechseln sind. Es ist daher durchaus möglich, dass der Schreiber des 13. Jahrhunderts, wenn er *percussura* schreibt, die ursprüngliche Form wieder hergestellt hat. Aber es kann als sicher gelten, dass es sich eben um eine Wiederherstellung handelt, nicht um die Wiedergabe der unmittelbaren Vorlage, von der er kopierte. Diese Deutung ist auch in ThLL (10.1:1834, l. 3) vorgeschlagen. Beide Termini ergeben einen möglichen Sinn: Man schüttelt das Sieb (*percussura*), aber das Sieb ist löchrig (*pertusura*). Die ursprüngliche lateinische Übersetzung hatte *percussura*, der Archetyp jedoch *pertusura.*

- διαμενεῖ wird außer in der Handschrift Z*, die *remanet* überliefert, in der gesamten Überlieferung mit der futurischen Form *remanebit* wiedergegeben. Ohne die Spezifizierung *durch* die Akzente kann das griechische διαμενει sowohl als Präsens (διαμένει) als auch als Futur (διαμενεῖ) gedeutet werden. An unserer Stelle dürften sich die Handschrift Z* oder ihre Vorlage dem griechischen Text angeglichen haben.
- σκύβαλα entspricht im Lateinischen *aporia* (var. *a porta, anxia* X, *confusio* Z*). Das griechische σκύβαλον bedeutet „Exkrement“, was sinngemäß nahe bei ἀπόρροια anzusiedeln ist, was *wiederum* hinter der lateinischen Form *aporria* steht.[46] Zwar ist selbstverständlich klar, dass der lateinische Übersetzer an dieser Stelle *aporia* meinte, das von dem griechischen ἀπορία, „ohne Weg“, abgeleitet ist, das jedoch in dem Zusammenhang keinen Sinn ergibt.

---

45. Zu *pertusura* siehe Deutsche Akademie der Wissenschaften zu Berlin, *Thesaurus Linguae Latinae* (Munich: de Gruyter, 1900–), 10.1:1833–1834; zu *percussura* siehe 10.1:1237.

46. Siehe dazu Georg Goetz, *Glossae codicum vaticani 3321, sangallensis 912, leidensis 67F*, Bd. 4 von *Corpus glossariorum latinorum* (Leipzig: Teubner, 1889), 201,27; Goetz, *Placidus: Liber glossarum [excerpta] Glossaria reliqua*, Bd. 5 von *Corpus glossariorum latinorum* (Leipzig: Teubner, 1894), 4,19 und 266,57; und Goetz, *Thesaurus glossarum emendatarum confecit Georgius Goetz: Pars prior*, Bd. 6 von *Corpus glossariorum latinorum* (Leipzig: Teubner, 1899), 82 (Index). Die wichtigsten Fakten sind in Deutsche Akademie, *Thesaurus Linguae Latinae*, 2:251,21–22, aufgenommen.

Aus allen drei Beispielen wird deutlich, dass die erste Hand der Handschrift Z (Metz, BM 7; Bibel von Angilram, vor 791) einen eigenen Text überliefert, der nach dem Griechischen revisiert wurde.[47]

11.2. Einige Forschungsdesiderate

(1) Wenn es stimmt, dass das Lob der Väter dem Sirachtext später hinzugefügt wurde, müsste man erwarten, dass der Abschnitt eine andere griechische Vorlage hatte, die Varianten anders verteilt sind und die Überlieferung weniger komplex ist. Die Variantenverteilung dürfte ein wichtiger Hinweis sein, ob man es mit einer anderen Tradition zu tun hat oder nicht. Allein die geringe Zahl der patristischen Belege beweist keineswegs, dass der Text nicht ursprünglich war. Dafür kann es andere Gründe geben: So handelt es sich um eine andere Textgattung als der übrige Sirachtext, nämlich um eine midraschartige Erzählung, deren Ereignisse aus anderem Kontext gut bekannt sind. Entsprechend geht z.B. auch Augustinus mit dem Text um, wenn er den ersten Teil der Sapientia häufig zitiert, den erzählenden zweiten Teil aber kaum. Eine gewisse Selbständigkeit des Textes[48] kann man eher daran erkennen, dass es Beispiele gibt, wo die Passage eigenständig überliefert wurde, und zwar in einigen griechischen und lateinischen[49] Handschriften und in einer arabischen.[50]

(2) Die Zuordnung des Buches an Salomo, die bei den lateinischen Vätern gängig war, bevor die Zuordnung zu Ben Sira üblich wurde, muss man wohl im Zusammenhang mit der *Oratio* Salomonis sehen, die in der lateinischen Tradition an das Sirachbuch angeschlossen wurde. Dadurch wird das Buch eng mit der sonstigen Weisheitsliteratur verbunden.

Die Rolle, die das Gebet des Salomo hier spielt, ist vergleichbar mit der des Psalms 151 im Psalter, der autobiographische Züge trägt, in dem also David von sich selbst spricht.[51] Die Unterschriften der Texte sind genauso zu beachten wie der Titel.[52]

---

47. Siehe Thiele, *Sirach (Eccesiasticus)*, 35.

48. Siehe Pierre-Maurice Bogaert, "Septante," in *DBS* 12.68:630.

49. St. Gallen 11, Vercelli XXII, Mailand, Ambr. E. 26 inf.

50. Richard Frank, *The Wisdom of Jesus Ben Sirach: (Sinai ar. 155. IXth/Xth cent.)*, CSCO 357 (Leuven: Secrétariat du CorpusSCO, 1974).

51. Pierre-Maurice Bogaert, "L'ancienne numérotation africaine des psaumes et la signature davidique du Psautier (Ps 151)," *RBén* 97 (1987): 153–62.

52. Pierre-Maurice Bogaert, "La datation par souscription dans les rédactions

Die römische Vulgata erlaubt folgende Thesen:[53]

(a) Die *Oratio Salomonis* (Sir 52) ist in den meisten Zeugen überliefert. Auffälligerweise fehlt sie in der spanischen Tradition (C Σ^{TC}) und in den frühen Theodulf-Bibeln (Θ^{HA}), die vermutlich von der spanischen Überlieferung abhängen.

(b) Die Erwähnung am Ende der Kapitula Ab ist in den Mailänder Zeugen überliefert.

(c) Im Amiatinus, Sangallensis 28 und den Mailänder Zeugen nennt das *Explicit* des Buches den Namen Salomos.

(d) Der Amiatinus nennt Salomo auch zu Beginn des 1. Kapitels.

(3) Es gibt keine einfache Erklärung für die komplizierte und komplexe Überlieferung, die schon in der römischen Vulgata, dann auch in der Vetus Latina sichtbar wird.

Die Komplexität besteht vom Beginn an: Die Abschnitte, die im hebräischen Text erhalten sind, weisen von Anfang an Varianten und Glossen auf. In der griechischen Überlieferung fehlt zunächst die Zuordnung zu Ben Sira, ebenso in der lateinischen Überlieferung. Das führt zu der Annahme, dass der Prolog ursprünglich fehlte und das Gebet des Salomo als Kolophon fungierte. Eine systematische Untersuchung, wie die griechischen Väter ihre Sirach-Zitate einführten, würde zweifellos zu interessanten Ergebnissen führen.

(4) Ziegler hat die Existenz einer hexaplarischen (*O*) und einer lukianischen (*L*) Rezension festgestellt. Die Existenz einer lukianischen Rezension bereitet keine Schwierigkeiten, zumal sie auf einen vollständigen Text hinweist, von dem aus die „Plusse" im Text erklärbar sind und von dem aus man grammatikalische Eigenheiten erklären kann.[54] Die hexaplarische Rezension hingegen ist schwierig nachzuweisen, wenn man die Bezeichnung so eng fasst, dass man darunter eine Bearbeitung des Origenes versteht; jener zeigte keinerlei Interesse an diesem Buch. Aller-

courte (LXX) et longue (TM) du livre de Jérémie," in *L'apport de la Septante aux études sur l'Antiquité : Actes du Colloque de Strasbourg 8–9 Novembre 2002*, hrsg. Jan Joosten (Paris: Cerf, 2005), 137–59.

53. Siehe BSR 12:127 und 373–75. Jetzt auch Pierre-Maurice Bogaert, "Les frontières du canon de l'Ancien Testament dans l'Occident latin, Appendice 2: Le Siracide salomonien dans les manuscrits," in *La Bible juive dans l'Antiquité*, hrsg. Rémi Gounelle und Jan Joosten, HTB 9 (Lausanne: Èditions du Zèbre, 2014), 94.

54. Joseph Ziegler, "Hat Lukian den griechischen Sirach rezensiert?," in *Sylloge*, 464–83.

dings deutet bis zum Kapitel 13 ein Teil der Handschriften darauf hin, dass Passagen unter Asterisk hinzugefügt wurden. Wenn die Bearbeitung auch nicht von Origenes stammt, so möglicherweise von anderen, die ähnliche Bearbeitungen durchgeführt haben. Dem Beispiel des Origenes folgend, der die parallelen griechischen Versionen von Theodotion, Aquila und Symmachus zusammengetragen hat, hat es wohl eine oder mehrere Versionen gegeben, die nicht direkt vom Hebräischen abhängen und die sich in dem Textbestand finden, der der Version Gr I hinzugefügt wurde.[55]

(5) Für das Studium des lateinischen Sirach sind vier Bereiche zu nennen:

(a) Ein erster Block umfasst den Bereich der Zuordnung des Buches innerhalb des Kanons, die Umstellung der Kapitel, das Vorhandensein bzw. Fehlen des Prologes, des Lobs der Väter und des Gebetes Salomos. Darüber hinaus muss man auch die weniger spektakulären Beobachtungen einbeziehen.

(b) Die Zusätze oder besser: die „Plusse" dürften wohl auf eine andere griechische Vorlage zurückgehen. Eine direkte Angleichung des lateinischen Textes an den hebräischen ist unwahrscheinlich; jedenfalls gibt es dafür noch keine überzeugenden Belege. Der griechische Text, der die Vorlage für die erste lateinische Übersetzung bildet, unterscheidet sich grundsätzlich von Gr I, was nicht nur in den „Plussen", sondern auch in dem übrigen Text zum Ausdruck kommt.

(c) Die lateinische Tradition erweist sich auch unabhängig von den „Plussen" als komplex, und wenn wir die direkte Handschriftenüberlieferung betrachten, stoßen wir auf eine große Zahl von Hinweisen auf eine Revision des griechischen Textes. In diesem Zusammenhang müssen u.a. die möglichen Übereinstimmungen des lateinischen Textes mit dem syrischen und hebräischen untersucht werden. Ist eventuell noch eine weitere griechische Textform, ein Zwischenglied, denkbar?

(d) Für die vereinzelten Varianten muss man von Fall zu Fall entscheiden, ob es sich um Fehler oder spontane Varianten handelt oder ob sie sich durch eine der bisher beschriebenen Möglichkeiten erklären lassen.

Bei der Erforschung des Sirachbuches geht es nicht darum, den ursprünglichen oder wenigstens besten Text, den man erreichen kann, wiederzugewinnen, sondern zu verstehen, wie sich der Text entwickelt

55. Joseph Ziegler, "Die hexaplarische Bearbeitung des griechischen Sirach," in *Sylloge*, 510–21.

hat. Selbstverständlich muss man versuchen, Schlüsse aus diesen Beobachtungen zu ziehen. Maurice Gilbert[56] konnte in einer beachtenswerten Studie über Sir 24 zeigen, dass sich die Zusätze gegenüber Gr I im griechischen Text und im lateinischen Text nur selten decken. Sie lassen sich in einem jüdischen Kontext erklären, in einem christlichen nicht.

(6) Es könnte sich lohnen, die Zitate der Sacra Parallela nicht nur nach ihren Entsprechungen mit den Versionen zu untersuchen, sondern auch nach ihrer Anordnung. Lässt es sich zeigen, dass die Sammlung der ursprünglichen Ordnung der Kapitel 30–36 folgt? Es sei außerdem darauf hingewiesen, dass die Kapitel 44–50 nur in einem einzigen Zitat in einer Handschrift (MP) belegt sind.[57]

Aus diesem Überblick wird deutlich, vor welche Herausforderungen die komplexe Textüberlieferung des Sirachbuches den Textkritiker stellt, welche Erkenntnisfortschritte schon gemacht wurden, aber auch, wie viele Frage noch auf eine Beantwortung warten.

56. Maurice Gilbert, "Les additions greques et latines à Siracide 24," in *Lectures et relectures de la Bible: Festschrift P.-M. Bogaert*, hrsg. J.-M. Auwers (Leuven: Leuven University Press, 1999), 195–207.

57. Wahl, *Sirach*, 167.

Plerique codices, nonnulli codices: Ambrose's Biblical Text; The Case of Ben Sirach and the Canticum Canticorum

Anthony J. Forte, SJ

Every reader of Ambrose of Milan is well-aware of his careful and diligent reading of the Scriptures.[1] No word of the *codices graeci et latini*[2] was left unscrutinized. Ambrose knew his Greek. He was not unacquainted with the works of Homer and Plato. He quoted, or at least alluded to, the works of Plotinus, Porphyry, Xenophon, Sophocles, and Euripides. In addition, he knew the exegetical works of important authors such as Philo, Origen, Basil of Caesarea, Athanasius of Alexandria, Didymus the Blind, Gregory of Nazianzus, Eusebius of Caesarea, Hippolytus, and so on.[3] Due to his proficiency in Greek, Ambrose read the versions of Aquila and Symmachus for the most part, as well as that of Theodotion. These

I would like to thank Camille Gerzaguet for allowing me to read her paper entitled "Ambroise de Milan et le texte des Écritures: Citer, comparer et traduire," which in the meantime appeared in *Le miel des Écritures*, ed. Smaranda Marculescu Badilita and Laurence Mellerin, Cahiers de Biblia Patristica Cahiers de Biblindex 1 (Turnhout: Brepols, 2015), 245–63. I appropriated the first part of the title of this paper from her study. *Plerique codices* occurs several times in Ambrose. See, for example, Ambrose (hereafter AM) *Job* 3.3.7 (252,20) and *Exp. Ps 118* 8.2 (150,1). For the occurrence of *nonnulli codices*, see *Exp. Ps. 37* 58 (182,12).

1. See Giorgio Maschio, *Ambrogio di Milano e la Bibbia*, Interpretare la Bibbia oggi. 3. Sez., Leggere la Bibbia alla luce della riflessione teologica 3 (Brescia: Queriniana, 2004).

2. See AM *Fid. Grat.* 5.16.193 (289,36) for a reference to *codices graeci* and AM *Job* 3.3.7 (252,21) for the use of the term *codices latini*.

3. See Cesare Pasini, ed., *Le fonti greche su Sant'Ambrogio*, Sancti Ambrosii episcopi Mediolanensis opera 24.1 (Milan: Bibliotheca Ambrosiana; Rome: Città Nuova Editrice, 1990).

were scrutinized, thanks to the Hexapla of Origen, which Ambrose knew as early as 386. All of these Greek versions were consulted and evaluated before Ambrose corrected and/or improved the Latin recensions at his disposal. He used as many texts as he could, including African texts, namely, those of Cyprian and Tertullian. Jerome's Hexaplaric recension of the LXX was a most important instrument because Jerome revised the Vetus Latina text(s) on the basis of the Hexaplaric recension. Ambrose was a competent reader of the codices and was able to distinguish and contrast those readings and translations that were of greater importance in order to help him make his own exegetical and philological decisions. He was not a textual critic in the modern sense, but he studied the Greek and Latin texts with great tenacity and with extreme care so as not to succumb to a banal and potentially erroneous interpretation. Every word had to be analyzed, evaluated, and interpreted in its context in order to arrive at the most probable and most convincing reading. More importantly, it was God himself who was the author of the sacred text, and Ambrose truly believed that "omnis scriptura divina dei gratiam spiret" (AM *Ps 1* 4 [4,19]).

According to Ambrose, the Latin texts acquired more authority in so far as they faithfully reflected the Greek, despite the fact that on occasion his Latin translations, or those appropriated from others, appear stiff and bereft of elegance. It must not be forgotten that some of the mistakes in his text of the Scriptures can perhaps be traced back to defective Greek and Latin manuscripts, as well as to his proclivity to sometimes (albeit rather infrequently) "correct" the text according to his version of the Bible.[4] Not only did the variety of Latin versions influence Ambrose's own text, but he read not a few exegetes who expounded allegorically as well as literally. Ambrose had a true dependence on other writers. This is significantly less true for Ambrose's comments on and use of Sirach than for the Canticum Canticorum,[5] but the context of the biblical text at hand must always be taken into consideration.

Ambrose's desire to present a Latin text that is, insofar as it is possible, a literal translation of the Greek, as well as his interest in interpreting texts

---

4. Cf. W. C. van Unnik, "De la règle Μήτε προσθεῖναι μήτε ἀφελεῖν dans l'histoire du canon," *VC* 3 (1949): 1–36.

5. Only once does Ambrose refer to this book of the Bible as Canticorum Canticum (AM *Ps 1* 6 [6,2]). It was his wont to use the plural, Cantica Canticorum (AM *Ps 118* 22.17 [496,24]).

allegorically, are the focus of the following pages. Examples from Sirach will be used to demonstrate Ambrose's efforts to present a biblical text that is faithful to his Greek Vorlage. This is especially apparent in singular readings. We often do not know where these surprising individual readings come from. Evidently, many have an affinity to the known biblical text while others transmit readings that are remnants of the Vetus Latina. Other readings are perhaps creations of Ambrose himself and have nothing to do with authentic biblical texts.[6] Again, it is most unlikely that Ambrose consciously altered a biblical text. This was not the praxis of Christian authors. Rather, it is more likely that we encounter readings that are extrabiblical and perhaps should be pointed out in the schema as Text-Type M.[7]

Ambrose's Latin text of Sirach lacks the originality and flexibility that other biblical texts portray. However, when his text contains innumerable allegorical interpretations, we can assume that Ambrose is borrowing from other writers. We know that he was well versed in Origen's commentary on the Canticum Canticorum and his text of this book of the Bible demonstrates his indebtedness to Origen's exegesis. In this paper I will also present some texts from the Canticum in order to show that Ambrose's interest in presenting a different text on occasion is not solely

6. See Hermann J. Frede, "Probleme des ambrosianischen Bibeltextes," in *Ambrosius episcopus: Atti del Congresso internazionale di studi ambrosiani nel XVI centenario della elevazione di sant'Ambrogio alla cattedra episcopale; Milano, 2–7 dicembre 1974*, ed. Giuseppe Lazzati, 2 vols., Studia patristica mediolanensia 6–7 (Milan: Vita e pensiero, 1976), 365–92 for a serious discussion of Ambrose's New Testament biblical texts. To my knowledge, there is no systematic treatment of Ambrose's biblical text(s) of the Old Testament.

7. Thiele did exactly this in his edition of Sir 1–24. I have avoided explicit references to the Text-Type M in the schema of my edition for the simple reason that I am editing Sirach and not Ambrose. Generally speaking, Text-Type D represents Pseudo-Augustinus's *Liber de divinis scripturis sive Speculum quod fertur S. Augustini*. Cf. B. Capelle, "Le cas du 'Speculum' augustinien 'Quis ignorat,'" *REAug* 2 (1956): 426–33; A. Vaccari, "Les traces de la 'Vetus Latina' dans le 'Speculum' de Saint Augustin," in *Studia Patristica 4: Papers Presented to the Third International Conference on Patristic Studies Held at Christ Church, Oxford 1959*, ed. F. L Cross, TUGAL 79 (Berlin: Akademie-Verlag, 1961), 228–33; Donatien de Bruyne, "Étude sur le Liber de divinis scripturis," *RBén* 43 (1931): 124–41; de Bruyne, "Étude sur le Liber de divinis scripturis," *RBén* 45 (1933): 119–41; Text-Type I indicates Chromatius's *Tractatus in Matthaeum*; Text-Type Z refers to a ninth-century manuscript housed in Metz at the Bibliothèque Municipale 7, and Text-Type J comprises the important eighth/ninth-century manuscript from Toulouse (MS 171), now in Paris in the Archives nationales AB XIX 1730.

an expression of his erudition, but rather that the texts he adopted served as a point of departure and foundation for his exegetical interests.[8]

In the very detailed and informative introduction to his Vetus Latina edition of Ben Sirach, Walter Thiele states that Ambrose's Latin biblical text, Text-Type M in the editions of the Vetus Latina, is often more in conformity with the Greek text that he had at his disposal. Thiele wrote: "Meist wird an solchen Stellen der griechische Text genauer wiedergegeben, und auch bei Varianten in der Wortwahl spielt die Rücksicht auf das griechische Wort eine Rolle."[9] It is not clear if Ambrose himself translated the Greek text at hand into Latin or whether he appropriated known Latin texts translated by others, which were in his view more acceptable because of their affinity to the Greek text. Some examples where Ambrose's biblical text demonstrates a more or less faithful rendering of the Greek text are as follows:

Sirach 8:10 (LXX) / 8:13 (Vulg.)

> LXX 8:10: μὴ ἔκκαιε ἄνθρακας ἁμαρτωλοῦ, μὴ [μήποτε] ἐμπυρισθῇς ἐν πυρὶ φλογὸς αὐτοῦ.
> Vulg. 8:13: non incendas carbones peccatoris arguens eos ne incendaris flamma ignis peccatorum.
> AM *Job* 2.5 (236,18): noli incendere carbones peccatoris, ne forte exuraris in igne flammae eius.

Ambrose's *noli incendere* and the Vulgate's *non incendas* are both faithful renderings of the Greek μὴ ἔκκαιε. The text of Ambrose does not include the expression *arguens eos* found in the Vulgate, but it transmits simply the words *carbones peccatoris*, which follow the text of the LXX (ἄνθρακας ἁμαρτωλοῦ). The negative particle *ne* in the text of the Vulgate and in Ambrose corresponds to the second μή of the LXX, while the variant reading μήποτε, found in MS 753, is reflected in Ambrose's *ne forte*. Another variant, ἐκπυρισθῇς, attested in MS V, is equivalent to Ambrose's

8. Eva Schulz-Flügel, who is presently editing the Canticum for both the Vetus Latina Institute and for the Göttingen Septuagint Project, very generously shared some of her research on the Canticum with me. We not only discussed the Canticum, but Schulz-Flügel provided innumerable examples of Ambrose's biblical text that I cite and expand upon in this paper.

9. See Walter Thiele, "Einleitung," in *Sirach (Ecclesiasticus)*, VLB 11.2 (Freiburg im Breisgau: Herder, 1987–2014), 141.

exuraris. It is to be noted that ἐμπυρισθῇς and ἔκκαιε here at Sir 8:10, as well as the verbal element ἐνεπύρισαν (49:6), are all rendered by some form of *incendere*: *incendas* (8:13a), *incendaris* (8:13b) and *incenderunt* (49:8). The expression *in igne flammae eius* used by Ambrose to translate ἐν πυρὶ φλογὸς αὐτοῦ includes the literal rendering of both ἐν and αὐτοῦ, which is omitted in the Vulgate. The Vulgate's *peccatorum* directly after *flamma ignis* is not attested in the LXX, and it is apparently for this reason that Ambrose's text omits it. The Sacra Parallela[10] contains the variant ἁμαρτιῶν, which renders the Vulgate's *peccatorum* comprehensible.

Sirach 11:27 (LXX) / 11:29 (Vulg.)

> LXX 11:27: κάκωσις ὥρας ἐπιλησμονὴν ποιεῖ τρυφῆς, καὶ ἐν συντελείᾳ ἀνθρώπου ἀποκάλυψις ἔργων αὐτοῦ.
> Vulg. 11:29: malitia horae oblivionem facit luxuriae magnae et in fine hominis denuntiatio operum illius.
> AM *Instit.* 21 (126): qua ratione hoc dixerit, superioribus docuit dicens quia in fine hominis nudantur opera eius.

Some of Ambrose's translations are far from being literal and careful interpretations of the extant Greek text. It is, of course, possible that he had a different Greek text. The beginning of LXX 11:27 (κάκωσις ὥρας ἐπιλησμονὴν ποιεῖ τρυφῆς) is equivalent to the Vulgate's *malitia horae oblivionem facit luxuriae magnae*. The Septuagint's use of ἀποκάλυψις in Sirach is not interpretated consistently by the Vulgate and Ambrose. The substantive ἀποκάλυψις is attested twice elsewhere (22:22 and 42:1) in the Septuagint of Sirach, and it is rendered as *revelatione* in both places. The Vulgate, on the other hand, translated ἀποκάλυψις at 11:29 as *denuntiatio*, but *denudatio* is likewise frequently attested in the Vulgate.[11] Another Vulgate reading at 11:29, *nudatio*, found in Fulgentius,[12] is a literal rendering of the LXX reading ἀποκάλυψις. Ambrose's preference for the verbal form *nudantur* is not noisome, since it does indeed reflect the Greek, but it is not in conformity with Ambrose's tendency to prefer a literal translation

---

10. Otto Wahl, *Der Sirach-Text der Sacra Parallela*, FB 16 (Würzburg: Echter, 1974), 68.

11. Thiele, *Sirach*, 396, reasons as follows: *vocem* denuntiatio *lectionem sinceram integramque interpretis latini esse iudico* (*contra editores* V^R *qui vocem* denuntiatio *ex* denudatio *degeneravisse aestimant*).

12. *Mitologiarum libri* 3 2.1 (39.4): in obitu hominis nudatio operum eius.

of the Greek. In this case it is very possibile that Ambrose had a different Greek Vorlage or had an older Latin text at hand that reflected the Hebrew rendering.[13]

Sirach 18:13 (LXX) / 18:12 (Vulg.)

> LXX Sir 18:13: ἔλεος ἀνθρώπου ἐπὶ τὸν πλησίον αὐτοῦ, ἔλεος δὲ κυρίου ἐπὶ πᾶσαν σάρκα·
> Vulg. Sir 18:12: miseratio hominis circa proximum suum misericordia autem dei super omnem carnem.
> AM *Exp. Ps. 118* 20.29 (459,16): misericordia enim (— *NT*) hominis in proximum suum, misericordia domini in omnem carnem.

The customary translation of ἔλεος in Sirach is *misericordia*. The Vulgate at Sir 18:12 transmits *miseratio* as an interpretation of the first ἔλεος but *misericordia* for the second. Could this be a simple desire on the part of the translator to vary his text (*varietas locutionis*)? There is an attestation of *miseratio* at Sir 17:27 (*miserationibus*), a reading that has no equivalent in the corresponding text of the LXX. Sirach 5:6 reads *et ne dicas miseratio Dei magna est multitudinis peccatorum meorum miserebitur* and does have a Greek *Vorlage*, not ἔλεος but οἰκτιρμός. The text reads: καὶ μὴ εἴπῃς Ὁ οἰκτιρμὸς αὐτοῦ πολύς, τὸ πλῆθος τῶν ἁμαρτιῶν μου ἐξιλάσεται. Note that the Vulgate (Sir 5:6) reads both *misericordia* and *miseratio* as interpretations of οἰκτιρμός.

The second word of Ambrose's text, *enim*, does not have a Greek Vorlage. Note, however, that two manuscripts of Ambrose's *Expositio Psalmi 118* (N and T) omit *enim* and thus Ambrose's text without *enim* is more in line with the LXX equivalent. The Latin word *circa* is not an exact rendering of the LXX's ἐπί.[14] Ambrose's *in* is a more faithful interpretation.

Ambrose's *misericordia domini* interprets the expression ἔλεος δὲ κυρίου but it does not include an interpretation of the particle δέ. This lacuna corresponds perfectly to the variant reading, that is, the omission of δέ by *l*, a sub-group of the Lucian reception. In addition, Ambrose's rendering of ἐπὶ πᾶσαν σάρκα as *in omnem carnem* and the Vulgate's *super omnem carnem*

13. See Thiele, *Sirach*, 396: cf. 𝕳 11.29b: "et finis hominis annuntiabit de eo" (*vox hebraica* > αποκαλυψις).

14. Cf. Deutsche Akademie der Wissenschaften zu Berlin, *Thesaurus Linguae Latinae* (Munich: de Gruyter, 1900–), 8:1114,21–22.

are both acceptable translations. We have another *in* plus the accusative as in 12a in Ambrose's text, and *super* (not *circa*) in the Vulgate.

Sirach 25:21 (LXX) / 25:28 (Vulg.)

> LXX Sir 25:21: μὴ προσπέσῃς ἐπὶ κάλλος γυναικὸς καὶ γυναῖκα μὴ ἐπιποθήσῃς.
> Vulg. 25:28: ne respicias in mulieris speciem et non concupiscas mulierem in specie.
> AM *Apol. Dav.* 12 (364,14): non *incidas* (*intendas X*) in mulieris speciem et non concupiscas mulierem; et (*TN*; ait *cet.*) alibi • 17 (367,20): noli in (— *TN*) speciem mulieris *intendere*/Prov 23:33 • pae 1.68 (151,12): non *intendat* (attendat Δ) saepius in (—Δ) formam mulieris meretricis • 1.70 (152,27): dixit quidem (— M; quidam *V*) propheta: nolo *intendas* in formam (forma *VP*) mulieris fornicariae. sed tamen dominus dixit.

Only here at LXX Sir 25:21 do we have an attestation of προσπίπτω. In my edition of this text,[15] I show that Text-Type D and Text-Type J interpret πρόσπιπτω differently: D renders the verb as *adtendas* while J translates the Greek literally with *incidas*.

The schema below helps the reader to realize immediately that the Greek προσπέσῃς corresponds only to *incidas*. Text-Type J (MS 171), as we have said above, is a literal translation of the Septuagint. It is unfortunate that so little of the manuscript is extant.

LXX	21	μὴ	προσπέσῃς
V	28	ne	respicias
			respicies
D		non	adtendas
			intendas
		noli	intendere
J		<*n*>e	incidas

15. Anthony J. Forte, ed., *Sir 25,1–28,24, Sirach (Ecclesiasticus): Pars altera*, VLB 11.2 (Freiburg im Breisgau: Herder, 2014), 22.

In order to explain the different elements, I formulated the problem in the critical apparatus as follows:

> respicias V • respicies ΣTQϰ^{V}, Paris lat. 11505 Reims 2; [PS-AU spe] 53 (a) • respicicias Π^{H}: *lapsu* • adtendas PS-AU spe • intendas AM pae 1,70; Dav alt 12 (Var) • intendere AM Dav alt 17 • *interpretes latini alium textum graecum legisse videntur, vide etiam* Sir 9,8 LXX καταμανθανε; Sir 41,27 ne respicias mulierem (*deest* 𝔊) • incidas 171; AM Dav alt 12: = 𝔊

The reading of the Vulgate, *respicias*, does not reflect the reading of the Septuagint. *Respicies* is also atttested in some other MSS, and is listed below *respicias* in the schema. Pseudo-Augustinus's *adtendas* (Text-Type D) likewise does not reflect the Greek. The two readings of Ambrose, *intendas* [AM *Paen.* 1.70; *Apol. Dav.* 12 (Var)] and *intendere* [AM *Apol. Dav.* 17], inserted below D's *adtendas*, suggest that the Latin translator perhaps had a different Greek Vorlage. The only correct rendering of the Greek προσπέσῃς is J's *incidas* (MS 171 and AM *Apol. Dav.* 12). Note that in the apparatus above, I make reference to Sir 9:8, καταμάνθανε, the reading of the LXX, while the Vulgate of this verse reads *circumspicias*.

***

Thiele offers other examples that I will develop and expand upon. For example, Thiele notes that αἰσχύνη and αἰσχύνεσθαι are for the most part translated in the Vulgata as *confusio* and *confundi*.[16] There are exceptions and most of these are found in Ambrose. Sirach 4:25 Vulg. reads *confusio* but the reading from AM *Exp. Ps. 37*, *verecundia*, likewise has a place in the schema of the critical edition.[17] Did Ambrose himself translate this text, or did he appropriate it from someone else? We simply do not know, and the following examples illustrate the impossibility of reaching a definitive conclusion. At AM *Exp. Ps. 43*, for example, Ambrose prefers *confusio* to *verecundia*.[18] The same phenomenon occurs at Sir 21:25 Vulg.: the Vulgate reads *confundetur*, while Ambrose's text translates αἰσχυνθήσεται (LXX

16. Cf. Thiele, *Sirach*, introduction, 140. Cf. 4:25: *confusio/verecundia* M; 4:31: *confundaris*; 13:8: *confundet*; 21:25: *confundetur/verecundatur* M; 22:31: *confundaris/erubescam* M / 22:31: *erubescas* M; 24:30: *confundetur*; 25:29: *confusio*; 29:19: *confusionem*; 41:20: *inreverentiam*; 41:21: *erubescite*; 51:24: *confundor*; 51:37: *confundemini*.

17. AM *Exp. Ps. 37* 51.3 (178,1): *scriptum est quia est verecundia adducens peccatum*.

18. AM *Exp. Ps. 43* 70.1 (312,1): *quemadmodum est confusio adducens pecca-*

21:22) as *verecundatur.*[19] Instead of adopting the Vulgate's *confundaris* at 22:31, Ambrose or some other translator whose translation Ambrose took over, considered *erubesco* to be a better and more appropriate solution.[20]

Another reading that Thiele mentions is the rarely attested word *infrunitus* (Sir 31:23 Vulg.) (*tasteless, senseless, silly*), a rendering of ἄπληστος (*insatiate, greedy*) (34:20 LXX).[21] The two citations from Ambrose that will appear in my Zeugenapparat and echo 31:23 Vulg. are from *De Cain et Abel*[22] and *De Helia et ieiunio.*[23] Neither text picks up the Vulgate's *infrunitus*, but they both introduce *edax* and *insatiabilis* in their place, while Pseudo-Augustinus's *Speculum*[24] maintains the reading of the Vulgate, *infrunitus*. Sirach 31:25 Vulg., however, appropriates *edax* by introducing *edendo* (ἐδέσμασιν, Sir 34:21) into the text. Both Ambrose[25] and Defensor[26] serve as witnesses to this reading.

We have some examples where Ambrose prefers not to adopt a Vulgate reading that constitutes a foreign word.[27] For example, at Sir 2:5 (LXX and Vulg.), Ambrose reads *fornace* instead of *in camino*, a literal translation of the Septuagint reading ἐν καμίνῳ. See also Sir 6:32 (*stolam gloria*), a literal rendering of the Greek στολὴν δόξης (6:31). Ambrose's rendering of στολὴν δόξης as *amictum gloriae* reflects this same tendency not to introduce foreign words into his biblical text.[28]

---

tum, ita est confusio quae peccatum abolet ... est etiam omnis confusio bona, quam pro Christi nomine subeas, et admodum gloriosa.

19. AM *Exh. virginit.* 72 (256): *quid enim tibi opus est vel ad proximam facile accedere? pes enim fatui facilis in domum proximi, qui autem sapiens est verecundatur.*

20. AM *Off.* 3.129 (202): *defer amico ut aequali nec te pudeat ut praevenias amicum officio; amicitia enim nescit superbiam; ideo enim sapiens dicit: amicum salutare non erubescas.*

21. Deutsche Akademie, *Thesaurus Linguae Latinae* 6:1497, 63–66: *infrunitus pertinet ad insolentiam, statum immoderatum.*

22. AM *Cain* 1.18 (354,25): *vigiliae enim et tormenta viro edaci.*

23. AM *Hel.* 26 (427,2): *vigiliae, inquit, et cholera et tortura viro insatiabili.*

24. Pseudo-Augustinus, *Liber de divinis scripturis sive Speculum quod fertur S. Augustini* 52 (527,9): *vigilia et cholera et tortio viro infrunito.*

25. AM *Cain* 1.18 (354,26): *si coactus fueris in edendo, surge et vome, et refrigerabit te et non adduces corpori tuo infirmitatem.*

26. Defensor, *Scintillarum liber* 54.7 (178): *si coactus fueris in edendo multum, surge de medio et vome, et refrigerabit te, et non adducis corpori tuo infirmitatem.*

27. Cf. Thiele, *Sirach*, 141: cf. AM *Exp. Ps. 118* 20.10.2 (449,31): *homines acceptabiles in fornace humilitatis.*

28. AM *Ob. Theo.* 52 (398): *sed amictum induti gloriae.*

During the initial phase of my work on Sirach for the Vetus Latina Institute, I erroneously thought that Ambrose's text of Sirach (Test-Type M) would exhibit a plethora of interesting readings. A cursory glance at Thiele's edition of Sir 1–24 and my recent edition of Sir 24–28:24 reveals a close connection between Ambrose's text and the readings of Text-Types D, I, Z, and J. Ambrose's Sirach does not transmit anything more than the Latin translations he had at his disposal. Of course, on occasion one encounters a different word order or formulation. Thiele summarized this phenomenon as follows: "Im allgemeinen nimmt Ambrosius in Sirach keine Sonderstellung ein; er belegt vielmehr die allgemeine lateinische Überlieferung in ihren verschiedenen Ausformungen und übernimmt dabei in der Regel deren Eigenarten in der Wortwahl und auch in—teilweise erheblichen—Abweichungen vom Griechischen."[29]

Some other unique readings from Sir 1–24 (Thiele) and from Sir 25–28 (Forte) are listed in the chart below:[30]

Sir	Vulgata	Ambrosius
3:33	extinguit	restinguet
3:34	tempore casus tui	die ruinae ×
6:26	et ne acedieris vinculis	nec taedieris ad vincula
8:16	quod si	si enim
10:28	liberi servient	multi serviunt liberi
18:5	minuere neque adicere	adicere neque minuere
18:6	quieverit	finierit
18:19	loquaris	loqui
19:2	sapientes	prudentes

29. Cf. Thiele, *Sirach*, 141.

30. The Vetus Latina edition of Sirach has been partially edited and published by Thiele (chs. 1–24) and Forte (chs. 25–28). Therefore, I have deemed it unnecessary to provide the exact references to the Ambrose readings in the right-hand column of this chart. The Ambrose readings are clearly presented in the Zeugenapparat of the Beuron editions. On the other hand, it was necessary to provide the exact citations from Ambrose below in the discussion of the Canticum, since the critical edition has not yet appeared.

21:25	peritus	sapiens
23:2	in cogitatu meo	× cogitationum mearum
23:6	concupiscentiae	cupiditatis
23:25	qui transgreditur	transgrediens
23:28	intuentes	deprehendentes
23:29	sperabit	putaverit
23:30	adprehendetur	comprehenditur
25:5	congregasti	collegisti / congregas
25:6	canitiae	incanae
25:28	respicias	intendas
26:14	neglexerit	praeterierit
27:14	narratio	fabula

***

The situation of Ambrose's text of the Canticum is quite different from that of Sirach. While only short segments of Sirach are quoted in Ambrose's works, it is astonishing to find that Ambrose has quoted the Canticum almost in its entirety. Ambrose took great liberty to make use of the various Text-Types, one right after the other. He consistently used the works not only of those who preceded him but also those of his contemporaries. Often Ambrose quotes many of the same passages in a variety of his writings and the very same biblical texts are presented in a different form by either replacing a word with a synonym or by allowing a grammatical divergence that represents some Greek version. Examples will be provided below. We do not know for certain what influence the Greek text of the Canticum had on Ambrose's Latin biblical text but we do know that Ambrose consulted not a few Greek manuscripts and even produced his own translations of them. Even though a phenomenon like word order that corresponds to the Greek text is evident, it is probably more prudent to conclude that Ambrose's text is the result of a combination of several

Latin texts that were at his disposal. Eva Schulz-Flügel formulated the problem in this way:

> [es] stellt sich heraus, daß Ambrosius sich ziemlich genau an einen ihm vorliegenden Text hält; wenn er den griechischen Text zu Hilfe nimmt, weist er meist selbst darauf hin, daß er sich bei der jeweiligen Version nicht um eine gängige lateinische handelt ... daß Ambrosius ... wohl kaum aus dem Kopf zitierte, sondern sich an eine Vorlage hielt.... Wir dürfen also Ambrosius als relativ verläßlichen Zeugen für bereits vorhandene Übersetzungen ansehen, auch wenn er selbst um die Verbesserung dieser Versionen bemüht war.[31]

Some examples of individual readings are as follows:

Canticles 1:14 (LXX) / 1:13 (Vulg.)

> LXX 1:14: βότρυς τῆς κύπρου ἀδελφιδός μου ἐμοὶ ἐν ἀμπελῶσιν Εγγαδδι.
> Vulg. 1:13: botrus cypri dilectus meus mihi in vineis Engaddi.
> AM *Exp. Ps. 118* 3.8.1 (44,24): nardum Cypri consobrinus meus, in uineis Engaddi.

In the text of Ambrose we read *nardum cypri* instead of *botrus cypri.* The LXX transmits βότρυς, the exact equivalent of the Hebrew אשכול. See Origen, *Comm. Cant.* 2 (171,2): *Idcirco autem singulatim et per ordinem primo 'nardum' suam, deinde 'guttam', post haec etiam 'botrum cypri' nominat, ut per eos gradus quosdam profectuum doceat caritatis.*[32] It is possible that Ambrose appropriated the reading, *nardum cypri*, from a defective manuscript of Hippolytus.[33]

Canticles 3:8 (LXX/Vulg.)

> LXX 3:8: πάντες κατέχοντες ῥομφαίαν δεδιδαγμένοι πόλεμον, ἀνὴρ ῥομφαία αὐτοῦ ἐπὶ μηρὸν αὐτοῦ ἀπὸ θάμβους ἐν νυξίν.
> Vulg. 3:8: omnes tenentes gladios et ad bella doctissimi uniuscuiusque ensis super femur suum propter timores nocturnos.

31. See Eva Schulz-Flügel, "Einleitung," in *Canticum Canticorum*, VLB 10.3.1 (Freiburg im Breisgau: Herder, 1992), 71.

32. Trans. Rufini.

33. This is the hypothesis of Schulz-Flügel.

AM *Virg.* 1.8.51: strictis armatis ensibus et eruditos proeliaribus disciplinis.

Ambrose reads *strictis armatis ensibus et eruditos proeliaribus disciplinis* instead of *omnes tenentes gladium et docti proelium*. This is most likely Ambrose's own formulation with Virgilian echoes (cf *Aen.* 2.330: *stricta … proelia*; *Aen.* 7.523: *strictis … ensibus*; *Aen.* 12.175: *pius Aeneas stricto sic ense*; *Aen.* 12.287: *strictis ensibus*).

Canticles 7:3 (LXX) / 7:2 (Vulg.)

LXX 7:3: ὀμφαλός σου κρατὴρ τορευτὸς μὴ ὑστερούμενος κρᾶμα· κοιλία σου θημωνιὰ σίτου πεφραγμένη ἐν κρίνοις·
Vulg. 7:2: umbilicus tuus crater tornatilis numquam indigens poculis venter tuus sicut acervus tritici vallatus liliis.
AM *Instit.* 14.89.5: venter tuus sicut acervus tritici minuti inter lilia.

We read *sicut acervus tritici minuti inter lilia* in Ambrose instead of the Vulgate reading, *sicut acervus tritici vallatus*[34] *liliis*. This is most likely an error in Ambrose's manuscript, or it could suggest that Ambrose read *minutus* (*small*) instead of *munitus* (*well protected, fortified, safe*), which is a paleographic possibility. The context indicates that Ambrose understood and intended to write *minutus*.[35]

Canticles 1:16 (LXX) / 1:15 (Vulg.)

LXX 1:16: Ἰδοὺ εἶ καλός, ὁ ἀδελφιδός μου, καί γε ὡραῖος· πρὸς κλίνη ἡμῶν σύσκιος.
Vulg. 1:15: ecce tu pulcher es dilecte mi et decorus lectulus noster floridus.
AM *Isaac* 4.27 (660,1): ecce es formonsus consobrinus meus equidem pulcher: adclinatio nostra opaca.

In many Vetus Latina texts we have a number of interesting interpretations of the Septuagint's ἀδελφιδός (*beloved*). The Text-Type K? and the Text-Type D transmit *frater* for ἀδελφιδός. The term *fraternus* belongs to the

34. In place of *vallatus*, Schulz-Flügel has conjectured *conseptus*, more in line with the Greek term πεφραγμένη.

35. See Deutsche Akademie, *Thesaurus Linguae Latinae* 8:1040,26sq. where the following authors are cited: Petronius, *Sat.* 32.1 (*minitussima* pro *munitussima*); Vulg. *Jos.* 11.13 (*munitissimam*); CAr in 1.4.3 (*munitissima*).

Text-Type I, while *fratruelis* is found in the Text-Type O (= Jerome). Other Latin interpretations for ἀδελφιδός, in addition to *pulcher* and *formonsus* above, are *frater, consobrinus, fraternus* and *fratruelis*. The following texts provide some examples of these other interpretations of the problematic term ἀδελφιδός.

> Cod. Salisburgensis (eighth/ninth century): vox ecclesiae. vide si speciosa frater meus, et quidam decorus; cubile nostrum condensum.[36]
> AM *Exp. Ps. 118* 5.9 (86,23): ecce bonus fraternus meus. ecce es bonus.
> Jerome, *Orig. Hom. Cant.* (48,24, 49,11): ecce es speciosus fratruelis meus.

This language, albeit enigmatic at times, is the result of Ambrose's own highly allegorical reflections on the person of Christ, ἀδελφιδός, the *beloved*, the son of the synagogue (as a Jew). According to Ambrose's allegoric interpretation, the synagogue is the sister of the church. Therefore, for the soul of a Christian, who is a child of the church, Christ is the beloved cousin (the son of his aunt), *consobrinus/fratruelis*.

A similar phenomenon appears at Cant 2:8. While the Vulgate reads *vox dilecti mei ecce iste venit saliens in montibus transiliens colles*, there are some passages in Ambrose where ἀδελφιδός is interpreted as *consobrinus* or *frater*. We encounter *vox consobrini* and *vox fratris* four times each.[37]

An even more interesting text is that of Cant 8:1. The Vulgate reads *quis mihi det te fratrem meum sugentem ubera matris meae*, which is an interpretation of the text of the Septuagint version which reads as follows: Τίς δῴη σε ἀδελφιδόν μου θηλάζοντα μαστοὺς μητρός μου; The different Latin versions of this verse are the consequence of the divergent Greek readings.[38] Ambrose has at least six different renderings of ἀδελφιδός, some of which contain doublets.[39] In this verse, the terms for the *beloved one* and *nephew*, ἀδελφιδός or ἀδελφιδοῦς, are rendered in the Vulgate as *frater*, as above.

---

36. *RBén* 38 (1926): 99.

37. For *vox consobrini*, see AM *Exp. Ps. 118* 6.5 (110,22, 111,2, 111,5, 111,8); *vox fratris*: see *Exp. Ps. 36* 66 (125,21); *Exp. Ps. 118* 12.14 (259,6), 22.12 (494,25), *Exp. Luc.* 3 (90.458).

38. Until the publication of Schulz-Flügel's Göttingen critical edition of the Canticum, the textual information provided in the hand-edition of Rahlfs-Hanhart will have to suffice. Their apparatus at Cant 8:1 (269) informs us that Codices Vaticanus (B), Sinaiticus (S), and "a few others" read *αδελφιδον*. Codex Venetus (V) reads *αδελφιδουν* (*ου* is always read instead of *ο*). All the other manuscipts read *αδελφιδε*.

39. For *te frater mi*: AM *Apol. Dav.* 9.47 (391,5); *te fratrem mihi*: AM *Instit.* 1.5.3;

Some individual examples where Ambrose takes advantage of several Text-Types are as follows:

Canticles 2:14 (LXX et Vulg.)

LXX 2:14: καὶ ἐλθὲ σύ, περιστερά μου ἐν σκέπῃ τῆς πέτρας ἐχόμενα τοῦ προτειχίσματος, δεῖξόν μοι τὴν ὄψιν σου καὶ ἀκούτισόν με τὴν φωνήν σου, ὅτι ἡ φωνή σου ἡδεῖα, καὶ ἡ ὄψις σου ὡραία.
Vulg. 2:14: columba mea in foraminibus petrae in caverna maceriae ostende mihi faciem tuam sonet vox tua in auribus meis vox enim tua dulcis et facies tua decora.
AM *Exp. Ps. 118* 22.17 (496,26): insinua mihi vocem tuam quia vox tua suavis est.

With reference to the term ἀκούτισόν με, the Latin translations vary depending on the Text-Type adopted. We read *insinua mihi* (Text-Type D or most likely the K reading) instead of *audiam* in the text of Ambrose quoted above: *insinua mihi vocem tuam quia vox tua suavis est.*

Another possible D or K reading is found in AM *Ep.* 13.4.6: *ostende mihi faciem tuam et insinua mihi vocem tuam.* Text-Type I transmits *auditam mihi fac*,[40] and Text-Type O reads *audire me fac*.[41] Another version of Cant 2:14, probably from Hippolytus, reads *exsurge secura integimento petrae* (AM *Isaac* 4.37 [663,22]), which is not unsimilar to Ambrose's *et ueni tu, columba mea, integimento petrae iuxta praemunitionem* (AM *Isaac* 4.37 [664,5]). Finally, the last element of the Vulgate text of Cant 2:14 reads *vox enim tua dulcis et facies tua decora*, which is similar to *quia vox tua suavis est et facies tua pulchra* (AM *Ex. Ps. 118* 6.33 [125.12]).

Canticles 6:7 (LXX) / 6:6 (Vulg.)

LXX 6:7: ὡς λέπυρον τῆς ῥόας μῆλόν σου ἐκτὸς τῆς σιωπήσεώς σου.
Vulg. 6:6: sicut cortex mali punici genae tuae absque occultis tuis.
AM *Ex.* 3.13.56 (99,5): ut cortex mali punici genae tuae et infra.

---

te fratrem frater: AM *Isaac* 8.70 (691,18) [doublet]; *te frater mihi*: AM *Myst.* 7.40 (105,52); *te fratrem*: AM *Exp. Ps. 118* 19.25 (435,2); *te frater fratrem mihi*: AM *Ob. Val.* 74 (363,3) [doublet]; AM *Ob. Val.* 75 (364,4) [doublet].

40. Cf. Origenis sec. trans. Rufini, *Commentarium in Cant. Cant.* 4 (231,23).

41. Cf. Origenis sec. trans. Hieronymi, hom. 2, par. 13 (60,22–24).

The curious reading at Cant 6:6, *sicut cortex mali punici genae tuae absque occultis tuis*, was probably not readily understood. There is only one attestation of *cortex mali punici* in Ambrose, but there is also a formulation of this expression in the plural: *cortices malorum punicorum*.[42] Perhaps the words *malum granatum* were more readily comprehensible. Ambrose uses this expression at least six times.[43]

There is a plethora of readings in Ambrose that are strikingly different from the readings of the Vulgate of the Canticum. Eva Schulz-Flügel has collected not of a few of these for her edition of the Canticum for the Vetus Latina Institute. I have selected some unique readings that in my view indicate that Ambrose not only had a different Greek Vorlage but also had innumerable Latin translations of the Canticum at his disposal. We will have to wait for Schulz-Flügel's edition for a complete listing of the variants and a systematic presentation of the patristic witnesses. In the meantime, the following list will suffice to give the reader a glimpse into Ambrose's extremely rich and unique variant readings. I suggest that these are mostly lost Vetus Latina readings but it is also very probable that some of the readings are Ambrose's own translations of his Greek Vorlage, given that it was not customary, as said above, for Christian writers such as Ambrose and Augustine to alter the transmitted biblical text.[44] I have given a reference to only one attestation in Ambrose where the reading is different from that of the Vulgate.

	Vulgata	Ambrosius
1:1	meliora ubera	bona[45]/optima[46] ubera
1:2	oleum effusum	unguentum exinanitum[47]
1:7	o pulchra inter mulieres	formonsa[48]/decora[49] in mulieribus
2:4	ordinavit in me caritatem	constituite in me dilectionem[50]

42. AM *Ob. Val.* 6 (332,11).

43. AM *Isaac* 5.48 (672,9).

44. Cf. van Unnik, "De la règle Μήτε προσθεῖναι μήτε ἀφελεῖν dans l'histoire du canon."

45. AM *Isaac* 3,9 (648,11).

46. AM *Exp. Ps. 118* 6.3 (6,21); 1.4 (7,7); 1.5 (8,2).

47. AM *Exp. Ps. 118* 1.5 (8,11).

48. AM *Exc.* 6.6.39 (230,11).

49. AM *Ex.* 6.9.56 (248,1).

50. AM *Exp. Ps. 118* 5.13 (88,25).

2:12	tempus putationis	tempus messis[51]/incisionis[52]/secandi[53]
4:1	capilli tui	capillamentum tuum[54]/capillatura tua[55]
4:9	vulnerasti cor meum	cor nostrum cepisti[56]
4:13	emissiones tuae paradisus	transmissiones tuae paradisus[57]
5:1	comedat fructum pomorum	manducet fructum pomorum[58]
5:3	expoliavi me tunica mea	exui tunicam meam[59]
5:10	dilectus meus candidus	fraternus meus candidus[60]
6:11	conturbavit me propter quadrigas Aminadab	posuit me currus Aminadab[61]
7:12	si floruit vinea	si floruit vitis[62]
8:2	dabo tibi poculum ex vino condito	potum dabo tibi a vino operosi[63]
8:7	extinguere caritatem	excludere caritatem[64]
8:9	propugnacula argentea	turres argenteas[65]
8:12	vinea mea ... ducenti his qui custodiunt fructus eius	vitis mea ... ducenti servantibus fructum[66]
8:14	fuge dilecte mi et adsimilare capreae	fuge frater meus et similis esto tu capreolae[67]

51. AM *Ex.* 4.5.22 (129,20).
52. AM *Exh. virginit.* 1.8.4.
53. AM *Isaac* 4.35 (663,13).
54. AM *Exp. Ps. 118* 15.12 (336,26).
55. AM *Spir.* 2.prol.14 (92,113).
56. AM *Exp. Ps. 118* 16.19 (363,17).
57. AM *Bon. mort.* 5.19 (721,5).
58. AM *Virg.* 1.8 (46,7).
59. AM *Isaac* 6.52 (675,21).
60. AM *Exp. Ps. 118* 11.56 (157,3).
61. AM *Isaac* 8.65 (687,23).
62. AM *Virg.* 6.34.7.
63. AM *Ob. Val.* 74 (364,6).
64. AM *Instit.* 17.113.5.
65. AM *Virg.* 2.6 (43,5).
66. AM *Exp. Ps. 118* 22.42 (508,16).
67. AM *Exp. Ps. 118* 22.44 (509,15).

***

In conclusion, we must never forget that for Ambrose there was nothing more important and more meaningful than the reading and the study of the sacred texts. The place for man to encounter God and to feel His presence is in the scriptures. This intuition is clearly articulated in one of Ambrose's letters when he wrote the following: *et nunc deambulat in paradiso deus, quando divinas scripturas lego.*[68] Whether by Ambrose's almost obsession to transmit a Latin biblical text faithful to the Greek Vorlage that he had at hand, as we have seen above in his treatment of the text of Sirach or by his attempt to teach and explain the Scriptures by means of his innumerable allegorical interpretations of an enigmatic text like the Canticum Canticorum, Ambrose has not failed us because his exegesis was carried out without any great pretence of his learning but rather with simplicity and clarity.

68. AM *Ep*. 33.3 (230,20).

Sir 51,1–12: Anhang oder Knotenpunkt?

Werner Urbanz

Die Verbindung von Weisheit und Gebet ist ein Spezifikum der Lehren des Sirachbuches. Reflexionen über und Praxis des Gebetes durchziehen das Buch und verdichten sich im lyrisch gehaltenen Finale.[1] Von den vielen Fragen, die dieses Kapitel aufwirft, soll im Folgenden jenen nach dem Zusammenhang und Verhältnis von Sir 51,1–12 mit dem Buchganzen nachgegangen werden.[2] Dabei werden einzelne Aspekte,[3] besonders

1. Walter Baumgartner, "Die literarischen Gattungen in der Weisheit des Jesus Sirach," *ZAW* 34 (1914): 193–94. Die hymnischen Teile des Buches sorgen nicht nur für Abwechslung, sondern vermögen „die Mannigfaltigkeit der Stimmungen einer höher entwickelten und darum komplizierteren Zeit wenigstens annähernd zum Ausdruck zu bringen" (195).

2. Zählung des Textes nach Friedrich V. Reiterer, *Zählsynopse zum Buch Ben Sira*, mit Renate Egger-Wenzel, Ingrid Krammer, Petra Ritter-Müller, and Lutz Schrader, Fontes et Subsidia ad Bibliam pertinentes 1 (Berlin: de Gruyter, 2003). Angabe der Textformen: SirH (hebräisch), SirG (griechisch), SirS (syrisch) und SirL (lateinisch) und tlw. mit hochgestellten Buchstaben für die entsprechenden Textzeugen z. B. SirH^{B} für hebräische Textform in Handschrift B aus der Geniza in Kairo. Wird nur auf eine Handschrift hingewiesen, wird die Abkürzung „MS" verwendet (z. B. MS B für: Handschrift B aus der Geniza in Kairo).

3. Eine umfassende Behandlung des Textes Sir 51,1–12 bietet Antonio José Guerra Martínez, *El poder de la oración. Estudio de Sir 51,1-12*, Asociación Bíblica Española 50 (Estella, Navarra: Verbo Divino, 2010). Eine breite Diskussion zu den verschiedenen Texten zeigt sehr anschaulich der Vorabdruck von Sir 51 in der geplanten Neuausgabe der Jerusalemer Bibel (La Bible en ses Traditions): Maurice Gilbert and Françoise Mies, "Siracide," *La Bible En Ses Traditions: Définitions Suivies De Douze Études*, hrsg. Ecole Biblique Jérusalem (Paris: Gabalda; Leuven: Peeters, 2010), 128–49 unter URL: http://tinyurl.com/SBL060467g. Wesentlich sind weiters die Beiträge von: Maurice Gilbert, "L'action De Grâce De Ben Sira (si 51,1–12)," in *Ce dieu qui vient: Études sur l'Ancien et le Nouveau Testament offertes au professeur Bernard Renaud à l'occasion de son soixante-cinquième anniversaire*, hrsg. Raymond Kuntzmann, LD 159

unter Berücksichtigung der hebräischen und griechischen Texttraditionen in den Blick genommen.[4] Pointiert formuliert könnte man fragen: Ist dieser Text einfach nur ein Anhang, ohne den das Buch auch gelesen und verstanden werden kann oder ist er ein Knotenpunkt wie jener am Ende eines Webteppichs, den man nicht einfach wegschneiden kann, ohne das ganze Gewebe, den Textus, aufzulösen?

(Paris: Cerf, 1995), 231–42 speziell zu Sir 51,1–12 und Maurice Gilbert, "Prayer in the Book of Ben Sira: Function and Relevance," in *Prayer from Tobit to Qumran: Inaugural Conference of the ISDCL at Salzburg, Austria, 5–9 July 2003*, hrsg. Renate Egger-Wenzel and Jeremy Corley, DCLY 2004 (Berlin: de Gruyter, 2004), 117–35, zur Frage nach den Gebeten in Sir. – Alexander A. Di Lella, "Sirach 51:1–12: Poetic Structure and Analysis of Ben Sira's Psalm," *CBQ* 48 (1986): 395–407 mit Blick auf SirH 51,1–12. – Jan Liesen, "First-Person Passages in the Book of Ben Sira," *PIBA* 20 (1997): 24–47. Otto Mulder, "Three Psalms or Two Prayers in Sirach 51? The End of Ben Sira's Book of Wisdom," in Egger-Wenzel und Corley, *Prayer from Tobit to Qumran*, 171–201 für das ganze Kapitel 51. – Maria Carmela Palmisano, "La Prière de Ben Sira dans les Manuscrits Hébreux et dans les Versions Anciennes," in *The Texts and Versions of the Book of Ben Sira: Transmission and Interpretation*, hrsg. Jan Joosten and Jean-Sébastien Rey, JSJSup 150 (Leiden: Brill, 2011), 281–96 zu den Gebeten Sir 36 und Sir 51,1–12 im Vergleich der Textformen. – Werner Urbanz, *Gebet im Sirachbuch: Zur Terminologie von Klage und Lob in der griechischen Texttradition*, HBS 60 (Freiburg im Breisgau: Herder, 2009), 250–80 für SirG.

4. Bezüglich der anderen Versionen ist besonders SirS zu nennen, der viele Lücken aufweist und vor allem die Aspekte der Klage streicht, welche das Gebet provozierten. Damit wird es aber zu einem Dankgebet, das bei jeglicher Rettung aus tödlicher Bedrohung verwendet werden kann; Maurice Gilbert, "Methodological and Hermeneutical Trends in Modern Exegeses on the Book of Ben Sira," in *The Wisdom of Ben Sira: Studies on Tradition, Redaction, and Theology*, hrsg. Angelo Passaro and Giuseppe Bellia, DCLS 1 (Berlin: de Gruyter, 2008), 6. Ähnlich Maurice Gilbert, "Oú en sont les études sur Ben Sira?," *Bib* 92 (2011): 168.—Maurice Gilbert, "The Vetus Latina of Ecclesiasticus," in *Studies in the Book of Ben Sira. Papers of the Third International Conference on the Deuterocanonical Books, Shime'on Centre, Pápa, Hungary, 18–20 May 2006*, hrsg. Géza G. Xeravits and József Zsengellér, JSJSup 127 (Leiden: Brill, 2008), 3–4 verweist darauf, dass in SirG und SirL die Unterschiede in der Anrede verschwinden. Zudem übernimmt SirL „strange readings" aus SirG (51,6a.10a).—Weitere Vergleiche zu SirS und SirL bei Palmisano, "La Prière," 294–94 sowie bei Guerra Martínez, *El poder*, 226–30 und im Kontext vieler Einzelauslegungen.

1. SirH^B 51,1–12d und seine Textgliederungsmerkmale

Seit der Veröffentlichung der Internetseite http://www.bensira.org/ wurde der Zugang zu digitalisierten Aufnahmen der hebräischen Textfragmente ungemein erleichtert.[5] Der Text Sir 51,1–12 findet sich in der mittelalterlichen Handschrift B aus der Geniza in Kairo.[6] MS B zeigt den Text in einer kolographischen Gliederung mit jeweils einem Sof Pasuq am zweiten Kolon-Ende.[7] Die Handschrift kennt an anderen Stellen Gliederungsanzeiger durch Leerzeilen,[8] tlw. auch durch Überschriften.[9] Auffallenderweise wird zwischen dem Ende von Kap. 50 und dem Beginn von Kap. 51 keinerlei Gliederung gesetzt. Der Kapitelwechsel vollzieht sich beinahe unscheinbar inmitten derselben Zeile nur im Rahmen des Kolonwechsels.[10] Josef Oesch, der sich in seinem Beitrag in der Festschrift für Johannes Marböck eingehend mit der Textdarstellung in den hebr. Handschriften beschäftigt hat, bemerkt vorsichtig dazu: „Singulär ist XXr10, wo der Text von 51,1 unmittelbar nach 50,28b mitten in der Zeile beginnt, am Ort, wo sonst das Spatium zwischen den beiden Kola steht. Sollte mit diesem engen Anschluss des Dankpsalms an das ›Schlusswort‹ in 50,27–29 der Eindruck vermieden werden, er gehöre nicht mehr zum Sirachbuch?"[11]

---

5. Veröffentlichung im Dezember 2013 durch Gary A. Rendsburg and Jacob Binstein vom Department of Jewish Studies der Rutgers University in New Brunswick, NJ, U.S.A.

6. Folio XX recto und verso (20r:10 bis 20v:11).

7. Für einen Überblick über die Textdarstellungen aller MS in SirH siehe Josef M. Oesch, "Textdarstellungen in den Hebräischen Sirachhandschriften," in *Auf den Spuren Der Schriftgelehrten Weisen: Festschrift für Johannes Marböck anlässlich seiner Emeritierung*, hrsg. Irmtraud Fischer et al., BZAW 331 (Berlin: de Gruyter, 2003), 307–24. Eine kolographische Textdarstellung wie SirH^B findet sich auch in SirH^M.

8. Als Bsp. listet Oesch, "Textdarstellungen," 320–22 eine Leerzeile vor 10,18; 11,10 (mit Ausradierung); 16,6 (mit Ausradierung); 38,1; 38,24; 42,9; 42,15; 51,13.—Diese Gliederungsebenen finden sich in den anderen hebr. MS nur zum Teil. Daher ist die Gliederung von MS B nur ein Element!

9. Oesch, "Textdarstellungen," 320–22. Überschriften nur in SirH^B vor 31,12 (מוסר לחם ויין יחדו) in der Mitte der ersten Zeile; 41,16 (מוסר בשת) zu Überschrift korrigiert und 44,1 (שבח אבות עולם). Einzig in einer Lakune in SirH^M könnte unter Umständen eine Überschrift angenommen werden; Oesch, "Textdarstellungen," 322 Anm. 60.

10. אהללך אלהי ישעי אודך אלהי אבי (*Kapitelwechsel*) כי יראת ייי חיים (SirH^B 20r:10).

11. Oesch, "Textdarstellungen," 316 Anm. 40. Eine hervorragende Zusammen-

Ein Blick auf die Einbettung von V 12, dem Ende des Textes in seinem Kontext von MS B zeigt ein leicht anderes Bild. In $SirH^B$ 20v:11–12 beginnt der folgende Textbereich, die sog. Litanei (51,12e+–zj+)[12] mit einer neuen Zeile. Die Besonderheit liegt aber hier in einem Zeichen am rechten Zeilenrand der Handschrift, direkt neben dem Beginn der Litanei: Dieses Zeichen, es sieht aus wie der hebräische Buchstabe Pe, der oben drei Punkte—vergleichbar mit dem Akzent S^{e}gōltā—direkt über dem Buchstaben, in nach oben spitzer „Dreiecksform“ trägt.[13]

Dieses Zeichen findet sich viermal in MS B: 36,1 (6v:0 in der Mitte über dem Text); 36,23 (6v:17 nach dem Gebet am Rand); 38,13 (8v:0 am oberen Blattrand in der Mitte über dem Text); 51,12e+ (20v:12 am rechten Blatt-Rand). Josef Oesch beurteilt die Zeichen aufgrund des anderen Schrifttyps als sekundäre Textgliederungsmerkmale, die sich übrigens in dieser Form nur in MS B finden.[14]

Vor 36,1 (6v:0) markiert das Zeichen klar den Einsatz einer neuen Einheit, welche ein Gebet ist, und auch deren Ende, bzw. der neue Abschnitt beginnend mit 36,23 (6v:17) wird so markiert.[15] Nach 51,12d und vor dem Beginn von 51,12e+ markiert es ebenfalls einen Übergang im Umfeld von Gebeten. Der Beleg oberhalb von 38,13 ist rätselhafter, weil er hier am Ende der Arztperikope (38,1–15) einen Akzent setzt, ohne dass man direkt einen neuen Abschnitt erkennen könnte.[16] Aufgrund der anderen drei Vorkommen, in welchen die Thematik Gebet eine Rolle

---

schau der Erklärungsversuche bietet Marko Marttila, *Foreign Nations in the Wisdom of Ben Sira: A Jewish Sage between Opposition and Assimilation*, DCLS 13 (Berlin: de Gruyter, 2012), 131–32.

12. Pancratius C. Beentjes, *The Book of Ben Sira in Hebrew: A Text Edition of All Extant Hebrew Manuscripts and a Synopsis of All Parallel Hebrew Ben Sira Texts*, VTSup 66 (Leiden: Brill, 1997), zählt 12a–o.

13. Oesch, "Textdarstellungen," 317 verweist darauf, dass die drei Punkte über dem Zeichen auf eine („damals“) bekannte Abkürzung hinweisen, welche Oesch bis dato noch nicht in anderen MS identifizieren konnte.

14. Einzig die Fragmente aus Massada ($SirH^M$) zeigen weitere Randzeichen; Oesch, "Textdarstellungen," 311–12.

15. Maria Carmela Palmisano, *"Salvaci, Dio dell'universo!" Studio dell'eucologia di Sir 36H,1–17*, AnBib 163 (Rome: Biblical Institute Press, 2006), 50 and 58.—Theophil Middendorp, *Die Stellung Jesus Ben Siras zwischen Judentum und Hellenismus* (Leiden: Brill, 1973), 126, sieht in diesem Zeichen auch einen Hinweis auf den sekundären Charakter des Gebets.

16. Vor 38,1 steht eine Leerzeile.

spielt, vermutet Oesch, dass es sich auch in 38,13 ähnlich verhält, und man das Zeichen verstehen könnte als einen Hinweis auf ein besonderes Stichwort wie z. B. עתר *flehen, beten* in 38,14. Oder es weist, da es auch etwas leichter und feiner geschrieben ist, auf den Textabschnitt über den Schriftgelehrten hin (38,24–41,15).[17]

Wir sehen also, dass das Ende des Textes Sir 51,1–12d bzw. der Anfang des nachfolgenden Textstückes im Unterschied zum Beginn markiert ist.

Hier sei auch kurz auf das Ende von Sir 51,12zj+, der in MS B angefügten Litanei geblickt. Dort wird vor 51,13 (in 21r:9) eine Leerzeile gesetzt, ein starkes Gliederungszeichen (das letzte vor dem prosaisch geschrieben Kolophon in 51,30). Damit schließt sich auch ein großer Bogen zur letzten vorherigen Leerzeile in 42,15 bzw. der Überschrift am oberen Seitenrand mit dem Beginn von 44,1 (שבח אבות עולם).

SirH 51,1–12d zählt also in MS B zum bezeichneten Großzusammenhang ab Sir 42,15[18] bzw. 44,1. Der direkte Übergang von Kap. 50 zu 51 könnte wirklich den Zusammenhang der Texte hervorheben wollen. Die Endmarkierung durch das gekennzeichnete Pe weist gerne auf Gebetstexte hin, zumindest eindeutig mit den Belegen in 36,1 und 36,23.

2. SirG 51,1–12d und seine Überschrift

Der Beginn von Sir 51,1 ist in den großen griechischen Unzial-Codices (B, S, A) durch eine eigene kleine Überschrift markiert: 51Ü: Προσευχὴ Ἰησου Υἱοῦ Σιραχ „Gebet des Jesus, des Sohnes des Sirach".[19] Rahlfs verweist in der

17. Oesch, "Textdarstellungen," 317. Vor 38,24 steht eine Leerzeile.

18. Maurice Gilbert, "The Review of History in Ben Sira 44–50 and Wisdom 10–19," *Rewriting Biblical History: Essays on Chronicles and Ben Sira in honor of Pancratius C. Beentjes*, hrsg. Jeremy Corley and Harm van Grol, DCLS 7 (Berlin: de Gruyter, 2011), 324 zu Sir 51,1–12 und 51,13–30: „these two texts also praise the Lord, which started in *Sir* 42,15. It seems to me that, at the time of Ben Sira, sacred history does not end with Simon, but with the wisdom master and his disciples".

19. Siehe dazu Georg Sauer, *Jesus Sirach / Ben Sira*, ATD.A 1 (Göttingen: Vandenhoeck & Ruprecht, 2000), 344 Anm. 2 mit der Diskussion um die Verfasserschaft von Sir 51.—Interessant ist weiter die Frage nach der Stellung des Sirachbuches in den Handschriften selbst; dazu Friedrich Vinzenz Reiterer, "Die Differenz zwischen Urtext und Ausgangstext: Beispiele zur Entwicklung der sirazidischen Versionen," in *From Qumran to Aleppo: A Discussion with Emanuel Tov about the Textual History of Jewish Scriptures in Honor of His 65th Birthday*, hrsg. Armin Lange et al., FRLANT 230 (Göttingen: Vandenhoeck & Ruprecht, 2009), 124 Anm. 5: Sir ist in B beinahe in der Mitte,

Anm. zu 18,30 auf mehrere Überschriften im Sir-Buch,[20] die er selbst nie oben im Text abdruckt, welche aber zu einem großen Teil (bei eindeutigerer Quellenlage) Ziegler in seine Wiedergabe (mit Unzialen) übernimmt und ihnen somit einen prominenten Platz einräumt.[21] Sir 51Ü markiert also nach 44,1, der Einleitung zum Väterlob, einen neuen Abschnitt, bzw. macht auf einen besonderen Inhalt aufmerksam. Dieser ist mit Προσευχή klar als Gebet benannt.[22] Genauer bestimmt wird es aber durch den Hinweis auf den Urheber, der hier als Jesus, Sohn des Sirach (ιησου υιου σ[ε]ιραχ) eingeführt wird. Damit wird auf den Prolog Sir 0,5 verwiesen, wo vom Großvater Jesus (ὁ πάππος μου Ἰησοῦς) die Rede ist, und zugleich wird tlw. das Kolo-

---

in S das vorletzte Buch vor Ijob und in A das vorletzte Buch vor PsSal.—Die Textgestaltung im Sinaiticus ist durch die neugestaltete Web-Seite nachvollziehbar: http://www.codexsinaiticus.org. Stelle: Sirach, 50:14–51:8 library: BL folio: 184b scribe: A.

20. Überschriften nach Rahlfs: Buch-Überschrift σοφια ιησου υιου σ(ε)ιραχ (S A); σοφια σειραχ (B); 18,30 εγκρατ(ε)ια ψυχης; 20,27 λογοι παραβολων; 23,7 παιδεια στοματος; 24,1 αινεσις σοφιας (B); σοφιας αινεσις (SA= Ziegler); 30,1 περι τεκνων; 30,14 περι υγιαιας (Bscompl.) (nicht in Ziegler); 30,16 περι βρωματων (B*S=Ziegler); περι υγιας (As†); 32,1 περι ηγουμενων (Bs[†]) (nicht in Ziegler); 33,25 περι δουλων (Bs) (nicht in Ziegler); 44,1 πατερων υμνος; 51,1 προσευχη ιησου υιου σ(ε)ιραχ.

21. Ergänzt wird der Hinweis aus Rahlfs durch die Buchüberschrift in den MS; darauf weist Mulder "Three Psalms," 175 hin.—Eine Übersicht zu einem griech. MS mit mehr Überschriften als bei Rahlfs bietet Hilaire Duesberg and Irénée Fransen, *Ecclesiastico*, La Sacra Bibbia (Torino: Marietti: 1966), 352–53 als Appendice IV „Titoli" Greci nach MS Γ51 vom Athos (vermittelt durch M. Richard). Hierbei einschlägig Sir 23,1 Εὐχή προς θεόν, Sir 36,1 Εὐχή προς ἐθνῶν und Sir 36,11–17 Εὐχή περὶ τοῦ Ἰσραήλ.

22. Eine genauere Bestimmung, was hier mit προσευχή verbunden wird bleibt noch offen. Inhaltlich geht es ja um die Schilderung der Not als auch um das Lob für die Errettung, weshalb man allgemein von Psalm sprechen oder auch die Begriffe Danklied bzw. berichtendes Loblied heranziehen könnte. Jan Liesen, *Full of Praise: An Exegetical Study of Sir 39,12–35*, JSJSup 64 (Leiden: Brill, 2000), 75 sieht 51Ü als ungewöhnliches Vorkommen von προσευχή im Sir-Buch, da es sonst eher im Klage- und Sündenkontext zu finden ist.—Siehe zur Beschreibung der Gattung sehr treffend Markus Witte, "Schriften (ketubim)," *Grundinformation Altes Testament: Eine Einführung in Literatur, Religion und Geschichte des Alten Testaments*, hrsg. Jan C. Gertz, UTB 2745 (Göttingen: Vandenhoeck & Ruprecht, 2010), 425–26.—Maurice Gilbert, "Wisdom and Cult according to Ben Sira," *Ben Sira: Recueil D' Études—Collected Essays*, BEThL 264 (Leuven: Peeters, 2014), 286 etwas anders: „the thanksgiving in 51,1–12 does not even have the literary structure of the psalms of that literary genre".—Herman Ludin Jansen, *Die spätjüdische Psalmendichtung ihr Entstehungskreis und ihr „Sitz im Leben": Eine literaturgeschichtlich-soziologische Untersuchung*, SNVAO.HF 3 (Oslo: Dybwad, 1937), 65 nennt ihn den klassischsten Psalm im Buche.

phon aus 50,27 mit Jesus, Sohn des Sirach, des Eleazar, des Jerusalemers (LXX.D)[23] (Ιησοῦς υἱὸς Σιραχ Ελεαζαρ ὁ Ιεροσολυμίτης) wiederholt.[24]

Die größte Nähe weist Sir 51Ü mit dem Titel des Gesamt-Buches in den griechischen MSS auf: σοφια ιησου υιου σ(ε)ιραχ. Damit wird ein großer Bogen an den Beginn des Buches geschlagen und eine Klammer um das ganze Buch gelegt. Die Weisheit (des Anfangs) wird aber am Ende in Sir 51 zum Gebet bzw. mit diesem in der Person des Jesus Sirach verbunden.

Interessant ist über das Sir-Buch hinausgehend die Frage, inwieweit der Begriff προσευχή sonst noch in Überschriften von Gebeten in der LXX Verwendung findet. In den Psalmen(-überschriften)[25] findet sich Προσευχὴ τοῦ Δαυιδ Ps 17(16); … τῷ Δαυιδ Ps 86(85); … τοῦ Μωυσῆ ἀνθρώπου τοῦ θεοῦ Ps 90(89); … τῷ πτωχῷ Ps 102(101) und in Ps 142(141) Συνέσεως τῷ Δαυιδ ἐν τῷ εἶναι αὐτὸν ἐν τῷ σπηλαίῳ· προσευχή. Aber auch außerhalb der Psalmen finden sich im AT noch Beispiele wie Jes 38,9 Προσευχὴ Εζεκιου βασιλέως τῆς Ιουδαίας und Hab 3,1 Προσευχὴ Αμβακουμ τοῦ προφήτου μετὰ ᾠδῆς. 2 Chr 33,18 und 19 erwähnt ein Gebet König Manasses (V18 καὶ τὰ λοιπὰ τῶν λόγων Μανασση καὶ ἡ προσευχὴ αὐτοῦ).[26] Damit zeigt sich

23. Eve-Marie Becker and Michael Reitemeyer, "Sophia Sirach," *Septuaginta Deutsch: Das Griechische Alte Testament in deutscher Übersetzung*, hrsg. Wolfgang Kraus and Martin Karrer (Stuttgart: Deutsche Bibelgesellschaft, 2009), 1090–1163.

24. Zur Gesamtproblematik der Namensnennung siehe Eve-Marie Becker et al., "Sophia Sirach: Ben Sira / Ecclesiasticus / Das Buch Jesus Sirach," in *Psalmen bis Daniel*, Bd. 2 von *Septuaginta Deutsch: Erläuterungen und Kommentare zum Griechischen Alten Testament*, hrsg. Martin Karrer and Wolfgang Krauss (Stuttgart: Deutsche Bibelgesellschaft, 2011), 2266 sowie Friedrich V. Reiterer, "Jesus Sirach / Jesus Sirachbuch / Ben Sira / Ecclesiasticus," in *"Die Vollendung der Gottesfurcht ist Weisheit" [Sir 21,11]: Studien zum Buch Ben Sira [Jesus Sirach]*, hrsg. Friedrich V. Reiterer, SBAB 50 (Stuttgart: Katholisches Bibelwerk, 2011), 13–14. Christian Wagner, *Die Septuaginta-Hapaxlegomena im Buch Jesus Sirach: Untersuchungen zur Wortwahl und Wortbildung unter besonderer Berücksichtigung des textkritischen und übersetzungstechnischen Aspekts*, BZAW 282 (Berlin: de Gruyter, 1999), 48, wirft die interessante Frage auf, ob man hier in Sir 50,27 wirklich davon sprechen kann, den ersten echten Verfassernamen der Bibel vor sich zu haben. Diese Beobachtung kommt aus dem Vergleich von SirH^{B} und SirS in 50,27, wo ja die Angaben des Verfassernamens in SirS fehlen und von daher die Frage auftaucht, ob bereits in GrI oder erst in GrII diese Angabe zu finden war.

25. Klammerziffern geben die LXX-Zählung wieder. Zit. nach Rahlfs.

26. Hier ergibt sich auch eine Verbindung zu Oden 12 (Προσευχὴ Μανασση) und dem ganzen Buch der Oden, reich an „Gebeten" (n. Rahlfs): 3,0 Προσευχὴ Αννας μητρὸς Σαμουηλ; Ode. 4,1 Προσευχὴ Αμβακουμ. Ode. 5,0 Προσευχὴ Ησαιου. Ode. 6,0

auf dieser Ebene, dass ein Überschriftstitel mit „Gebet“ keine Ausnahme in der LXX darstellt, wenngleich (dies) nicht sehr häufig zu finden ist, ja nicht einmal in den Psalmen. Aus den genannten Stellen werden aber Davidsbezüge (Ps 17; 86; 142) deutlich. Ebenso hätte der Bezug auf Mose (Ps 90) einen besonderen Charme für einen Weisheitslehrer, dem die Tora sehr am Herzen liegt. Man denke eventuell neben Ps 90 auch an das Buch Dtn mit dem Lied (Dtn 31,30–32,44) und Segen (Dtn 33,1–29) des Mose in der Finalposition des Buches.

Die Überschrift am Beginn von Sir 51 in den griechischen MSS hebt diesen Text hervor. Die Titulierung als *προσευχή* ist singulär in den Überschriften des Buches und auch thematisch von den sonst stärker an weisheitlichen Traktaten geprägten Titeln unterschieden. Insofern wird ein besonderer Akzent gerade am Buchende gesetzt und damit auch ein großer Bogen zurück sowohl in die erste Unterschrift in 50,27 als auch an die Überschrift des Buches in den griechischen MSS bzw. bis in den Prolog (0,5) hinein gezogen.

Anfang und Ende sind hier also sehr stark verwoben, auch im Hinblick darauf, wer nochmals das letzte Wort hat und in welcher Form er es hat.

3. Die Einordnung von Sir 51,1–12d in der wissenschaftlichen Diskussion

Welchen Stellenwert hat Sir 51,1–12 für die Struktur bzw. in der Redaktionsgeschichte des Sirachbuches? Marböck hat das ganze Kapitel 51—übrigens in Parallele zu Sir 24—treffend als „crux“ im Hinblick auf diese Themen bezeichnet.[27] Viele Fragen zur Komposition(sgeschichte) des Buches sind im ganzen ja noch offen, und manche Thesen wurden vorgelegt.[28]

Προσευχὴ Ιωνα. Ode. 7,0 Προσευχὴ Αζαριου. Ode. 9,0 Προσευχὴ Μαριας τῆς θεοτόκου. Ode. 9,26 Προσευχὴ Ζαχαριου. Ode. 11,0 Προσευχὴ Εζεκιου. Ode. 12,0 Προσευχὴ Μανασση. Ode. 13,0 Προσευχὴ Συμεων.

27. Johannes Marböck, “Structure and Redaction History of the Book of Ben Sira. Review and Prospects,” in *The Book of Ben Sira in Modern Research: Proceedings of the First International Ben Sira Conference 28–31 July 1996, Soesterberg, Netherlands*, hrsg. Pancratius C. Beentjes, BZAW 255 (Berlin: de Gruyter, 1997), 78.

28. Einen guten Überblick bieten dazu Katja Tesch, *Weisheitsunterricht bei Ben Sira: Lehrkonzepte im Sirachbuch und ihre Relevanz für heutiges Lernen im Religionsunterrich*, BBB 169 (Göttingen: V&R Unipress, 2013), 60–62, Marttila, *Foreign Nations*, 15–16, Bradley C. Gregory, *Like an Everlasting Signet Ring: Generosity in the Book of*

Bezüglich der gliedernden Elemente des Buches—ich folge hier zunächst Marböck—werden klassisch Weisheitsperikopen als gewichtige Marksteine gesehen.[29] Weiter weisen die sog. autobiographischen Notizen (Ich-Texte: vgl. 16,24–25; 24,30–33; 33,16–18.19; 39,12.32; 50,27Gr; 51,13–22.27 sowie Gebete in der 1. Person wie 22,27–23,6; 51,1–12)[30] sowie ein äußerer (1,1–10; 51,13–30) und innerer (2,1–18; 51,1–12) Rahmen auf gliedernde Elemente hin.[31] Marböck sieht gerade Gebetstexte an gewichtigen Positionen im Buche verteilt (vgl. u. a. 2,18 u. 51,1–12;

Sirach, DCLS 2 (Berlin: de Gruyter, 2010), 19–24 sowie Charles Buttigieg, "The Book of Ben Sira: Connecting the Jews All Over the Greek World," *ScrB* 44 (2014): 12–13. Besonders einschlägig und umfangreich Jeremy Corley, "Searching for Structure and Redaction in Ben Sira: An Investigation of Beginnings and Endings," in *The Wisdom of Ben Sira. Studies on Tradition, Redaction, and Theology*, hrsg. Angelo Passaro and Giuseppe Bellia, DCLS 1 (Berlin: de Gruyter, 2008), 21–47 bes. 34–35 Anm. 43.—Lutz Schrader, *Leiden und Gerechtigkeit: Studien zu Theologie und Textgeschichte des Sirachbuches*, BBET 27 (Frankfurt am Main: Lang, 1994), 58–68 fasst die „ältere" Diskussion gut zusammen.—Vgl. auch den Ansatz zur Gliederung des Gesamtbuches von Michael Reitemeyer, *Weisheitslehre als Gotteslob. Psalmentheologie im Buch Jesus Sirach*, BBB 127 (Berlin: Philo, 2000), 17–48.—Auf den hypothetischen Charakter aller Rekonstruktionen weist deutlich Marttila, *Foreign Nations*, 16 hin.—Benjamin G. Wright, "Preliminary Thoughts about Preparing the Text of Ben Sira for a Commentary," *Die Septuaginta—Text, Wirkung, Rezeption. 4. Internationale Fachtagung Veranstaltet von Septuaginta Deutsch (LXX.D), Wuppertal 19.–22. Juli 2012*, hrsg. Wolfgang Kraus and Siegfried Kreuzer, WUNT 325 (Tübingen: Mohr Siebeck, 2014), 106 fragt hierbei zurecht ob unsere Vorstellungen vom Schreiben und Entstehen eines Buches für das Verständnis dieses Prozesses hilfreich sind.

29. Johannes Marböck, *Jesus Sirach 1–23*, HthKAT (Freiburg im Breisgau: Herder, 2010), 27: Sir 1,1–10; 4,11–19; 6,18–37; 14,20–15,10; 19,20–30; 24; 32,14–33,18; 38,24–39,11; 51,13–30.—Einen Blick auf die Gliederungseinheiten verschiedener moderner Autoren und syrischer MS werfen Konrad Jenner and W. Th. van Peursen, "Unit Deltimitations and the Text of Ben Sira," in *Studies in Scriptural Unit Division*, hrsg. Marjo C. A. Korpel and Josef M. Oesch, Pericope 3 (Assen: van Gorcum, 2002), 144–201.

30. Frank Ueberschaer, *Weisheit aus der Begegnung. Bildung nach dem Buch Ben Sira*, BZAW 379 (Berlin: de Gruyter, 2007), 299, betont ebenfalls die Bedeutung der Selbstaussagen, meint aber in Anm. 9 dazu: „Eine Ausnahme sind die Gebete in Sir 23,1–6; 36,1–17; 51,1–12, in denen Ben Sira ebenfalls ein ›Ich‹ bzw. ein ›Wir‹ verwendet. Dabei handelt es sich wahrscheinlich jedoch um eine literarische Verwendung der 1.Person, wie sie sich auch in den Psalmen findet, und nicht um eine autobiographisch auswertbare."

31. Johannes Marböck, "Das Buch Jesus Sirach," in *Einleitung in das Alte Testament*, hrsg. Erich Zenger and Christian Frevel; 8. Aufl., KStTh 1,1 (Stuttgart: Kohlhammer, 2012), 499.

22,27–23,6; 36,1–17; 42,15; 44,1–2; 45,26–27; 50,22–24).[32] Sir 51,1–12 ist also in zweifacher Hinsicht bedeutsam, als Gebetstext und als Gebetstext in 1. Person (vgl. Sir 36 als Wir-Gebet).

Im Rahmen einer Redaktiongeschichte spielt Sir 51,1–12 als Text im Schlusskapitel eine Rolle. Wenn man mehrere Editionen des Buches annimmt, stellt sich die Frage, ab wann Sir 51,1–12 dazu gehört. Bei Corley in seiner fünfstufigen Editionsrekonstruktion ist es ab der dritten Stufe (1,1–38,23 und 51,1–30) dabei.[33] Bei Roth ist es Teil der Erstausgabe (1,1–23,27 und 51,1–30 in Parallele zum Sprüchebuch).[34] Damit verknüpft stellt sich auch verschärft die Frage, ob das Buch in seiner Anordnung, und damit die Texte in Kapitel 51 bzw. zumindest Teile dessen, von dem Jerusalemer Weisen stammt oder nicht, und wenn nicht von ihm, von wem dann?[35] Hier gibt es eine große Breite an Positionen: Für Otto Mulder ist Ben Sira „undoubtedly the author of this individual psalm of thanksgiving“[36] in

---

32. Marböck, *Jesus Sirach*, 499.—Vgl. Corley, "Searching for Structure," 34–36 und seine acht Einheiten beginnend und endend mit Weisheitsperikopen (als Adaptation von Patrick William Skehan and Alexander Di Lella, *The Wisdom of Ben Sira: A New Translation with Notes*, AB 39 (New York: Doubleday, 1987), xiii–xvi und in Bezugnahme auf John D. Harvey, "Toward a Degree of Order in Ben Sira's Book," *ZAW* 105 (1993): 52–62.—Den hohen Stellenwert der Gebete für den Gesamttext streichen viele Arbeiten der „Gilbert-Schule“ heraus: Gilbert, "Prayer," ; Nuria Calduch-Benages, *En el crisol de la prueba. Estudio exegético de Sir 2,1–18*, Asociación Bíblica Española 32 (Estella, Navarra: Verbo Divino, 1997); Liesen, *Praise*; Palmisano, *"Salvaci"*; Renato de Zan, *Il culto che Dio gradisce: Studio del "Trattato sulle offerte" di SirGr 34,21–35,20*, AnBib 190 (Rome: Gregorian & Biblical Press, 2011).

33. Corley, "Searching for Structure," 41–44: (1) 1,1–23,27 und 51,13–30; (2) 1,1–32,3 und 51,13–30; (3) 1,1–38,23 und 51,1–30; (4) 1,1–43,33 und 51,1–30; (5) 1,1–51,30.

34. Wolfgang Roth, "On the Gnomic-Discursive Wisdom of Jesus Ben Sirach," *Semeia* 17 (1980), 60.—Vgl. dazu auch Gilbert, "Oú en sont les études," 173, wo er den Zusammenhang von Sir 1–2 und Sir 51 betont (1//51,13–30 und 2//51,1–12).

35. Vgl. u. a. Tesch, *Weisheitsunterricht*, 64–65.—Middendorp, *Stellung*. Ausführlich bei Guerra Martínez, *El poder*, 21–33.—Bénédicte Lemmelijn, "Wisdom of Life as Way of Life: The Wisdom of Jesus Sirach as a Case in Point," *OTE* 27 (2014): 458–59 übt sich in großer Zurückhaltung bezüglich der Gliederungsversuche. Ähnlich auch Richard J. Coggins, *Sirach*, Guides to Apocrypha and Pseudepigrapha (Sheffield: Sheffield Academic, 1998), 25.

36. Mulder, "Three Psalms," 180 und 196: „Ben Sira should be conceived as the poet of the closing part of his book (42:15–51,30), not only of the Praise of the Creator and the Praise of the Fathers, but also of the Appendix with three psalms at the end of his book in Sir 51, based on content and the delimiter model“.

SirH 51,1–12.[37] Oftmals findet man einen Kompromiss, indem in Sir 51,1–12 „ein persönliches Bekenntnis Sirachs aus einer späteren Lebensphase“[38] gesehen wird und somit zwar Sirach als Autor gerettet, aber zugleich auch eine gewisse Unterscheidung zum Buch-Rest nicht weggewischt wird.[39] Sir 51 wird somit eher zu einem Anhang[40] oder Nachtrag[41] bzw. zu einer Erweiterung.[42] Ein eleganter Vorschlag und eine zutreffende Lösung ist es wohl, von Sir 50,25–51,30 einfach als „Schluss“ des Buches zu sprechen.[43]

---

37. Vgl. auch Núria Calduch-Benages, "Trial Motif in the Book of Ben Sira With Special Reference to Sir 2,1–6," in Beentjes, *Book of Ben Sira in Modern Research*, 148–49. Sie betont den Aspekt des Weisen als Beispiel für seine Schüler—mit starkem Bezug zu Sir 2,1—und nennt es (149) ein „personal testimony“ „for I believe the prayer is autobiographical“.—Pancratius C. Beentjes, "God's Mercy: 'racham (pi.)', 'rachum' and 'rachamim' in the Book of Ben Sira," in *Happy the One Who Meditates on Wisdom“ (Sir. 14,20): Collected Essays on the Book of Ben Sira*, CBET 43 (Leuven: Peeters, 2006), 243 „one should consider Sir 51:1–12 authentic because of its language, form and contents“.

38. Odo Camponovo, *Königtum, Königsherrschaft und Reich Gottes in den frühjüdischen Schriften*, OBO 58 (Freibourg: Universitätsverlag; Göttingen: Vandenhoeck & Ruprecht, 1984), 135.—Marböck, "Das Buch Jesus Sirach," 503 erwähnt nur die Authentizitäts-Diskussion bzgl. Sir 36,1–17; 51,13–30b; „anders steht es bei der in Hs B überlieferten Litanei 51,12a–o“.

39. John G. Snaith, *Ecclesiasticus or the Wisdom of Jesus Son of Sirach*, CNEB (Cambridge: Cambridge University Press, 1974), 257 „ch. 51 was added later—probably by Ben Sira himself because of the similarity of style with the rest of the book“.

40. Norbert Peters, *Das Buch Jesus Sirach oder Ecclesiasticus*, EHAT 25 (Münster: Aschendorff, 1913), 437 nennt Sir 51 einen „Anhang“; wie in seinem Musterbuch Spr 31,10ff „so setzt er selbst einen Psalm als Anhang an den Schluß, der selbst wieder in seiner zweiten Hälfte (51,13–30) ein separates alphabetisches Lied ist. Das Kapitel vor 50,27 zu rücken (Fr) ist ebenso unberechtigt wie seine Echtheit zu bezweifeln“.—Von einem Anhang spricht auch Thierry Legrand, "Jesus Sirach," in *Einleitung in das Alte Testament: Die Bücher der Hebräischen Bibel und die alttestamentlichen Schriften der katholischen, protestantischen und orthodoxen Kirchen*, hrsg. Thomas Römer et al. (Zürich: Theologischer Verlag, 2013), 752, in dessen Buchgliederungsübersicht Sir 51 leider nicht extra gelistet wird.

41. Rudolf Smend, *Die Weisheit des Jesus Sirach* (Berlin: Georg Reimer, 1906), 495: „Aber sie wollen als ein Nachtrag hingenommen sein, und sie dem Grossvater abzusprechen, besteht kein Grund. Vielmehr zeugt ihre Sprache und Form, aber auch ihr Inhalt (vgl. zu V. 12 add.) laut für ihre Echtheit“.

42. Burkard M. Zapff, *Jesus Sirach 25–51*, NEchtB 39 (Würzburg: Echter, 2010), 399 nennt Sir 51 das „erweiterte Sirachbuch“.

43. Markus Witte, "Jesus Sirach (ben Sira)," in *Grundinformation Altes Testament: Eine Einführung in Literatur, Religion und Geschichte des Alten Testaments*, hrsg. Jan

Freilich gibt es auch noch genügend Stimmen, die gegen eine Autorschaft Sirachs für diese Kapitel votieren.[44] Immer wieder taucht auch die Vermutung auf, der Enkel sei der Autor[45] oder habe zumindest das Material, das er vorfand, zusammengestellt.[46]

Für manche Auslegenden wird sogar ein Sitz im Leben sichtbar. Gilbert kann sich Sir 51,1–12 als Gebet in einer Zeremonie im Tempel vorstellen[47] und trifft sich damit auch mit Oda Wischmeyer, für die sich in Sir 51,1–12 der priesterlich-levitische Tempelgottesdienst der nachexilischen Zeit spiegelt.[48] Smend, geht davon aus, dass ein Großteil des

---

C. Gertz, UTB 2745 (Göttingen: Vandenhoeck & Ruprecht, 2010), 557.—Reitemeyer, *Weisheitslehre*, 47, spricht von Sir 51 als „überhöhenden Schlusspunkt auf der hymnischen Ebene".

44. Daniel J. Harrington, *Jesus Ben Sira of Jerusalem. A Biblical Guide to Living Wisely*, Interfaces (Collegeville, MN: Liturgical Press, 2005), 80: „But nothing in the hymn itself demands that it was written by Ben Sira, and in tone and content it is quite different from anything that Ben Sira says about himself in the body of the book".—Sauer, *Jesus Sirach*, 346: „Die Inhalte, die Ben Sira sonst in Gebeten vorträgt, sind andere, vgl. 22,27–23,6 und 36. Man darf annehmen, dass dieses Gebet eine spätere Zutat und ein Anhang an die Reden Siras darstellt".—Für Heinz-Josef Fabry, "Jesus Sirach und das Priestertum," in *Auf den Spuren Der Schriftgelehrten Weisen: Festschrift für Johannes Marböck anlässlich seiner Emeritierung*, hrsg. Irmtraud Fischer et al., BZAW 331 (Berlin: de Gruyter, 2003), 278, findet sich der Inhalt des Gebetes sonst in der Botschaft des Siraziden nicht wieder. Die Selbstaufforderung in 51,12c–d entspricht ganz der Selbstaufforderung „der aaronidischen Priester, Gott zu loben, wie sie bereits in Sir 45,25 vorliegt. Die vorliegende Selbstaufforderung zum Gebet könnte also von dorther initiiert sein und auf aaronidische Verfasser zurückgehen".—Middendorp, *Stellung*, 116.

45. Smend, *Weisheit*, 495, erwähnt die Synopse des Athanasius, die (wohl aufgrund des Ende in 50,27–29) den Enkel als Verfasser der beiden Lieder sieht.

46. Schrader, *Leiden*, 74, geht zwar nicht vom Enkel aus, doch vermutet er im Sinne einer Schultradition, dass „derjenige, der das Sirachbuch um Kapitel 51 erweiterte, den Psalm im schriftlichen Nachlaß des Verfassers vorfand."—Schrader, *Leiden*, 73–74, und Middendorp, *Stellung*, 115–16, vergleichen Sir 51 auch mit den Hodajot aus Qumran.

47. Gilbert, "L'action de Grâce," 239–40.—Etwas anders in Gilbert, "Wisdom and Cult," 286, wo er die drei Gebete erwähnt „without any connection with liturgical worship".

48. Oda Wischmeyer, *Die Kultur des Buches Jesus Sirach*, BZNW 77 (Berlin: de Gruyter, 1995), 269.—Im Kontext einer liturgischen Praxis von Sir 51 sei die Verwendung des syro-hexaplarischen Textes von SirS 51,6–11 in westsyrischen Lektionaren für die neunte Stunde am Karfreitag erwähnt; W. Th. van Peursen, "Ben Sira in the Syriac Tradition," in Joosten and Rey, *The Texts and Versions of the Book of Ben Sira*, 158.

Buches auf mündliche Vorträge zurückgeht, sei es in der Schulstube, oder auch öffentlich z. B. Sir 31,21–36,22 als Parallelgottesdienst der Frommen im Tempel. „Dort wird er auch den Psalm 51,1–12ff. rezitiert haben.“[49] Anknüpfend an die Frage nach einem mündlichen Vortrag sei auch die These von Katja Tesch erwähnt, die anregend die Frage diskutiert, ob nicht Teile von SirH auf Unterrichtsmanuskripte zurückgehen[50] und somit an der Grenze zwischen Mündlichkeit und Schriftlichkeit stehen.[51]

Ähnlich wie Jansen[52] sieht aber auch Sauer keine Bestimmbarkeit, „zu welchem Zeitpunkt Ben Sira dieses so ganz anders geartete Gebet gesprochen haben könnte.“[53] Für Smend hingegen ist ein historischer Kontext durchaus vorstellbar. Das Gebet beziehe sich auf eine Not, „die an das Ende von Sirachs Leben fällt“ und nennt die Ära Seleukos‘ IV.[54]

Als eine weitere Möglichkeit wird eine Art der „Kollektivierung“ des Gebets angenommen,[55] wenn Smend meint: „Nach alledem muss Israel

---

49. Smend, *Weisheit*, xxxvi.

50. Tesch, *Weisheitsunterricht*, 45, im Rückgriff auf u. a. Marböck, “Das Buch Jesus Sirach,” 503.—Ueberschaer, *Weisheit*, 208–11, spricht ausgehend von Sir 39,12–16 davon, dass gerade im Singen von Psalmen/Hymnen eine Form der Aneignung von Lerninhalten stattfindet, welche vielfältige Schichten des Bewusstseins zu erreichen vermag.

51. Tesch, *Weisheitsunterricht*, 151. Tesch selbst geht auf Sir 51 direkt nicht ein.

52. Jansen, *Psalmendichtung*, 137: „In Dankgebeten wie Ps. Sal. 16, Sir 51,1–12, die nicht an die gottesdienstlichen Rahmen gebunden sind, und in Klagegebeten … finden wir keine Änderungen; das ist ja ganz natürlich, da die Dichter durchaus keine erbaulich-didaktischen Zwecke darin verfolgten.“

53. Sauer, *Jesus Sirach*, 346.

54. Smend, *Weisheit*, 496.—Middendorp, *Stellung*, 116 setzt es in die Zeit der Makkabäer, verwandt den Dankgebeten aus Qumran, aber älter als diese. „Das Dankgebet gab m.E. dem Lehrbuch Ben Siras in einer veränderten Zeit einen neuen Akzent. Dieser ermöglichte die weitere Verwendung des Buches in einer fremdenfeindlichen Zeit, als das Gottesverhältnis wieder inniger und persönlicher erlebt wurde. Es spricht nichts dagegen, dass schon die Vorlage des Enkels das Gebet an seiner jetzigen Stelle enthalten hat.“ Den Aspekt der „Überarbeitung für eine Neuauflage“ skizziert in der Darstellung Middendorps auch Ueberschaer, *Weisheit*, 9.

55. Vinzenz Hamp, *Sirach*, EB 13 (Würzburg: Echter: 1954), 140: „Hier wie dort ist der Sinn zunächst wohl individuell zu verstehen, nimmt jedoch im Gemeindegebet gern, besonders in der Danksagung, universelle Züge an: Die Rettung des Beters deckt sich mit dem Ruhm des gesamten Volkes.“—Vgl. auch Josef Knabenbauer, *Commentarius in Ecclesiasticum cum appendice. Textus „Ecclesiastici“ Hebraeus descriptus secundum fragmenta nuper reperta cum notis et versione litterali Latina*, CSS 2.6 (Paris: Lethielleux 1902), 467: „Precatur itaque Sapiens nomine totius populi Dei et docet

der Betende sein, und die Farblosigkeit und Unklarheit der Schilderung erklärt sich wie in so vielen Psalmen aus der Personifikation des Volkes".[56] Die Gemeinde wird im Umfeld des Todes Seleukos IV. von den Samaritanern oder Tobiaden verleumdet.[57]

Interessant ist aus meiner Sicht, dass einige Elemente der zuvor genannten Forschungsthesen zuletzt wieder aufgenommen, aber unter anderen Prämissen interpretiert werden. Als ein Beispiel sei nur Judith Newman genannt, die nicht nur die mündliche Seite der Überlieferung betont,[58] sondern—anders als die Frage nach der Authentizität[59]—die Frage nach der Rolle des Jesus Sirach in seinem Buch als konstruierter Autor-Stimme aufwirft.[60] Dies wirkt sich auch auf Sir 51,1–12 aus: Dort (einem Text in 1. Person) „hören" wir den konstruierten Autor und die Beispielfigur des Ben Sira,[61] die ein Identifizierungsangebot auf der Suche nach Weisheit und Paideia darstellt.[62] Die Erweiterungen des Buches werden als eine Fortsetzung des Dialoges durch Gebet und der liturgischen „Performance" zwischen dem Weisen und dem Allerhöchsten verstanden.[63] Damit wird eine Weitergabe, eine Traditionskette gebildet, welche

---

Deo maximas esse agendas gratias laudesque deferendas, quia suum populum oppressum saepe et fere conculcatum benigne tutatus sit et liberaverit."

56. Smend, *Weisheit*, 496.

57. Vgl. dazu auch Hamp, *Sirach*, 140, der von „Sykophantentum vor den heidnischen Machthabern" spricht.

58. Judith H. Newman, "Liturgical Imagination in the Composition of Ben Sira," in *Prayer and Poetry in the Dead Sea Scrolls and Related Literature: Essays in Honor of Eileen Schuller on the Occasion of Her 65th Birthday*, hrsg. Jeremy Penner et al., StTDJ 98 (Leiden: Brill, 2012), 316 und bes. Anm. 15.

59. Auch Marttila, *Foreign Nations*, 1–10, mahnt hier zu einer gewissen Zurückhaltung.

60. Newman, "Liturgical Imagination," 314, auch im Rückgriff auf Benjamin G. Wright, "Ben Sira on the Sage as Exemplar," in *Praise Israel for Wisdom and Instruction: Essays on Ben Sira and Wisdom, the Letter of Aristeas and the Septuagint*, JSJSup 131 (Leiden: Brill, 2008), 165–82.

61. Newman, "Liturgical Imagination," 324.—Vgl. auch S. 319–23 "Ben Sira as Teacher and Model of Prayer."

62. Newman, "Liturgical Imagination," 325: „But the question of who has the last word is something of a trick question because the book seems to have invited others to add to the collection upon attaining their own wisdom." Dies auch im Blick auf die vielen „Abschlüsse" im Buch.

63. Ibid., 325.

vom Weisen auf seine Schüler und von diesen auf die Gemeinschaft über Generationen hinweg weitergeknüpft werden kann.[64]

In diesem Zusammenhang spielt Kap. 51 mit seiner Gebetssprache in 51,1–12 und den Tempelbezügen in 51,13ff eine wesentliche Rolle, ist es doch das Schluss-Statement des Buches—so etwas wie eine *ultima vox*.[65]

4. Stichproben zu Text-Bezügen von Sir 51,1–12d ins Sirachbuch hinein und darüber hinaus

Wenn man sich mit dem Themenkomplex der Verknüpfung von Sir 51,1–12 mit dem Buchganzen beschäftigt, ist eine Frage jene nach den Verbindungen des Gedankengutes und des Vokabulars mit dem Buchganzen. Im Bezug auf Sir 51 wird ja auch oft von einem musivischen Stil, einem Mosaikstil im Blick auf die Auswahl und Bezugnahme auf andere (bereits kanonische?) Texte, besonders die Psalmen gesprochen.[66] Im Folgenden sollen ein paar ausgewählte Stichproben aus Sir 51 solche Verbindungs-

---

64. Ibid., 326: „The work represents the triumph of the sage, and a triumph of the liturgical imagination to carry the community on in diaspora and beyond Temple destruction".

65. Ibid., 324: „one has to look beyond the review of the ancestors to the finale of the book to determine who has the last word. This is important because like the beginning of a text, its ending is also a powerful statement."—Vgl. dazu auch Matthew J. Goff, *Discerning wisdom: The Sapiential Literature of the Dead Sea Scrolls*, VTSup 116 (Leiden: Brill, 2007), 250, im Bezug auf Sir 51,13–30: „Even if Ben Sira did not write Sir 51:13–30 the poem is an appropriate conclusion to his instruction".

66. Schrader, *Leiden*, 71–73. Als Fundgrube für „Parallelstellen" erweisen sich Salomon Schechter and Charles Taylor, *The Wisdom of Ben Sira: Portions of the Book Ecclesiasticus from Hebrew Manuscripts in the Cairo Genizah Collection* (Cambridge: Cambridge University Press, 1899), 25.66–67, sowie George H. Box and William O. E. Oesterley, "The Book of Sirach," hrsg. Robert H. Charles, APOT 1 (Oxford: Clarendon 1913), 512–14.—Baumgartner, "Die literarischen Gattungen," 197–98, urteilt zuweilen recht hart: „Etwas Originelles sucht man in seiner Lyrik vergebens. Selbst in dem persönlichen Dankliede kommt er über die übliche steife Bildersprache nicht hinaus und vermag uns darum auch seine Person nicht näher zu bringen. Die Beziehungen der lyrischen und prophetischen Gattungen ist nicht sein Verdienst, sondern liegt im Zug der Zeit. Gelegentlich hat er dabei stark fehlgegriffen". Für Middendorp, *Stellung*, 136, hätte eine Abtrennung der als sekundär erkannten Anhänge (Sir 36,1–17 und Sir 51) den Vorteil, dass dann Sirach wird „freigesprochen werden müssen vom Makel des Epigonen, der mechanisch und phantasielos biblische Texte zusammenfügt, wie dies gerade in den Gebeten sinnenfällig geschehen ist".

linien und auch deren „Stärke“ verdeutlichen.[67] Welche Beziehungen können Lesende auf der Basis der vorliegenden Texte aus Sirach zu anderen biblischen Texten ziehen? Zugleich wird dies sowohl anhand von SirH und SirG untersucht, um eventuelle Unterschiede sichtbar zu machen.[68]

4.1. Stichprobe 1: Sir 51,1a: „Ich will dich loben“

Bereits das erste Wort in Sir 51,1a zeigt besondere Linien auf. Die exakte Form aus SirH אהללך (1.Sg. und enklitisches Personalpronomen) „*ich will dich loben*“ findet sich nur mehr in Ps 22,23 und Ps 35,18. Verändert man die Suche auf die übrigen Formen mit 1.Sg. Präfixkonjugation (אהללה) wird die Basis auch nur etwas breiter: In SirH sind da Sir 51,11a und 12c zu nennen (אהללה). In den Psalmen sind es 56,5.11; 69,31; 109,30; 145,2; 146,2.[69]

Für SirG 51,1a ergibt sich ein völlig anderes Bild. Schon die ganze Phrase ἐξομολογήσομαί[70] σοι, κύριε „*ich will dich loben, Herr*“ findet sich recht

67. Die Vergleiche werden anhand konkreter Formen und Formulierungen versucht. Im Blick ist nicht eine Klärung, ob Sirach andere biblische Texte „zitiert“. Vielmehr soll von der Ebene der vorliegenden Textfassungen aus beobachtet werden, welche Bezüge herstellbar sein könnten.—Markus Witte, “Der ‚Kanon‘ Heiliger Schriften des Antiken Judentums im Spiegel des Buches Ben Sira/Jesus Sirach,” in *Kanon in Konstruktion und Dekonstruktion: Kanonisierungsprozesse religiöser Texte von der Antike bis zur Gegenwart. Ein Handbuch*, hrsg. Eve-Marie Becker and Stefan Scholz (Berlin: de Gruyter 2012), 243 Anm. 67, spricht von „mit ‚biblischer‘ Sprache gesättigten Gebete[n]“ und bietet einen Überblick zur methodisch abgesicherten Suche nach dem Gebrauch von Traditionsliteratur in Sir wie von P. C. Beentjes entwickelt.

68. Detaillierte Untersuchungen bei Guerra Martínez, *El poder*, Palmisano, “La Prière,” 293–94 und Mulder, “Three Psalms.”—Grundsätzlich ist aber (und gerade bei Sir 51,1–12) zu betonen, dass SirH und SirG als jeweils eigene literarische Größen zu bewerten sind: Pancratius C. Beentjes, “Some Major Topics in Ben Sira Research,” in *“Happy the One Who Meditates on Wisdom” (Sir. 14,20)*, 5: „literary entities of their own“.—Vgl. dazu auch die Betonung bei Franz Böhmisch, “Die Textformen des Sirachbuches und ihre Zielgruppen,” *Protokolle zur Bibel* 6 (1997): 91, die Theologie jeder Textform erst zu nehmen und sich deutlicher mit der Frage der Zielgruppenorientierung auseinander zu setzen.

69. Vergleiche zwischen SirH 51,1–2 und 1QH XI 20–21 siehe bei Émile Puech, “Ben Sira and Qumran,” in *The Wisdom of Ben Sira: Studies on Tradition, Redaction, and Theology*, hrsg. Angelo Passaro and Giuseppe Bellia, DCLS 1 (Berlin: de Gruyter, 2008), 95, und Guerra Martínez, *El poder*, 104.

70. Antonino Minissale, *La versione greca del Siracide. Confronto con il testo*

häufig: 2 Sam 22,50; Ps 9,2; 35(34),18; 86(85),12; 111(110),1; 119(118),7; 138(137),1. Ohne direkt verbundenes κύριε kommt es noch vor in: SirG 51,12; Ps 18(17),50; 30(29),13b; 43(42),4c; 52(51),11; 57(56),10; 71(70),22; 108(107),4; 118(117),21; 118(117),28a; 118(117),28c; 139(138),14, womit sich eine sehr breite Textverknüpfung ergibt.

Untersucht man die jeweils griechischen und hebräischen „Äquivalente" zu den genannten Stellen ergibt sich folgendes Bild: Als Äquivalente für Formen von אהללה (1.Sg. Präfixkonjugation) erscheint meist αἰνέσω (Sir 51,11a.12c; Ps 35,18; 56,11; 69,31; 109,30; 145,2; 146,2) bzw. ἐπαινέσω (Ps 56,5). Jeweils nur einmal stehen ὑμνήσω (Ps 22,23) und eben die Stelle in Sir 51,1a mit ἐξομολογήσομαί.

Betrachtet man nun umgekehrt die hebräischen Äquivalente zur Phrase ἐξομολογήσομαί σοι im Griechischen, findet man beinahe konkordant immer אודך also eine Form von ידה im H-Stamm: 2 Sam 22,50; Ps 9,2; 18(17),50; 30(29),13b; 35(34),18; 43(42),4c; 52(51),11; 57(56),10; 71(70),22; 86(85),12; 108(107),4; 111(110),1; 118(117),21.28a.28c; 119(118),7; 138(137),1; 139(138),14.[71] Insofern ist die Parallele in Sir 51,1a mit אהללך singulär und beachtenswert.[72]

Die direkten lexematischen Formen führen in SirH und SirG also in andere Textbereiche hinein. Auffallend ist, dass die Vergleiche in SirG zu einem größeren Stellenspektrum (besonders in den Psalmen) als in SirH führen. Auch bei einem Vergleich der ansonsten üblichen Äquivalente zeigt SirH eher seltene Verwendungsmuster an.

---

ebraico alla luce dell'attività midrascica e del metodo targumico, AnBib 133 (Rome: Pontifical Biblical Institute, 1995), 45 Anm. 21, verweist auf Aspekte der Bedeutung und Vorkommen von Sündenbekenntnissen.

71. In Sir 51,12c steht einem ἐξομολογήσομαί (siehe die Varianten bei Rahlfs und Ziegler) ein הודיתי gegenüber. Damit gibt es auch einen sehr guten Stichwortanschluss zur anschließenden Litanei mit den 14 Vorkommen von הודו.

72. Dies mag auch zu der gerne postulierten Umstellung geführt haben, אהללך als den stärkeren Ausdruck an die zweite Stelle zu setzen und die Lücken in 1b mit אוֹדך zu ergänzen; vgl. u. a. Smend, *Weisheit*, 497, Aloys Fuchs, *Textkritische Untersuchungen zum hebräischen Ekklesiastikus: Das Plus des hebräischen Textes des Ekklesiastikus gegenüber der griechischen Übersetzung*, BibS[F] 12.5 (Freiburg im Breisgau: Herder, 1907), 97–98.112, und weiters Conleth Kearns, *The Expanded Text of Ecclesiasticus: Its Teaching on the Future Life as a Clue to Its Origin; Enlarged with a Biographical Sketch of Kearns by Gerard Norton; An Introduction to Kearns' Dissertation by Maurice Gilbert; Bibliographical updates (1951–2010) by Nuria Caldúch-Benages*, DCLS 11 (Berlin: de Gruyter, 2011), 95.

4.2. Stichprobe 2: Sir 51,2a und die verschiedenen Exodusbezüge

In SirH 51,2a fällt die Form פדה auf. Die Wurzel findet sich im Sirachbuch nur noch in 51,12a (ויפדני): Gott hat losgekauft, erlöst und befreit. Die bedrohlichen Umstände werden mit Tod (ממות 2a)[73] und allem Bösen (מכלרע 12a) beschrieben. Verfolgt man die Vorkommen der Form (2. Sg. פדית) in anderen Teilen der Bibel wird man ebenso in Kontexten von Gebeten fündig (Mose: Dtn 9,26; die Ältesten des Volkes: Dtn 21,8; David: 2 Sam 7,23 par. 1 Chr 17,21; Nehemia: Neh 1,10; Ps 31,6; 71,23). Diese beziehen sich—bis auf die Psalmenzitate—auf die Rettung im Rahmen des Exodus, also aus einer großen Not.

Die Bezüge von SirG weisen in die gleiche Richtung, nur mithilfe anderer Stellenbezüge. Die beiden Epitheta Gottes in SirG 51,2a *σκεπαστής* und *βοηθός* finden sich so auch—in umgekehrter Reihenfolge—im Schilfmeerlied von Ex 15,2 LXX:[74] Ex 15,2 weist mit dem Stichwort *σωτηρία*/Rettung[75] auf das ähnliche Lexem *σωτήρ*/Retter, das auch in SirG 51,1b steht.[76] Wie in der Exodusfassung tauchen die drei Begriffe ebenso im Gebet der Judit in Jdt 9,11 auf und verweisen damit auf eine breitere Wirkungsgeschichte.[77] In Jdt 9 wird die tätige Wirkmacht, welche Gott im

73. Vgl. zu den Todesbildern in Sir 51 sowohl in SirH als auch SirG; Jean-Sébastien Rey, "L'espérance Post-mortem Dans Les Différentes Versions Du Siracide," in Joosten and Rey, *Texts and Versions of the Book of Ben Sira*, 269–71.

74. Ex 15,2 LXX/Rahlfs: *βοηθὸς καὶ σκεπαστὴς ἐγένετό μοι εἰς σωτηρίαν·οὗτός μου θεός, καὶ δοξάσω αὐτόν, θεὸς τοῦ πατρός μου, καὶ ὑψώσω αὐτόν.*

75. Das Lexem findet sich in Sir nur in der Beschreibung Josuas in Sir 46,1.

76. SirG 51,1b *σωτῆρά* ist mit SirH 51,1a ישעי wohl in Korrelation zu sehen. Ausgehend von Ex 15,2 (LXX) *θεὸς τοῦ πατρός μου* ist auch SirH 51,1b אלהי אבי gut integrierbar (vgl. auch Jdt 9,12); Guerra Martínez, *El poder*, 220. An diesem Beispiel zeigt sich auch, dass auf der Suche nach Bezugnahmen der Texte in Sir 51 die Verse 1–2 zusammenhängend zu betrachten sind, ohne gleich eine Umstellung der Kola zur „Angleichung“ vornehmen zu müssen. Zum bereits erwähnten Bezug zu Jdt 9,12 wäre noch die Wendung *σὺ εἰσάκουσον τῆς δεήσεώς μου* zu ergänzen, welche beinahe identisch in SirG 51,11c zu finden ist.

77. Bei Barbara Schmitz, *Gedeutete Geschichte. Die Funktion der Reden und Gebete im Buch Judith*, HBS 40 (Freiburg im Breisgau: Herder, 2004), bes. 304–7 bzw. zum Konnex von Jdt 9 und Ex 15 280–289.—Judith H. Newman, *Praying by the Book: The Scripturalization of Prayer in Second Temple Judaism*, EJL 14 (Atlanta: Scholars Press, 1999), 117–54, bringt einen weiten Bezugsrahmen zum Gebet von Jdt 9 ein und untersucht auch „typologische“ Momente in den Rettungsschilderungen. Aspekte aus älteren Erzählungen werden dabei typologisch wiederverwendet und auf eine gegen-

Exodus gezeigt hat, angerufen.[78] Das Danklied des Mose und des Volkes für die erfolgte Rettung in Ex 15 wird im Sirachbuch zum Dankgebet des Weisheitslehrers für die erfolgte Rettung und—als Teil seines (Lehr) Buches—auch zu einem nachahmenswerten Gebet für seine Rezipienten. Sirach wird zum paradigmatisch Betenden und mit seinem Buch zum „Medium".[79]

Sir 51,2 verknüpft das Gebet Sirachs mit jenem des Mose und des Volkes aus Ex 15 (bes. in SirG) und jenen Gebeten des Mose und der Ältesten in Dtn 9,26 und Dtn 21,8 (SirH). Sirach betet wie David (SirH 2 Sam 7,23 // 1 Chr 17,21), Nehemia (SirH Neh 1,10) und Judit (SirG Jdt 9,11–12).

4.3. Stichprobe 3: Das Gebetsvokabular als Verbindung zu anderen Buchteilen

Der immer wieder angenommene sekundäre Charakter von Sir 51,1–12 wird häufig damit begründet, dass das Gebet Inhalte, Themen und Begriffe verwendet, welche sonst in Sir unüblich seien.[80] Dies weise darauf hin, dass der Text eine spätere „Zutat" zum Buche sei.[81] Hier tauchen wir freilich wieder in die zuvor erwähnten Buchkompositionsfragen ein. Eine Analyse des verwendeten Gebetsvokabulars in SirG stellt aber vielfältige Bezüge zum Buchganzen her.[82]

---

wärtige Situation angepasst (154). In diesem Kontext erwähnt sie auch die Schilderung Davids in Sir 47,4–5 (153). Im Gebet von Sir 51,1–12 klingen zwar auf sublime Art und Weise Exodusbezüge an, doch wird hier die Vergangenheit nur dezent zur Grundlage und Vorlage des eigenen Betens und der damit verbundenen gegenwärtigen existentiellen Erfahrung; Newman, *Praying*, 117, betitelt das ganze Kapitel zur Jdt 9 als „The Past as Blueprint for Present".

78. Vgl. Matthew Goff, "Recent Trends in the Study of Early Jewish Wisdom Literature: The Contribution of 4QInstruction and Other Qumran Texts," *CurBS* 7 (2009): 393.

79. Werner Urbanz, "Die Gebetsschule des Jesus Sirach: Bemerkungen zu Inhalten, Subjekten und Methoden des Gebets im Sirachbuch," *Protokolle zur Bibel* 18 (2009): 43.

80. Vgl. die bereits genannten Angaben in Anm. 44.

81. Eventuell wirken hier auch noch Grundannahmen zu den literarischen Gattungen nach. Gattungswechsel und -unterschiede werden literarkritisch und redaktionsgeschichtlich verwertet. Gebete gelten demnach als sekundär verdächtig (vgl. Jona 2).

82. SirG bietet sich grundlegend an, weil das ganze Buch vorhanden ist. Eine Ausnahme bildet die Litanei in $SirH^{B}$ 51,12e+–zj.

Das in den Rahmenteilen (51,1.11–12) häufige Lobvokabular (Formen von ἐξομολογέω in 1a.1c.11b.12c und αἰνέω 1b.11a.12c u. ä.) findet sich auch in anderen Buchteilen und dort an prominenten Stellen.[83] In Sir 15,9–10 ist vom dem sündenfreien, in Weisheit gesprochenen Lob die Rede, in Sir 17,10.27a.28b vom Lob des Schöpfers als grundlegender Ordnung der Schöpfung und Zeichen der Lebendigkeit des Menschen. In 39,5–6 wird der Lobpreis als wesentliche Haltung des Weisen beschrieben, die in 39,14–15 angesichts der Werke Gottes zu einer angemessenen Reaktion des Menschen in Dankbarkeit wird. Im Bilde Davids 47,8–10 sind diese Züge eingewoben, wonach dieser über sein eigenes Loben hinaus in den gottesdienstlichen Vollzügen Echoräume und Partizipationsmöglichkeiten eröffnet (vgl. 50,18a). Und auch das Buchende ist vom Lob Gottes geprägt (51,22b.29b).

Gebets-Lexeme, welche dem Bereich der Klage zuordenbar sind, tauchen besonders in den weiterführenden „Schritten aus der Not" ab V 8 auf. Die Erinnerung an das Erbarmen des Herrn (8a) führt über eine flehende Anrufung Gottes in Lebensgefahr (9–10: 9b δέομαι; 10a ἐπικαλέω) zu einem Lobgelübde (11a–b) und letztlich bis zur Schilderung der Erhörung der Bitte (11c δέησις). Die Anrufung Gottes in 10a mit ἐπικαλέω zieht einen weiten Bogen durch das ganze Buch hin nach 2,10d. Dort in einem paränetischen Traktat (2,1–18) über die Gottesfurcht eingebettet, wird gefragt, ob Anrufungen Gottes in Not bei den früheren Geschlechtern unbeantwortet blieben? Die Antwort gibt das Buch selbst im Lob der Väter. Gott reagiert auf das Schreien Josuas (46,5a), Samuels (46,16a), Davids (47,5a) und jenes der Bewohnerinnen und Bewohner Jerusalems mit Jesaja (48,20a). In Sir 51,10a tut es der Weise selbst und antwortet positiv aus der eigenen Erfahrung heraus.[84] Mit δέομαι (9b) und δέησις (11c) lassen sich weitere Verknüpfungen beobachten. Häufig im Kontext von Sünde zu finden (17,25b; 21,1b; 28,2b.4b; 39,5c.e) oder als Ausdruck eines Flehens in schwierigen Lebenslagen (21,5a; 26,5b;[85] 35,16b.20b; 36,22a; 37,15a; 38,14a; 50,19a) sind besonders die Bezüge zum kollektivem Rettungsgebet

83. Eine detaillierte Übersicht findet sich in Urbanz, *Gebet*, 133–34.

84. Nuria Calduch-Benages, *Un gioiello di sapienza: Leggendo Siracide 2*, Cammini nello Spirito, Biblica 45 (Milan: Paoline Editoriale Libri, 2001), 92. Dies betont auch besonders Gilbert, "Prayer," 122–24 unter Rückgriff auf Calduch-Benages, „Trial Motif".

85. Lectio varians ἐδεήθην bei Rahlfs gegenüber dem ἐφοβήθην bei Ziegler.—Vgl. dazu Urbanz, *Gebet*, 80–82.

in Sir 36 nicht unbedeutend. Ebenso ist die Zeichnung des idealen Weisen in 39,5–6 in Farben einer intensiven Gebetsbewegung vom Flehen (V 5) hin zum Dank (V 6) gehalten.

Somit erweist sich gerade das Gebetsvokabular als wesentliche Verbindung von Sir 51,1–12 in viele Teile des Buches hinein und dient damit—vielleicht auf recht sublime Art—zur Bildung von tragenden Themen-Clustern im Buch, die seinen Gedankengang sinnerhellend begleiten und didaktisch stimulieren.[86] Damit betreibt Sirach neben dem Beispiel in Sir 51,1–12 und mit den anderen Gebeten eine „Integration der Welt des Betens in die Weisheit".[87]

5. Zusammenschau

Das Gebet in Sir 51,1–12 scheint doch etwas mehr zu sein als nur ein Anhang zum Buch. Es ist Teil des Buches, sowohl in Form als auch Inhalt und Pragmatik. Auf der Ebene der ältesten MS wird die enge Verbindung mit Sir 50 (SirH) bzw. die Brückenfunktion hin zum Prolog und dem Buchtitel (SirG) deutlich. In seiner literarischen und inhaltlichen Form als Gebet ist Sir 51,1–12 am Buchschluss passend plaziert. Das Gebetsvokabular zieht lange und breite Fäden quer durch das Buch: Dies wird nicht nur in Bezug auf 2,10 deutlich und dessen Bezügen zu Josua (46,5), Samuel (46,16) und David (47,5) im Väterlob. Besonders in den Zügen des weisheitlich geprägten Menschen (15,9–10; 39,5–6) und in den hohen Entfaltungen der Schöpfungsordnung (17,10.27–28) hin zum Lob, zeigt sich eine Dynamik, welche in Sir 51,1–12 und dem nachfolgenden Text bzw. den nachfolgenden Texten ein passendes Finale findet. Im Sinne der weisheitlichen Lehre und Pädagogik, welche von einer Praxis des Gebets durchtränkt ist, dankt man am Ende eines Buches, in dem Gelingen als auch Gefahren des menschlichen Lebensvollzuges vielfältig thematisiert wurden, dafür,[88] dass man vor einem Weg in den Abgrund bewahrt

86. Marböck, *Jesus Sirach*, 268.

87. Hermann Spieckermann, *Lebenskunst und Gotteslob in Israel. Anregungen aus Psalter und Weisheit für die Theologie*, FAT 91 (Tübingen: Mohr Siebeck, 2014), 118. Mit Rückgriff auf Kemper Fullerton, "Studies in the Psalter," *The Biblical World* 37 (1911): 128, und dessen Betonung der besonders engen Verbindung zu den Psalmen, sei es weil zur selben Zeit entstanden oder weil Sirach ein sorgfältiger Imitator ist.

88. Markus Witte, "‚Weisheit' in der alttestamentlichen Wissenschaft: Ausgewählte literatur- und theologiegeschichtliche Fragestellungen und Entwicklungen,"

wurde.[89] Gebete sind in biblischen Büchern oftmals Schaltstellen oder Knotenpunkte, welche strategisch platziert sind, um an wichtigen Stellen einen Dialog mit Gott zu suchen und zugleich auch die Lesenden aufzufordern, sich Gott zuzuwenden.[90] „Gebet, Bekenntnis, Reflexion sind ineinander verschlungen"[91], gerade auch in der Gebetsschule des Sirachbuches. Sein Finale ist sein Vermächtnis.

ThLZ 137 (2012): 1174, spricht von einem „vielfältigen Gespräch … über Grunderfahrungen menschlicher Existenz" dessen Vielzahl sprachlicher Ausdrucksformen „weiß, dass die Rede von Gott und der Welt unterschiedliche Gestalten annehmen muss, um gehört zu werden".

89. Svend Holm-Nielsen, "Religiöse Poesie Des Spätjudentums," *ANRW* 19.1:163.

90. Georg Fischer, "Gebete Als Hermeneutischer Schlüssel zu biblischen Büchern - Am Beispiel von Jeremia," in *Congress Volume: Ljubljana, 2007*, hrsg. André Lemaire, VTSup 133 (Leiden: Brill, 2010), 236–37. Fischer sieht in Gebeten einen „Schlüssel für das Verständnis biblischer Bücher", die „unter hermeneutischer Rücksicht eine zentrale Rolle" spielen".

91. Andreas Wagner, "Strukturen Des Gebets Im Alten Testament," in *Orakel Und Gebete. Interdisziplinäre Studien zur Sprache der Religion in Ägypten, Vorderasien und Griechenland in hellenistischer Zeit*, hrsg. Johannes Diehl und Markus Witte, FAT 2/38 (Tübingen: Mohr Siebeck, 2009), 213.

Contributors

James. K. Aitken, PhD., geb. 1968, Reader in Hebrew and Early Jewish Studies, Faculty of Divinity, University of Cambridge/GB

Pierre-Maurice Bogaert, OSB, Dr. theol., geb. 1934, Professor em. für Altes Testament an der L'Université catholique de Louvain, Belgien (übersetzt von Bonifatia Gesche, OSB, Mariendonk)

Franz Bömisch, geb. 1965, Religionslehrer, Diözese Linz

Anthony Forte, SJ, Dr., Professor (Dozent) für Griechisch, Latein und Geschichte am Pontificium Institutum Biblicum und Gastprofessor für Textkritik am Pontificium Institutum Augustianum, Roma/Italien

Jan Joosten, Dr. theol., geb. 1959, Regius Professor of Hebrew, University of Oxford

Otto Kaiser, Dr. theol. Dr. h.c. mult., geb. 1924, Professor em. für Altes Testament an der Philipps-Universität Marburg

Siegfried Kreuzer, Dr. theol., geb. 1949, Professor für Altes Testament und Biblische Archäologie, Kirchliche Hochschule Wuppertal/Bethel, Hochschule für Kirche und Diakonie

Jean-Sébastien Rey, Dr. theol., geb. 1977, Professor für Biblische Exegese an L'Université de Lorraine-Metz, Centre de recherche écriture

Werner Urbanz, Dr. theol., geb. 1974, Ass.-Prof. am Institut für Bibelwissenschaft des Alten und Neuen Testaments der Katholischen Privatuniversität Linz

Knut Usener, Dr. phil., geb. 1959, apl. Professor für Griechisch und Latein, Kirchliche Hochschule Wuppertal/Bethel, Hochschule für Kirche und Diakonie

Oda Wischmeyer, Dr. theol., Dr. h.c., Professorin em. für Neues Testament an der Friedrich-Alexander-Universität in Erlangen-Nürnberg

Markus Witte, Dr. theol., geb. 1964, Professor für Exegese und Literaturgeschichte des Alten Testaments an der Humboldt-Universität zu Berlin

Benjamin G. Wright, PhD., geb. 1953, University Distinguished Professor am Department of Religion Studies der Lehigh University, Bethlehem/USA

Burkard M. Zapff, Dr. theol., geb. 1960, Professor für Alttestamentliche Wissenschaft an der Katholischen Universität Eichstätt-Ingolstadt

Index of Selected Biblical References

Deuterocanonical Works

CPSIA information can be obtained
at www.ICGtesting.com
Printed in the USA
BVOW09s2225110917
494595BV00001B/3/P

9 781628 371826